The New Authoritarianism

Vol. 2: A Risk Analysis of the European Alt-Right Phenomenon

Edited by Alan Waring

THE NEW AUTHORITARIANISM

Vol. 2: A Risk Analysis of the European Alt-Right Phenomenon

Edited by Alan Waring

ibidem-Verlag
Stuttgart

Bibliographic information published by the Deutsche Nationalbibliothek
Die Deutsche Nationalbibliothek lists this publication in the Deutsche Nationalbibliografie; detailed bibliographic data are available in the Internet at http://dnb.d-nb.de.

Bibliografische Information der Deutschen Nationalbibliothek
Die Deutsche Nationalbibliothek verzeichnet diese Publikation in der Deutschen Nationalbibliografie; detaillierte bibliografische Daten sind im Internet über http://dnb.d-nb.de abrufbar.

ISBN-13: 978-3-8382-1263-0

Printed in the United States of America

Dedication

This two-volume book is dedicated in memoriam to the Lord Peter Temple-Morris QC, who inspired and encouraged the editor to embark on the project. Originally scheduled to contribute the Foreword, throughout 2017 and into 2018 he battled with much fortitude against increasingly severe illness and operations and became too frail to write. Sadly, he died aged 80 on May 1, 2018.

Lord Temple-Morris's British parliamentary career as an MP ran from 1974 to 2001, for the most part as a Conservative of the liberal 'One Nation Tories' group, before crossing the floor of the House to Labour in 1997. He entered the parliamentary upper chamber (House of Lords) in 2001. His strong distaste for authoritarianism (which he saw as increasingly prevalent in the Conservative Party), and an equally strong belief in justice and moderation, characterised his world-view. Serving variously on the Justice and Foreign Affairs Select Committees and others, he was also a key member of the British-Iranian All-Party Parliamentary Group from 1989 to 2005, and in 1990 launched the British-Irish All-Party Parliamentary Group. He is credited with a substantial contribution to the Northern Ireland peace process that culminated in the 1998 Good Friday Agreement.

This book is a fitting tribute to his sense of justice and moderation and 'jaw-jaw' approach to difficult political issues, especially in foreign policy areas.

Contents

List of Figures and Tables

Figures

Tables

List of European Cases

UK

Other Countries

List of Abbreviations and Acronyms

ADL	Anti-Defamation League (US)
AfD	Alternative für Deutschland (Alternative for Germany, political party)
AKEL	Progressive Party for the Working People (communist party in Cyprus)
BCE	Before Current Era
BNP	British National Party
BP	British Petroleum
CIA	Central Intelligence Agency
CPS	Crown Prosecution Service (UK)
CVE	Countering Violent Extremism
EC	European Commission
ECB	European Central Bank
ECHR	European Court of Human Rights
ECJ	European Court of Justice
EDL	English Defence League
EEC	European Economic Community
EHS	Environment, Health, and Safety
EP	European Parliament
EU	European Union
FBI	Federal Bureau of Investigation
FN	Front National (France)
FPÖ	Freiheitliche Partei Österreichs (Austrian Freedom Party)
FvD	Forum for Democracy (Netherlands)
GDP	Gross Domestic Product
IMF	International Monetary Fund
IRGC	Islamic Revolutionary Guard Corps (Iran)
IS	Islamic State
ISIS	Islamic State in Iraq and Syria

KKK	Ku Klux Klan (US)
LDPR	Liberal Democratic Party of Russia
LGBT	Lesbian, Gay, Bisexual, Transsexual
MEP	Member of European Parliament
MMR	Measles, Mumps, and Rubella
MP	Member of Parliament
NATO	North Atlantic Treaty Organization
Neo-con	Neo-conservative (US)
NHS	National Health Service
NIHCE	National Institute for Health and Care Excellence (UK)
NPL	National Policy Institute (US)
Obamacare	Patient Protection and Affordable Care Act 2010 (US)
ONS	Office for National Statistics (UK)
ÖVP	Österreichs Volkspartei (Austrian People's Party)
PCA	Paris Climate Accord
PEGIDA	Patriotische Europäer gegen die Islamisierung des Abendlandes (far-right German movement)
PRC	People's Republic of China
PVV	Partij Voor Vrijheid (Party for Freedom in Netherlands)
QRA	Quantified Risk Assessment
RNU	Russian National Unity party
RWA	Right Wing Authoritarianism
SDO	Social Dominance Orientation
SPÖ	Sozialdemokratische Partei Österreichs (Austrian Social-Democratic Party)
TPP	Trans Pacific Partnership

UHC	Universal Health Care
UK	United Kingdom (of Great Britain and Northern Ireland)
UKIP	United Kingdom Independence Party
UN	United Nations
UNCAC	United Nations Convention Against Corruption
UNFCCC	United Nations Framework Convention on Climate Change
US	United States (of America)
VVD	Dutch Liberal Party
WWI	World War One
WWII	World War Two

Foreword

This edited two-volume collection of papers comes at a crucial time for Europe, the United States, and the wider world. Momentous economic and political changes of the last few years continue to have impacts. Waring, a prominent author in risk, its assessment and management, provides the reader with a refreshingly different analytical focus for the phenomenon of resurgent authoritarianism now evident in populist and radical right-wing politics. The subject matter is controversial, and the temptation to descend into polemic is resisted by the weight of scholarly analysis from such a range of distinguished international authors. My close personal and professional relationship with Alan may have affected my view of this book, but it has been a long time since I felt that I craved to read a book chapter after chapter! The Alt-Right's vivid relationship, with both current events and perseverant effects, makes it a living book. I feel honoured to have had the opportunity to be one of its first readers.

The New Authoritarianism's eminently qualified contributors bring to the task an eclectic range of specialisms and expertise on the subject matter. The book also comes with some unique features. It is the first book on the Alternative Right to explicitly frame the narrative around a risk analysis. The expected political analysis, which so often on its own can seem rather sterile, is encompassed within a much broader structured analysis focused on risks for various parties—society, governments, sectors, individual citizens, and the Alt-Right themselves. In addition, there is a special early chapter examining the psychological aspects of the Alt-Right phenomenon, which include the promulgation of fear as a political tactic, the psychological characteristics of nationalist and supremacist ideology, as well as how best to consider allegations of mental instability and personality disorder against particular politicians.

The book's working definition of the Alt-Right is twofold: (1) as an ideology, the spectrum of right-wing world-views outside traditional conservatism, which begins with a dissatisfaction with the mainstream political process and character and frustration by perceived impotence of traditional conservatism, and runs through populist, hard-right, ultra-right, and extreme-right ideology; (2) as an identifiable group, those having such world-views.

The New Authoritarianism book seeks to explain the Alt-Right phenomenon on a global level as well as nationally. Chapters show that the Alt-Right ideology is shared transnationally—with prominent examples not just in the US but also in all western democracies, as well as Russia and other nationalist authoritarian regimes. Evidence of considerable transnational collaboration between Alt-Right groups in different countries is discussed. The range of chapters in this Volume covers Britain, France, Germany, Austria, Netherlands, Norway, and Russia—and far-right activities in Hungary and Italy are also addressed. Two case study chapters address lone actor far-right terrorism (the murder of Jo Cox MP in Britain, and the bombing atrocity and subsequent massacre in Norway by Anders Breivik), and other chapters address more recent extremist atrocities.

The chapter on Brexit analyses the fragile, problematic relationship of the European Union with the UK and reveals how Alt-Right activists (both populist and far-right) sought to exploit widespread genuine concerns among British voters about some aspects of EU membership and persuade such voters in the Brexit referendum that their only salvation from their fears would be to vote for Brexit. The book argues that, for the Alt-Right, a Brexit result was merely a stepping stone towards their desire for permanent, nationalist right-wing authoritarianism in Britain and an end to the multi-culturalism and cosmopolitanism encouraged by the EU.

The book's message is that the over-riding thrust of the Alt-Right in western democracies is to achieve a permanent Alt-Right stamp on the governance of each country. They seek to achieve this by persuading, subverting, and as necessary bullying, mainstream and populist conservatism to shift its center of political gravity firmly towards the far-right. The objective of fascist movements in the 1930s to overthrow the state and replace it with a totalitarian regime has been modified to one where the Alt-Right today are largely content (at least in the short-term) to exert a modifying and attenuating influence on electable mainstream conservative governments i.e. to get the latter to 'correct' themselves and become more nationalist and authoritarian e.g. democratically elected regimes in Austria, Hungary, Germany.

The book argues that to achieve this the Alt-Right seek the normalization and public acceptability of their nationalist and white supremacist ideology, and so Alt-Right leaders and opinion formers are typically keen to portray their ideology and policies as a reasonable, fair, just, and necessary response to what they assert are dangerous liberal ideas and weak mainstream governance. The Alt-Right portray themselves as society's saviours, as the only protection against being overwhelmed and destroyed by foreigners, immigrants and their alien ideas, creeds, and cultures.

The book asserts with evidence that, in the Alt-Right coda, any and all means are permissible in pursuit of their ends e.g. deliberate dissemination of lies, fake news, and invented 'alternative facts'; seeking to replace representative democracy by direct democracy. Both flagrant and subtle defamation in the form of fake global conspiracy propaganda against Jews and Muslims is commonplace, especially using the Internet and social media, the subversion of which the book examines critically in detail. For the far- and extreme-right elements, intimidation, hate crimes, and violence are also acceptable tactics, and the book examines numerous examples.

At the conclusion of each of nine chapters in Part 2, in which specific examples of the Alt-Right phenomenon are addressed, a summary list of risks is included. Towards the end of the book, these risks are collated and individually analysed heuristically for impact, probability and risk rating in a special chapter, making this a unique contribution to an examination of the Alt-Right. As the author emphasizes, this is neither a definitive risk analysis nor the pronouncements of a 'Risk Oracle' and the assessment is open to debate. This chapter, in effect, becomes a reference utility and one that is available for application, debate, and further development by anyone who wishes to use it.

The penultimate chapter examines the overall strengths, weaknesses, opportunities, and threats in relation to the Alt-Right, and posits five different potential scenarios for the Alt-Right's future. While one scenario suggests that the current democratic status quo could be retained, the other four are increasingly authoritarian of which the final two involve Alt-Right coups d'état. A prognosis is made for which of the scenarios are more likely to occur in which countries.

The book's final chapter includes detailed discussion of a range of strategies for combatting what the chapter's authors conclude is an Alt-Right threat to democracy. These include legislation and judicial strategies; Internet and social media; education; political and economic strategies; and grassroots and mass action. The book ends on a call for 'muscular moderation' to combat the Alt-Right threat, a difficult but nonetheless compelling challenge.

George Boustras
Professor in Risk Assessment
Director of the Center of Risk and Decision Science (CERIDES)
European University Cyprus
Editor-in-Chief, *Safety Science* (Elsevier)

Acknowledgements

In addition to the authors themselves, the editor would like to thank the following for their support and various contributions to this book.

For contributing the Foreword, advising on, and reviewing the book's development:

- Professor George Boustras, Professor in Risk Assessment and Director of the Center for Risk and Decision Science (CERIDES), European University Cyprus.

For encouraging the creation of this book from its earliest inception:

- Emeritus Professor Matthew Feldman, Director of the Centre for Analysis of the Radical Right (CARR); formerly Emeritus Professor at the Centre for Fascist, Anti-Fascist and Post-Fascist Studies at Teesside University, UK.
- The Lord Peter Temple-Morris QC (see Dedication).
- Paul Sheils, formerly managing partner of a leading law firm, London.

For advising on the book's development and reviewing drafts of various chapters:

- Professor Ali Ansari, Professor of Modern History and Founding Director of the Institute for Iranian Studies, St Andrews University, Scotland.
- Associate Professor Dr Ian Glendon, School of Applied Psychology, Griffith University, Gold Coast Campus, Queensland, Australia.
- Dr Clodagh Harrington, Senior Lecturer, De Monfort University, member of the Political Studies Association's American Politics Group and the Trump Project research group.
- Dr Roger Paxton, contributing author, reviewer and tireless mentor to the editor throughout.
- Long-standing friends and political observers: Liz Buck, avid reader of books; Lynne Jalalian, public and environmental health lecturer; Gavin Jones, author, columnist and social commentator; Susan-Marie Kelly, retired editor and American citizen.

Dr Anton Shekhovstov, Valerie Lange and colleagues at ***ibidem*** Verlag for their support, guidance, professionalism, and efficiency throughout the lengthy publishing process.

Last, but by no means least, my wife Mehri, who put up with numerous periods of my detachment from family life during the creation of this book.

Introduction: Risk and the Alt-Right

By Alan Waring

The Book's Target Readership

Readers of this book are likely to fall into a broad spectrum of professional groups that have, in some way or other, a need to unravel and consider the impact of resurgent nationalism and ultra-conservative agendas on risk issues affecting governments, institutions, corporations, the judiciary, businesses, the media, individual citizens and others, as well as protective strategies against such threats. In addition to a wide range of scholars and academics, such readers will include risk analysts and risk managers of various kinds, politicians and political analysts, intelligence officers, corporate security specialists, corporate ethics and integrity managers, economists, investment analysts, lawyers, journalists, psychologists, sociologists, and civil society leaders and professionals.

Students on a range of Masters and other post-graduate courses are also likely to find the book of value, in such subjects as business administration, risk management, security and counter-terrorism, corporate ethics, government administration, political science, and international relations.

The Book's Rationale

This book considers, from a risk perspective, the current phenomenon of the new Alt-Right authoritarianism that began to emerge in the first decade of the 21st century, and whether it represents 'real' democracy or an unacceptable hegemony potentially resulting in elected dictatorships and abuses. Potential threats and risk exposures, whether to democracy, human rights, law and order, social welfare, racial harmony, the economy, national security, the environment, or international relations, are identified and analysed. Potential strategies to limit threats that might arise from Alt-Right ideology and activities are proposed. The book acknowledges the particular relevance of and contribution to its analysis by such authors as Lyons (2017a and b), Michael (e.g. 2003, 2016, 2017), and Neiwert (2017) on the American right-wing and the emergent Alt-Right phenomenon, and, on the right-wing in Europe, Eatwell and Goodwin (2010), Feldman and Pollard (2016), Goodwin (2011), and Wodak (2015 and passim).

It is axiomatic to state that life, liberty and the pursuit of happiness are fundamental to a democratic society. The American constitution cites these fundamentals explicitly, but they are implicit to all democratic societies. Democratic freedoms naturally threaten the very existence of dictatorships, totalitarian states and pseudo-democracies, as well as putative states run by terrorists such as Da-esh/IS (Islamic State). None of these can exist unless they impose abusive and degrading conditions on their populations, so as to cow them into submission. Although the existence of coercive and often barbaric regimes may seem self-evident, and there are plenty of examples, perhaps a less obvious threat comes from internal extremists within democratic societies who seek radical change by undermining or destroying basic freedoms. While these obviously include IS followers, others just as insidious and dangerous are lurking among us. Ironically, some of the worst internal extremists are those who justify themselves and their often draconian and abusive acts by claiming to offer the public true democracy, true freedom, true security, and true protection against alleged threats. The label Alternative Right or Alt-Right has arisen in recent years to encompass not only the spectrum of beliefs, values, attitudes, opinions, and positions within the Alt-Right worldview, a view more strident, authoritarian, and harsher than conventional conservatism and now regarded by many as extremist, but also the exponents of Alt-Right ideology.

The new Alt-Right authoritarianism that is sweeping the western world could easily be described as neo- or proto-fascist in general character. Traditionally, the fascism label has been applied almost exclusively to right-wing authoritarianism, such as Hitler and Nazism, the Pinochet regime in Chile, the Orban regime in Hungary, and by some even to the Trump administration in the US. However, by virtue of some of its tactics, it could apply equally to left-wing extremism, such as the Chavez and Maduro regimes in Venezuela and the totalitarian regime in North Korea. As a further example, the widely reported bullying and anti-Semitism by authoritarians now controlling the hard-left Momentum faction within the British Labour Party has all the tactical hallmarks of fascism (see e.g. Fisher 2018; Maguire and Fisher 2018; Zeffman 2018). Although this book focusses very much on the Alt-Right (because of its current rapidly growing presence across the west), one should nevertheless also be alert to neo-Marxist extremism wherever it flourishes, to right-wing authoritarian regimes in the non-western world, as well as to IS extremism.

The so-called Brexit Referendum in June 2016, whereby the UK electorate voted by a small margin in favour of leaving the European Union, was a prominent example of the Alt-Right ideology and agenda at work. The pro-Brexit campaign was infused with Alt-Right ideas, language and propaganda. Indeed, there was acknowledged close collaboration between the UK Independence Party (UKIP), the populist prime mover for Brexit, and leading figures and organizations within the Alt-Right movement in the US. Fear of immigrants and concern about allegedly weak immigration controls became the main driving force of the pro-Brexit campaign, along with slogans about allegedly incompetent and overbearing interference in British life by an unelected elite of EU leaders and officials in Brussels. An authoritarian tableau broadly similar to pro-Brexit played out in the Trump campaign in the 2016 US presidential election (see Vol 1). The common theme of Brexit and Trump supporters was that 'the Establishment', i.e. government and the traditional political parties, were not listening to them about their concerns on such things as immigration, national control, job losses from cheap imports or jobs moving abroad. Some of these complaints may well be valid up to a point. However, as the respected *Times* columnist and former British Conservative MP Matthew Parris wrote in January 2017, many of their complaints do not bear much scrutiny in factual terms. He later described the anti-foreigner jingoistic attitudes of the populist Alt-Right in Britain (or 'the shadow', as he called them) as "something brutish, something authoritarian, something mean" (Parris 2018). False beliefs and exaggerated fears among an electorate about immigrants, for example, are easy for skilled demagogues to whip up into nationalistic frenzy whereby voters become convinced that their only salvation is to vote for the authoritarian candidate who will 'protect' them. However, whatever the merits of their grievances, they have absolutely no right to demand pathological solutions and political leaders have absolutely no right to offer them much less deliver them.

It is often said that truth is the first casualty of war. That could equally apply to politics. It is generally accepted that politicians and their acolytes are likely to cherry pick 'the truth' and massage it and finesse it to their best advantage. Presenting their best case is, perhaps, the acceptable face of politicians. The public tolerates it. However, what has been emerging in recent years, and very much so in the US Presidential Election campaign of 2016, is the 'post-truth' phenomenon, an altogether different proposition. Post-truth refers to the deliberate fabrication and dissemination of plausible but false news stories, or stories comprising a mixture of fact and damaging fiction, in order to assist in a black propaganda campaign against a political target. Fake news became a weapon-of-choice of the Alt-Right movement in support of Donald Trump's presidential campaign, perhaps unsurprisingly in view of the fact that one of his campaign directors was Steve Bannon, the doyen of Alt-Right propaganda and former editor of *Breitbart News*, the leading Alt-Right promotional medium. Potentially damaging fake news stories were disseminated about Trump's electoral rival Hillary Clinton. See, for example, Neiwert (2017).

Since President Trump's inauguration, however, it became evident that the post-truth fake news tactic had become an integral part of his Presidential policy, whether from his own mouth, his *Twitter* account, or a variety of official spokespersons. The world was expected to swallow unabashed such demonstrable falsehoods as: a non-existent terrorist massacre at Bowling Green, Kentucky, the number of people celebrating Trump's inauguration near the Lincoln Memorial far exceeding those at President Obama's 2009 inauguration, and an accusation that the media barely covered terrorist attacks in Nice, Paris, Berlin and some 75 other locations. Furthermore, when challenged, the lies were either denied, or brazenly repeated, or dismissed as trivial errors. It is instructive that Steve Bannon was appointed by President Trump as his Chief Strategist in his inaugural cabinet, along with other senior Alt-Right representatives. The implications of the widespread use of fake news and fake facts by the Alt-Right political machine are addressed in more detail in chapter 11 of Vol 1.

A common agenda of the Alt-Right movements across the west is to stop immigration. Some, and especially the more extreme elements, also wish to go further and enforce the repatriation or expulsion of all non-whites and non-Christians, particularly Muslims. The Fidesz government of Viktor Orban in Hungary and Italy's 5 Star and Lega parties are three contemporary examples that advocate a variety of extreme actions. The leaders of Britain First, in their official policy manifestos, public statements and recorded intimidatory behaviour towards ethnic minorities, are clearly inspired by Adolf Hitler and Nazi ideology. A number of British National Party, Britain First, and English Defence League members have been convicted of offences, some violent, involving hate crimes and promulgating racial hatred. The hard-right National Action group and its supporters have been proscribed by the British government as a terrorist organization.

In addition to the hard-right, the UK Independence Party (UKIP) became a relatively softer rallying point for large numbers of disaffected conservatives who felt that the Conservative Party, their natural 'home', had been too weak on immigration controls and stopping perceived excessive interference by the EU in British daily life. Under UKIP's charismatic former leader Nigel Farage, and using anti-immigrant rhetoric, UKIP and its allies managed to persuade sufficient British voters to vote for a British exit from the EU (or Brexit) in the 2016 referendum (see chapters 3 and 4). Citizens with views allied to the far- and extreme right-wing groups voted tactically for UKIP candidates in elections and have been keen Brexit supporters. The strident anti-immigrant rhetoric of some Brexit demagogues and their allies in the right-wing media is arguably incitement to violence. After the referendum pro-Brexit result, there was as an upsurge of hate crimes against foreigners and ethnic and religious minorities in the UK, including at least two murders. Just before the referendum, an anti-immigration obsessive with a history of far-right extremist views murdered the anti-Brexit Labour MP Jo Cox, as described in chapter 5.

The Editor's Perspective

Throughout the book, the editor and primary author applies an analytical concept called 'world-view' that has proven over many decades to be a very useful descriptive and analytical tool for understanding the stance of particular individuals or particular groups. The modern world-view concept, or *Weltanschauung* in the original German, is ascribed to the late 19th century German philosopher Dilthey although it has antecedents in the philosopher Kant. According to Kluback and Weinbaum (1957), who provided an introductory glimpse of Dilthey's proposition, world-view refers to a complex set of perceptions, attitudes, beliefs, values and motivations that characterize how an individual or group of people interpret the world, their own existence and how the two inter-relate. World-view represents a set of characteristic biases from which it is possible to predict the likely stance and behaviour of those who hold a particular world-view. However, only a small proportion of world-view as personally expressed by the individual is conscious, and pre-conscious processing (Dixon 1981) largely determines overall world-view and actions as observed by others.

As expressed above, the editor understands the world-view concept in the way typically used in the social sciences by sociologists and psychologists (see, for example, Burrell and Morgan 1979) and by other disciplines such as systems science (see, for example, Ackoff 1971; von Bertalanffy 1992; Checkland 1981; Checkland and Scholes 1990). The fine structure of world-view as recognised by such disciplines is lost in the ill-defined and variable colloquial use of the term, where it may mean simply 'attitude' or 'stance'.

In addition, the disciplined use of world-view recognizes that, in ascribing a particular world-view to a particular individual or group, the analyst is influenced by his or her own world-view used as a lens or viewing instrument seeking to reveal the world-view characteristics of the subject or subjects. This process of abduction (Denzin 1978) is bound to be affected by inherent biases of the viewer. No observer, researcher, analyst or commentator can ever be free of bias, no matter how hard they may try to be 'objective'. The art is to try to make the objectifier's biases as explicit as possible so that readers may judge to what extent these may have affected the analysis and conclusions.

The editor values order and justice in society and believes that extremism of whatever kind is not only an affront to order, justice, and humanity but represents a real threat to democracy and, in some instances, national security. A liberal conservative, who in the Brexit context might be labelled a Eurosceptic Remainer, he rejects Alt-Right authoritarianism and extremism as much as he does that of the Marxist hard-left or any other group.

Risk and the Alt-Right Context

In contrast to other books on the Alt-Right, this book is not just a philosophical, sociological, political, or economic examination of the phenomenon but is also explicitly a risk analysis. The risk concept itself is, of course, not without controversy and the risk analysis and assessment discipline encompasses the spectrum of both pure and opportunity/speculative risks (Waring and Glendon 1998; ISO, 2018; Waring 2013). Assessment techniques appropriate to pure risks areas such as engineering, fire, safety, white collar crime and credit control may not be appropriate to speculative risk areas such as political risk, investment, HR strategy, IT strategy, foreign policy, and international relations, where more qualitative and heuristic assessment methods come to the fore (Glendon and Clarke 2016; Shrader-Frechette 1991). This book therefore adopts a primarily qualitative and heuristic approach to the Alt-Right risk narrative, using a risk assessment technique applied systematically in chapter 12.

In pursuing a risk analysis, this book recognizes that there should be no *a priori* assumptions about what risk exposures exist in a particular context or who is 'at risk' from them. Certainly, it may be convenient to assume that the Alt-Right represents a source of threat(s) to various likely parties who, therefore, may be subject to a variety of risk exposures as a result. However, such a uni-directional model is unrealistic and, indeed, a cogent analysis must also consider what risk exposures affect imputed risk sources themselves. For example, although many may regard the Alt-Right as a threat to democracy, and be alarmed at the perceived threat posed by electoral successes by populist and hard right-wing parties in recent years, the speed with which the latter voting successes may go into sharp reverse shows up a major risk exposure for such parties. For example, by May 2017 the number of UK Independence Party elected officials at both national and local levels had all but disappeared in less than a year and political oblivion beckoned. Similarly, the far-right Party for Freedom of Geert Wilders in Holland and the Front National of Marine Le Pen in France were both defeated in general elections in 2017, following years of growing success. Dubious credibility, relentless unpleasant rhetoric from such parties, and their propaganda based on fear and faked facts, are likely to eventually combine to motivate rejection at the ballot box. The risk of hubris and no longer being acceptable or taken seriously by an electorate is a political risk faced by any Alt-Right (or indeed any) party but, of course, electoral demise does not eliminate their ideology or its core supporters.

The Book's Style, Content, Authors and Structure

This book follows academic discipline and seeks to provide evidence and references to support particular statements or at least make clear any necessary distinctions between facts, assertions, arguments and opinions. However, with such a controversial subject, and potential evocation of strong emotions (whether for or against a particular ideology or exponents of it), there is a temptation for authors to slip into polemical expression in their narratives. Indeed, there is currently an unresolved debate among academics about whether traditional scholarly neutrality must be maintained or whether authors could legitimately take a strong for/against position and use polemic in support of it. The editor took the view that the traditional approach should prevail. However, should any traces of polemic remain, he takes full responsibility for any criticism that may arise.

The potential scope for the content of a book such as this is huge and, if fully comprehensive, its size would be prohibitive. Moreover, with the inherently fast-moving nature of current affairs and developments, it is not possible to capture all relevant events and to be up-to-date, which in any event is the task of journalists and the news media. From systems science, a holistic approach only requires to include the perseverant essence of the whole and not every ephemeral component of the whole (von Bertalanffy 1972; Checkland 1981). Therefore, in deciding on content, the editor has taken a selective approach to a number of areas in an attempt to provide a reasonably representative coverage of key issues.

The book is fortunate to benefit from contributions from an eclectic group of thirteen authors with backgrounds in psychology, sociology, history, political science, international relations, and risk analysis, who variously have specialised in studies of the populist and far-right in the United States, UK, mainland Europe and elsewhere. A number have also been engaged in comparative studies of the populist right and far-right in different countries. Details of the authors' affiliations are presented in the section About the Editor and Authors.

The book is in three parts. Part 1 on the nature of Alt-Right ideology comprises two chapters. Chapter 1 considers how best to define the evolving Alt-Right phenomenon. Chapter 2 examines the psychology, and especially the emotional origins and motivations, of the Alt-

Right as an aid to understanding their behaviour and potentially predicting future actions.

Part 2 comprises nine chapters that examine how the Alt-Right ideology has been absorbed and framed by various groups in a selection of European countries including Russia, in which this ideology has made some inroads into society and, in some cases, has achieved a degree of political, if not electoral, success.

Part 3 Conclusion comprises three chapters that synthesise the various analyses from Parts 1 and 2. One chapter provides systematically a common risk analysis and assessment framework to all the risks identified in Part 2. The penultimate chapter considers how far Alt-Right ideology and practice represent a threat to democracy and western civilisation, and makes a prognosis for how the Alt-Right phenomenon might develop and how far it is likely to increase its influence. The final chapter identifies potential strategies to limit the Alt-Right threat in so far as it may exist.

References

Ackoff, R.L. 1971. "Towards a System of System Concepts". *Journal of Management Science* 17(11), 661–671.

Beck, U. 1992. *Risk Society—Towards a New Modernity.* London: Sage Publications.

Burrell, G. and Morgan, G. 1979. *Sociological Paradigms and Organizational Analysis.* London: Heinemann.

Checkland, P. 1981. *Systems Thinking, Systems Practice.* Chichester: John Wiley & Sons.

Checkland, P. and Scholes (1990). *Soft Systems Methodology in Action.* Chichester: John Wiley & Sons.

Denzin, N.K. 1978. *The Research Act.* New York: McGraw-Hill.

Dixon, N. 1971. *Pre-Conscious Processing.* Chichester: John Wiley & Sons.

Douglas, M. 1992. *Risk and Blame: Essays in Cultural Theory.* London: Routledge.

Eatwell, R. and Goodwin, M. (eds). 2010. *The New Extremism in 21st Century Britain.* Abingdon, Oxford: Routledge.

Feldman, M. and Pollard, J. 2016. "The Ideologues and Ideologies of the Radical Right: an Introduction". *Patterns of Prejudice*, November 2, 2016. DOI 10.1080/0031322X.2016.1244148.

Fisher, L. 2018. "Antisemites Will Destroy Labour, Senior MPs Warn". *The Times.* March 27, 2018. Pages 1–2.

Glendon, A.I. 1987. "Risk Cognition". In W.T. Singleton and J. Hovden (eds), *Risk and Decisions*, pages 87–107. Chichester: John Wiley & Sons.

Glendon. A.I. and Clarke, S. 2016. *Human Safety and Risk Management: a Psychological Perspective*. 3rd edition. Boca Raton, FL: CRC Press/Taylor & Francis.

Goodwin, M. 2011. *Right Response. Understanding and Countering Populist Extremism in Europe*. London: Chatham House.

ISO. 2018. *ISO 31000 Risk Management—Guidelines*. Replaced ISO 31000 (2009). Geneva: International Organization for Standardization.

Janis, I.L. 1982. *Groupthink: Psychological Studies of Policy Decisions and Fiascos*. 2nd edition. New York: Houghton and Mifflin.

Kahneman, D. 2003. "Maps of Bounded Rationality: Psychology for Behavioural Economics". *American Economic Review* 93(5), 1449–1475.

Kluback, W. and Weinbaum, M. 1957. *Dilthey's Philosophy of Existence: Introduction to Weltanschauungslehre*. Translation of an essay. London: Vision Press.

Lyons, M.N. 2017a. *Ctrl-Alt-Delete: The Origins and Ideology of the Alternative Right*. Somerville, MA: Political Research Associates.

Lyons, M.N. 2017b. *Insurgent Supremacists: The US Far Right's Challenge to State and Empire*. Oakland, Ca: PM Press.

Maguire, P. and Fisher, L. 2018. "No More Talk, Jewish Leaders Warn Corbyn". *The Times*. March 27, 2018. Page 10.

Michael, G. 2003. *Confronting Right-Wing Extremism and Terrorism in the USA*. Abingdon, Oxon UK: Routledge.

Michael, G. 2016. "The Seeds of the Alt-Right, America's Emergent Right-Wing Populist Movement". *The Conversation*, November 23, 2016. http://theconversation.com.

Michael, G. 2017. "The Rise of the Alt-Right and the Politics of Polarization in America". *Skeptic Magazine*, February 1, 2017. Altadena, Ca. The Skeptics Society.

Morgan, G. 1986. *Images of Organization*. London: Sage.

Neiwert, D. 2017. *Alt-America—The Rise of the Radical Right in the Age of Trump*. London: Verso.

Parris, M. 2018. "There's a Brutish Jingoism Afoot in Britain". Comment. *The Times*. March 24, 2018. Page 25.

Shrader-Frechette, K.S. 1991. *Risk and Rationality: Philosophical Foundations for Populist Reforms*. Berkeley: University of California Press.

Simon, H.A. 1972. "Theories of Bounded Rationality". In *Decisions and Organization*, edited by C.B. MaGuire and R. Radner, 161–176. Amsterdam: North Holland Publishing Co.

von Bertalanffy, L. 1992. "The History and Status of General Systems Theory". *Acad. Management Journal* 15(4), 407–426.

Waring A.E. 2013. *Corporate Risk and Governance: an End to Mismanagement, Tunnel Vision, and Quackery*. Farnham, UK: Gower/Routledge.

Waring, A.E. and Glendon, A.I. 1998. *Managing Risk: Critical Issues for Survival and Success into the 21st Century*. Aldershot, UK: Thompson/Cengage.

Wodak, R. 2015. *The Politics of Fear. What Right-Wing Populist Discourses Mean*. London: Sage.

Zeffman, H. 2018. "Tensions in Labour Erupt Over Rising Abuse of Jews". *The Times*. April 18, 2018. Pages 1–2.

Part 1:
The Nature of the Alt-Right Ideology

Chapter 1:
Defining the Evolving Alt-Right Phenomenon

By Alan Waring

Abstract

This chapter examines right-wing world-views outside the realms of traditional conservatism, which are more strident, more intolerant and increasingly extreme the further to the right is their location. Populist-, far- and extreme-right parties and groups in European societies and others (e.g. Russia) are identified and characterised by nationalist, nativist, anti-liberal, anti-immigrant, anti-Muslim, anti-Semitic, and white supremacist rhetoric and policies. The Alt-Right emergence in several EU countries and Russia is examined and transnational collaboration between Alt-Right groups in different countries is discussed. Collectively labelled as the Alternative Right or Alt-Right, such groups typically have a strong desire to legitimize and normalise their ideology for electoral appeal purposes. Noting the difficulties in defining the evolving Alt-Right, a working definition is proposed.

Key words: Alt-Right, ideology, nationalism, nativism, transnational, Trump.

The Conservative Tradition

Conservatism, in a general sense, refers to adherence to traditional, normative values and a reluctance to welcome change. In a political context, conservatism or the so-called 'right-wing' exhibits such characteristics as these found within the population, but also extends the general concept to extol the virtues of individual endeavour and self-reliance as well as favouring free enterprise, private ownership, low taxation, and socially conservative ideas. Conservatism emphasizes personal responsibility and eschews collectivism and any kind of socialist or left-wing agenda, such as an emphasis on public spending, high taxation of businesses and high earners, trades union power and a de-emphasis on defence spending.

Traditional conservatism has never been monolithic and has always included identifiable co-existing factions, ranging from the more liberal centre-right (e.g. the so-called Mainstreet Republicans in the USA; the One Nation Conservatives, Tory Reform Group and Conservative Party Europhiles/Brexit Remainers in the UK); through to right-wing conservatives, such as the Paleoconservatives, NeoCons, Tea Party and latterly Trumpists in the USA, and the Thatcherites, Eurosceptics and EU Brexiteers in the UK.

Further right still, and outside the realms of traditional conservatism, exist world-views that are more strident, more intolerant and increasingly fascist the further to the right is their location. Ultra-right parties and groups in western societies are characterised by strongly nationalist, nativist, anti-liberal, anti-immigrant, anti-Muslim and white supremacist rhetoric and policies, for example in the UK, the British National Party, Britain First and English Defence League. Similar parties and groups have arisen in many countries. Some, in view of their extremist and violent proclivities, are classed as terrorists e.g. National Action proscribed in the UK, and Aryan Nations and National Alliance in the USA (FBI, 2002). Lyons (2017a and b), Michael (2003; 2008; 2014; 2016; 2017), and Neiwert (2017) refer to a range of right-wing extremist groups in the United States. However, as discussed below, it should be noted that, although attention to the far-right is typically focussed on the west, far-right characteristics are also evident in many non-western countries.

The Alternative Right

The so-called Alt-Right (short for Alternative Right) is generally considered to encompass the spectrum of right-wing conservative world-views outside mainstream conservatism that begins with those who have become dissatisfied with the mainstream political process and character and frustrated by what they regard as the impotence of traditional conservatism. This spectrum ranges from the populist Alt-Right to all those having a hard-right, ultra-right or extremist ideology. ADL (2018) described in detail a less extreme group within the Alt-Right, which it termed the Alt-Lite. However, although informative, this distinction appears to be more pedantic than substantive. Although coined initially with reference to populist right-wing and far-right groups, ideas, and activities in the United States, the term Alt-

Right has since been extended to cover similar characteristics evident in western countries generally, as well as in non-western countries such as Russia and Ukraine.

The term Alt-Right, although adopted originally in the US by Gottfried (2008) (see later), has taken on a more global coverall meaning but is not used as such everywhere e.g. in the UK. This has led to confusion in the UK, where some people call Britain First, for example, a far-right group, others call it extremist, while others call it populist. In Italy, Lega and 5 Star are often called populist yet their rhetoric and policies appear much more far-right, and some might argue extremist.

The author decided to use the term Alt-Right in this book in a coverall way simply to ensure that the spectrum of right-wing views outside and beyond mainstream conservative parties is fully captured. That spectrum ranges from populist parties not far removed from mainstream conservatism but definitely outside it, all the way through more authoritarian far-right parties and groups frequently prepared to advocate if not use violence, up to and including extremists and proscribed terrorists. The membership of UKIP, the populist Alt-Right party in the UK, undoubtedly includes many who actually profess views much more akin to the far-right Britain First and EDL—there is abundant evidence of this referred to in various chapters. Indeed, even within the mainstream Conservative Party in Britain, there have been allegations of Conservative MPs promoting far-right views e.g. Humphries (2018). Inclusion of populist parties under the Alt-Right label is necessary, therefore, since (a) the delineations between such parties and more far- and extreme-right groups are not sharp (in policy, member views, or rhetoric), and (b) there is persistent pressure by far-right groups on the more populist and even mainstream right-wing parties to shift their centre of political gravity rightwards e.g. infiltration of UKIP by Britain First and EDL activists; senior UKIP figures making racist and anti-Islamic statements reflecting BF and EDL policy and contrary to UKIP policy.

However, although the Alt-Right term is usually applied in a coverall shorthand way as above, and is how it is applied in this book, it should be noted that there are also Alt-Right characteristics evident in other countries, regimes, ethnicities, and religions. For example, the Duterte regime in the Philippines may be described as far-right authoritarian, repressive, and proto-fascist. In Myanmar, although attempting to adopt some strands of democracy following decades of absolute military dictatorship, in 2016–2017 the Bhuddist nationalist regime engaged in wholesale atrocities against, and ethno-religious cleansing of, Rohingya Muslims. Many countries in the Middle East, Central Asia, and Africa exhibit far-right characteristics in the form of quasi- or actual dictatorships, anti-democratic repression, judicial abuses, and human rights abuses. Similar charges have been aimed at North Korea and China, both of which are formally communist states i.e. far-left rather than far-right. Then there is the IS/Al Ghaeda/Boko Haram bloc of Islamist extremists who, while flying a false Muslim flag for justification, portray authoritarian, repressive, and proto-fascist characteristics strikingly similar to those of the ultra-right in the west, many of whom fly a false Christian flag for justification. For example, Michael (2006) has examined such similarities regarding the US far-right and, in particular, the seemingly paradoxical conceptual convergences between, on the one hand, neo-Nazis, Holocaust deniers, and white separatists, and, on the other hand, Islamist extremists in a number of countries. The paradox is sharpened by the fact that the Alt-Right generally in the west is anti-Muslim, and professed Islamists are generally anti-Christian. However, they share a common hatred of Jews, Israel and American foreign policy. Nevertheless, it is reported that Geert Wilders, leader of the right-wing racist Party for Freedom in Holland is a "serious case of philo-Semitism" and is very pro-Israel (Engelhart 2013)—see chapter 9. Another paradox is the upsurge in anti-Semitism in the British Labour Party, especially among the hard-left Momentum group, which contradicts the traditional anti-racist philosophy of the Labour Party (see e.g. Fisher 2018a; Maguire and Fisher 2018; Zeffman 2018).

Whereas the ideologies, strategies, tactics, and justifications used by authoritarian, repressive, and fascistic entities of whatever declaration and in whichever country appear to be remarkably similar (despite their often purported inimical differences), the scope of this book is limited to the Alt-Right as conventionally understood i.e. western countries (primarily US and European) and non-western European countries (e.g. Russia).

Table 1.1 in Appendix 1.1 lists prominent examples of Alt-Right groups in a range of European countries. The list in Table 1.1 is incomplete. New small groups arise from time to time and frequently groups alter their name or merge with other groups, especially in the United States (see e.g. Neiwert 2017). While it may appear that Alt-Right groups enjoy a large membership or level of support, typically each one has followers in the hundreds or low thousands. For example, in the US the estimated number of KKK (Ku Klux Klan) members and committed supporters in June 2017 was some 3,000 spread across 42 local groups (or Klans) in 33 states (ADL 2017). This small total compares with a national membership of some 4 million in the 1920s and between 6,000 and 10,000 in the early 1990s—see also chapter 3 in Vol 1. Similarly, in the UK, the populist UKIP's membership peaked at 45,999 in 2015 before falling to 39,000 in 2016 and into 2017 (Keen and Apostolova 2017), and to 21,000 in early 2018 (ONS 2018). The British National Party (BNP) also fell from a peak membership of just over 10,000 in 2010 to less than 3,000 in 2016. Even at their peak, such numbers were relatively small compared to those of the mainstream British political parties and, over a period of many years, both UKIP and BNP failed to enjoy any sustained electoral success at either local or national level, as discussed further in chapters 3 and 4.

The Alt-Right is neither a political party nor is it a movement in the sense of a cohesive movement or a group having a defined philosophy, constitution, organization, policy, membership and so on. To that extent, it may be described as a phenomenon whereby large numbers of individuals, across a broad spectrum beyond and to the right of conventional conservatism and conservative political parties, share an ideology based primarily on racism and white supremacy, anti-immigration, and antipathy to perceived government interference in the daily lives of citizens. Of course, not all Alt-Right supporters are white or believing in white supremacy. For example, a number of prominent Alt-Right supporters are from ethnic minorities e.g. some former *Breitbart News* staffers. Nagle (2017) described the Alt-Right as a meta-group of semi-divergent right-wing sub-cultures in broad coalition seeking to overturn and replace the established order in society. Some argue that the Alt-Right is like a religious cult in some respects, as evidenced by the idolisation of particular zealots and their expressed ideas and by the invention of obscurantist language and symbols that only committed supporters are likely to understand (see, for example, Sonnad and Squirrell 2017). However, Neiwert (2017) argued that the Internet has revolutionised communication between disaffected right-wingers, especially young people, to such an extent that they are now able to rapidly encourage each other towards radicalisation and, for some, to extremism. The anarchic revolutionary zeal of some younger recruits to the Alt-Right and their fixated, self-absorbed immersion in on-line obscurantism formed the substance of the examination by Nagle (2017). Such 'new elite' elements are likely never to be regarded as more than an eccentric and largely incomprehensible oddity by the majority of populist Alt-Right supporters. As potential recruiters and persuaders of mainstream conservatives to move decisively rightwards into the Alt-Right, the very eccentricity, secretive language and esoteric condescension they display to outsiders is likely to weaken their appeal.

Neiwert (2017) also explained in some detail that, in common with earlier manifestations of the American populist radical right such as the Patriots and the Tea Party, the US Alt-Right movement has conjured up an alternative universe to that of verifiable reality, with alternative explanations for an entire world of known facts, and eagerness, even passion, for believing in easily disprovable falsehoods and conspiracies involving these (Kahan et al 2017; Shermer 2018). Some examples are discussed in chapters 9 and 10 of Vol 1.

Although the Alt-Right spectrum in each country is unique, a common pattern permeates them all to a greater or lesser degree:

- Racism, specifically white supremacy, anti-Semitic, and anti-Muslim world-view.
- Anti-immigrant priorities.
- Anti-central government/anti-federalist world-view.
- A fundamentalist world-view, both religious and political.
- Anti-establishment/anti-government conspiracy theories.
- Strident right-wing fanaticism that often spills over into social settings, Internet and social media in the form of hectoring and propaganda rants.
- An over-riding hatred for such groups as non-whites, ethnic minorities, non-Christians (especially Jews and Muslims), immigrants, foreigners, liberals, socialists and other left-wingers, federalists, mainstream politicians, and bankers and financiers.
- An over-riding scepticism about established science or facts of any kind that do not support, or that contradict, ideological positions and beliefs of the Alt-Right, and a willingness to believe in an alternative universe of invented 'facts' that support Alt-Right contentions (see e.g. Kahan et al 2017; Shermer 2018).

For example, as noted earlier, it is commonplace to hear some (but not all) UKIP supporters in the UK espouse racist, nativist, anti-immigrant and anti-Muslim positions that do not form part of official UKIP policy. This is anecdotal evidence that the Alt-Right is not monolithic and there is no fixed dogma spanning the entire phenomenon. However, the further to the right is the political party or group of an Alt-Right supporter, the more likely it is that all eight characteristics will be exhibited.

From their experimental study of how different political groups in the US respond to information, Kahan et al (2017) concluded that scepticism about truth and accuracy is (a) very much dependent on subject matter context, and (b) is biased by the individual's pre-existing beliefs. Confirmation bias looms large in how individuals select some facts and ignore others so as to support their prejudices (Dror and Fraser-Mackenzie 2008). The eight characteristics may also be commonly linked psychologically to an authoritarian pre-disposition manifested by low curiosity, lack of open-mindedness, dislike of surprise or challenging information, taking comfort in rigid hierarchies of social and political order, feeling insecure about diversity and liberalism, and a dislike of and unwillingness to accept change that challenges their world-view.

Other more particular subsets occur that are not listed in Table 1.1. For example, one strand of Alt-Right followers are misogynists who believe that not only are they victims of government-led suffocation of their individual rights and freedoms but also that they are specifically victims of a conspiracy by government, liberal elites and feminism to downgrade men's dominant role in society, an alleged transgression that they stridently seek to combat (see e.g. ADL 2018).

The 'them' against 'us' character evident in all the Alt-Right rhetoric and posturing across the range of different issues in the Alt-Right agenda points to an underlying paranoia in their perception of threats (real or imagined) facing them. The psychology of fear and risk and its importance to understanding the Alt-Right world-view and predictions of Alt-Right behaviour is addressed in detail in chapter 2.

The Alt-Right Emergence in the United States

Resurgent nationalism in the US, including the emergence of the Alt-Right phenomenon, is addressed in detail in chapter 3 of Vol 1 and the following is a brief introduction. Lyons (2017a and b), Michael (2016; 2017), and Neiwert (2017) provided an extensive descriptive summary of the Alt-Right 'movement' in the US and its rapid evolution as an increasingly populist phenomenon, from lowly beginnings and small numbers of supporters in 2008 to the unexpected electoral success of Donald Trump in November 2016 as US President. ADL (2018) provided mini-biographies of leading Alt-Right (and Alt-Lite) figures, and indicated how interconnected they and the many sub-groups and factions are. Openly committed to an Alt-Right agenda (if, indeed, he was fully aware of the full implications), and contemptuous of both the traditional conservatism of the Republican Party and, of course, the Democrats, Trump made no secret of his view that many traditional Republicans were too close ideologically to Democratic thinking. His rambling book (Trump 2015) represented a classic 'salvation' proposition used in sales and marketing, in which buyers are told that they have a major problem (which may be true, or an exaggeration or completely untrue) and that only the company's product will solve the problem and save them: Trump asserted that America is crippled and that only he knows how to "make America great again".

Nevertheless, Trump himself did not emerge politically from the Alt-Right. Rather, it is more likely that the headline-grabbing issues promoted by the Alt-Right became a convenient opportunistic vehicle for Trump's election campaign. Trump is not a career politician and was much more interested in using the presidency to advance and promote the Donald J. Trump brand as part of a long-term business strategy. Moreover, as Lyons (2017a) and Neiwert (2017) asserted, the Alt-Right movement also judged support for Trump as an opportunity both to promote their agenda, and to weaken the Republican Party. A kind analysis is that, as President, Donald Trump became an unwitting Trojan horse for the Alt-Right, whereas a less kind analysis (e.g. Neiwert 2017) suggested that Trump was well aware of his Alt-Right role and remained more than happy to pursue an Alt-Right agenda. Either way, with no formal party and no electoral candidates, it could be argued that in the election of Trump the Alt-Right achieved a bloodless political coup of staggering proportions.

According to Michael (2017), in 2008 Paul Gottfried, a conservative academic, while addressing the H.L. Mencken Club on "The Decline and Rise of the Alternative Right", implied that the 'alternative right' was a dissident far-right ideology that rejected mainstream conservatism. The latter address (Gottfried 2008) is a somewhat self-absorbed pseudo-intellectual dissection of the minutiae of what Gottfried claimed to be wrong with the right-wing in America, in particular his distaste for what he regarded as a perfidious neo-con hegemony that had marginalised Gottfried himself, and had subverted right-wing conservatism. He asserted that "We are convinced that we are right in our historical and cultural observations while those who have quarantined us are wrong". In arguing for a vigorous resurgence of a viable true right-wing based on this certitude, and on an equal certitude of white racial superiority (e.g. "the fact that not everyone enjoys the same genetic precondition for learning"), ironically Gottfried's elaborate discourse undermined his fervent expectation that he was creating the basis "to gain recognition as an Intellectual Right". The so-called intellectual basis for the Alt-Right appears to be little more than an attempt to gain falsely some measure of credibility, respectability and social acceptability for what was, and is, a set of prejudiced beliefs in the primacy of inequality and the fostering of racial discrimination and white supremacy.

Nevertheless, from such small beginnings in 2008, the Alt-Right momentum in the United States took off following the appointment in 2011 of the voluble right-wing intellectual Richard Spencer as head of the National Policy Institute (NPL), a white nationalist 'think tank' founded in 2005. Spencer and his coterie of NPL writers have published prolifically on the white supremacist philosophy and agenda under the *Radix* imprint e.g. Spencer (2012). Gottfried, MacDonald and the Spencer writers arguably are the closest that the Alt-Right gets to the creation of an appearance, albeit dubious, of rational intellectual discourse.

However, the pretence of intellectualism was not central to the rapid rise of the Alt-Right. The cleverness of the Alt-Right 'movement' in the US, or at least those Alt-Right leaders in positions to manipulate public opinion, was to capture the growing disillusionment of broad swathes of the population about the ability, indeed willingness, of the traditional mainstream political parties to address effectively concerns about jobs, tax, the economy, health care, education etc. and lay the blame for it at the door of: (a) an allegedly weak and self-serving political establishment in cahoots with big business, and (b) the alleged predations of immigration and globalisation. The introduction in 2016 of Donald Trump, a business tycoon with no political background or experience of office, as a renegade Alt-Right Republican candidate for the Presidency, with such populist slogans as "Making America Great Again" and "draining the establishment swamp in Washington", and "We're gonna build a wall" (referring to a border wall to keep out illegal immigrants from Mexico and Central and South America), was sufficient to coalesce all strands of disaffected voters and get him elected in November 2016. Surrounded by an Alt-Right dominated cabinet and team of officials and advisers, the Alt-Right ideology and agenda could now be enacted.

Evidence has emerged that extremist elements in the US have taken advantage increasingly of right-wing populist advances since 2008 (e.g. Johnson 2012). For example, the white supremacist KKK that had been relatively quiescent for decades actively supported Donald Trump's presidential election campaign and, following his election, became more vociferous in openly praising Trump and his anti-immigrant, anti-Muslim, and anti-liberal policies. After several decades, the KKK and other far-right groups re-engaged in street protests and marches to promote their ideology. At such events, their members and supporters openly gave the Nazi salute, noisily expressed their hatred for non-whites, immigrants and ethnic minorities, gave adulation to Trump, and engaged in violent hate crime against anyone daring to challenge their views. For example, on August 11, 2017, there was a torch-lit Unite the Right march of white supremacists through the centre of Charlottesville in Virginia. From video evidence, some were armed with clubs and firearms. David Duke, a still-active former KKK leader, was reported to have said about the march: "We're going to fulfil the promises of Donald Trump to........ take our country back".

A young white supremacist drove his car at speed into peaceful counter-protesters, killing one person and injuring 19 others. According to eye witness reports, the ramming was deliberate. The suspect was arrested and charged with second degree murder and other offences. However, President Trump's response to the incident was one of equivocation in which he blamed "many sides" for such hatred, bigotry and violence (White House 2017a). Curiously, Trump's televised statement made on August 12, 2017 was not listed in the White House official statements. Only following widespread condemnation from

Congress members, the mayor of Charlottesville, mainstream politicians both Republican and Democrat, the media and commentators, did the White House issue a clarification on August 14 mixed within a statement on foreign trade. Also televised, this statement (White House 2017b) suggested that in his original condemnation Trump had automatically implied white supremacists etc.: "Of course, that includes white supremacists, KKK, neo-Nazi and all extremist groups". Nevertheless, both his implication that the violence of the perpetrator had a moral equivalence with the relatively peaceful behaviour of the victims, and his reluctance to condemn the perpetrator and his allies as domestic terrorists, led many to question whether the President covertly agreed with such right-wing extremists. After 48 hours of increasing political pressure, Trump issued a third statement in which he unequivocally condemned white supremacists, the KKK and neo-Nazis for their violent behaviour. Nevertheless, the following day, during a White House press conference scheduled to outline the president's infrastructure policy and development, he launched into a lengthy tirade against the media in which he re-iterated and amplified his original assertion that anti-fascist demonstrators were equally to blame for the violence in Charlottesville. Blaming the victims of fascism for their own demise is a well-exercised tactic of the far-right, for example denial of the Nazi Holocaust against the Jews in WWII, while nonetheless stating that any harm that might have befallen them was entirely their own fault for having parasitic characters that naturally attracted hatred.

The renewed aggression of US far-right extremists and their vocal support for Trump and his policies suggested that they felt encouraged and emboldened by an Alt-Right dominated Trump administration to enact their ideological beliefs, secure in their presumption that Trump agreed with them and was likely only ever to grudgingly censure their actions if and when forced to do so. The resurgent far-right in the USA is discussed in more detail in chapter 3 of Vol 1.

The Alt-Right Emergence in the UK

In the UK too, from 2004 onwards and especially after 2010, an increasing number of right-wing supporters of the Conservative Party withdrew their support for the Party in protest at what they regarded as policies that were a betrayal of such right-wing values as national independence (from alleged domination by the EU), strict immigration controls, low taxation, reduced public spending, and toughness on law and order. A particular cause for their ire was their perception that increasingly the EU (of which the UK has been a member since 1973) was imposing EU laws, regulations and diktats on the UK that were both unacceptable and often dysfunctional. Allied assertions included imposition of un-British constraints on British courts by the EU, the European Court of justice and European Court of Human Rights, which it was alleged forced British courts to be unduly lenient on a range of issues, such as benefits for asylum seekers and discrimination of various kinds, often finding in favour of plaintiffs and claimants whom right-wingers judged to be undeserving or fraudulent.

UKIP (see chapter 3), which since its birth in 1993 has always been openly hostile to the EU, gradually became a haven for disaffected conservatives. However, the founder Alan Sked resigned in 1997, apparently over what he felt was racist and far-right infiltration of the party. Indeed, in 2006 the Conservative MP David Cameron who would later become Prime Minister, described UKIP members as "fruitcakes, loonies and closet racists, mostly". Regardless of poor electoral showing over many years, UKIP attracted a steadily increasing proportion of votes and eventually gained a number of local council seats and, in 2014, its first British MP. Somewhat perversely for a dedicated anti-EU party, by 2014 UKIP also had 24 Members of the European Parliament (MEPs), although it became apparent that the UKIP purpose in gaining such seats was not to enhance the EP in any way but to destroy it from within. Destruction from within is very much in line with the 'entryist' non-reform strategy and tactics advocated by both the hard-left (e.g. the former Militant Tendency of the 1970s and 80s and international Marxists within the UK Labour Party) and the hard-right (e.g. white nationalists in the US such as Sallis (2014) as described by Lyons (2017a)).

Led from 2006 by the charismatic and acerbic orator Nigel Farage, UKIP became the flagship for all those on the right seeking the UK's withdrawal from the EU as a means (as they saw it) to re-establish British sovereignty, remove unwanted EU legislation and diktats, recover control of the UK's borders, and stop the free movement of citizens of EU countries into the UK. UKIP masterminded a relentless campaign of anti-EU propaganda and lobbying, culminating in the UK Referendum of 2016 to determine whether the British people wanted to remain in or leave the EU. The 'leavers' won by 52% to the 'remainers' at 48%—a small but clear majority and sufficient to ensure that the 2-year process for exiting the EU (so-called 'Brexit') would begin. However, having succeeded in championing Brexit to the stage of the UK government formally starting the actual Brexit process, UKIP then found itself as somewhat 'a party without a cause' and, in the UK General Election of 2017 and Local Elections of 2017 and 2018, it was soundly trounced. With former Conservative supporters or other mainstream party 'converts' to UKIP returning to vote for their original parties, UKIP failed to win a single parliamentary seat and lost most of its local council seats. The party was left in disarray with its future uncertain, although it is likely to continue as an Alt-Right lobbying and rallying focus for those beyond the right wing of the traditional Conservative Party.

In addition to the populist UKIP, more extreme right-wing groups (see chapter 4) include British National Party (BNP), Britain First, English Defence League, For Britain, Generation Identity, and the proscribed terrorist group National Action. BNP's electoral successes have been weak and patchy, never managing to gain a British parliamentary seat but from time-to-time holding some local council seats and two European Parliament seats. Since 2014, when it lost its only remaining European Parliament seat, BNP has been in marked decline.

The Trans-National Appeal of the Alt-Right

Although the histories of the American and the UK right-wings are significantly different, ideologically they have much in common. It is unsurprising that openly there was considerable sharing of ideas on strategy, tactics, marketing, and public relations between UKIP leaders and the Trump team and coterie of the US Alt-Right, both during the lead up to the UK's EU Referendum and to the US Presidential Election. UKIP leaders, such as Nigel Farage and Arron Banks, had frequent meetings in the United States with Trump's senior team members, and Farage even gave a personal endorsement to Trump at one of the latter's major campaign rallies.

The close involvement of US Alt-Right protagonists in UK politics continued into 2018 on British soil e.g. attendance by Steve Bannon at populist- and far-right gatherings, support for the far-right EDL and its former leader Tommy Robinson by Bannon (LBC 2018) and congressman Paul Gosar (Fisher 2018b), and unofficial meetings between John Bolton and British right-wing politicians (Fisher 2018b). Bannon referred to Robinson , a person with multiple criminal convictions, including those connected with his political activities, as "the backbone of this country" (LBC 2018). As Aaronovitch (2018) noted, "The anti-Muslim street-brawler Tommy Robinson, who in times past would have been shunned entirely, is now spoken of by some on the right who should know better as a rough hero of the new struggle". Bannon was also accused of plotting with the German far-right (Charter 2018) and, while in France, he told a far-right Front National rally to wear "as a badge of honour" accusations of racism (Pasha-Robinson 2018).

The recognition of common cause, and the sharing of information and ideas on advancing their individual agendas, evolved transnationally (Engelhart 2013) to the extent that the erstwhile notion of the Alt-Right ideology being a purely American matter no longer holds. Far-right political parties across Europe (many predating the rise of the US Alt-Right) have promoted agendas and policies broadly similar to those of the Trump administration and those of the US far-right. The nationalist, anti-immigrant, anti-Muslim, anti-globalisation rallying cries of Front National in France, Party for Freedom in the Netherlands, AfD and PEGIDA in Germany, Northern League/Lega and 5 Star in Italy, Freedom Party and People's Party in Austria, and Fidesz and Jobbik in Hungary, for example, are in tune with those of the British and the US Alt-Right. In July 2018, the US Alt-Right evangelist Steve Bannon announced a plan to create a European foundation named The Movement, intended to promote and support populist- and far-right political groups across Europe, with an initial objective of forming an Alt-Right 'supergroup' of MEPs within the European Parliament (Alexander 2018). Viktor Orban, the Hungarian far-right Prime Minister much praised by Bannon and supported by Poland and the ruling far-right coalition in Austria, has openly described the pan-European far-right program as "anti-immigrant, anti-multicultural and stand[ing] for the Christian family model" and, further, stated "Christian democracy is by definition not liberal. It is illiberal" (Waterfield 2018). Whether Bannon's subversive zeal in seeking to export to Europe his brand of far-right political and social revolution will be successful is uncertain, although Rikfind (2018) concluded it will fail as far as the UK is concerned. Nevertheless, in urging the mainstream political right to "guard against its lunatic fringe", Aaronovitch (2018) noted that "Farage is the clearest example of a trend towards what could be called 'Orbanisation'—a belief that the nation state and its indigenous culture are under threat externally from international institutions and internally from migrants, especially Muslims".

Also uncertain is whether Bannon's zeal will eventually bring him into conflict with state authorities in the various European countries. Clearly, by openly supporting individuals and political groups having a history of intimidation, violence, and public order offences, the risk that he will become to be regarded as a threat to public order, public safety, and possibly national security, is heightened. For example, a number of far-right foreigners (see e.g. Hosenball 2018) have been barred from entering the UK as being not in the public interest, and one in particular for an intention to meet Tommy Robinson, the far-right leader so praised by Bannon.

Moreover, the common ideology of the US and European Alt-Right movements is also in tune with much of the autocratic and increasingly far-right populist character of the Russian administration of Vladimir Putin (see chapter 11). For example, in March 2017, Putin sent an envoy to Italy to sign a mutual cooperation pact with the far-right Northern League and also made a similar pact with the far-right Freedom Party in Austria (see chapter 6). During the US Presidential campaign, Putin openly expressed his admiration for Donald Trump, as did many of the deputies in the Russian Duma. There is, of course, the on-going unresolved controversy as to whether the Russians covertly attempted to subvert the presidential election to favour Trump and whether Trump and/or any of his team cooperated unlawfully in any way with the Russians to influence the election outcome or US foreign policy in a way that ultimately would favour Russian strategic interests.

The far-right parties in these various countries also share another characteristic: the strong desire to legitimize and make respectable their ideology and agenda by presenting them as being fair, virtuous and reasonable, and offering real democracy, real freedom and real security to the population—or at least to the majority who are white, non-immigrant and non-Muslim or of other minority religion. The far-right have sought to draw intellectual legitimacy for their cause from individuals who variously have sought to present the Alt-

Right ideology as a necessary and inevitable antidote to alleged harmful liberalism, for example, Richard Spencer (e.g. *Radix Journal*), Jared Taylor (e.g. Taylor, 1993), Samuel Huntington (e.g. Huntington 2004), Glenn Beck (e.g. Beck 2015) and Kevin MacDonald (e.g. MacDonald 2002; 2004).

There is some dispute as to whether the contemporary upsurge of the Alt-Right is qualitatively similar to that of fascism in the 1930s. For example, academics such as Niall Ferguson argued that it is not (Ferguson 2012; Long 2016; McDougall 2016), whereas others have argued that although recent contexts are different to those of the 1930s the underlying ideology is broadly the same (Engelhart 2013; McDougall 2016). Moreover, the strategies and tactics of the Alt-Right today have evolved and become more sophisticated and nuanced compared to fascism of the 1930s. Whereas in the 1930s, the fascist goal was to gain absolute control of the state, the Alt-Right now in the main do not appear to be seeking a totalitarian takeover but instead seem content for now to exert such a powerful influence on mainstream conservativism that it 'corrects itself' and shifts its centre of political gravity firmly towards the far-right. Rather than coup by force, it is more about subversion of mainstream conservatism to ensure a permanent Alt-Right stamp on national governance.

Chapter 2 delves further into the emotional and motivational character of the evolving Alt-Right and how it is possible for seemingly different, even opposing, interests between different countries to have so much in common. Also examined are the world-views informing some of the inconsistent, if not misleading, claims of many far-right parties to represent freedom, democracy and benign policies while at the same time promoting policies advocating repression and denial of human rights for disfavoured classes of person.

Defining the Alt-Right

Both Lyons (2017a and b) and Michael (2016; 2017) suggested that defining the Alt-Right precisely is difficult because it is a continually evolving phenomenon. What emerges is that the Alt-Right, is a somewhat chaotic melange of disaffected, disgruntled and angry people. Neiwert (2017) referred in particular to the 'producerist' core of the populist Alt-Right (i.e. angry citizens who see themselves as hard-working patriots sandwiched between a nefarious, oppressive, corrupt elite of corporate owners, officials and politicians above them and a parasitic underclass of feckless, lazy, immoral, unpatriotic and undeserving 'others' beneath them). No more is this anger exemplified than in the utterances and publications of Milo Yiannopoulos (Neiwert 2017), a British-born former staffer on *Breitbart News*, the Alt-Right media organ—although ADL (2018) categorized him as Alt-Lite. Yiannopoulos is a notorious self-publicist who deliberately courts media attention by making outrageous statements on a number of topics. When he made a controversial statement that could have been interpreted as advocating underage sex, the company originally contracted to publish his book *Dangerous* (Simon & Schuster) withdrew and the author eventually self-published it (Yiannopoulos 2017). Bubbling, visceral anger was also evident in such leading Alt-Right exponents as Steve Bannon, President Trump's former chief strategist, and Dr Sebastian Gorka, a former national security adviser and former Deputy Assistant to the President (see chapter 5 in Vol 1). In TV media interviews, for example, neither person sought to disguise their angry contempt for public accountability or being questioned pointedly on matters of public interest (e.g. Gorka interviews on *BBC Newsnight* January 31, 2017 and *CNN* July 24, 2017).

The outward anger towards their objects of hatred that characterises the Alt-Right is also frequently directed internally within Alt-Right groups and between them. For example, in the US, the KKK leadership has periodically engaged in destructive power struggles. In the UK, similarly these have occurred within UKIP, BNP, EDL, and Britain First. Over the period 2014 to 2017, UKIP appeared to be in a permanent state of self-destructive in-fighting (see chapter 3). In 2014, BNP's entire membership list was leaked onto the Internet by a disgruntled official. Senior officials of BNP and Britain First have traded angry accusations, and defections between the groups appear to have damaged mutual good will. Self-destructive behaviour evident within and among the Alt-Right is addressed in chapter 2.

A definition of the Alt-Right raised by Michael (2017) derived from Gottfried, namely 'a dissident far-right ideology that rejects mainstream conservatism' is probably no longer adequate to express the Alt-Right in its current evolved state. The editor's own definition, namely as an ideology, 'the spectrum of right-wing world-views outside traditional conservatism, which begins with a dissatisfaction with the mainstream political process and character and frustration by perceived impotence of traditional conservatism, and runs through populist, hard-right, ultra-right, and extreme-right ideology', is probably also inadequate but may serve as a working definition for the purposes of this book. For example, how does one satisfactorily capture the characteristic indignant anger in a definition of the Alt-Right? Redefinition may well become necessary as the Alt-Right evolves further.

References

Aaronovitch, D. 2018. "Right Must Guard Against its Lunatic Fringe". *The Times.* August 9, 2018. Page 21.

ADL. 2017. *Despite Internal Turmoil, Klan Groups Persist.* Anti-Defamation League. KKK Report CR1573. June 2017. New York: ADL.

ADL. 2018. *From Alt Right to Alt Lite: Naming the Hate.* Anti-Defamation League. New York: ADL. https://www.adl.org/. Accessed January 31, 2018.

Alexander, H. 2018. "Steve Bannon Announces Plan for European Foundation to Back Right-Wing Political Groups". *The Telegraph.* July 21, 2018. https://www.telegraph.co.uk.

Beck, G. 2014. "Glenn Beck: Obama's Idea of Leveling the Playing Field". www.glennbeck.com/content/articles/article/198/42443.

Beck, G. 2015. *It Is About Islam: Exposing the Truth About ISIS, Al Qaeda, Iran and the Caliphate.* New York: Threshold Editions/Simon & Schuster.

Charter, D. 2018. "Bannon Plots with German Far Right". *The Times.* March 8, 2018.

Dror, I.E. and Fraser-Mackenzie, P.A.F. 2008. "Cognitive Biases in Human Perception, Judgment, and Decision Making: Bridging Theory and the Real World". In *Criminal Investigative Failures.* edited by Kim Rossmo, 53–67. Abingdon Oxon UK: Taylor & Francis.

Engelhart, K. 2013. "The Rise of the Far Right in Europe". *Maclean's.* November 30, 2013. http://www.macleans.ca/.

FBI. 2002. "Domestic and International Terrorist Threat to the United States". Testimony of Dale L. Watson, Federal Bureau of Investigation, to Senate Select Committee on Intelligence. Washington DC. February 6, 2002.

Ferguson, N. 2012. "Europe's New Fascists—Populism Takes an Ominous Turn". August 10, 2012. *Niall Ferguson.* www.niallferguson.com.

Fisher, L. 2018a. "Antisemites Will Destroy Labour, Senior MPs Warn". *The Times.* March 27, 2018. Pages 1–2.

Fisher, L. 2018b. "I'll Be Back if This Betrayal Continues, Promises Farage". *The Times.* July 14, 2018. Page 11.

Gottfried, P. 2008. "The Decline and Rise of the Alternative Right". Address to H.L. Mencken Club AGM, November 21–23, 2008. Reproduced December 1, 2008 by *Taki's Magazine*. www.tkimag.com.

Hosenball, M. 2018. "British Authorities Ban Three Foreign Right-Wing Activists". *Reuters*. March 12, 2018. https://reuters.com/.

Humphries, W. 2018. "Tory MP Attacked for Anti-Muslim Post". *The Times*. March 27, 2018. Page 10.

Huntington, S. 2004. *Who Are We? The Challenges to America's National Identity*. New York: Simon & Schuster.

Johnson, D. 2012. *Right Wing Resurgence: How a Domestic Terrorist Threat is Being Ignored*. Lanham, Maryland: Rowman and Littlefield Publishers.

Kahan, D.M., Jamieson, K.H., Landrum, A.R. et al. 2017. "Culturally Antagonistic Memes and the Zika Virus: an Experimental Test". *Journal of Risk Research*, 20(1), 1–40.

Keen, R. and Apostolova, V. 2017. *Membership of UK Political Parties*. House of Commons Briefing Paper SN05125. 28 March 2017. London: House of Commons.

LBC. 2018. "Steve Bannon Clashes with *LBC*'s Political Editor Theo Usherwood Over Tommy Robinson". *LBC News*. July 15, 2018. https://www.lbc.co.uk.

Long, J. 2016. "Interview with Niall Ferguson and Yiannis Varoufakis". Jackie Long. *C4 News*. November 10, 2016. www.channel4.com.

Lyons, M.N. 2017a. *Ctrl-Alt-Delete: The Origins and Ideology of the Alternative Right*. Somerville, MA: Political Research Associates.

Lyons, M.N. 2017b. *Insurgent Supremacists: The US Far Right's Challenge to State and Empire*. Oakland, Ca: PM Press.

MacDonald, K.B. 2002. *Culture of Critique: An Evolutionary Analysis of Jewish Involvement in Twentieth Century Intellectual and Political Movements*. 2nd edition. Bloomington IN: Author House.

MacDonald, K.B. 2004. "Understanding Jewish Influences: a Study in Ethnic Activism". *Occidental Quarterly*, November 2004.

Maguire, P. and Fisher, L. 2018. "No More Talk, Jewish Leaders Warn Corbyn". *The Times*. March 27, 2018. Page 10.

McDougall, J. 2016. "No, This Isn't the 1930s—But Yes, This is Fascism". *The Conversation*. November 16, 2016. https://theconversation.com/.

Michael, G. 2003. *Confronting Right-Wing Extremism and Terrorism in the USA*. Abingdon, Oxon UK: Routledge.

Michael, G. 2006. *The Enemy of My Enemy: The Alarming Convergence of Militant Islam and the Extreme Right*. Lawrence KA: University Press of Kansas.

Michael, G. 2008. *The American Far Right*. Gainesville, FL: University of Florida.

Michael, G. (ed). 2014. *Extremism in America*. Gainesville, FL: University of Florida.

Michael, G. 2016. "The Seeds of the Alt-Right, America's Emergent Right-Wing Populist Movement". *The Conversation*, November 23, 2016. http://theconversation.com.

Michael, G. 2017. "The Rise of the Alt-Right and the Politics of Polarization in America". *Skeptic Magazine*, February 1, 2017. Altadena, Ca: The Skeptics Society.

Nagle, A. 2017. *Kill All Normies: Online Culture Wars from 4Chan and Tumblr to Trump and the Alt-Right*. Arlesford, Hants UK: Zero Books.

Neiwert, D. 2017. *Alt-America—The Rise of the Radical Right in the Age of Trump*. London: Verso.

ONS. 2018. *Electoral Statistics for the UK*. March 22, 2018. London: Office of National Statistics.

Pasha-Robinson, L. 2018. "Steve Bannon Tells French National Front Rally: 'Let Them Call You Racists..... Wear it as a Badge of Honour'". *The Independent*. March 12, 2018. https://www.independent.co.uk.

Rifkind, H. 2018. "The Bannon Revolution will Stop at Calais". *The Times*. March 13, 2018. Page 23.

Sallis, T. 2014. "Democratic Multiculturalism: Strategy and Tactics". *Counter-Currents Publishing*, November 19, 2014. http://www.counter-currents.com/2014/11/democratic-multiculturalism/.

Shermer, M. 2018. "For the Love of Science—Combating Science Denial with Science Pleasure". *Skeptic*. January 2018, page 73. www.scientificamerican.com.

Sonnad, N. and Squirrell, T. 2017. "The Alt-Right is Creating its Own Dialect. Here's the Dictionary". *Quartz*, October 30, 2017. https://qz.com/1092037/.

Spencer, R. 2012. *The Great Erasure: The Reconstruction of White Identity*. Ed. R. Spencer. Radix Vol 1. National Policy Institute. Arlington, VA: Washington Summit Publishers.

Taylor, J. 1993. *Paved with Good Intention: the Failure of Race Relations in Contemporary America*. New York: Carroll and Graf Publishers.

Trump, D.J. 2015. *Crippled America: How to Make America Great Again*. New York: Threshold Editions/Simon & Schuster.

Waterfield, B. 2018. "Next EU Election will Finish Liberal Elite, Says Orban". *The Times*. July 30, 2018. Page 25.

White House. 2017a. *Statement by the President of the United States*. August 12, 2017. https://www.youtube.com/watch?v=_uIVkdWZAWk

White House. 2017b. *Statement by the President of the United States*. August 14, 2017. Office of the Press Secretary. https://www.youtube.com/watch?v=Uqfg96W4T5U

Yiannopoulos, M. 2017. *Dangerous.* Self-published. New York: Dangerous Books.

Zeffman, H. 2018. "Tensions in Labour Erupt Over Rising Abuse of Jews". *The Times.* April 18, 2018. Pages 1–2.

Appendix 1.1 Alt-Right Representative Groups and Parties

It should be noted that the categories in Table 1.1 are not mutually exclusive and it is possible, indeed likely, that a particular group may be classified under more than one category.

Table 1.1: Alt-Right Exemplars in European Countries

Country	Populist	Separatist/ Anti-Central Government	White Supremacist/ Christian Identity/Nativist/ Anti-Muslim/ Anti-Semitic	Neo-Nazi /advocating nationalist policies akin to Third Reich	Extremist Militias (examples)	Officially Classified Terrorist or Proscribed Group (proscribing authority indicated)
UK	UKIP; One Nation	UKIP*; One Nation* (*separatism from EU)	National Action; Britain First; English Defence League; British National Party; Scottish Dawn; NS131; For Britain; Generation Identity; System Resistance Network	National Action; Britain First; English Defence League; British National Party; Scottish Dawn; NS131; For Britain; Generation Identity; System Resistance Network	National Action; Scottish Dawn; NS131; Generation Identity; System Resistance Network	National Action* (*proscribed 2016, Home Office). Scottish Dawn;** NS131** (**proscribed 2017, Home Office).

France	Front National		Front National; Nomad 88; Bloc Identitaire	Front National; Nomad 88; Bloc Identitaire		Nomad 88
Netherlands	Party for Freedom; Forum for Democracy		Party for Freedom; Forum for Democracy; Identitair Verzet; Erkenbrand; Falanx Nederland; Voorpost	Party for Freedom; Dutch People's Union; Netherlands National Youth; Erkenbrand; Falanx Nederland; Voorpost	Falanx Nederland; Voorpost	
Germany	AfD	National Democratic Party; Identitarian; Reichsbürger (Reich Citizens' Movement)	AfD; PEGIDA; Freital; Reich Citizens' Movement; National Socialist Under-ground; Third Way	PEGIDA; Freital; Reich Citizens' Movement; National Socialist Underground; Kameradschaften	Reichsbürger (Reich Citizens' Movement)	Freital; Reich Citizens' Movement; National Socialist Under-ground
Austria	Freedom Party		Freedom Party	Freedom Party; VAO		VAO
Italy	Lega Nord; Five Star	Lega Nord	Lega Nord	Movimento Sociale-Fiamma Tricolore; Veneto Fronte Skinheads		Fronte Nazionale; Ordine Nuovo

				Fronte Nazio-nale; Ordine Nuovo		
Greece			Golden Dawn	Golden Dawn		
Cyprus			ELAM	ELAM		
Poland			National Radical Camp; All-Polish Youth; National Rebirth of Poland; National Move-ment	National Radical Camp; All-Polish Youth; National Rebirth of Poland; National Move-ment		
Hungary	Fidesz		Fidesz; Jobbik	Jobbik; Magyar Garda	Magyar Garda	
Russia	United Russia		United Russia; Russian National Socialist Party; Russian National Unity Party; LDPR; Pamyat	Russian National Socialist Party; Russian National Unity Party; LDPR; Pamyat		

Sources: official websites of listed organizations and groups; Home Office.

Chapter 2: Psychological Aspects of the Alt-Right Phenomenon

By Alan Waring and Roger Paxton

Abstract

This chapter seeks to make sense of the harsh, non-egalitarian, Alt-Right ideology and world-view, the often indignant and angry authoritarian rhetoric that characterises them, and the Alt-Right's internal contradictions, such as claiming to offer freedom to some but also advocating loss of freedom and human rights to others. The relationship between psychological factors and political preferences are discussed in terms of personality (notably the 'the Big 5 theory', Right-Wing Authoritarianism, Social Dominance Orientation, and the 'dark triad' of narcissism, Machiavellianism, and psychopathy), the psychology of fear and risk (notably fear of foreigners and immigrants, globalisation and job losses, and experts), motivation, and the political psychology of anger. Also examined is the issue of confirmatory bias and its relevance to alternative or fake facts and political preferences. Allegations of personality disorders against Alt-Right leaders (e.g. Trump) are discussed but cautioned as unproven and unsafe.

Key words: Alt-Right, psychology, personality, motivation, emotion, risk

Making Psychological Sense of the Alt-Right

The over-riding impression given by Alt-Right leaders, opinion formers and followers is one of anger and indignation, of disaffected and disgruntled people who are determined to bring about radical change in the political system, national governance and society. However, it is not at all clear that there is a coherent political logic and structure to what is evidently a fairly chaotic melange of frequently contradictory emotions, attitudes and motivations within the Alt-Right 'movement'.

As noted in chapter 1, the Alt-Right is more a collection of people having a broadly shared world-view than being a well-defined movement. However, the term 'movement' will suffice for this book's purposes.

Some individuals of the Alt-Right want to change the existing political system and so-called establishment, others want to destroy it and replace it with a white nationalist dictatorship or even no government at all. Some in the US Alt-Right, for example, cite an anti-Semitic justification for their cause, others are anti-Muslim and yet others are anti-Hispanic, and some are totally against all non-white, non-Christian and non-US born citizens. Some favour an isolationist and non-interventionist America, whereas others demand that the US crushes militarily any foreign group or country that dares to challenge the United States or in some way represents a perceived threat. Some are strongly in favour of homophobic policies, while others are themselves openly gay (for example, the Alt-Right commentator and author Milo Yiannopoulos). Some are misogynist and anti-feminist and champion men's rights at the expense of women's, whereas others are neutral or indifferent. See, for example, Lyons (2017a and b) on the array of differing Alt-Right values and motivations.

So, in the absence of any theoretical or practical coherence presented by the Alt-Right itself, how can sense be made of the Alt-Right phenomenon?

At a high level of abstraction, one might observe that the Alt-Right world-view represents a conscious rejection of and reaction to what Fukuyama (1989; 1992) referred to as "the universalization of western liberal democracy as the final form of government". In essence, the Alt-Right assertion is that, on the contrary, not only has western liberal democracy failed as the ultimate form of successful government, but also it is the cause of what are portrayed as intolerable injustices to those who should rightfully inhabit and control the world i.e. those having an Alt-Right world-view. The Alt-Right dystopian view of the present, whatever the merits of their analysis and however exaggerated some of their negative assertions, is necessary for them to project in order to be able to justify the solutions they put forward. In a curious way, the Alt-Right stance against liberal democracy is not that dissimilar to the neo-Marxist slur against the 'neo-liberal' policies of western democracies and the post-modernist accusations of Ulrich Beck (1992) against the collective power of western governments, industry and the establishment to perpetuate an unfair distribution of risks in society.

But, where do such negative world-views come from? Some might argue that there is an inherent desire of white people to assert their supposed superiority over all other races, whereas others might argue that it is common-sense to protect oneself against such 'obvious' threats as being swamped by mass immigration, losing one's job owing to globalisation and 'unfair' foreign competition, being exposed to perceived violent crime from immigrants, or being exposed to terrorist attacks by immigrants. All such beliefs and anxieties, including those that may have some degree of factual foundation, are paranoid in nature. To understand such anxieties and paranoia, and the attitudes, motivations and political preferences stemming from them, it is necessary to appreciate the psychological factors involved.

Psychological Factors and Political Preferences

Do people coolly weigh up the appeal of different political parties or candidates to decide which will most advance their economic interest, and then vote accordingly? Much evidence shows that political preferences are rarely so straightforward. Several kinds of psychological factor affect political affiliation. These are briefly reviewed before turning specifically to the psychology of the Alt-Right. The central question is: are there particular psychological factors that make people susceptible to the appeal of the Alt-Right?

Personality (an individual's characteristic enduring ways of thinking, feeling and behaving) was famously linked to extreme right-wing views through the concept of the authoritarian personality (Adorno et al 1950). The latter presented evidence for the existence of a 'potentially fascist' personality type—one associated with susceptibility to authoritarian and anti-democratic political beliefs. The book was subsequently widely criticised on various methodological grounds (Martin 2001), and is now generally seen as of only historical interest. However, much recent research has shown reliable links between personality and political preferences, using the Big 5 theory (McCrae and Costa 2003), the most broadly supported current personality theory. The Big 5 dimensions are extraversion, agreeableness, conscientiousness, neuroticism and openness to experience. The most consistent finding, from American and European studies, is that people on the political right are low in openness to experience (Caprara and Vecchione 2013). Other recent research in this area has focussed specifically on the relationship between personality and right-wing attitudes, and confirmed that at least two dimensions are involved. Right Wing Authoritarianism (RWA) (Altemeyer 1996) and Social Dominance Orientation (SDO) (Sidanius and Pratto 1999) are two constructs that have been widely investigated and shown to be reliably related to right-wing ideology. RWA is a personality characteristic comprising three traits: authoritarian submission, authoritarian aggression and conventionalism (Altemeyer 1998). RWA involves belief in coercive social control, obedience to and respect for conventional authority, and traditional moral and religious conformism (Duckitt and Sibley 2010). SDO is a general attitude concerning preference for equal versus hierarchical relationships between social groups. People scoring highly on SDO believe in social and economic inequality rather than equality, and in the right of powerful groups to dominate weaker ones (Duckitt and Sibley 2010). Extensive research from North America and elsewhere shows that RWA and SDO are strong predictors of a range of social attitudes associated with right-wing ideologies, including social and economic conservatism, generalized prejudice, nationalism, ethnocentrism and anti-democratic views (Altemeyer 1998; Duckitt 2006; Sibley et al 2006; Roccato and Ricolfi 2005).

Another personality concept that appears relevant to the psychology of political preferences is the 'dark triad' of Machiavellianism (manipulativeness), narcissism (egocentricity and grandiosity) and (subclinical) psychopathy (callousness and impulsivity) (Paulhus and Williams 2002). These three dimensions are psychometrically independent (i.e. they do not measure the same thing) but appear to share a core of callous manipulation (Furnham et al 2013). Substantial evidence shows the dark triad is related to a range of antisocial behaviours (Jones and Paulhus 2011). There is currently little on its relationship to politics but one important study is mentioned below, and its deployment in political psychology is likely to grow. The edited collection of papers in Cruz and Buser (2017) also addresses specifically the topic of narcissism in the Trump era.

A few studies have investigated links between RWA and SDO and other personality features such as the Big 5 mentioned above. Some suggest that conscientiousness and lack of openness to experience fuel RWA, and others that a lack of agreeableness and lack of openness are at the root of SDO (Caprara and Vecchione 2013; Sibley and Duckitt 2008), but these relationships remain uncertain. Regarding the dark triad, unsurprisingly perhaps, all three measures correlate negatively with agreeableness (Jakobowitz and Egan 2006). Overall, the evidence summarised above shows strong links between personality and political views.

Closely related to personality is motivation (the particular factors that drive the individual). Caprara and Vecchione (2013, 39) summarise the evidence on the relationship between motivation and personality as follows: "People's predispositions and needs are turned into habits and values, depending on their early socialization and personal experiences. Likewise, situations provide the challenges and opportunities that allow values to turn into habits and action". Personality is thus one of a range of factors influencing each person's political affiliation, and motivation is another. 'Needs' and 'motives' are sometimes used synonymously, and political conservatism is related to a high need for cognitive closure, that is, a tendency to process information in such a way as to maximize stability and reduce change and uncertainty (Jost et al 2003). Social and moral values are an important motivational category here, and Jonathan Haidt's moral foundations theory is prominent in this literature. From extensive research Haidt (2012) showed how very different moral value systems underpin the widening left-right ideological divisions in American politics. Haidt demonstrated that six 'foundations' underlie both moral judgements and political preferences in America and elsewhere. The foundations are: 1 care/harm, 2 liberty/oppression, 3 fairness/cheating, 4 loyalty/betrayal, 5 authority/subversion, and 6 sanctity/degradation. For liberals, foundations 1 and 3 are important, and they have little concern about the others. The more right-wing the person's preferences the more the others are salient. A second very important finding from Haidt's research is that people at opposing ends of this moral spectrum differ not just in terms of preference or affiliations but also in their ability to understand or respect the other's views as representing a moral standpoint at all. This finding will receive further attention in the final chapter (14) when potential strategies to limit the Alt-Right threat are considered.

Closely linked to both motivation and needs is emotion, as, for instance, when people seek to maximize stability and reduce uncertainty they clearly do so to avoid negative emotions. Fear is the emotion that has been most studied within political psychology (Brader and Marcus 2013), and below the authors show how evoking fear in order to change opinions or bolster support has been a common tactic used by Alt-Right politicians.

The Psychology of Fear and Risk

Glendon and Clarke (2016), albeit it with a human safety focus, provided a detailed exposition of the current state of knowledge on the psychology of risk, in which fear forms a component. Previously only partly integrated areas of the subject, such as risk cognition, emotions, individual factors and external factors such as social environment, are now organized into an integrated multilevel framework of five levels:

Table 2.1: A Multi-Level Psychological Framework for Exploring Risk

Psychological Level	Illustrative Variables
Socio-cultural	Peer/family influences, socialization, social environment, political/economic circumstances, organizational memberships/policies/values.
Individual differences	Age, gender, personality, habits, motivation, attitudes, experience, disposition (e.g. risk-taking tendencies, anti-social tendencies, narcissism, sociopathic/psychopathic disorders).
Risk-related behaviours	Task difficulty/complexity, skills, abilities, training, moderating controls—in a range of situations (e.g. drug-taking, drinking excess alcohol, engaging in anti-social activity, promoting ethnic hatred), workload, fatigue, distractions.
Cognitions and affect	Memory, learning, risk perception, decision-making, judgement, mood, biases, stress, awareness, understanding, emotions (e.g. fear, anger, hate).
Neural correlates	Developmental stage, processing efficiency, attentional capacity, integrated reward/affect circuitry, decision-making circuits, response/behavioural inhibition.

Source: adapted from Fig 1.1 of Glendon and Clarke (2016).

Earlier authors (Glendon 1987; Glendon, Clarke and McKenna 2006; Waring and Glendon 1998), introduced the term 'risk cognition' as an all-encompassing label for the sense-making activities of the brain relating to risk (whether risk in general, or specific categories or specific exposures). Glendon and Clarke (2016) suggested that 'risk perception' rather than risk cognition would be a more suitable term, as it incorporates both sensory perception of risk (seeing, hearing etc) and cognitive perception of risk (thinking, awareness, appraisal etc) including threat perception.

The emotion of fear relates to a feeling within the individual of a lack of control and uncertainty about the nature and/or scale and/or outcome of a particular perceived risk (threat). The greater the feeling of lack of control and uncertainty, the greater the fear that the perceived uncontrolled threat will become realised and will cause unacceptable harm to the individual and probably to others he or she loves or values. For example, an individual who feels great uncertainty about uncontrolled immigration and its potential consequences, and who is unable to conceive of any effective controls ever being implemented, may fear a negative, even terrible, outcome.

However, an individual's perception of a particular threat, and his or her estimate of how large the risk is and how likely it is to be realised, may not accord well with reality. Such perception is notoriously faulty, and typically individuals tend to greatly inflate their estimation of threats they particularly fear. Social amplification of risk (Kasperson et al 1988; Pidgeon et al 2003) is a factor in this phenomenon. Two such perceived threats are those associated with immigration and Muslims. Studies have shown that people typically over-estimate by orders of magnitude both the numbers of immigrants in the population and the proportion of the population who are Muslim. For example, the UK's Office for National Statistics (ONS 2017) reports for the year 2016 that net UK migration fell to +248,000, of whom some 53.6% were EU citizens. The number of asylum applications was 36,846 of which 32% were granted. The report states that, based on National Insurance and taxation, in March 2017 of those in employment 88.9% were British citizens, 7.3% were EU citizens and 3.9% were non-EU citizens. Another report (ONS 2015) states that, of the stable resident population of the UK, 13.3% (8.6m) were born abroad and 8.7% (5.6m) were of non-British nationality.

Yet, despite such official data which many would accept as reasonably accurate, an international survey of public perceptions of immigration (Ipsos MORI 2014) showed that in every country surveyed respondents grossly over-estimated immigrant numbers. For example, whereas the actual proportion of immigrants in the UK population is 13%, respondents in the UK believed it to be 24%. Similarly in the US, respondents estimated the US immigrant level at 32% as against an actual 13%. Nevertheless, a report from a right-wing policy group (Palmer and Wood 2017) asserted that in the UK immigration figures are far higher than in ONS reports, owing to illegal immigration. On the more specific topic of the proportion of the population that is Muslim, UK respondents to the Ipsos MORI survey believed it to be 21% in the UK as against an actual 5% while US respondents believed that 15% of their population was Muslim whereas it is only 1%. See also Duffy and Frere-Smith (2014) and British Future (2014).

Ignorance of facts and possession of wildly inaccurate, or even simply faulty or biased information, on perceived threats is likely to fuel fears and encourage inappropriate or even extreme responses. This is seen as an opportunity for exploitation by politicians, policy advisers, and opinion formers, and no more so than those of the Alt-Right or even mainstream conservatives who claim to offer the public true security and true protection against such alleged threats as immigrants, Muslims, asylum seekers, globalization, unfair foreign trade, and liberalism and socialism in a variety of guises. Wodak (2015) discussed the right-wing politics of fear explicitly. Right-wing media, politicians, demagogues and intellectuals knowingly play their part in the social amplification of risk and promulgation of fear and then offering control solutions. While some solutions may have some merit (e.g. encouraging greater integration and assimilation of immigrants into society; appropriate trade tariffs and anti-dumping policies), clearly any solution that appears to offer some kind of salvation or magic antidote, particularly to perceived threats subject to many complex and difficult-to-control variables, is unlikely to deliver its promise. Waring and Glendon (1998) and Waring (2013) warned of the caution required when considering the adoption of any proposed salvation model of risk control.

Kakkar and Sivanathan (2017) conducted a large-scale survey in which respondents were asked to indicate their preference for the character and style of national political leaders under a number of different hypothetical circumstances of threat e.g. economic uncertainty, increased unemployment, terrorist attack. They argued that the results showed that the psychological threat imposed by an individual's environment increases the appeal of an external agent who might help to assuage this threat and the "psychological sense of lacking control over one's life". Specifically, they argued that to assuage this threat, people prefer a leader who is perceived to be decisive, authoritative, and dominant as opposed to one who is respected, knowledgeable, admired, and permissive. This survey provided a potentially plausible explanation for why authoritarian leaders such as Trump, Putin, Marine Le Pen (and even Hitler and Mussolini in their day) have proven popular.

Nevertheless, individual attitudes to risks are multi-dimensional and complex and preferences expressed in attitude surveys, while suggestive, are open to other interpretations and are not necessarily compelling. Revealed preferences are usually more significant. As Waring and Glendon (1998) noted, actual risks, perceived risks and expressions of concern about them are fully coincident in only two of eight possible combinations. What a person says about a particular risk may not match either what they actually believe or what they do in relation to the risk. Also, individuals themselves are frequently inconsistent in what they report about risks, both qualitatively and over time (see Schulz 2010; Waring and Glendon 1998, 33–35). Confirmation bias or self-biasing to confirm pre-conceptions (Dror and Fraser-Mackenzie 2008; Nickerson 1998; Zimmerman 2011), whether conscious or pre-conscious, also may play a significant part in framing attitudes towards objects of fear, as discussed later in this chapter. There is a tendency for individuals to seek out information that appears to confirm their pre-existing beliefs about matters of importance to them, while ignoring or rejecting information that appears to disconfirm those beliefs.

There is much to say about anxiety and fear in the origins of the Alt-Right. A number of specific fears feature frequently in the rhetoric and expressions of concern emanating from the Alt-Right, namely:

- Fear of foreigners and immigrants
- Fear of globalization and job losses
- Fear of experts

The following three sections briefly examine these fears.

Fear of Foreigners and Immigrants

One of the memorable expressions widely used by UKIP supporters and those of the far-right during the Brexit Referendum campaign in 2016 was "Give me back my country", an expression also used by Trump supporters during the 2016 US presidential campaign. This plea encapsulated the belief of such people that their respective country was being taken over by foreigners and immigrants. Indeed, the much-used term in the UK has been 'swamping', indicating that they feel that the indigenous British population is being swept over by a relentless tide of immigrants.

Such a fear is not new. Anti-immigrant emotions have been prominent in the UK for at least a century. At the turn of the 20th century, the British Brothers League was spewing out anti-immigrant propaganda about Jews newly arriving from the continent, in terms remarkably similar to those of the Alt-Right towards the immigrants of today. Others, such as the Chinese, faced similar antipathy in the same era. In the 1930s, Europeans, especially Jews seeking asylum in Britain from the Nazis, were made to feel unwelcome by right-wing elements—see, for example, Kushner and Valman (2000) and Magens (1971) on the so-called Battle of Cable Street on October 4, 1936. The latter was a provocative march by an estimated 2,000–3,000 of Oswald Mosley's Black Shirts of the British Union of Fascists, flanked by some 6,000 police officers deployed apparently to keep the peace, who tried to intimidate and force out Jewish immigrants from the East End of London.

As raised above, the various official UK government reports on current immigration (e.g. ONS 2015 2017; Home Office 2014a) show that such a belief of being swamped is not based on current reality and the Ipsos MORI (2014) report suggests that those who fear immigration typically grossly inflate the number of immigrants they believe are in the country compared to the actual number. Since the number of immigrants who are in the country illegally are not recorded and can only be estimated, no one can say for sure how many there are. Illegal immigrant numbers would, necessarily, be additional to the official figures based on legal migrants. Estimates of illegal immigrants by right-wingers, whether members of the public or research bodies (e.g. Palmer and Wood 2017), are likely to be higher than reality for the same reasons that estimates of legal immigrants are inflated. However, the legitimacy of any case against illegal immigrants should be based on their lack of legal right to be in the country and not on any alleged damage to the economy, even though there may be an element of truth in the assertion, for example in relation to undeclared earnings.

Second order fear-based assertions (typically unsupported factually) of the Alt-Right arising from the primary fear of immigration include:

- Crime inevitably increases since immigrants are inherently more criminally orientated. This is the essence of the official statements and policies of the Trump administration e.g. a justification to build a wall between Mexico and the US to keep immigrants from Central and South America out of the US.
- Muslim immigrants inevitably increase the threat of terrorism i.e. conflating the fear of Muslims and immigrants with the fear of terrorism. This is the essence of the statements and policies of the Trump administration to justify banning immigrants from a number of predominantly Muslim countries (see chapter 10 in Vol 1).
- Immigrants take away the jobs of indigenous citizens by accepting lower pay. This may be true of lower paid unskilled manual jobs. However, in view of their relatively small proportion of the population, any job losses would also be relatively small.
- Immigrants are unfairly granted generous welfare benefits and public housing when they have not contributed to National Insurance and taxation, while indigenous claimants who have contributed are rebuffed; they are not only undeserving, but they also typically engage in benefits fraud.
- Immigrants refuse to integrate, learn the host country's language, and accept its values. This is almost exclusively a problem relating to older immigrants and those coming from poorly educated and conservative backgrounds.
- In the UK, swamping by immigrants is resulting in the British national identity being altered permanently into a diluted multi-ethnic, multi-cultural chimera. As the ONS and Ipsos MORI data show, this assertion appears to be unsupported

> when looking at the UK overall, although there are undoubtedly 'hot spots' of high concentrations of immigrants where it may appear that such an assertion has some foundation.

All such fears and assertions, repeated often enough, add to the social amplification of the risks of immigration.

Fear of Globalisation and Job Losses

President Trump has made the objectives of keeping jobs in America, cutting foreign imports and promoting US-made goods as high priorities. There is nothing intrinsically wrong or sinister about such objectives. However, the practical problems of achieving them are major. Moreover, in seeking to achieve them, there are likely to be unintended adverse consequences.

Since the early 1990s, the growth of globalization, or the location of capital, production units, labour sources and sourcing of goods wherever in the world is the most cost-effective and cost-efficient, has become the de facto position of international trade. National governments have accepted that their economies have to work within such an environment. There are undoubted benefits from globalization, such as access to markets, cost and price reduction, corporate efficiency etc. However, by sourcing goods abroad rather than locally and outsourcing production abroad rather than locally, there is an almost inevitable threat to local jobs and to local companies that are unable or unwilling to follow suit.

The fear of globalization and the potential adverse consequences of it, particularly among blue-collar workers in the US, is based on real examples of factory closures and job losses across America's industrial centres, although factors other than globalization per se are almost certainly also involved. For example, companies become uncompetitive because they fail to adapt to changing markets, to new technology and new production methods, to the need to upgrade their employee skills base. This remains the case regardless of sourcing and outsourcing overseas. There are multiple threat issues arising from globalization and Le Coze (2017) emphasizes the systemic nature of such threats.

Fear of Experts

Antipathy towards the 'Establishment' and the elites among them is a hallmark of the Alt-Right but not exclusively so. As O'Rourke put it in his polemical deconstruction of the 2016 US presidential election, it was a 'War of Incivility':

> "The war is not between Republicans and Democrats or between conservatives and progressives. The war is between the frightened and what they fear. It is being fought by the people who perceive themselves as controlling nothing. They are besieging the people they perceive as controlling everything. We are in the midst of a Perception Insurrection, or, depending on how you perceive it, a Loser Mutiny". (O'Rourke 2017, 189)

Experts feature prominently among the elites that the Alt-Right apparently fear, as they demonstrate quite openly in their negative comments about experts. Trump advertises his rejection of experts, when it suits him, as a badge of honour and some of his cabinet members and advisers appear to be of like mind. The Trump administration's rejection of expert knowledge, advice and opinion includes:

- Rejection of scientific expertise on global warming. Scott Pruitt, Trump's appointee as the head of the now much diminished Environmental Protection Agency, has stated that carbon dioxide is not the primary contributor to global warming (see chapter 9 in Vol 1). Trump announced on June 1, 2017 that the US would formally withdraw from the international Paris Climate Accord that aims to attenuate the causes of global warming. Trump also slashed the budget of the National Oceanic and Atmospheric Administration.
- Trump publicly stated his disbelief in the safety of vaccines and in particular the MMR (Measles, Mumps, Rubella) vaccine given routinely to children worldwide. Moreover, he has publicly endorsed Andrew Wakefield, a British former doctor who in 2010 was struck off by the UK's General Medical Council for falsifying and manipulating research data to show that use of the MMR vaccine significantly increased the risk of autism. Wakefield called for parents to refuse MMR vaccinations for their children. Trump's support for Wakefield directly contradicts the policy of the US government's Centers for Disease Control and directly interferes with MMR prevention.

- Trump diminished the role of the Council of Economic Advisers and, in August 2017, dismissed its two key committees following multiple resignations of business leaders who were committee members in protest at Trump's public statements.
- Trump has publicly suggested that the accuracy and quality of reports from the US intelligence agencies are suspect.

In the UK, Michael Gove MP, a former UK Justice Minister and appointed in June 2017 as Secretary of State for Environment, Food and Rural Affairs, has a reputation as a right-wing Conservative who to all intents and purposes is an Alt-Right exemplar within a mainstream British Conservative government. Mimicking the anti-elites and anti-experts stance of the Trump administration, in the febrile lead-up to the EU Referendum, Gove revealed clearly his antipathy towards experts. In June 2016, in an interview on *Sky News*, he stated that people in the UK had had "enough of experts" and, further, they had had "enough of organizations with acronyms saying that they know what is best and getting it consistently wrong". He further lambasted the International Monetary Fund (IMF) as being elitist, distant and unaccountable. Clearly embarrassed by adverse media and public reaction to his comments, he later tried to play them down.

At the surface level, the rejection by the Alt-Right of facts, and sources of facts, that do not fit their ideology and narrative (see Dror and Fraser-Mackenzie 2008; Kahan et al 2017; Nickerson 1998; Schulz 2010; Shermer 2018; Zimmerman 2011 on confirmation bias, certitude, and responses to factual error) represents a fear of being found out and discredited in the minds of the public at large. It is a fear that experts will be listened to and that Alt-Right ideological dogma and policy positions that do not accord with scientific or other expert-based facts will be rejected by the public. Experts, unless they happen to fit the Alt-Right narrative, are seen by them as meddlesome and dangerous. The Alt-Right's penchant for generating fake facts to counter actual facts is relevant to their desire to discredit experts whose information is inconvenient—see chapter 11 in Vol 1. However, as noted elsewhere in this book, attempts to discredit the counter-arguments or positions of opponents by using fake facts are not exclusive to the Alt-Right, although they tend to be more vocally aggressive, strident, and laden with personal invective seeking to discredit the character of individual experts.

However, at a deeper level, there are broader fear-related social-psychological processes at work. Both Bate (1999) and Durodié (2002; 2005a and b) suggested that increasingly since the 1970s there has developed in the population a growing suspicion of experts. In the modernist era after the Industrial Revolution and up to the early 1970s, governments, state agencies and the scientific community were largely accepted by the public as the authoritative source of factual information, direction and guidance on such matters as health, medicines, food safety, disease prevention and control, nuclear safety, as well as a broad range of other matters affecting their lives. Now, in the post-modernist era, large numbers of people are unconvinced and not persuaded by such official and expert advice e.g. rejection by some parents of the MMR vaccine for their children. Douglas (1992, 11) also noted "the baffling behaviour of the public" in ignoring or even doing the opposite of expert advice.

It could be argued that such contrary responses may reflect an increasing disillusionment in society with science and its ability to deliver effective public safety, health and social improvements. For example, so-called alternative medicines and alternative therapies having no or dubious scientific validation are increasingly popular. Coupled with such rejection may be an increasing disillusionment with and decreasing engagement with established political structures and processes. Politicians, their officials and the risk experts they employ or commission exert both obtrusive and unobtrusive power to identify, scope, define, measure, assess, and evaluate risks and determine risk treatments and methods (Hardy 1985; Dekker and Nyce 2014). Other legitimate voices, including the anticipated beneficiaries of such expertise and official decisions, may be drowned out or ignored. Beck's dystopian anti-establishment view of risk in modern society, with Durodié concurring (Beck 1992; Durodié 2002; 2005a and b), was that the erstwhile unchallenged authority and acceptance of official and expert positions in the modernist era had given way to a much less deferential, less trusting, more cynical and more contrarian, even antagonistic, populace. Durodié extended his argument to assert that the population's cynicism has created an increasing disengagement and detachment from the traditional political process in favour of populist tactics, a development also noted by Paxton (2017).

The Political Psychology of Anger

Anger has been less often investigated, but is another negative emotion of great importance in political psychology, particularly because of its motivational effects, or 'action tendencies' (Frijda 1986). Different emotions are associated with different actions, and fear and anger, in particular, have different effects on both risk perception and risk-taking behaviour. For instance, in a nationwide American study Lerner and colleagues (Lerner et al 2003) found that after the 11th September terrorist atrocity of 2001 people whose main emotional response was fear perceived greater risks and took more precautionary actions than those who responded primarily with anger. The angry group perceived less risk and took fewer precautions. Similarly, Brader et al (2010) showed that, compared with people who were mainly fearful, citizens who were angry when faced with a potentially fatal viral outbreak were more likely to take legal or other action against those responsible. Fearful people took preventive or protective measures. Further insights on the relation between emotions and action come from the theory of affective intelligence (Marcus et al 2000) which deals with the effects of different emotions on decision making. Much evidence supports the claim of the theory that anxiety or fear increases attention to contemporary pertinent information, whereas both anger and enthusiasm lead to reliance on pre-existing beliefs. The political judgements of anxious people are more influenced by media messages and campaign information than those of angry or enthusiastic people, whose judgements are more tied to predispositions or existing attitudes (e.g. Parker and Isbell 2010).

Personality, Values and the Alt-Right

The Alt-Right ideology, summarised earlier, is consistent with the values shown by Haidt (2012) to be most important to conservatives: liberty/oppression (a concern with resisting perceived domination); loyalty/betrayal (nationalism and localism rather than the universalism favoured by the left); authority/subversion (respect for traditional hierarchical relationships); and sanctity/degradation (respect for traditional religious and national symbols). Conservatives and liberal share concern with fairness/cheating, but this similarity is superficial, because of the elasticity of the concept of fairness. Haidt demonstrates that for liberals fairness is connected with equality whereas for conservatives it means proportionality; rewards should be in proportion to contributions. However, all this is only to say that the Alt-Right is essentially conservative in its values. What distinguishes the Alt-Right psychologically from other ideological conservatives?

A survey of 447 American Alt-Right adherents carried out following the 2016 American election provides important information on measures of personality, emotions and motivation. Forscher and Kteily (2017) used a battery of psychological tests and compared the scores of the Alt-Right group with those of a group of 382 non-adherents. Alt-Right supporters were higher on the dark triad traits and SDO, they reported higher levels of aggression, and exhibited extreme levels of intergroup bias, including overt dehumanization of ethnic minority groups. Forscher & Kteily's analysis revealed two subgroups of their Alt-Right participants; one more populist and anti-establishment, and the other more supremacist and motivated to maintain existing hierarchies. As discussed in chapter 13, this distinction parallels two rhetorical strands typically used by populist radical right leaders: attacking and blaming both a remote elite establishment and some supposedly alien group, usually identified by religion or ethnicity. At this point, it should be noted that Donald Trump as a Presidential candidate and as President has repeatedly used these rhetorical devices to generate anger and thus divert attention from current opposing information and re-evoke prejudices in order to strengthen and motivate his support base: "crooked Hillary", "lock her up", "the fake media", "build the wall", and so on.

Other Psychological Factors Evident in the Alt-Right Phenomenon

The issue of confirmation bias was raised earlier in this chapter (see Dror and Fraser-Mackenzie 2008; Nickerson 1998; Zimmerman 2011). Confirmation bias may be defined as the result of seeking out and/or interpreting information that tends to confirm the individual's preconceptions about a particular topic, while also avoiding, ignoring or rejecting information that tends to disconfirm those preconceptions (see also Kahan et al 2017; Shermer 2018). Although confirmation biasing is frequently a conscious process, a large degree of pre-conscious processing is likely to be involved (Dixon 1981). Such cognitive bias is likely to result in systematic error i.e. the individual's beliefs, while reinforced, may not born out by the facts. How that individual responds to factual challenges to his or her beliefs, backed up as they are by 'incontrovertible evidence' of their 'unassailable truth' collated by the individual's confirmation biasing activities, has been examined by Schulz (2010) in her book *Being Wrong*. What is evidenced in much of the Alt-Right's rhetoric, especially from the Trump administration, has a close fit with the five defence strategies that Schulz argued individuals adopt in the face of challenges on truth, especially on evidence of success or failure, summarised in Table 2.2 below.

Table 2.2: Individual Defence Strategies in the Face of Challenge on Success or Failure

Defence	Defensive Narrative for Failure	Example
Time-frame	Unconditional prediction that a certain thing would happen by a particular time failed to be born out, but it was only a delay and it will happen sooner or later. It is not a failure.	Trump's predictions on: building the wall between USA and Mexico to deter illegal immigrants and make Mexico pay for it; repeal and replacement of Obamacare health care legislation (Affordable Care Act) by Trump's own bill.
Near miss	Unconditional prediction that a certain thing would happen that did not, but it almost did and so the prediction was a pretty good one. It is not a failure.	Trump's predictions on: building the wall between USA and Mexico to deter illegal immigrants and make Mexico pay for it; repeal and replacement of Obamacare health care legislation (Affordable Care Act) by Trump's own bill; $1trillion new investment promised for infrastructure versus maximum $200bn actual Federal funds for infrastructure (Chao 2017).
Unexpected event	Unconditional prediction that a certain thing would happen which did not. It almost happened as predicted, save for a	On US troops in Afghanistan:

	completely unforeseeable occurrence out-of-left field. It is not a failure.	Trump's U-turn on his promise not to increase troops; national security review cited (August 21, 2017).
Transference and blame	I was only wrong because of you. I failed because I placed too much trust in the advice and actions of others. You people would not do as I wanted or directed. It is a failure but you are to blame.	On the Russia conspiracy allegations, Trump's sacking of : General Mike Flynn; FBI Director James Comey; Trump's and his team's critical rhetoric against: Attorney-General Jeff Sessions, Chief of Staff Reince Priebus; Trump's cancellation* of the Singapore summit of June 2018 with North Korea's Kim Jong-un, which Trump blamed on China (*subsequently reinstated); Trump's blaming of his enforced separation of children from undocumented migrant parents on Obama and the Democrats for failing to support his Mexican Wall project.
Innocence and precautionary wisdom	I made the best judgement I could on the basis of what information had been given me. Erring on the side of caution, and 'better safe than sorry', I had no alternative. It may be a failure but I am innocent of any wrongdoing.	US President G W Bush and UK Prime Minister Tony Blair's decision to invade Iraq on the basis of WMD (weapons of mass destruction) threat (although clearly not an Alt-Right example).

Source: based on discussion in Schulz (2010).

Transference and blame became especially prominent in the Trump White House, particularly when the latter's attempts to avoid or block in-depth FBI investigation into alleged improper contacts by various Trump officials (including his son Donald Trump Jr and son-in-law Jared Kushner) with Russian officials and go-betweens during the Presidential election campaign, allegedly seeking to influence the election outcome in Trump's favour. The *Twitter* attacks on the Attorney-General Jeff Sessions by Trump in July 2017, describing him on 24th July as "weak" and "beleaguered", in effect for acting correctly and ethically in not replacing the acting FBI Director by a Trump-compliant alternative, were unprecedented for a sitting US President (see chapter 5 in Vol 1).

There then followed over several weeks a succession of highly publicised resignations (some forced) from the White House staff , including the Chief Press Secretary, Sean Spicer, and Chief of Staff, Reince Priebus, precipitated by the appointment of former hedge fund entrepreneur Anthony Scaramucci. Within days, Scaramucci was publicly denigrating both Sessions and Preibus on *Twitter* and in media interviews, including a particularly foul-mouthed vitriolic outburst on 27th July in an interview with *The New Yorker* magazine (Lizza 2017) in which he implied that Priebus had leaked to the press information damaging to the President, and implied in very coarse terms that Steve Bannon, Trump's then Chief Strategist, was a self-absorbed, self-serving, political parasite feeding off the President.

Being in denial and selectively biasing information received is part of a particular individual's psychological defence strategy. It is fear-related in multiple ways—the fear that the beliefs they hold dear may be weak or delusional, the fear that the basis of their own identity will collapse if their beliefs are crushed, the fear that weak or delusional beliefs masquerading as strong and valid ones may be exposed to public ridicule or anger, and so on. Public approval ratings, voter disapproval and ballot box risks weigh heavily in the Alt-Right psyche. The fear that in the US, for example, President Trump and his Alt-Right political agenda might only be a short-term 'wonder' and might be swept away early is too terrible for Alt-Right populists to acknowledge as a possibility. Therefore, the Alt-Right has adopted a 'by hook or by crook' approach to the task of Trump staying in power. False facts and fake news propaganda are all part of that approach to denial of verified facts and challenges to weak or delusional beliefs of the Alt-Right. See chapter 11 in Vol 1 for further discussion on post-truth and fake news.

Paxton (2017) echoed much of the foregoing on the psychology of the far-right. Of course, it should be noted that denial, transference, blaming, lying and so on are not exclusive attributes of the Alt-Right. These are also features of many political parties, movements and individuals. However, with the Alt-Right, such features have become core characteristics to such an extent that the public anticipates it as normative conduct of Alt-Right politicians, commentators and supporters. For the Alt-Right, the 'truth is what I say it is' is perfectly acceptable since the end justifies the means. Paxton noted the wide acceptance of the dishonesty of post-truth politics and a lack of concern about morality in public life that Trump's presidential victory has brought.

Much has been written about embedded social inequalities allegedly providing a root cause in modern times of many societal problems including poverty, criminality, clinical depression, substance abuse, extremism and so on. However, whereas there may well be associations between inequalities and such problems, such associations do not prove causation. Nevertheless, it may be posited that inequalities may lead, among those allegedly adversely affected, to feelings of powerlessness to alter their conditions and situation for the better, which in turn may lead to anomie, hopelessness and disaffection. Although such theories may have some validity, they raise a paradox as far as the Alt-Right is concerned. A fundamental principle of the far-right is that of maintaining inequalities—between races, between religions, between owners of capital and the proletariat, between rich and poor, between political authority and the compliant masses (see, for example, MacDonald 2002; Beck 2014). Yet, many of the disfavoured groups in such inequalities are the very people who voted for President Trump in decisively large numbers. They apparently accepted his promises to save them from their situation, but with little apparent awareness of either the fundamental inequality basis of Alt-Right ideology or the practical difficulties Trump would face in delivering their salvation.

Others, such as Glynos and Mondon (2016), have noted an 'enjoyment' motivation of far-right supporters, whereby they and their fellow supporters share a jealously guarded sense of 'rightful ownership' of 'their' country. They indignantly rail against all those whom they perceive have robbed them of their enjoyment of such entitlement, such as liberals, elites, immigrants, and Muslims. An enjoyment is also evident in vituperative far-right rhetoric in which their dystopian assertions of danger from immigrants and Muslims may also be projections of wish fulfilment—despite expressing fears of public disorder and violence involving immigrants and Muslims, they actually want this to happen as a means of accelerating the enforced departure of such people from 'their' country.

The Issue of Alleged Personality Disorders

There has been widespread media speculation (e.g. Lexington 2016; Pavia 2017) concerning whether President Trump is suffering from some form of personality disorder that might explain some of his often bizarre and outrageous behaviour. For example, his almost daily habit of issuing comments via his *Twitter* account that use very un-presidential language and frequently contain wild allegations, invective against anyone he believes has crossed him, and slurs against high profile persons (politicians, government officials, journalists, actors, singers, film stars etc) is unique and unprecedented from a President (see chapter 11 of Vol 1 for examples).

Trump's *Twitter* attack on the Mayor of London, while the latter was grappling with the immediate impact of another terrorist outrage in London on June 3, 2017 (the London Bridge/Borough Market attack), provides another poignant example of his personality and character. Mayor Sadiq Khan had made a public statement advising Londoners that they would "see an increased police presence here today and over the course of the next few days. There's no reason to be alarmed". This statement was clearly referring to the potential alarm that people might have in seeing large numbers of armed officers in a country where armed police are the exception not the norm, Britain still being a relatively non-violent society with strict gun control, unlike the US for example. Trump responded on *Twitter*: "At least seven dead and 48 wounded in terror attack and mayor of London says there is no reason to be alarmed!"

The mayor's office immediately corrected Trump's interpretation but this just provoked a further *Twitter* outburst from him: "Pathetic excuse by London mayor Sadiq Khan, who had to think fast on his 'no reason to be alarmed' statement. MSM <mainstream media> is working hard to sell it!"

The reaction in the UK (political, public, media) was one of outrage at what was generally interpreted as a wilful, or certainly negligent, misinterpretation of Khan's words by Trump and then compounded by an even worse second *Twitter* comment (see, for example, Aaronovitch 2017). Public anger swelled, not only at the attitude displayed by Trump to the London emergency, but also his thinly veiled swipe at the Mayor of London because he is Muslim. The sub-text in Trump's attack on Khan appeared to be 'If the Mayor had not been a

Muslim, this terror attack would have been dealt with correctly. What was London thinking of in appointing a Muslim as Mayor?'

Some commentators have suggested that Trump may be a narcissist and/or psychopath (see Cruz and Buser 2017). Indeed, on June 21, 2017 in an outburst of supreme irony, none other than Kim Jong-Un, the leader of the Democratic Republic of North Korea and a notably unstable and cruel personality, described President Trump as a psychopath. If such a diagnosis were true, clearly it would have major implications for whether his decision-making and actions could be trusted not to be reckless or damaging to the nation. Entertaining though such speculation may be, it rarely comes from individuals entitled to render a qualified opinion about such matters, let alone from anyone who has actually undertaken a psychiatric examination of him. Concurring with the psychiatrist and political psychologist Jerrold Post (2015) and with Klitzman (2016) and Singer (2017) and the so-called Goldwater Rule, this book takes the view that it is unsafe and improper to characterize Trump as suffering from any specific personality disorder. Various psychologists in Cruz and Buser (2017) suggested there is evidence in Trump of a strongly narcissistic trait but this does not necessarily connote a personality or mental disorder. Post (2015), Klitzman (2016), and Banschuk (2014), also pointed out that the trait of narcissism is evident in most people to some extent and is not necessarily dysfunctional or destructive. Positive narcissism reveals itself in ambitious achievers. For a discussion on whether presidential narcissism can ever be positive, see Schwartz-Salant (2017). Clinical discussion on psychopathic disorders is presented in APA (2013); Hare (2003; 2016); Hirstein (2013); Kiehl and Buckholtz (2010); and Walton (2007a and b; 2010). For non-clinical analyses of Trump's conduct, see Green (2017), Krugman (2017), Neiwert (2017), Nutt (2017), Warner (2017) and Wolff (2018).

Trump's evident flamboyance, egocentricity, insistence on winning, and immature reactions to perceived rejection or insult, are more consistent with those of another businessman turned politician, Silvio Berlusconi the former Prime Minister of Italy (Post 2015; Haglund et al 2017). As Singer (2017) observed, Trump carries around "the longest selfie-stick in the world". Larres (2017) also referred to Trump's enduring self-promotion in his turbulent administration.

Of course, Trump's shocking assertions and provocative language may have been all part of a deliberate façade or act, a drama that he carefully orchestrated so as to ensure high profile publicity. A speculation by some (see, for example, Krushcheva 2017) is that in foreign policy matters, such as North Korea, Trump may have been deliberately acting when he threatened their annihilation. This is a speculated application of the 'madman theory' of war and diplomacy attributed to President Richard Nixon and his collaborator Henry Kissinger in the late 1960s (Burr and Kimball, 2015; Wellen 2013).

The same caution also applies to the characterization of some other Alt-Right leaders who have also displayed a variety of signs of apparent personality disorder. Whether any of them will ever undergo a psychiatric examination whose results will become available publicly is unlikely. It is more likely that control and deterrence of their potential excesses will come via electoral failures, policy failures, congressional stumbling blocks, and legal procedures such as congressional inquiries, prosecutions, civil law suits and, for the US President, potential invocation of the 25th Amendment or potential impeachment.

At the populist level, Alt-Right supporters are generally a disgruntled, fearful and angry group who believe that most of the problems of their country are caused by foreigners and, more especially, immigrants and, more especially still, Muslims. In the vernacular, the more extreme Alt-Right exponents appear to be maladjusted personalities with a massive chip on their shoulder. While some will actively support far-right groups and attend their rallies and protest marches, far more show their support in on-line blog comments to newspapers or on social media. The relentless on-line outpouring of vile anti-immigrant, anti-foreigner, anti-Semitic, and anti-Muslim invective is indicative of a deep-seated paranoia and possibly some level of personality disorder in such comment authors.

Conclusion

Many of the far-right in different countries claim to promote freedom, democracy and benign policies while, confusingly, promoting policies advocating repression and denial of human rights for disfavoured classes of person. Some far-right parties even have the word 'freedom' in their title—see chapters 6 and 9 for specific examples. Such confusion needs to be seen against the febrile, visceral emotions of disgruntlement, frustration, hatred and anger that characterize the Alt-Right as a whole. They do not appear to care about such internal confusion. What matters to them is to win political control or, failing that, act as a thorn in the side of the mainstream political parties, to be a noisy nuisance, encourage hate crimes and to weaken and subvert the mainstream parties. The behaviour of UKIP and far-right parties in the UK (see chapters 3 and 4), Front National in France (see chapter 8 and Mondon, 2013; 2014; 2015), the Freedom Party in Austria (see chapter 6), and AfD in Germany (see chapter 7) exemplifies their 'end justifies the means' approach based on promulgation of fear.

Internal confusion is also evident in many of the Alt-Right also being heavily involved in Christian fundamentalism and taking authoritarian or even extreme positions against abortion, scientific theories of evolution, multi-culturalism, immigration, and liberal modernism in general. Many Alt-Right supporters seem at ease with, on the one hand, portraying themselves as fully-committed Christians, while, on the other hand, espousing and enacting very un-Christian aspects of Alt-Right ideology. For example, the prominent Alt-Right Republican senatorial candidate in Alabama in 2017, Roy Moore, openly argued that homosexuality should be made illegal, Muslims should not be allowed to serve in Congress, and that he was standing as the candidate of Christian values. Meanwhile, he stood accused by eight women of various past acts of sexual misconduct, including at least one involving an underage 14-year-old girl, all of which he denied.

In the UK, although UKIP has sought to portray itself as a non-racist party, the many instances of gaffes by its officials, candidates and supporters caught on camera making actual or thinly disguised racist comments are matched only by the party's many official denials. Party officials are adamant that their policies have nothing to do with exploiting fear of immigrants and Muslims to gain populist votes.

The emotional and motivational commitments of the Alt-Right are so focussed on fear-based issues such as immigration and race that they typically fail to develop any coherent and comprehensible policies on the major issues of concern to the public, such as the economy, health, employment, pensions, and education.

References

Aaronovitch, D. 2017. "You're Not Welcome in My City, Mr President". *The Times*. London. 8 June 2017.

Adorno, T., Frenkel-Brunswik, E., Levinson, D., and Sanford, R. 1950. *The Authoritarian Personality*. New York: Harper.

Altemeyer, R.A. 1996. *The Authoritarian Specter*. Cambridge, MA: Harvard University Press.

Altemeyer, R.A. 1998. "The Other 'Authoritarian Personality'". In *Advances in Experimental Social Psychology*, edited by M.P. Zanna. Vol. 30, 47–91. New York: Academic Press.

APA. 2013. *Diagnostic and Statistical Manual of Mental Disorders*, 5th edition. Arlington, Va: American Psychiatric Association.

Bate, R. 1999. *What Risk? Science, Politics and Public Health*. Oxford: Butterworth-Heinemann.

Beck, G. 2014. "Glenn Beck: Obama's Idea of Leveling the Playing Field". www.glennbeck.com/content/articles/article/198/42443.

Beck, U. 1992. *Risk Society—Towards a New Modernity*. London: Sage Publications.

Brader, T., Groenendyk, E.W. and Valentino, N. 2010. "Fight or Flight? When political Threats Arouse Public Anger and Fear". *Proceedings from Annual Meeting of the Midwest Political Science Association*, Chicago Ill.

Brader, T. and Marcus, G.E. 2013. "Emotion and Political Psychology". In *The Oxford Handbook of Political Psychology* (2nd ed.), edited by L. Huddy, D.O. Sears & J.S. Levy. Oxford: Oxford University Press.

British Future. 2014. *How to Talk About Immigration*. November 2014. London: British Future.

Caprara, G.V. and Vecchione, M. 2013. "Personality Approaches to Political Behaviour". In *The Oxford Handbook of Political Psychology* (2nd ed.), edited by L. Huddy, D.O. Sears & J.S. Levy. Oxford: Oxford University Press.

Chao, E. 2017. "Chao to Senate: Trump Infrastructure 'Principles' Coming Soon". *CNN report*. May 17, 2017. edition.cnn.com.

Cruz, L. and Buser, S. (eds). 2017. *A Clear and Present Danger: Narcissism in the Era of President Trump*. Asheville NC: Chiron Publications.

Dekker, S.W.A. and Nyce, J.M. 2014. "There is Safety in Power, or Power in Safety". *Safety Science* 67, 44–49.

Dixon, N. F. 1981. *Pre-Conscious Processing*. Chichester: John Wiley & Sons.

Douglas, M. 1992. *Risk and Blame: Essays in Cultural Theory*. London: Routledge.

Dror, I.E. and Fraser-Mackenzie, P.A.F. 2008. "Cognitive Biases in Human Perception, Judgment, and Decision Making: Bridging Theory and the Real World". In *Criminal Investigative Failures,* edited by Kim Rossmo. 53–67. Abingdon Oxon UK: Taylor & Francis.

Duckitt, J. 2006. "Differential Effects of Right Wing Authoritarianism and Social Dominance Orientation on Outgroup Attitudes and their Mediation by Threat From and Competitiveness To Outgroups". *Personality and Social Psychology Bulletin*, 32, 1–13.

Duckitt, J. and Sibley, C.G. 2010. "Personality, Ideology, Prejudice, and Politics: A Dual Process Motivational Model". *Journal of Personality*, 78, 1861–1894.

Duffy, B. and Frere-Smith, T. 2014. *Perception and Reality: 10 Things We Should Know About Immigration in the UK.* January 2014. London: Ipsos-MORI Social Research Institute.

Durodié, B. 2002. "Trust Comes from Expertise". In *Science: Can We Trust the Experts?* edited by T. Gilland. 17–38. Abingdon, UK: Hodder & Stoughton.

Durodié, B. 2005a. *The Concept of Risk. Risk Case Studies.* Nuffield Trust Global Programme on Health, Foreign Policy and Security. London: Nuffield Trust.

Durodié, B. 2005b. "Limitations of Public Dialogue in Science and the Rise of 'New' Experts". In *The Changing Role of the Public Intellectual*, edited by D. Cummings. 82–92. Oxford: Routledge.

Forscher, P.S. and Kteily, N. 2017. "A Psychological Profile of the Alt-Right". *Open Science Framework*, August 10, 2017. https://mfr.osf.io.

Frijda, N.H. 1986. *The Emotions.* Cambridge: Cambridge University Press.

Fukuyama, F. 1989. "The End of History". *The National Interest*, 16, 3–18.

Fukuyama, F. 1992. *The End of History and the Last Man.* New York: Free Press.

Furnham, A., Richards, S.C. and Paulhus, D.L. 2013. "The Dark Triad of Personality: A 10 Review". *Social and Personality Psychology Compass*, 7(3), 199–216.

Glendon, A.I. 1987. "Risk Cognition". In *Risk and Decisions*, edited by W.T. Singleton and J. Hovden. 87–107. Chichester: John Wiley & Sons.

Glendon. A.I. and Clarke, S. 2016. *Human Safety and Risk Management: a Psychological Perspective.* 3rd edition. Boca Raton, FL: CRC Press/Taylor & Francis.

Glendon, A.I., Clarke, S. and McKenna, E. 2006. *Human Safety and Risk Management.* 2nd edition. Boca Raton, FL: CRC Press/Taylor & Francis.

Glynos, J. and Mondon, A. 2016. *The Political Logic of Populist Hype: The Case of Right-Wing Populism's 'Meteoric Rise' and its Relation to the Status Quo.* Populismus Working Papers No. 4. Thessaloniki: Populismus.

Gove, M. 2017. "Interview with Donald Trump". *The Times*. January 16, 2017. https://thetimes.co.uk/article/full-transcript-of-interview-with-donald-trump-5d39sr09d.

Haidt, J. 2012. *The Righteous Mind: Why Good People are Divided by Politics and Religion*. London: Allen Lane.

Hardy 1985. "The Nature of Unobtrusive Power". *Journal of Management Studies*. 22(4), 384–399.

Hare, R.D. 2003. *Manual for the Revised Psychopathy Checklist* (2nd edition). Toronto, Canada: Multi-Health Systems.

Hare, R.D. 2016. "Psychopathy, the PCL-R, and Criminal Justice: Some New Findings and Current Issues". *Canadian Psychology*, Vol 57(1), Feb 2016, 21–34.

Hirstein, W. 2013. "What is a Psychopath?" *Psychology Today* blog column. January 30, 2013.

Home Office. 2014a. *Impacts of Migration on UK Native Employment: an Analytical Review of the Evidence*. Occasional Paper 109. March 2014. London: Home Office.

Home Office. 2014b. *The Reasons for Migration and Labour Market Characteristics of UK Residents Born Abroad*. Occasional Paper 110. September 2014. London: Home Office.

Ipsos MORI. 2014. *Perception and Reality: Public Attitudes to Migration*. London: Ipsos MORI Social Research Institute.

Jakobowitz, S. and Egan, V. 2006. "The Dark Triad and Normal Personality Traits". *Personality and Individual Differences*, 40(2), 331–339.

Jones, D.N. and Paulhus, D.L. 2011. "Differentiating the Dark Triad with the Interpersonal Circumplex". In *Handbook of Interpersonal Psychology: Theory, Research, Assessment and Therapeutic Intervention*, edited by L.M. Horowitz and S. Strack. Hoboken, New Jersey: Wiley.

Jost, J.T., Glaser, J., Kruglanski, A.W. and Sulloway, F.J. 2003. "Political Conservatism as Motivated Social Cognition". *Psychological Bulletin*, 129, 339–375.

Kahan, D.M., Jamieson, K.H., Landrum, A.R. et al. 2017. "Culturally Antagonistic Memes and the Zika Virus: an Experimental Test". *Journal of Risk Research*, 20(1), 1–40.

Kakkar, H. and Sivanathan, N. 2017. "When the Appeal of a Dominant Leader is Greater Than a Prestige Leader". *Proceedings of the National Academy of Sciences*, doi: 10.1073/pnas.1617711114.

Kasperson, R.E., Renn, O., Slovic, P. et al. 1988. "The Social Amplification of Risk: a Conceptual Framework". *Risk Analysis*, Vol 8 No 2, 177–187.

Kiehl, K.A. and Buckholtz, J.W. 2010. "Inside the Mind of a Psychopath". *Scientific American Mind*, Sept/Oct, 22–29.

Kushner, T. and Valman, N. 2000. *Remembering Cable Street: Fascism and Anti-Fascism in British Society*. London: Vallentine Mitchell & Co.

Le Coze, J-C. 2017. "Globalization and High-Risk Systems". *Policy and Practice in Health and Safety*, Vol 15 (1), 57–81.

Lerner, J.S., Gonzalez, R.M., Small, D.A. and Fischhoff, B. 2003. "Effects of Fear and Anger on Perceived Risks of Terrorism: A National Field Experiment". *Psychological Science*, 14(2), 144–150.

Lexington 2016. "Normalizing Narcissism". The Lexington column. *The Economist*, August 20, 2016, page 36.

Lizza, R. 2017. "Anthony Scaramucci Called Me to Unload About White House Leakers, Reince Priebus, and Steve Bannon". *The New Yorker*, July 27, 2017. www.newyorker.com.

Lyons, M.N. 2017a. *Ctrl-Alt-Delete: The Origins and Ideology of the Alternative Right*. Somerville, MA: Political Research Associates.

Lyons, M.N. 2017b. *Insurgent Supremacists: The US Far Right's Challenge to State and Empire*. Oakland, Ca: PM Press.

MacDonald, K.B. 2002. *Culture of Critique: An Evolutionary Analysis of Jewish Involvement in Twentieth Century Intellectual and Political Movements*. 2nd edition. Bloomington, IN: Author House.

Magens. 1971. Oral testimony of Mrs Magens, eye witness to the Battle of Cable Street, London, 1936. Interviewed by A.E. Waring in Stamford Hill, London.

Marcus, G.E., Neuman, W.R. and MacKuen, M.B. 2000. *Affective Intelligence and Political Judgement*. Chicago: University of Chicago Press.

Martin, J.L. 2001. "The Authoritarian Personality, 50 Years Later: What Lessons are There for Political Psychology?" *Political Psychology*, 22, 1, 1–26.

McCrae, R.R. and Costa, P.T. 2003. *Personality in Adulthood: A Five-Factor Theory Perspective* (2nd ed.). New York: Guilford Press.

Mondon, A. 2013. *The Mainstreaming of the Extreme Right in France and Australia: A Populist Hegemony?* Aldershot UK: Ashgate.

Mondon, A. 2014. "The Front National in the Twenty-First Century: From Pariah to Republican Democratic Contender". *Modern and Contemporary France*, 1–20.

Mondon, A. 2015. "Populism, the People and the Illusion of Democracy—the Front National and UKIP in a Comparative Context". *French Politics*, 13(2), 141–156.

Nickerson, R.S. 1998. "Confirmation Bias: a Ubiquitous Phenomenon in Many Guises". *Review of General Psychology*, 2, 175–220.

ONS. 2017. *Migration Statistics Quarterly Report, May 2017*. Office for National Statistics, Home Office and Department for Work and Pensions. London: ONS.

ONS. 2015. *Statistical Bulletin: Population of the UK by Country of Birth and Nationality*. London: ONS.

O'Rourke, P.J. 2017. *How the Hell Did This Happen? The US Election of 2016.* London: Grove Press UK.

Pavia, W. 2017. "Psychiatrists' Verdict: a Man Incapable of Guilt with Inner Rage". *The Times,* May 20, 2017, page 33.

Paxton, R. 2017. "Democracy in Danger. How Can Psychology Help?" *The Psychologist,* June 2017.

Parker, M.T. and Isbell, L.M. 2010. "How I Vote Depends on How I Feel: The Differential Impact of Anger and Fear on Political Information Processing". *Psychological Science,* 21(4), 548–550.

Paulhus, D.L. and Williams, K.M. 2002. "The Dark Triad of Personality: Narcissism, Machiavellianism and Psychopathy". *Journal of Research in Personality,* 36(6), 556–563).

Pidgeon, N., Slovic, P. and Kasperson, R.E. (eds). 2003. *The Social Amplification of Risk.* Cambridge, UK: CUP.

Post, J. M. 2015. *Narcissism and Politics: Dreams of Glory.* Cambridge: Cambridge University Press.

Roccatto, M. and Ricolfi, L. 2005. "On the Correlation Between Right-Wing Authoritarianism and Social Dominance Orientation". *Basic & Applied Social Psychology,* 27, 187–200.

Schulz, K. 2010. *Being Wrong: Adventures in the Margin of Error.* London: Portobello Books.

Shermer, M. 2018. "For the Love of Science—Combating Science Denial with Science Pleasure". *Skeptic.* January 2018, page 73. www.scientificamerican.com.

Sibley, C.G. and Duckitt, J. 2008. "Personality and Prejudice: A Meta-Analysis and Theoretical Review". *Personality and Social Psychology Review,* 12, 248–279.

Sibley, C.G., Robertson, A. and Wilson, M. 2006. "Social Dominance Orientation and Right Wing Authoritarianism: Additive and Interactive Effects". *Political Psychology,* 27, 755–768.

Sidanius, J. and Pratto, F. 1999. *Social Dominance: An Intergroup Theory of Social Hierarchy and Oppression.* Cambridge: Cambridge University Press.

Walton, M. 2007a. "Leadership Toxicity—an Inevitable Affliction of Organizations?" *Organizations and People,* 14(1), 19–27.

Walton, M. 2007b. "Toxic Leadership". In *Leadership: The Key Concepts.* edited by J. Gosling and A. Marturano. Oxford: Routledge.

Walton, M. 2010. "Senior Executives: Behavioural Dynamics". *HRM Review.* August 2010, 10–18.

Waring, A.E. and Glendon, A.I. 1998. *Managing Risk: Critical Issues for Survival and Success into the 21st Century.* Aldershot, UK: Thompson/Cengage.

Waring, A.E. 2013. *Corporate Risk and Governance.* Farnham, UK: Gower/Routledge.

Wodak, R. 2015. *The Politics of Fear. What Right-Wing Populist Discourses Mean*. London: Sage.

Zimmerman, M. 2011. "Confirmatory Bias". In *Encyclopaedia of Clinical Neuropsychology*. Page 661. New York: Springer.

PART 2:
THE ALT-RIGHT
IN SELECTED EUROPEAN COUNTRIES

Chapter 3: Brexit and the Alt-Right Agenda in the UK

By Alan Waring

Abstract

This chapter examines the development of the Brexit campaign and its gradual emergence as a populist platform and metaphor for Alt-Right ideology. The origins of the Eurosceptic agenda and the Brexit movement are discussed in detail e.g. fears of immigration and perceived adverse effects; EU incompetence, fraud and corruption; overbearing EU bureaucracy; taxpayer bailouts of ailing EU member states; EU refusal to reform; pressure for political rather than economic union. The manipulation of the Brexit campaign and referendum by UKIP and other Alt-Right supporters using fear-based arguments is analysed. The paradox of UKIP's success in relation to Brexit and its subsequent electoral demise is discussed. Risks are systematically identified.

Key words: Brexit, Eurosceptic, Alt-Right, UKIP, Farage, immigration

The Brexit Project

The formal process of the exit of Britain from the European Union, generally abbreviated to 'Brexit', began on March 29, 2017 following a national referendum in the UK on June 23, 2016, seeking to indicate whether the voting population wanted to leave or not, which resulted in a small but clear majority for leaving the EU. Considerable numbers of Conservative Party voters supported the Brexit campaign but so too did significant numbers of Labour Party supporters. However, at the populist level, it was undoubtedly the relentless rhetoric of the numerically small UK Independence Party and its Alt-Right credo and agenda that persuaded sufficient voters of all political parties to vote 'leave' in the referendum. Moreover, parties and groups further to the right than UKIP, while relatively small in voting numbers, also backed the referendum vote for Brexit.

This chapter examines the development over some years of the Brexit campaign and its gradual emergence as a populist platform and metaphor for expression of some aspects of Alt-Right ideology. The chapter does not take a position on whether Brexit is a good or bad proposition, nor does it seek to examine in any detail the asserted arguments for and against Brexit, although mention of some of these is inevitable in places in order to clarify a particular issue. The chapter also does not examine the success or failure of on-going UK-EU negotiations for Brexit, which began on March 29, 2017 and which will not be complete until at least 2019, other than to consider potential risk implications for different outcomes and different groups.

Britain's EU Membership

Britain's accession to the European Economic Community (EEC) occurred in January 1973, following two previous attempts to join during the 1960s that had been blocked by President de Gaulle of France. Britain joined eight other countries in the EEC, which was essentially a body based on common trade interests. Within two years of joining, British Prime Minister Harold Wilson held a referendum on Britain's continued EEC membership, in which the electorate voted by 67.2% to 32.8% to remain in the EEC (UKParl 2013).

In 1987, the Single European Act was signed by the existing EEC member states to enable the creation of an area without frontiers in which the free movement of goods and persons, services and capital, would be ensured. It took another six years for that Act to bring into formation the new European Union via the Treaty on European Union, the so-called Maastricht Treaty, signed on February 7, 1992 and the EU establishment on January 1, 1993. On establishment, the number of member states was 12. By 1995, the membership was 15 which eventually grew to 28 by 2013.

Among the major initiatives seeking to fulfil the overall stated intentions of the EU was, firstly, the Schengen Agreement in March 1995 between, initially, seven EU member states to enable travellers of any nationality to travel between Schengen signatory states without passport control at the frontiers. Whereas some additional EU states have subsequently joined the Schengen scheme, a significant number of others (including the UK) have remained outside it.

A second major initiative was the creation in 1999 of the common euro currency (€) and its introduction in 2002. However, as with the Schengen Agreement, not all member states chose to adopt the euro currency. Initially, there were eleven that adopted the euro, which eventually rose to 19 out of the 28. Britain was among those that chose to stay outside the euro currency.

However, the scope for which aspects of the EU its member states are allowed to reject is very limited. Notwithstanding the opt-out provisions on the Schengen and euro currency topics, the single market requires that member states ensure the four EU freedoms: the free movement of goods, services, people and money. Since its inception, tens of thousands of EU laws in the form of regulations have been drawn up (with the close involvement of all member states in their drafting and finalisation) that apply across the EU. In addition, EU Directives require member states to implement their substance in their own legislation. Further, EU jurisdiction on a very broad range of issues takes ultimate precedence over courts in individual member states via, for example, the European Court of Justice and the European Court of Human Rights.

The representative body for citizens of member states, the European Parliament, considers and votes on EU legislation drawn up by the EU Commission as well as debating issues raised by European citizens. Citizens elect to the European Parliament members (MEPs) representing their local constituency.

While the constitution and processes of the EU may appear uncontroversial, in reality all of the topics mentioned above (common currency, Schengen and migration, EU laws, EU courts, and the European Parliament) have been the objects of growing complaint within EU member states but most strongly in Britain. The gradual crystallisation of a broad spectrum of unease, frustration and resentment about the EU among the British population into an informal anti-EU 'movement' became more prominent from around 2004 onwards, aided and abetted by the propaganda activities of the UK Independence Party (UKIP)—see below.

The Origins of a Eurosceptic Agenda and Brexit Movement

Many citizens of EU Member States believe that the EU is, and can only ever be, a force for good and that the 500-plus million citizens of its

28 Member States should be grateful for all the many benefits that it is argued the EU bestows upon them. This view is supported by a significant number of business leaders, professionals and academics (see, for example, Campos and Coricelli 2015; Campos et al 2014), as well as official European Commission surveys such as Eurobarometer (2015; 2016). As a common trading bloc, the EU provides huge trading advantages to its member states and citizens. Those trading advantages were the prime focus of the original EEC (European Economic Community) from which the EU emerged and with a much enlarged agenda in the areas of common legislation, currency union and free movement of goods, services, people and capital.

In addition, for many citizens of mainland EU member states, the horrors wreaked across Europe in the 19th and 20th centuries as a result of disastrous national rivalries and divisions and two World Wars are sufficient evidence of the need for a unifying entity such as the EU. Many EU citizens, especially those old enough to remember WWII and the scourge of Nazism, or the Cold War and the Iron Curtain, firmly believe that the EU has been largely responsible for general peace in Europe since 1945. The Eurobarometer (2016) survey showed that overall 66% of respondents agreed that the EU is a "place of stability" in a troubled world and that the majority of respondents in all Member States shared this view. This belief that EU has kept the peace may not be entirely well-founded (e.g. arguably the combination of the NATO military alliance and US backing has been the biggest deterrence to intra-European military conflicts and those between Russia and the west), and may not be shared widely outside Europe. Moreover, Bickerton (2015) argued that the EU has contributed little to peace-building per se in post-WWII Europe and has instead concentrated on economic and financial integration as a stepping stone to political integration. However, EU foreign policy is continually hampered by difficulties in securing agreement among the 28 members, leading to risks of delays, policy dilution, and 'lowest common denominator' policy. National interests and divisions between member states militate against the EU becoming a superpower and against EU security strategy.

Nevertheless, the perceived role of the EU as European peace-generator remains a strongly unifying belief for many in Europe and does have some substance in the areas of economic strength and development of shared values and approaches to many common issues and the breaking down of harmful barriers arising from ethnicity, religion, and toxic nationalism. Pan (2016) likened the EU dream to that of the cosmopolitanism of the Holy Roman Empire and, by extension, to the *civis romanus sum* concept attributable to Cicero i.e. the notion of common belonging across the EU and entitlement to protection afforded by virtue of common citizenship. A 'United States of Europe' was the ardent wish of such post-WWII European leaders as Winston Churchill, Konrad Adenauer in West Germany (1949–1963), Jean Monnet, Robert Schuman and the other 'founding fathers' of the EU (FF 2017). In their vision, the EU would exhibit all the structures and processes of a federated state in which the independent powers and freedoms of member states would be subordinate to the overarching requirements of the EU in Brussels. Such a desire was consistent with the belief that full political, economic, and monetary union would greatly strengthen the EU bloc and heighten the security of all member states. Indeed, there has even been a move to create an EU military force, separate and distinct from NATO, although this remains unfulfilled.

However, Bickerton (2015) asserted that the EU had migrated a long way from the founding fathers' vision in the 1950s to a current reality in which the euro currency zone (Eurozone) had created divisions and potential sources of crisis and conflict e.g. between productive and unproductive national economies within the EU, between the stronger northern industrialized economies and the weaker southern agrarian/tourist economies. Berman (2016) also questioned the guaranteed inevitability of a greater and more perfect EU. See later for examples and how these topics affected perceptions of the EU in the UK.

Despite an undoubtedly strong support for the EU among its citizens, from the early 1990s and even earlier some activists and politicians believed that the EU was a fatally flawed concept. As the first decade of the new millennium progressed, many others began to fear that, whatever the noble intentions may have been, the grand EU 'European experiment' had gone disastrously wrong (Waring 2016). There were growing calls across Europe from both mainstream and fringe politicians, as well as activists and disaffected voters, for either radical reform of the EU or for their country to quit the EU. The most strident and persistent of such calls were within the UK, where traditionally suspicion of foreigners has been prevalent and national sovereignty has always been jealously guarded by its citizens.

The following sub-sections examine some of the reasons for the evident growing disillusionment in the UK about the EU.

Immigration and its Perceived Second-Order Effects

Despite official data to the contrary (ONS 2015; 2017), an international survey of public perceptions of immigration (Ipsos MORI 2014) showed that in the UK respondents estimated immigrant numbers at 24% of the population against an actual level of 13%. On the more specific topic of the proportion of the population that is Muslim, UK respondents to the Ipsos MORI survey believed it to be 21% as against an actual 5%. See also Duffy and Frere-Smith (2014), British Future (2014) and Home Office (2014a).

The rhetorical plea by the Alt-Right during the Brexit Referendum campaign to "Give me back my country" and references to "swamping" implied a belief that the UK was being taken over by foreigners and immigrants. Second order fear-based prejudicial assertions arising from the primary fear of immigration (as discussed in chapter 2) featured prominently in the developing pro-Brexit rhetoric to justify leaving the EU:

- Crime inevitably increases since immigrants are inherently more criminally orientated.
- Muslim immigrants inevitably increase the threat of terrorism i.e. conflating the fear of Muslims and immigrants with the fear of terrorism.
- Immigrants take away the jobs of indigenous citizens by accepting lower pay.
- Immigrants are unfairly granted generous welfare benefits and public housing when they have not contributed to National Insurance and taxation, while indigenous claimants who have contributed are rebuffed; they are not only undeserving, but they also typically engage in benefits fraud.
- Immigrant numbers put undue pressure on the NHS, education provision and public services.
- Immigrants refuse to integrate, learn English and (in the UK) accept British values.
- In the UK, swamping by immigrants is resulting in the British national identity being altered permanently into a diluted multi-ethnic, multi-cultural chimera.

Cultural concerns, such as loss of national identity and other supposed immigration effects as a result of EU membership, featured strongly in responses to the British Social Attitudes survey 33 for 2015, reported in June 2016 (Curtice 2016a): "Cultural concerns (of which immigration may, it seems, be just a part) are at the heart of the debate about Britain's membership of the EU". Pan (2016) referred to the increasing tensions and struggle between, on the one hand, individual libertarianism and democratic nationalism—the nation states view held by UKIP and the Leave campaign, for example—and, on the other hand, imperial multiculturalism perceived to be imposed by the EU's 'borderless' migration rules. Biggar (2017) specifically accused the EU's alleged imperialism and its "impatience, highhandedness and inflexibility" as being the root cause of Brexit. See also Pabst (2016).

Sustained repetition of all such assertions and fears about immigration contributed to a social amplification of such risks (Kasperson et al 1988; Pidgeon et al 2003), as was apparent during the slow gestation of the Brexit movement from around 2004 onwards, its gradual acceleration after 2010, and eventually into the Brexit referendum campaign. The study by Carvalho et al (2015) of patterns of politicization in the debate on UK immigration over the period since 1995 demonstrated the strong influence of extensive and intensive coverage by large circulation tabloid newspapers on the British public's beliefs about and attitudes towards immigration into the UK. The study showed a clear association between negative news coverage on immigration and integration and the salience of negative public opinion about it. It also showed that the immigration debate remained highly polarized over the period 1995 to 2009 (when the data collection ended). However, the study was more cautious about ascribing all anti-immigration sentiments in the UK to either racism or support for far-right ideology:

> "It is possible to oppose forms of new immigration without being stigmatized as extreme right-wing; and some views which mirror BNP ideology, such as support for strong leadership, might reflect an apolitical desire for 'low cost signalling' rather than authoritarianism. On the other hand, many people have developed the discursive abilities to hide views, or package them in liberally acceptable ways, and forms of 'banal patriotism' remain pervasive in traditional portrayals of national identity (Billig 1995)". (Carvalho et al 2015).

This view concurs with the findings of Curtice (2015) and Curtice and Evans (2015). Nevertheless, in an extended survey on social attitudes in Britain, Kelley et al (2017), reported that over the period 1983 to 2013 the proportion of respondents admitting to being racially prejudiced remained static at approximately 25%. This percentage remained unaltered in March 2017 i.e. after the Brexit referendum. Moreover, of those who admitted racial prejudice, those who voted for Brexit constituted nearly double those who did not (34% as against 18%). Similarly, of those who admitted racial prejudice, Conservative voters were 33% and Labour voters were 18%. The figures for UKIP and other right-wing voters are not identified.

The Carvalho et al study also demonstrated the ephemeral nature of media attention and the transience of its effects (unless continually repeated), with a number of distinct oscillations over the 14-year period of the study when media attention was focussed intermittently on issues other than immigration and integration, thus suggesting that social amplification of risks may not always perseverate. See also Allen (2016) on press coverage of immigration and the Brexit issue.

Another oddity surfaced as a result of the Brexit debate, namely immigrants into the UK from EU countries were seen as more problematic than from non-EU countries, despite the fact that they were only a fraction of the annual totals. This negative perception of there being large numbers of EU immigrants became amplified on accession of Romania and Bulgaria as EU Member States in 2007. Undoubtedly, public opinion was shaped firstly by media coverage suggesting that the UK would be swamped by cheap labour, unemployed benefit seekers and criminals from these two countries, and then by articles claiming to provide evidence to support such fears (e.g. Slack 2007 and later Petre and Walters 2013). In addition, the potential for Turkey gaining accession to the EU threw up an image of large numbers of Turkish citizens being enabled to travel freely to the UK. Indeed, UKIP's then leader Nigel Farage implied that some 75 million Turks would descend on the UK. The fact that Turkish EU accession was by no means guaranteed and was in any event many years ahead, plus the high unlikelihood of the whole Turkish population wanting to move to the UK, became lost in the political and media rhetoric.

Despite there being no direct connection with migration of EU citizens into the UK, the asylum seeker and economic migrant crisis in mainland Europe, resulting from displacements and escape from wartorn areas such as Iraq, Afghanistan, Syria, Libya and many other countries into the mainland EU, added to fears and anxieties of the British public about UK immigration via the EU. These included fears (later shown to be well-founded) that the mass of asylum seekers might be infiltrated by opportunistic IS/Da-esh terrorists trying to get into mainland EU and then into the UK. By 2015, there had been 1.32m asylum applications in the EU and in 2016 it was a similar figure (Eurostat 2017), the vast majority in mainland EU countries having these migrants arriving across the EU's southern borders. All of this added to pro-Brexit propaganda.

EU Bailouts of Ailing Member States

One of the benefits of EU membership is the bailout facility when a Member State gets into such serious financial difficulties that it is in danger of national insolvency. However, bailouts come with a price. For example, the multiple EU bailouts of Greece from 2010 onwards and its on-going economic crisis resulted in austerity measures imposed on the Greek population. Such measures directly challenged the wishes of Greek voters who democratically elected the anti-austerity Syriza party into government in two successive elections. Ignoring the primary responsibility of the Greek population and its succession of elected governments for preventing and avoiding national insolvency and to accept austerity and drastic reforms as a necessary consequence of debt default, the fact remains that the bailout programme over-rode democracy in Greece. Although the EU was only one party to the bailout programme (the others being the International Monetary Fund—IMF and the European Central Bank—ECB), it was the EU that the Greek population blamed not only for their austerity demise but also for their original indebtedness (sic). There were populist calls for Greece to quit the EU—a so-called Grexit. Moreover, particular EU states were singled out for popular invective. Germany and Chancellor Angela Merkel bore the brunt of the anger and vilification, with popular demands repeated by Greek politicians for Germany to make massive restitution payments for alleged underpayment of its WWII reparations to Greece. The widespread autistic hostility (d'Estree and Shapiro 1971; Newcomb 1947) evident in the Greek population's reaction, cast the EU as an institution and Germany and its Chancellor as villains. Trust in the EU among Greeks plummeted to 20% (Eurobarometer 2016).

A similar picture developed in Cyprus, whose communist AKEL government over its five-year term to 2013 created a €17bn government deficit and resulted in the collapse of one bank (Laiki), the near collapse of the country's largest bank (Bank of Cyprus), and the near bankruptcy of the state. The new centre-right government in March 2013 under Nicos Anastasiades immediately signed a bailout agreement with the Troika (EU, ECB and IMF) which, like the Greek bailout, imposed strict terms on Cyprus to implement drastic reforms and austerity measures. The programme also included an across-the-board debt 'haircut' of all bank deposits in excess of €100,000. The term 'deposits' referred not only to savings accounts but also to current accounts, whether or not interest-bearing. This unprecedented debt recovery action partly resulted from Troika concerns (Deloittes 2013; Lascelles 2013; Moneyval 2013) that Cyprus banks had been (a) attracting large deposits by offering indefensibly high interest rates (typically 5% or more in 2012) while failing on a massive scale to ensure that borrowers serviced their loans, (b) imprudently maintaining bank assets of some €150bn that dwarfed Cyprus GDP of barely €18bn, (c) over many years providing mortgages and property-related loans without due diligence checks and often involving corrupt relationships, resulting in a massive bad debt portfolio, and (d) through lax due diligence checks, providing opportunities for large-scale money laundering e.g. Russian organised criminals, and the Raja case (Waring 2013a, 117) involving alleged laundering through Cyprus banks of some of the €479m in bribes allegedly obtained by an Indian former minister from the Indian telecoms industry.

Thousands of bank account holders lost their balances in excess of €100,000 and, in some cases, individual losses were millions of Euros. These included highly educated and professional people who simply could not comprehend how their accounts had been 'raided' and apparently lawfully. The author, who was resident in Cyprus at the time, knew many such victims. As in Greece, the Cypriot population blamed the Troika, and especially the EU, Germany and Angela Merkel, for their predicament.

Perhaps unsurprisingly, the image of profligate and badly managed EU member states apparently abusing EU funds on a massive scale, through bailouts to which British taxpayers were indirectly contributing, did not help the Britain Stronger in the EU (otherwise known as the Remain campaign) in the Brexit referendum.

Institutional Incompetence, Fraud and Corruption

Many argue that the EU as an institution has become corrupted. On one plane, the EU is perceived by many to exhibit the 'corrupted spirit' (see Waring 2013b, 115) of an apparently uncaring leviathan run by hordes of faceless, nameless, self-serving bureaucrats in Brussels and Strasbourg. These officials, on the so-called EU 'gravy train', are perceived, accurately or not, as pursuing as their main priority their own careers and financial enlargement, while being paid vast salaries and benefits (often tax-free) out of tax payers' money supplied via Member States. Nevertheless, despite receiving such largesse, there is anecdotal evidence that EU officialdom is often slow, evasive, equivocal, and sometimes abjectly incompetent.

On top of corruption of the spirit, there is also recorded evidence of actual fraud and corruption. Vast sums of EU money are unaccounted for. Stretching back to the 1990s, there has been a series of scandals such as the Eurostat scandal uncovered in 2003, in which for more than a decade Planistat officials had been diverting millions of € for their personal gain (see Mahoney 2003). The Eurostat internal audit service eventually discovered it but the OLAF (European Anti-Fraud Office) report on it was deliberately delayed for years, apparently at the behest of three EU Commissioners.

An internal audit by the European Parliament uncovered widespread fraud by MEPs in relation to the allowances that they claimed (Galvin 2008). In 2013, the Austrian MEP Ernst Strasser was convicted for receiving corrupt payments for influence in the EU (Pancevski 2013). Sentenced to 4 years in jail, this was overturned on appeal but reinstated in 2014 with a lesser sentence of three-and-a-half years (Politico 2014).

The scale of the fraud and corruption problem (estimated to amount to tens of billions of Euros per annum, and possibly more) within the EU institution, and the on-going struggle to control and eradicate it, has been recognized by the EU Commission (e.g. EC 2014). However, progress remained limited (see, for example, EC 2013; Brandt and Svendsen 2013). To the 500m citizens of the EU, this may have looked like a self-serving reluctance that undermined the moral authority of the EU. In the UK, such revelations added to the growing scepticism about the EU.

Perceived Unaccountable Overbearing Inertia

Many accuse the EU of pretending to enshrine democratic values and promote fairness and human rights for all its citizens, while in reality also imposing an authoritarian paternalism summed up as 'the EU knows best what is good for you' or even 'EU imperialism' (Biggar 2017). This perceived overbearing super-state paternalism will also be familiar to citizens of Member States which have ever had either a communist or hard-left party or a nationalist party, in either partial or complete control of their government policy e.g. Cyprus (AKEL), Greece (Syriza), Hungary (Fidesz), Scotland (SNP).

A paternalistic ideology has been driving EU legislation, especially in areas of law, social welfare, consumer protection and so on. Few would dispute that there have been some benefits from various EU regulations and directives (see, for example, respondents' perceptions in Curtice and Evans 2015). However, the deserved plaudits in some areas have been overshadowed by highly criticised absurdities in others. For example, the micro-management diktats from Brussels on such parochial matters as banning bent bananas, proscribing short or bent cucumbers, forbidding British pubs to sell beer in pint measures, and banning sales of noisy vacuum cleaners, have attracted much ridicule. Forcing the UK to pay benefits and provide housing to EU migrant claimants, as soon as they enter the UK, erupted into a national scandal that undoubtedly boosted the 'Leave' vote in the Brexit referendum. No matter what are the facts, the lasting perception among British citizens from all this was that they were yet further examples of unwarranted and unacceptable interference in their lives by overbearing EU busybody bureaucrats in Brussels. Curtice (2016a) noted the perception in the UK of EU 'meddling', whereas Biggar (2017) went further to accuse it of outright imperialism.

There seemed to be a lack of awareness in the EU headquarters and leadership that the EU was being perceived by UK voters as persistently acting in an overbearing, coercive and arrogant manner towards them, and that such a perception demanded urgent counter-action on their part. The EU elites in Brussels may have had the legal authority to act as they did but, in the eyes of British voters, their arrogant disregard for the concerns of ordinary citizens undermined their own moral authority and legitimacy. In short, the perceived dismissive behaviour of the EU towards the legitimate concerns of the

British population inflicted great damage on its image and perceived trustworthiness, and the EU's failure to recognize the need to repair that public relations damage contributed significantly to the pro-Brexit mood.

If perceptions of over-weaning micro-management intrusions were not enough, at the more macro and strategic levels the EU appeared to be struck down by "a kind of collective catatonia, a policy and executive constipation" (Waring 2016). This is exemplified by the EU's disarray when faced with crises, such as financial bailouts for weaker Member States verging on bankruptcy and the large-scale influx of migrants from outside the EU. The migrant crisis and the absolute need to secure the EU's borders, from both a perceived endless mass of would-be migrants and terrorist insurgents taking advantage of the crisis, put a heavy strain on the Schengen accord and the EU's internal borderless travel scheme. Out of sovereign self-interest, some Member States re-imposed border controls temporarily against the Schengen accord. In 2017, a leaked diplomatic paper reportedly showed that both France and Germany were seeking, in exceptional circumstances, suspension of the Schengen accord for periods of up to four years (Waterfield 2017).

Many UK voters, as evidenced in the Brexit referendum, strongly believed that the UK should have full control over its own borders and immigration policy, and perceived (accurately or not) that continued EU membership would necessarily undermine that independent control to the UK's detriment, and would allow economic migrants from the EU to continue to enter the UK unchecked.

Failure of EU Subsidiarity Principle

The principle of subsidiarity provides for EU legislation issued in the form of Directives to be implemented by the Member States through their own legislation and enforced locally. The Directives are arrived at through a fairly rigorous consultation and drafting system seeking to ensure final acceptance by every Member State. The implementation and enforcement of such legislation is devolved entirely to each Member State, and this appears to represent a particularly benign and enlightened approach that recognises the sovereign integrity of each Member State and shows a high degree of trust in them.

However, subsidiarity relies entirely on each Member State implementing a particular Directive and enforcing it i.e. acting responsibly. Regrettably, history shows that whereas some Member States do act responsibly in this regard, others do not. Some have a very lax and laissez-faire attitude towards EU Directive enforcement, the various major hazard Directives being an example. For example, the Polyviou Report into the Mari-Vassilikos disaster of July 2011 was highly critical of both lack of local compliance with the EU Seveso II Directive and the local enforcing authority's absent supervision (Polyviou 2011; Waring 2013b). The glaring weakness of subsidiarity lies in the fact that the EU centrally has no over-arching monitoring, auditing and supervisory function over what a Member State does or does not do to implement a Directive and has no mandate to establish one. Each Member State is left 'on its honour' to implement a Directive correctly. Such trust is not always warranted.

While the general public in the UK may not have been aware of the dysfunctional subsidiarity issue, many professionals and business people were aware that, whereas the UK generally abided by the requirements of EU Directives, some other EU Member States were virtually ignoring them without any accountability. Indignation at the manifest unfairness of the EU Directive system vis-à-vis the UK added to antipathy towards the EU.

Perception of EU Refusal to Reform

The economic argument to stay in the EU was strong but such events as the difficult and costly bailouts for Greece, Cyprus, and Portugal and the unresolved EU migration crisis cast doubts on for how long, or whether, the economic strength of the EU could be assured. The inability and unwillingness of the EU to institute radical reform, and its steadfast refusal to allow the UK to eradicate the alleged widespread abuse of its state welfare system by economic migrants from poorer EU countries, turned increasing numbers of UK citizens against the EU. EU leaders dismissively telling Britain that it must accept the EU's decision on benefit payments to EU migrants added to the discontent.

The Brexit Remain campaign (or Britain Stronger in the EU) and its many supporters believed that self-reform was possible and that it would be better for the UK to remain inside so as to be able to spearhead the reforms. However, it became increasingly apparent that the EU leadership and Commission were in denial about its weaknesses and lacked the political will to reform it in any substantive way. The patrician aura and arms-length imperial elitism exhibited by EU leaders and commissioners had created a distinct impression that they regarded themselves not only as unaccountable but also rightly so.

The former UKIP leader Nigel Farage, (also an MEP), took great delight in using opportunities during debates in the European Parliament to remind such assembled patricians that none of the 500 million citizens of the EU had elected them yet they held sway over policies and vast expenditure that impacted every citizen. See, for example, *YouTube* (2013). Moreover, he reminded them that few of them had ever had "a proper job", thus implying that both their competence credentials and their right to be in such powerful positions unelected were suspect. Farage, a skilful orator, knew how to articulate the thoughts and concerns of the ordinary citizen and sought to demonstrate that he, at least, was in touch with the 'reality' of the ordinary citizen whereas the EU patricians were not. He advised them that, as they were incapable of substantive reform, the only solution would be the ultimate dissolution or destruction of the EU. This may be one possible outcome among several (Patel and Reh 2016).

Manipulation of Brexit by UKIP and the Far-Right

The term 'Eurosceptic' arose early in the Brexit campaign as a shorthand descriptor for all those who had doubts about the UK's continuing EU membership. However, before long, Eurosceptic became the general term for anyone who definitely wanted the UK to quit the EU, although Curtice (2016a) challenged this absolutist meaning, pointing out that in the 2015 British Social Attitudes survey whereas 65% of respondents were Eurosceptics, 60% still backed the option to remain in the EU.

Nevertheless, public support for the populist anti-immigration ideas and slogans of UKIP gathered momentum during the 2010–2015 period of the campaign to secure a Brexit referendum (see, for example, Curtice 2015), when they received much backing from the right-wing press. In 2013, Conservative Party anti-EU rebels obtained a conditional government agreement for a Brexit referendum before the end of 2017. After the European Union Referendum Act 2015, UKIP support increased during the referendum campaigning, both as part of the official Vote Leave campaign and the unofficial Leave.EU/Grassroots Out campaign, although its message was somewhat dwarfed by the official Vote Leave campaign that was targeting ordinary voters across the mainstream parties. After the Brexit referendum in 2016, however, public support for UKIP evaporated, as evidenced by the party losing its last remaining UK parliamentary seat in the 2017 General Election and most of its council seats in 2017 local authority elections, and more still in 2018. However, as Curtice (2016a and b) reported, although from 2012 onwards UK respondents were significantly more Eurosceptic than in earlier years, in 2015 two thirds of them still favoured remaining in the EU. By the time of the referendum, the Eurosceptic mood had hardened sufficiently in favour of Brexit to secure a Brexit win and, according to Curtice (2016b), actually increased after the referendum. Nevertheless, actual UKIP supporters, whether committed members (then some 40,000—Keen and Apostolova 2017) or transient supporters, in addition to far-right supporters, never amounted to more than a small minority (probably less than 5%) of the 17.41m Leave voters. Clearly, if Euroscepticism increased after the referendum yet UKIP lost almost all its seats in the 2017 general and local elections, it tends to confirm that UKIP accounted for only a small proportion of Eurosceptics.

A series of instances from 2013 onwards provoked questions about the honesty, integrity and competence of UKIP officials and candidates, as well as allegations of racism. For example, the UKIP party leader Paul Nuttall was found to have been untruthful in his 2017 general election candidacy registration and separately in his claimed credentials and achievements. The manifesto (UKIP 2017a, 37) contained a statement that "clothing that........prevents intake of essential vitamin D from sunlight is not liberating" and therefore UKIP policy would be to ban face coverings by Muslim women. At least 30 UKIP officials or candidates were variously identified by the press as making allegedly racist statements or comments about immigrants or ethnic or religious minorities (e.g. *Mirror Online* May 19, 2013; *New Statesman* December 19, 2014; *Mail Online* December 11, 2014, March 1, 2015, February 11, 2016). After the Referendum and the Article 50 Brexit trigger, the party attracted further controversy in the candidature of Anne Marie Waters (UKIP 2017b), who openly described Islam as evil and who co-founded the anti-Islam group Pegida UK (for more on the

German far-right origins of Pegida, see chapter 7) with Tommy Robinson, the former leader of the far-right English Defence League (Roberts 2017)—see also chapter 4. Such instances attracted negative attention, including increasing ridicule, from sections of the media that previously admired UKIP.

The fickleness of the media is matched by the fickleness of the electorate. What an individual says about a particular risk or opportunity may not match either what they actually believe or what they do in relation to the risk and also varies, both qualitatively and over time (see Schulz 2010; Waring and Glendon 1998). This fits with the thesis that apparently increasing support for UKIP in UK elections during the lead up to the referendum vote came from disaffected supporters of the Conservative Party and Labour Party who were temporarily supporting UKIP as a form of protest against perceived weaknesses on immigration and national control issues in their own usual party of choice. Such temporary support suggests that, while sharing some nationalist beliefs and prejudices on immigration and race with the Alt-Right, these particular voters did not see themselves as extremists and were in denial about having any kind of fascist mentality. Anecdotal evidence supports this contention, although data from Curtice (2015) show that those professing to be UKIP supporters express a significantly more authoritarian attitude than do others.

Supporters of such far- and extreme-right groups as NF, BNP, Britain First, and EDL, although small in number, also typically have voted tactically for UKIP candidates in UK general and local elections. Unsurprisingly, like UKIP, such groups backed the Leave campaign. Although UKIP officially bans its members from also being members of such parties, a small number of ex-members of NF, BNP and EDL are recorded as having infiltrated positions within UKIP itself (Walters et al 2016). Some UKIP officials have also been expelled for praising or promoting BNP and EDL statements on race, religion and immigration. Nevertheless, leadership candidate Waters stated openly that she advocated lifting the UKIP ban on members from such parties as BNP and EDL [she later quit UKIP to form with Tommy Robinson the far-right For Britain group, with anti-immigrant and anti-Muslim views akin to those of Britain First; she also co-founded Pegida UK, an offshoot of the German Pegida anti-immigrant/anti-Muslim movement].

Unexpectedly, in 2017 UKIP elected as its leader a more traditional establishment figure Henry Bolton, who made clear that he disavowed far- and extreme-right views and would not allow UKIP to become a quasi UK Nazi party. Nevertheless, within months, Bolton was embroiled in January 2018 in a scandal involving his young partner making racist remarks against the fiancée of Prince Harry and Bolton's future as UKIP leader looked doubtful. In a vote of no confidence, Bolton was voted out as UKIP leader by the membership in February 2018, and in March 2018 he launched a rival party called One Nation. That aside, clearly, if candidate Waters had won the UKIP leadership election, it would probably have heralded a policy shift towards the far-right and away from its previously more populist tenor. Senior UKIP members had indicated that, in the event of her becoming leader, they and a number of other senior UKIP figures (including MEPs and possibly Nigel Farage the former leader) would probably quit the party and establish a new populist right-wing party. The latter would focus on ensuring that the British government achieved an uncompromisingly hard-line Brexit in 2019 that fulfilled all the expectations, as asserted by Mr Farage, of those who voted Leave in the referendum. A parallel concern about a far-right takeover of UKIP's German counterpart AfD (see chapter 7) occurred in September 2017 when, having just won over 90 seats in the German Bundestag, the AfD chairperson Frauke Petry resigned citing her dismay at the party's 'anarchic' character and its drift towards far-right extremism (*YouTube* 2017; Charter 2017).

By April 2018, under a new leader Gerard Batten, UKIP membership was reported (ONS 2018) to have fallen to 21,000 from 49,000 in 2016 and was on the verge of bankruptcy. In the local government elections of May 2018, the number of UKIP candidates fielded had fallen by 75% compared to 2014 (Fisher 2018a), and the party lost a further 123 seats with only 3 elected. Batten's apparent strategy for UKIP revival (Hamilton 2018), as laid out at its annual conference in September 2018 (*Huff Post* 2018), centred on a distinctly rightward shift in policies to those closely aligned with EDL, Britain First and the far-right in general (see chapter 4), including a strident anti-Muslim and anti-immigrant tone, removal of human rights laws and legal protections, and nationalist/nativist discrimination based on religion, ethnicity, and country of origin. In October 2018, Batten, along with Lord Pearson the former UKIP leader, also fêted Tommy Robinson, the former far-right EDL leader and Pegida UK activist, with a meal at the House of Lords (Simpson 2018). In November 2018, Batten appointed Robinson as his personal adviser on rape gangs and Islam, apparently seeking to reinforce political rhetoric that rape is an inextricable consequence of Islam (Masters 2018). His persistent call to welcome the controversial far-right Tommy Robinson into UKIP membership was still under consideration by the party at the time of writing.

Batten's appointment of Robinson drew wide condemnation, including censure from Nigel Farage, the former UKIP leader (Masters 2018), who subsequently quit in protest at both Batten's openly far-right policies and his adulation of Robinson. The confluence of UKIP and far-right groups was further demonstrated by a pro-Brexit march in London on December 9, 2018, at which both Batten and Robinson spoke and flags of UKIP and the far-right anti-Muslim group Generation Identity (see chapter 4) were flown, while banners and placards variously invoked the German word *Lügenpresse* ['lying press'] used by the Nazis and a 'Jo Cox False Flag' accusation [apparently implying that Jo Cox MP had not been murdered by a far-right extremist—see chapter 5] (Burgess 2018).

Aaronovitch (2018) warned of Farage's 'Orbanisation' fear-based model, and the liberal conservative Matthew Parris (2018) also warned that the apparent mass defection of UKIP voters to primarily the Conservatives presaged an Alt-Right 'hard Brexit' momentum building within the Conservative Party and, in response, harsher policies so as to assuage "the dark heart of British nativism". He continued that, despite UKIP's continuing electoral obliteration, "..... Farageism has done well. The more Farageist the local electorate, the better the Tories have fared. It is futile for people like me to deny it: the collapse of UKIP does not represent a collapse of the populist right, but a growing realisation by former UKIP voters that their best hopes for the kind of policies UKIP used to promise now lie with the Conservative Party". Such political realignment to normalise far-right policies within mainstream parties is similar to the 'poldering' principle that has already arisen in Dutch politics (see van der Valk in chapter 9, and Bruning 2016).

The Alt-Right in general in the UK were ecstatic at the Brexit referendum result as, in their eyes, it provided a validation of their nationalist and anti-immigration agenda. Of course, Brexit per se could only enable controls to be placed on the free movement of actual EU migrants into the UK and would have no impact on the majority immigration from elsewhere. However, it became evident that some Alt-Right supporters genuinely but naively misunderstood Brexit propaganda which may have wrongly implied that immediately after a Brexit win a programme of immigrant repatriation and deportation would begin, not just against EU migrants but all 'unwanted foreigners'. As it clearly did not begin (and was never likely to), anger and frustration built up rapidly among them after the referendum, exhibiting itself as an upsurge of hate crimes against foreigners and ethnic and religious minorities. Hundreds of reported cases across the country include Muslims and Asians being harassed, assaulted and spat at in the street and told to leave the country, and foreigners beaten up because they were speaking a foreign language or just looked foreign. Although such hate crimes subsided somewhat, it is likely that there will be a further upsurge around the time of the actual Brexit date, when once again nationalists may feel emboldened and disinhibited by the Brexit symbolism to demonstrate their hatred.

Conclusion

From the perspective of those UK citizens who are both physically and psychologically distant from the EU headquarters and EU mainland, the weaknesses evident in the EU, both as an institution and in the attitudes and behaviour of some of its mainland Member States, increasingly called into question the wisdom of the UK remaining an EU member. Both during the developing Brexit referendum campaign and since the referendum result, pro-Brexit supporters generally conceded that a Brexit may cause the UK short-term economic damage but, overall, expected that it would bring long-term salvation to the UK—economically, politically, and socially (Curtice 2016a). It is unclear whether this expectation will be born out.

The tenor and progress of the formal Brexit negotiations between the UK and the EU, following the referendum result in June 2016 and the triggering of the Article 50 requirement on March 29, 2017, have resulted in much debate, speculation, comment, prediction and argument in political circles, the media, and the public. Discussions of Brexit risks abound in such discourses. However, these are beyond the scope of this chapter and this book. Rather, this chapter's conclusion focusses (a) on identifiable risks to various parties that result from the UK Alt-Right's stance on Brexit, and (b) on risks to the UK Alt-Right constituents themselves.

UKIP and the far-right groups sought to use the Brexit movement and campaign as a Trojan horse to achieve their broadly common nationalist agenda, namely a permanent Alt-Right timbre to the governance of Britain. By both capturing and developing the public's anti-EU mood, notably through the skilful demagoguery of their leader Nigel Farage, the populist UKIP catalysed the Leave campaign. Nevertheless, although most pro-Brexit voters identified well with the desire for stricter immigration controls and removing Britain from the clutches of a profligate, badly managed and dictatorial EU, few bought into UKIP's more questionable nationalist aims and policies, or indeed those of the far- and extreme-right.

The evidence so far is that the Alt-Right's hope and expectation that a Brexit referendum win would ensure a kind of Alt-Right utopia for Britain, even considering the continued increase in Euroscepticism after the referendum (Curtice 2016b), is unlikely to be fulfilled. As Parris (2018) noted, the closest the Alt-Right may get to achieving some of their aims is through the hard-line 'Brexiteer' right-wing group operating within the mainstream Conservative Party, and a large influx of former UKIP supporters will strengthen their position. Although arguably having more in common with UKIP, these MPs have been savvy enough to appreciate that by remaining inside the Conservative Party they had a real power base, whereas by joining UKIP or other right-wing party it would most likely result in their political oblivion. Even inside the Conservative Party, they were unlikely ever to attain more than factional, but nonetheless influential, status.

Thus, despite Brexit becoming a virtual certainty, UKIP and the far-right are likely to remain a collection of noisy, but nonetheless minority, Alt-Right protesters. Nevertheless, their small numbers and overall weak political influence belie the potential of some of the far- and extreme-right to be not just political irritants and agitators but also ideological extremists capable of violence (see chapters 4 and 5).

In summary, the identifiable threats/risks include the following, which are assessed further in chapter 12:

Risks from the Alt-Right's Stance on Brexit

Risk 1. Societal division and polarisation

Anti-immigrant rhetoric encouraging blame allocation and an insular, defensive world-view, leading to increased division and polarisation in society.

Risk 2. Pressure on mainstream parties for nationalist 'Alt-Right friendly' policies

Pressure on government for Alt-Right orientated nationalist policies if Brexit negotiations with EU succeed (i.e. so-called 'soft Brexit') and harsher nationalist policies if Brexit negotiations fail (i.e. so-called 'hard Brexit').

Risk 3. Pressure for harsher immigration policy

Pressure on government for harsher immigration policy if post-Brexit economy declines (e.g. potential GDP fall, stagflation, higher living costs, higher unemployment, business closures, businesses relocate abroad).

Risk 4. Encouragement of violence and hate crimes

Potential encouragement for extremist nationalist elements to engage in violence and other hate crimes against immigrants, ethnic and religious minorities, or political opponents of nationalism.

Brexit-related Risks for the UK Alt-Right

Risk 1. Electoral oblivion for UKIP

The Brexit goal having been achieved, electoral oblivion for UKIP as a result of its loss of relevance.

Risk 2. Financial backers abandon UKIP

Post-Brexit withdrawal of major financial backers of UKIP, frustrated by the party's poor electoral showing and organisational and political incompetence.

Risk 3. Alt-Right increasingly perceived as fringe agitators

Strident and inflammatory rhetoric from the Alt-Right post-Brexit against immigrants and minorities steadily losing its appeal to Eurosceptics, thereby ensuring the Alt-Right remain as fringe agitators.

Risk 4. Alt-Right fails to achieve permanent nationalist stamp on UK governance

Failure by Alt-Right to impose a permanent nationalist timbre on UK governance post-Brexit.

References

Aaronovitch, D. 2018. "Right Must Guard Against Its Lunatic Fringe". *The Times.* August 9,2018. Page 21.

Allen, W.L. 2016. *A Decade of Immigration in the British Press.* Report. The Migration Observatory. Oxford: University of Oxford. www.migrationobservatory.ox.ac.uk.

Berman, A.B. 2016. "Critical Theory of the Contemporary: Brexit, Immigration, and Populism". Telos Scope, October 26, 2016. *Telos,*Vol 2016, No. 176.

Bickerton, C. 2015. "Opinion: Can the EU Keep the Peace in Europe? Not a Chance". *Research Discussion.* Cambridge UK: University of Cambridge. www.cam.ac.uk.

Biggar, N. 2017. "Europe's Imperial Ambitions Led to Brexit". Comment. *The Times,* September 4, 2017, page 24.

Billig, M. 1995. *Banal Nationalism.* London: Sage.

Brandt, U.S. and Svendsen, G.T. 2013. "Why Does Bureaucratic Corruption Occur in the EU?" *Public Choice,* Vol 157 (3–4), 585–599.

Bruning, H. 2016. "Polder and Politics". *Open Democracy.* February 25, 2016. https://www.opendemocracy.net/.

Burgess, K. 2018. "Thousands on the Street to Oppose Brexit Marchers". *The Times.* December 10, 2018. Page 9.

Campos, N. and Coricelli, F. 2015. "Why did Britain Join the EU? A New Insight from Economic History". *Vox,* February 3, 2015. Centre for Economic Policy Research. CEPR Policy Portal. http://voxeu.org.

Campos, N., Coricelli, F. and Moretti, L. 2014. *Economic Growth and Political Integration: Estimating the Benefits from Membership in the European Union.* CEPR Discussion Paper 9968. London: Centre for Economic Policy Research.

Carvalho, J., Eatwell, R. and Wunderlich, D. 2015. "The Politicization of Immigration in Britain". Chapter 8. In *Support for and Opposition to Migration in Europe.* Edited by W. van der Brug et al. London: Routledge.

Charter, D. 2017. "Chaos Reigns: AfD Co-Leader Disowns her 'Anarchic' Party". *The Times.* September 26, 2007. Page 31.

Curtice, J. 2015. "A Revolt on the Right? The Social and Political Attitudes of UKIP Supporters". *British Social Attitudes 32.* London: National Centre for Social Research.

Curtice, J. 2016a. "How Deeply Does Britain's Euroscepticism Run?" *British Social Attitudes 33.* June 2016. London: National Centre for Social Research.

Curtice, J. (2016b). "The Vote to Leave the EU. Litmus Test or Lightning Rod?" *British Social Attitudes 34*, London: National Centre for Social Research.

Curtice, J. and Evans, G. 2015. "Britain and Europe: Are We All Eurosceptics Now?" *British Social Attitudes 32*, London: National Centre for Social Research.

Deloitte's. 2013. *Deloitte Italy's Special Assessment of the Third Party Audit Money Laundering Assessment of the Effective Implementation of Customer Due Diligence Measures with Respect to Cyprus Deposits and Loans.* June 14, 2013. Milan: Deloitte's Italy.

d'Estree, T.P. and Shapiro, I.L. 2017. "Interpersonal Conflict". Conflict Resolution Vol 1. *Encyclopedia of Life Support Systems.* Paris: UNESCO.

Eurobarometer. 2015. *The Main Challenges for the EU, Migration, and the Economic and Social Situation.* Project number EB/EP 84.1. Parlemeter 2015—Part 1. European Parliament.

Eurobarometer. 2016. *Public Opinion in the European Union.* Standard Eurobarometer 86, Autumn 2016, First Results. Project number 2016.8131. D-G Communication. Brussels: EU Commission.

Eurostat. 2017. *Asylum Statistics.* European Commission. https://ec.europa.eu/eurostat/. Accessed September 13, 2017.

FF. 2017. "The Founding Fathers of the EU". https://europa.eu. Accessed September 9, 2017.

Fisher, L. 2018a. "UKIP Puts Up 75% Fewer Candidates for Councils". *The Times.* April 7, 2018. Page 2.

Fisher, L. 2018b. "I'll Be Back If This Betrayal Continues, Promises Farage". *The Times.* July 14, 2018. Page 11.

Galvin, R. 2008. *Audit of the Parliamentary Assistance Allowance.* Internal Report No. 06/02 to the Institution's Internal Audit Service. European Parliament.

Hamilton, F. 2018. "EDL Founder Jailed for Court Rant". *The Times.* May 30, 2018. Page 7.

Huff Post. 2018. "UKIP Are Now Truly a Far-Right Party". *Huffington Post.* September 21, 2018. https://www.huffingtonpost.co.uk.

Kasperson, R.E., Renn, O., Slovic, P. et al. 1988. "The Social Amplification of Risk: a Conceptual Framework". *Risk Analysis*, Vol 8 No 2, 177–187.

Keen, R. and Apostolova, V. 2017. *Membership of UK Political Parties.* House of Commons Briefing Paper SN05125. March 28, 2017. London: House of Commons.

Kelley, N., Khan, O. and Sharrock, S. 2017. *Racial Prejudice in Britain Today.* British Social Attitudes Survey. Brentwood, Essex: National Centre for Social Research.

Lascelles. 2013. *Independent Commission on the Future of the Cyprus Banking Sector*. Final Report. October 13, 2013. Chairman David Lascelles. Nicosia: Central Bank of Cyprus.

Mahoney, H. 2003. "Commission Admits Huge Eurostat Fraud". *EU Observer*, July 9, 2003. https://euobserver.com.

Masters, J. 2018. "Anti-Islam Activist Tommy Robinson Appointed as UKIP Adviser". *CNN*. November 23, 2018. https://edition.cnn.com/2018/11/3/uk/tommy-robinson-ukip-gbr-intl/index.html.

Moneyval. 2013. *Special Assessment of the Effectiveness of Customer Due Diligence Measures in the Banking Sector in Cyprus. Moneyval* Committee. Strasbourg: Council of Europe.

Newcomb, T.M. 1947. "Autistic Hostility and Social Reality". *Human Relations*, Vol 1 No 1, 69–86.

Pabst, A. 2016. "Brexit, Post-Liberalism, and the Politics of Paradox". *Telos*, Vol 2016, No. 176, 189–201.

Pan, D. 2016. "European Union and Holy Roman Empire". *Telos*, Vol 2016, No. 176, 202–208.

Pancevski, B. 2013. "Jail for Corrupt MEP Exposed by The Sunday Times". *The Times*, January 20, 2013.

Parris, M. 2018. "UKIP Defectors Will Drag May Farther Right". *The Times*. May 5, 2018. Page 25.

Patel, O. and Reh, C. 2016. *Brexit: The Consequences for the EU's Political System*. UCL Constitution Briefing Paper No. 2. The Constitution Unit. London: UCL.

Petre, J. and Walters, S. 2013. "Exposed: What they DIDN'T Tell You About the New Wave of Migrants Heading for Booming Britain". *Mail on Sunday*. December 28, 2013. www.dailymail.co.uk/news/article-2530503.

Pidgeon, N., Slovic, P. and Kasperson, R.E. (eds). 2003. *The Social Amplification of Risk*. Cambridge, UK: CUP.

Politico. 2014. "Strasser Convicted Again". European Voice. *Politico EU*. 19 March 2014. www.politico.eu.

Roberts, R. 2017. "UKIP Leadership Hopeful Anne Marie Waters Opens Door to Tommy Robinson Joining Party". *The Independent*. September 5, 2017.

Simpson, J. 2018. "Tommy Robinson Treated to Subsidised Meal at House of Lords". *The Times*. October 25, 2018. Page 13.

Slack, J. 2007. "Romanians Living in UK Carrying out 1,000 Crimes in Six Months". *Daily Mail*. September 19, 2007. www.dailymail.co.uk/news/article-482557.

UKIP. 2017a. *General Election Manifesto, June 2017*. UK Independence Party. Newton Abbott, Devon: UKIP.

UKIP. 2017b. *UKIP Leadership: Final List of Candidates Announced.* August 13, 2017. UK Independence Party. Newton Abbott, Devon: UKIP.

UKParl. 2013. *Parliament and Europe.* Living Heritage. April 2013. www.parliament.uk.

Walters, S., Owen, G. and Cahalan, P. 2016. "The Neo-Nazi with a Swastika on Her Breast". *Mail on Sunday.* Mailonline June 4, 2016. www.mailonline.co.uk/news/article-3625503.

Waring, A.E. 2013a. "The Banks and Due Diligence". The Risk Watch column. *Financial Mirror,* May 22–28, 2013, page 4.

Waring, A.E. 2013b. *Corporate Risk and Governance: an End to Mismanagement, Tunnel Vision and Quackery.* Farnham UK: Gower/Routledge.

Waring, A.E. 2016. "A Dysfunctional EU: What Future?" The Risk Watch column. *Financial Mirror,* February 10–16, 2016, page 6.

Waterfield, B. 2017. "Berlin and Paris Threat to EU's Free Movement". *The Times.* September 15, 2017, pages 1–2.

Webber, E. 2018. "Farage Quits UKIP Over 'Far-Right' Fixation'". *The Times.* December 5, 2018. Page 11.

YouTube. 2013. "Nigel Farage—Confronts Herman van Rompuy, José Manuel Barroso and Martin Schulz". Compilation. April 27, 2013. https://www.youtube.com/watch?v=bJHETdxwv8Y.

YouTube. 2017. "Bundestagswahl 2017: Frauke Petry will AfD-Fraktion nicht angehören". September 25, 2017. https://www.youtube.com/watch?v=uNNFOAgBOKw.

Chapter 4: The Politics of Cultural Despair: Britain's Extreme-Right

By Emily Turner-Graham

Abstract

This chapter examines the cultural despair that has suffused far- and extreme-right politics in Britain for nearly a century, and their proposed solution by enforced destruction of a purportedly corrupt society, its institutions and norms and replacement with a pure, reborn nation. British far-right history is traced from the pre-WWII era, with detailed examination of such contemporary extremist parties and groups as the British National Party, English Defence League, Britain First, National Action, and Generation Identity. Cultural despair, alienation, and a frustration with political failure, among British far- and extreme-right groups, may spur a re-alignment of support resulting in more extremist groups becoming dominant. Risks are systematically identified.

Key words: Britain, far-right, extreme-right, political ideologies, crimes, risks.

The Politics of Cultural Despair

In 1961, German-American historiographer Fritz Stern wrote *The Politics of Cultural Despair: a Study in the Rise of the Germanic Ideology*. It is "a study in the pathology of cultural criticism" (Stern 1974, xi) and examines the ideological role played by the German nineteenth and early twentieth century right-wing writers Paul de Lagarde, Julius Langbehn and Arthur Moeller van den Bruck in laying the foundation for the physical practicalities of Hitler's Third Reich. As such, Stern charts "the *political* organization of cultural hatreds and personal resentments" (Stern 1974 xvi, his italics).

With a striking contemporary resonance for today's extreme right, Stern depicts philosophical arguments woven by "guardians of what they thought was an ancient tradition, they attacked the progress of modernity—the growing power of liberalism and secularism" (Stern 1974 xi). Lagarde, Langbehn and Moeller van den Bruck were "heroic vitalists who denigrated reason and logic" (Stern 1974, xi). They lamented the nineteenth century's loss of faith and its replacement with the more nebulous notions of liberalism, desiring "a new community of believers, a world with fixed standards and no doubts, a new national religion that would bind all Germans together" (Stern 1974, xii). "I have no use for abstract truth I want to bind and liberate my people" Lagarde stated, seeing nationalism and "a new folk-rootedness" as the only solution (Stern 1974, xiii). They proclaimed a heady, irrational mixture of "cultural despair and mystical nationalism" (Stern 1974, xiii).

Their "[i]deology of [r]esentment" and "sentimental brutality" (Stern 1974, xxi and xxix) was written with

> [g]reat fervor and passion [,] [t]hey condemned or prophesied, rather than exposited or argued, and all their writings showed that they despised the discourse of intellectuals, depreciated reason, and exalted intuition. Humorless and murky, their prose was fitfully lit up by mystical, but apodictic epigrams. (Stern 1974, xiv)

Further, they argued,

> Man is not primarily rational, but volitional; he is not by nature good nor capable of perfectability; the politics of liberal individualism rest on an illusion; evil exists and is an inherent aspect of human life[.] (Stern 1974, xviii)

Their despair led them to a desire for the destruction of society as it stood. They were "Luddites, who in their resentment of modernity sought to smash the whole machinery of culture" (Stern 1974, xvii). Finally,

> National Socialists gathered together millions of malcontents, of whose existence the conservative revolutionaries (*Lagarde, Langbehn and Moeller van den Bruck*) had for so long spoken, and for whose relief they had designed such dangerous and elusive ideals. (Stern 1974, xxx)

The language and ideas of cultural despair have long motivated the extreme-right. This chapter examines this key and continuous thread in the case of Britain, charting first its history then, in more detail, its representation and subsequent threat today. With the advent of the Internet, which has been so expertly employed by the extreme-right to "shar[e] advice, pool[...] resources and collaborat[e] to common aims" (Gaston 2017), the very real danger posed by philosophical hatred depicted so widely and so viscerally will be made clear as Britain's right-wing extremists continue their long ideological mission to "privilege, protect and defend" (Gaston 2017). This chapter does not consider the UK Independence Party (UKIP), which portrays itself as a moderate populist right-wing party and is covered in chapter 3. However, as noted there and elsewhere in the book, there has been considerable unofficial fluidity of cross-party allegiances and even membership between UKIP and far- and extreme-right parties and groups. To that extent, while up to mid 2018 not officially espousing far- and extreme-right views and policies, UKIP nonetheless harbours numerous individuals holding such views. The series of pro-EDL statements and actions by UKIP leader Gerard Batten in 2018, and his stated enthusiasm for and appointment of the far-right former EDL leader Tommy Robinson as his adviser, indicated that UKIP was becoming officially increasingly a far-, if not extreme-right party.

The 'Sacred Flame': the Ideological Ancestors of Today's Extreme Right

"A desperate situation": the British Union of Fascists

> Together in Britain we have lit a flame that the ages shall not extinguish. Guard that sacred flame my brother Blackshirts until it illuminates Britain and lights again the paths of mankind. (Mosley 1938)

The path of the contemporary far- and extreme-right in the United Kingdom essentially starts with Oswald Mosley's British Union of Fascists [*hereafter BUF*] in 1932. Although there were other British groups influenced by Mussolini's Fascists and Hitler's National Socialists, some as early as the 1920s, Mosley's movement was the most noteworthy. Troubled by the deep social tumult of the Interwar years as well as (like Mussolini and Hitler) having been profoundly affected by the First World War, Oswald Mosley entered parliament in 1918. By 1925, he was already describing Britain's situation with the language of despair.

> [We are in] a desperate situation. We have reached a supreme crisis in the history of humanity. We stand, indeed, at the cross-roads of destiny. For good or ill, we live in an epic age. Once again the lash of great ordeal stings an historic race

> into action. Once more the soul of man is on the march...we must awaken and mobilize our country to save itself by heroic gestures before the sands of time and fate run out. (Mosley quoted by Sykes 2005, 54)

Although espousing an ideology based initially upon that of the Italian *Fascisti*, Mosley stressed that his was not a mere application of foreign ideas. As such, Tudor England was put forward by the BUF as its local precursor, with its goal of national unity through a centralised authoritarian state. Mosley also cited Oliver Cromwell as having instigated "the first fascist age in England" and the BUF's corporatist economic policy reflected England's Medieval guild system. Yet Mosley also insisted on what are now stereotypical trappings of the extreme right—he was to be referred to as The Leader (much like *Il Duce* and *der Führer*), to be greeted with "Hail Mosley!", the BUF headquarters in London was named The Black House (vis-à-vis Hitler's *Braunes Haus* in Munich) and its members were Blackshirts, kitted out in a uniform of black tunic and trousers for men and black tunic and skirt for women.

So too, the BUF promised a "Greater Britain" with a particular focus upon unity between Catholic and Protestant befitting their professed commitment to traditional Christian values. They argued too that culture made for differences between races and nations. This view was closer to that of the Italian Fascists rather than the biological racism of Hitler's National Socialists. As the 1930s progressed however, and Mosley altered the name of the party to the British Union of Fascists and National Socialists and became increasingly Spenglerian in his view, an anti-Semitic tone becoming far more prominent.

In keeping with a despair-laden theme, Mosley argued that Fascism would need to not just change people, but remake them anew—"we must...set to work to make new men" (Mosley in Sykes 2005, 55). Further, echoing Mussolini's notion of a newly-forged 'Trenchocracy', Mosley stated

> For this age is dynamic and the pre-war age static...[t]he types which have emerged from the pre-war and post-war periods are so different they can scarcely understand each other's language...[t]his is not an age of dreams and fancies; it is an age of iron, in which an iron spirit and iron will are needed by men to cut their path through to victory...(Mosley in Sykes 2005, 56)

Mosley believed that the destruction of Britain as it had been prior to the First World War was not only preferable but necessary for a Fascist phoenix to rise from its ashes. This apocalyptic stance has set the tone for many extreme-right groups since, such as the very recent example of National Action, as shall be discussed.

There was no question that Mosley's Fascism—as with arguably all extreme-right parties—would be brought with violence. The chaotically ferocious 1934 rally at the Olympia stadium in London made clear the BUF's *modus operandi* with a "level of violence that shocked the audience and raised a sceptre that haunted the BUF for the rest of its existence" (Sykes 2005, 66). The Battle of Cable Street in East London in 1936 consolidated the BUF's violent image as being reliant upon "the good old English fist" (Bloom 2010, 300).

Mosley's Fascism was at once arcane and modern, in a manner that can be seen oft repeated by the extreme right. Emphasising Fascism's modernity, Mosley stated in the 1934 edition of *The Greater Britain*, "Fascism is a thing of the spirit. It is the acceptance of new values and of a new morality in a higher and nobler conception of the universe" (Sykes 2005, 72). It sought to draw together "the concepts of struggle, the will and the superman" of Nietzsche with "the service, duty and sacrifice" characteristic of Christianity. (Sykes 2005, 72) in fact, Mosley's new Fascist man was "the aristocratic crusading Christian knight in modern dress; the corporate state, feudalism industrialised; fascism, the church militant secularized." (Sykes 2005, 72). The BUF was banned in 1940 and Mosley and many of his followers were interned.

"In the Grip of Degenerative Forces": the National Socialist Movement and the National Front

Following the War, Mosley established the Union Movement, which called for the development of a united European nationalism—"Eurofascism" (Griffin 1995, 313)—rather than narrow, country-based nationalist movements. The large-scale non-white immigration from Britain's colonies to the British motherland provided ample impetus for a renewed wave of racism. Of all the myriad far- and extreme-right groups formed in Britain during the post-war period, the first incarnation of the British National Party (1960–1967), the National Socialist Movement (1962–1968) and the National Front (1967–) are amongst the most notable due to their membership of John Tyndall and Colin Jordan, two highly influential figures in Britain's post-war extreme-right. Openly advocating neo-Nazism, Jordan was appointed "World Führer" of the World Union of National Socialists with the

American neo-Nazi and leader of the American Nazi Party, George Lincoln Rockwell, as his deputy.

Tyndall attempted to recast his neo-Nazism as a uniquely British nationalism, arguing that there was a distinct, white British race and that there was a Jewish conspiracy to pollute that race with large-scale immigration. Tyndall advocated an authoritarian state in Britain, which would deport all non-whites, engage in a eugenics program and re-establish the British Empire in a conquered Africa. Tyndall led the National Front (NF) from 1972 until a falling-out in 1980 and in 1982 formed the current British National Party (BNP). He proclaimed it to be a "racial nationalist party which believes in Britain for the British, that is to say racial separatism" (Tyndall quoted by Goodwin 2011, 37). He was successfully challenged for the leadership of the BNP in 1999 by Nick Griffin. Tyndall continued the extreme-right theme of cultural, societal and political despair in language modern in its references but also historical in its use of a biological racism.

> We live in a state that is terminally sick, in the manner of a political, economic, social and spiritual AIDS. Lacking the built-in immunity that is to be found in all healthy body-organisms, it is vulnerable to every germ and shock that the world climate may blow its way...The political rot...is only a part of a much more general rot. Our entire national life is in the grip of degenerative forces, which barely leave one small area of affairs unaffected, as they run amok like maggots invading a diseased carcass...(Tyndall quoted in Griffin 1995, 368–9)

"The Art of the Possible": the British National Party

The BNP followed the NF's ideological line under John Tyndall's leadership of the former. Nick Griffin, who served as the BNP's leader from 1999–2014 sought to moderate the party's policies and in so doing widen its appeal. In embracing a more populist position, Griffin hoped to replicate the success of Jean-Marie Le Pen's *Front-National* in France and Austria's *Freiheitliche Partei Österreichs* led by Jörg Haider (Copsey 2007, 67). With either cynicism, pragmatism or both, Griffin argued "The very first step is to look at the things we do, or condone, that make us unelectable" (Copsey 2007, 68). Further, "[o]f course we must teach the truth to the hardcore, but when it comes to influencing the public, forget about racial differences, genetics, Zionism, historical revisionism and so on" (Copsey 2007, 68) rather than focus on "idealistic, unobjectionable, motherhood and apple pie concepts" (Copsey 2007, 68). In short, Griffin's approach was to play the long game—

> Politics is always the art of the possible, so we must judge every policy by one simple criterion: Is it realistically possible that a decisive proportion of the British people will support it? If not, then to scale down our *short-term* ambitions to a point at which the answer becomes 'yes' is not a sell-out, *but the only possible step closer to our eventual goal.* (Copsey 2007, 80, italics in original)

As such, it focussed on rising immigration rates and sought out local community issues. This change in emphasis led to the BNP's greatest period of success during the 2000s with over fifty seats in local government, one seat on the London Assembly and two Members of the European Parliament, making the most successful far-right party in British history. It now has one local government councillor.

The BNP's ideological emphasis has turned to Islamophobia (and away from the NF's anti-Semitism). Griffin stated:

> *This* is the threat that can bring us to power. *This* is the big issue on which we must concentrate in order to wake people up and make them look at what we have to offer all around. (Copsey 2007, 77, italics in original)

Its 2016 manifesto sought to "defend our traditional Christian faith [*and*] [b]an Sharia law...[*and*]...the burqa" (BNP 2016). It also stood for economic protectionism and Euroscepticism and opposed such cornerstones of 'political correctness' as feminism and LGBT rights. It advocated a move away from liberal democracy and, in a return to its ancestral espousal of biological racism, argued for the existence of a global policy of white genocide. Its manifesto noted the need to

> [e]nd the disgraceful culture of discrimination which has resulted in a great many native Londoners having been pushed out of their city because of rising rents, and the favouring of foreigners. So-called 'white flight' from London has not happened by accident, it's a result of successive governments favouring and putting foreigners first at the expense of native Londoners. The BNP will change all that by introducing Local Connection Assessment tests to ensure qualification for being placed on local housing lists. Each applicant must demonstrate historical association with the area by birth, family or employment. Special consideration will be extended to ex-servicemen and their families, and the most vulnerable of our people including those that are homeless and those suffering from domestic abuse. (BNP 2016)

There has not been any real change to the BNP's core values. Rather it has been repackaged. Instead of blatant racism, issues of cultural identity are highlighted and the "right to difference"—we love and must protect our own people, rather than we hate and must attack other people (Copsey 2007, 71).

"No Surrender to the Taliban": the English Defence League

The English Defence League (EDL) was formed in 2009 as the United Peoples of Luton. It has been argued that the EDL, and its key allies such as Casuals United, mark a change of sorts in far- and extreme-right protest in Britain.

> [T]he EDL and Casuals United, while sharing some characteristics with establish[ed] far-right parties, mark a different manifestation of the fusing of football hooligan casual culture and extremist politics...(Garland and Treadwell 2010, 20)

It is in this way that they have been argued to "pose the most significant threat to community cohesion in Britain's inner-cities since the heyday of the National Front in the mid-to-late 1970s" (Garland and Treadwell 2010, 20). In March 2009, the extreme Islamist organisation Al-Muhajiroun had held a concurrent protest against a welcome-home parade through Luton of the Royal Anglian Regiment, who had recently returned from a tour of duty of the Helmand province in Afghanistan. Amid numerous counter-protests, local football 'firms' [*groups of football hooligans*] and their membership of football 'casuals' decided that an organised response was required.

Stephen Yaxley-Lennon was the EDL's original leader. He assumed the name Tommy Robinson, after the football hooligan associated with Luton's MIG (Men-in-Gear) football 'firm'. Yaxley-Lennon [*hereafter Tommy Robinson*] repeatedly stated that the EDL were not anti-Islam but anti-Islamic extremism, yet many supporters of the EDL were known to be anti-Islam and exhibited these views in their choice of targets. The hostility of many football 'firms' to the IRA in the 1970s and 1980s meant that their chant was often "No surrender to the IRA". For the EDL, this became "No surrender to the Taliban", as well as "You can shove your fucking Allah up your arse" and "Give me a gun and I will shoot the Muzzie scum" (Garland and Treadwell 2010, 32). Clearly, the perspective of many within the EDL (and Casuals United) is politicised and ethnically-focussed.

Despite their protests that: "[w]e are an alliance of British Football Casuals of various colours/races who have come together in order to create a massive, but peaceful protest group to force out Government to get their act in gear..." (Garland and Treadwell 2010, 22), there is much to suggest that their vision of the way of life they are defending in Britain is of a very specific, homogeneous type. "See that", commented one EDL protester, pointing to a St George's flag. "[T]hat makes me proud, it's what being English is all about, but where I come from that isn't seen anymore. The Pakis have taken over the churches and turned them into mosques, now what the fuck is that about, eh?" (Garland and Treadwell 2010, 29). Similarly Tommy Robinson has referred to "our Christian culture" and stated "[w]e will combat militant Islam wherever it raises its ugly, paedophilic, disturbed, medieval fucking head" (Garland and Treadwell 2010, 29). Likewise, though the EDL leadership burnt a Nazi flag prior to a 2009 demonstration to underline their apparent anti-racist position, only a week later, Welsh Defence League members burnt an anti-Fascist flag and gave Nazi salutes. This encapsulates the long-running gap between the professed opinions of the EDL through their leadership and the views expressed on the street by various members of the rank-and-file. So too, the black-and-white, us-and-them mentality exhibited here certainly speaks once more to a despairing, exclusivist position. Numerous cases of violent disorder throughout the British Isles have involved the EDL, often of an ethnically targeted nature. The fact that the EDL and their allies were able to form a ready street army of sorts, given they were already organised as football 'firms', makes this track record especially alarming. In 2011, the EDL joined with an offshoot of the BNP, the British Freedom Party, through which EDL members would be able to stand as candidates in elections. They enjoyed little success in their electoral efforts. In 2012, Robinson expressed a desire to form a pan-European group, the European Defence League, and certainly a number of 'defence leagues' have developed in other countries. They were even cited by Anders Behring Breivik, the Norwegian mass killer, as comrades [the EDL has denied this].

The significance of the EDL, as Matthew Goodwin points out, when compared with the far- and extreme-right groups of the 1970s, has been that the Islamophobia they profess taps into a rich vein of not dissimilar argument already in the mainstream media, thus broadening the EDL's acceptability and voice. This is notable, given the lack of mainstream resonance found for the extreme-right's anti-Semitism in the 1970s (Taylor 2010 https://www.theguardian.com/uk/2010/may/28/english-defence-league-protest-bnp). The Labour MP Jon Cruddas similarly described the EDL as

> "a dangerous cocktail of football hooligans, far-right activists and pub racists...a bigger threat than the BNP...providing a new white nationalist identity through which they can understand an increasingly complex and alienating world. In a similar way to how football hooligans once coalesced around support for Ulster loyalism and hatred of the IRA, the followers of the EDL genuinely believe they are "defending" their Britain against the threat of Islam. What makes the EDL much more dangerous is how it reflects a wider political and cultural war". (Cruddas 2010, https://www.theguardian.com/uk/2010/oct/10/john-cruddas-english-defence-league)

While Paul Jackson does concede that the EDL *is* anti-Nazi, it is nonetheless "in conflict with liberal democratic principles" (Jackson 2012). In 2013, Tommy Robinson and another key EDL member, Kevin Carroll, left the organisation, suggesting it had taken too extreme a turn. Tommy Robinson has served jail terms for assault and also has convictions for contempt of court, drug offences, using someone else's passport, and mortgage fraud (Lusher 2017). His latest conviction on May 29, 2018 (for contempt of court, relating to wilfully defying a court order not to publicly name defendants and witnesses in a case not yet concluded) resulted in a 13-month jail term (Hamilton 2018a). This alleged contempt also involved manifestly racist overtones to Robinson's apparent motive for naming the defendants and witnesses who were of Asian origin. This conviction was later quashed on procedural grounds on appeal and a retrial ordered which, at the time of writing, was still under review by the Attorney General. Robinson is still regarded as their champion by many on the far- and extreme-right in Britain.

While the EDL has continued on, it has failed to have the presence that it once held, although it could be argued that it has laid the groundwork for another street-based, anti-Islam movement, Britain First.

"We Want Our Country Back": Britain First

Britain First (BF) is an extreme-right British political organisation formed in 2011 by a former member of the BNP, Jim Dowson, and an ex-BNP councillor, Paul Golding. BF can be seen as direct ideological descendants to the street protesting, trenchant Islamophobia of the EDL, although BF take their position one step beyond the EDL, officially stating they are "anti-Islam in the UK", not only anti-Islamic extremism (Fransen quoted in Bladen-Ryal 2015). BF dismiss comparisons with their ideological confrères. "The BNP was racist and the EDL was drunken hooligans" states Golding (Golding quoted in Zand 2015). Golding has led BF since its foundation and its deputy leader is Jayda Fransen—notable given that women rarely hold leadership roles in the far- or extreme-right. Jim Dowson, an anti-abortion activist and Christian fundamentalist, is believed to have been the driving force behind BF's foundation and a major financial supporter. Two other BNP organisers, Andy McBride and Kevin Edwards (the latter of whom was also a BNP councillor), were also instrumental in the foundation of Britain First. The apocalyptic tone of much of BF's discourse is summarised well in this remark from Dowson—

> "Remember the forces of Islam once got as far as Vienna. Now they are as far as John O'Groats in Scotland and more and more are coming in. This is not political. This is a fight between good and evil, black and white, a fight of the Cross, a fight of Christ". (Dowson quoted in Gable 2016)

Their claimed Christian identity is also clear, albeit a simplistic one referencing the medieval Crusades in the manner of the likes of Anders Behring Breivik. Dowson left the group in 2014, yet his views as a founder have clearly left their ideological mark. The militancy at the core of BF is underlined in such comments as that of Jayda Fransen—"if you don't respect the values of this country, and the law of this country, and the monarchy, then you don't deserve to be here, so we would also hang you for treason." (Fransen quoted in Zand 2015). This is in keeping with the openly militaristic character of the group, also seen in the recruiting and training ex-soldiers, and unlawfully wearing political uniforms in their early, highly controversial days.

BF campaigns primarily against the 'Islamisation' of the United Kingdom and advocates the preservation of what it regards as traditional British culture. In its initial period of operation, it attracted widespread attention with its vocal and provocative protests outside the homes of Islamic extremists, its 'Christian patrols' and 'invasions' of British mosques, which will be discussed in detail shortly. BF has also been noted for its successful online activism, with social media followers far exceeding the major political parties of Britain in numbers. These factors have given it a presence above that of the plethora of smaller but similar voices.

BF's stated aim is to protect "British and Christian morality" and it is "committed to preserving our ancestral ethnic and cultural heritage" while it also "supports the maintenance of the indigenous British people as the demographic majority within our own homeland", that "genuine British citizens will be put first in housing, jobs, education, welfare and health" (Britain First 2018).

BF's contention with Islam is against the doctrine and religion of Islam itself as an ideology.

> The Koran and Islamic doctrine promotes hatred, violence and intolerance against non-Muslims. "Jihad" is the most talked about issue in the Koran. Women are oppressed in Islam. The death penalty applies to homosexuals. Marriage to children is allowed. Muslims who died fighting non-Muslims are promised 72 virgins in paradise. Sharia Law prescribes stonings and amputations. Halal slaughter is barbaric and evil. We are against these principles of Islam, not individual humans who have been led astray by this barbaric "religion". (Britain First 2015)

In the manner of many extreme-right populist movements across the Continent, BF also claimed its objective "to save this country and our people from the EU, [*the*] politically correct, multicultural insanity that is now engulfing us"(Britain First 2015). Further,

> The European Union is a left-wing, socialist political project that will eradicate all individual national identities in Europe under an avalanche of mass immigration and political correctness. The EU will destroy political independence across Europe, leaving every country ruled from Brussels by an unelected bureaucracy. In opposing the EU, we and our European sister nations are striving to maintain our ancient cultures and freedoms. (Britain First 2015)

Yet, they assert that they are not racist because "Britain First is home to thousands of patriots from ethnic minorities from all over the world who share our defence of British values and culture. The word 'racism' was invented by a communist mass murderer to silence European opposition to 'multi-culturalism', so we do not recognise its validity" (Britain First 2015). The raising of the Communist spectre brings to mind the fear of Cultural Marxism so strongly a part of contemporary extreme-right discourse.

Paul Golding disputed interpretations that Jesus was pacifistic or liberal. He justified his belief by citing Jesus' apparent violence against the money lenders in the temple and his statement that he "did not come to bring peace but a sword" (Matthew 10:34). This is a view that could be optimistically described as a sort of 'muscular Christianity' or, more negatively, in step with the National Socialist belief in a militant 'positive Christianity'. Christian denominations across the UK have condemned BF's beliefs as blasphemous to Christian teachings.

In May 2013, following the murder of British soldier Lee Rigby by Islamic extremists in a London street, BF released a video threatening to place controversial Islamist cleric Anjem Choudary, who was accused of radicalising Rigby's killers, under citizen's arrest if the Metropolitan Police would not arrest him. In February 2014, BF began their notorious 'Christian patrols' in the East London borough of Tower Hamlets, an area noted for its largely Muslim population. The Christian patrols were designed to counter the already established Muslim patrols in Tower Hamlets. Around a dozen or so BF activists recorded themselves holding a banner proclaiming "We Are the British Resistance" and drinking cans of beer outside a mosque to 'bait' Islamic extremists operating in the area. They also went into mosques, challenging anyone they came across. A video uploaded onto social media showing these activities gained national media attention in the UK and the patrol was condemned by a number of both Muslim and Christian leaders.

In May 2014, members of Britain First forced their way into ten Bradford mosques, as well as mosques in Glasgow, Luton and East London. They circulated information regarding Muslim grooming gangs allegedly in the area, accusing Muslim community elders of failing to stop the gangs, while handing out Army Bibles and proselytising Christianity, telling one mosque attendee to "reject the false prophet Muhammad and read the Bible". They also went to a Labour Party office to inform them that "they [*Muslims*] had been warned" (*BBC* 2014). In response, the Labour Member of Parliament for Bradford West, George Galloway said, "This is a grave and national issue. We demand full police action and protection of mosques and worshippers" (Brown 2014). It is speculated that Jim Dowson's departure was due to Paul Golding's initiation of this infamous policy of mosque 'invasions', which Dowson allegedly denounced as "provocative and counterproductive…unacceptable and unchristian…[and] just as bad as [*Islamic extremist*] Anjem Choudary" (Dearden 2014).

In 2015, BF offered "solidarity patrols" in areas of London with high Jewish populations, while blaming anti-Semitism on Islam. The Community Security Trust, an organisation particularly concerned with anti-Semitism, has warned Jews not to become involved with BF, and has likened this policy to similar ones by the English Defence League and the BNP, saying that all of these groups were opposing Muslims more than supporting Jews, acting on the notion that 'my enemy's enemy is my friend'.

In July 2014, Britain First entered the Crayford Mosque in South London, demanding that its segregated entrances be removed, with Golding saying, "When you respect women, we'll respect your mosques" (Dearden 2014). Two addresses were raided during the police investigation of this action, which led Britain First to protest at Bexleyheath Police Station. They sought to gain publicity by claiming that Golding was arrested for this protest, although the Metropolitan Police said that they had spoken with him and no arrests had been made. Golding was jailed for eight weeks in December 2016 for breaking a court order banning him from entering mosques or encouraging others to do so.

In November 2015, BF claimed that its *Facebook* page had over a million 'likes', more than any other British political party and even the then British Prime Minister, David Cameron. At the end of November, *Facebook* briefly closed the BF page for breaching its community guidelines. The group also had to remove two photos published without permission. By October 2017, it had 2 million *Facebook* followers.

Paul Golding, in a 2015 *BBC* report, stated "We are just leagues ahead in terms of advanced social media...[*compared with*]... all the other political movements in this country" (Golding in Zand 2015). Benjamin Zand, the *BBC* reporter on the story, added, "*Facebook* is their biggest platform, garnering thousands of comments and shares." Zand concluded "It's safe to say that they're [*BF*] not going to have real power any time soon, but their *Facebook* and street marches mean they do have some influence."

However, there have also been allegations that BF sometimes garners those likes unethically, with catch-all posts such as 'click if you support our troops' on sites that are not clearly labelled as being affiliated to BF. They often posted simple memes which appealed to broad themes of patriotism and nationalism. Using this approach, they were able to become the second-most 'liked' page in *Facebook* UK's politics and society category, the top spot having been taken by the British royal family (Hern and Rawlinson 2018). There have also been allegations of the photo-shopping of some images. There have been posts which falsely labelled Afghanistan's first female police officer, who was murdered by the Taliban, as a terrorist, and posts falsely linking the burqa and terrorism (Meredith 2014). In March 2015, an American veteran stated his intention to sue for libel after the group shared a photo-shopped image of him. In the original image, the veteran was holding a sign reading "Boycott bigotry"—in the version shared by Britain First the sign reads "Boycott bigotry and kill all non-Muslims" (Faridi 2015). This sort of information manipulation has been labelled as a form of "domestic terrorism". The influential sweep of the material BF posted online was made clear in November 2017, when the American President, Donald Trump, retweeted several videos from Fransen's *Twitter* feed.

Britain First registered with the Electoral Commission on January 10, 2014, aiming to become "the sort of party you could vote for" (Fransen 2015). During the European elections of that year, Britain First controversially registered the phrase "Remember Lee Rigby" for use in their campaign. The chair of the Electoral Commission later issued an apology "for the offence that has been caused" by accepting the so-named registration (*Huffington Post* 2014). When questioned by the *BBC's* Andrew Neil about the offence caused to Lee Rigby's mother, Paul Golding said "We apologise to the mother of Lee Rigby, but it was a major act of terrorism, it was a big public event. He was a public serving soldier" (Golding in *BBC* 2014).

BF stood candidates for the 2014 European elections in Wales and Scotland. It encouraged English supporters, in the absence of a BF candidate, to instead vote for the English Democrats or UKIP, while warning against voting for the BNP. The party came eighth of eleven candidates in Wales, with 6,633 votes (0.9%), and seventh of nine in Scotland with 13,639 votes (1.02%).

Britain First stood its first parliamentary candidate for the Rochester and Strood by-election on November 20, 2014, nominating its Deputy Leader, Jayda Fransen. The party had been active in nearby Gillingham, in opposition to a planned mosque. Royal Mail refused to deliver a leaflet for the party because it believed it to be illegal. The company said it could refuse to carry election mail if it considered the contents threatening or abusive. UKIP won the by-election. BF finished ninth of thirteen candidates, with 56 votes (0.14%), finishing below the Monster Raving Loony Party. On September 27, 2015, Paul Golding announced that he would stand as a candidate in the 2016 London mayoral election. He received 31,372 or 1.2% of the vote, coming eighth of twelve candidates. During the victory speech of Labour's Sadiq Khan, he turned his back.

The impact of groups such as BF and the extreme-right in general was made tragically clear on June 16, 2016, when Labour MP Jo Cox was fatally shot and stabbed outside a library in Birstall, by a man who eyewitnesses said shouted "Britain first" as he carried out the attack. One witness told *BBC News* that he was uncertain whether the suspect was shouting "Britain first" or "put Britain first" (*BBC* 2016). BF issued a statement denying any involvement or encouragement in the attack and suggested that the phrase "could have been a slogan rather than a reference to our party" (Boyle 2016). Yet, continuing with their militant tone, Paul Golding condemned the attack saying, "[*w*]e hope that this person who carried it out is strung up by the neck on the nearest lamp post. That's the way we view justice" (Forster 2016).

In November 2017, BF was statutorily deregistered as a party by the Electoral Commission. In March 2018, Jayda Fransen was sentenced to 36 weeks imprisonment and Paul Golding to 18 weeks for harassing and abusing people they incorrectly believed were involved in an ongoing rape trial. They distributed leaflets and made videos which endangered the trial against three Muslim men and a teenager. The presiding judge believed they were using the case "for their own political ends" by "draw[ing] attention to the race, religion and immigrant background of the defendants" (Dearden 2018). The all-important BF *Facebook* page was closed down in the same month, as were Fransen and Golding's individual *Facebook* pages.

"Death to Traitors": National Action

National Action (NA) is an openly neo-Nazi British group, and equally with BF can be seen as a successor to the EDL. NA can also be seen as a successor to the NF and the BNP. Although the precise details of the group's formation are not entirely clear, Benjamin Raymond, Alex Davies, Ashley Bell and Jack Renshaw are all known to be founding and/or influential members of NA since its formation in 2013. It was proscribed as a terrorist organisation by the British government in December 2016. However, it continued to meet secretly in 2017 and it allegedly splintered into new, non-proscribed groups such as NS131 and Scottish Dawn. These two groups have also since been proscribed. On September 5, 2017, it was widely reported that four serving male members of the British Army had been arrested under the Terrorism Act 2000 on suspicion of being members of National Action. A fifth man was reported to have been detained in Cyprus. As a result, three men, including two British soldiers, were charged with terrorism offences. On September 27, 2017, eleven men were arrested in further raids across England and Wales. On January 3, 2018, six people—five men and a woman—were arrested on suspicion of being concerned in the commission, preparation and instigation of acts of terrorism, namely on suspicion of being a member of a proscribed organisation, National Action.

NA revered Thomas Mair, the murderer of Labour MP Jo Cox (see chapter 5), with the online quip "Only 649 MPs to go!" (Home Office 2017, 16), as well as a photo of Mair captioned "Don't let this man's sacrifice go in vain" (Home Office 2017, 16). NA also changed their online slogan to "Death to traitors, freedom for Britain!"—the 'name' Mair gave himself when he appeared in court. NA also showed support for the 2016 attack on an Orlando (Florida) gay nightclub. The proscription of NA in December 2016 made them the first extreme-right group to be proscribed since the BUF in the 1940s and also showed that the British government acknowledge the current rise of the extreme-right. The government's counter-terrorism Prevent programme received 323 extreme-right referrals in the year 2014–2015 and 561 from 2015–2016 (De Simone 2016).

NA primarily targets young people, paying particular attention to Britain's large university student population. Benjamin Raymond stated that the group's aim was to "build an organisation which has more intelligent people [*in it*]...a university educated far-right" (Nye 2015). Similarly, Gerry Gable, founder of the anti-fascist magazine *Searchlight*, has observed "They're not looking to attract thickos who just want a fight. They want thinkers who are prepared to die for National Socialism" (Gable in Filfilan 2015). NA are attempting to place themselves within the tradition of 'warrior philosophers', a notion which particularly appeals to the extreme-right, lauding as it does masculinity and the capacity to fight while also allowing for an astute intellect (a characteristic not often perceived to be present in the extreme-right). Ernst Jünger is one such example.

The organisation grew out of the youth wing of the British National Party and describes itself as like the BNP but more radical, a "revolutionary nationalist" organisation. With its youthful membership, it has masterfully instigated and maintained a strong Internet presence, both on blogs and social media. Many of their statements are formed as attention-grabbing sound bites, as illustrated by the group's founder Ben Raymond. "The idea of what is extreme, what is unreasonable, what is disgusting to society, changes…I'm a love preacher! You can't have hate without love. And if you love something, you…hate whatever is a threat to it" (Nye 2015).

Oswald Mosley has been cited as an influence on National Action, as well as Alexander Raven Thomson—'ideologue' of the BUF, the Spanish interwar fascist José Antonio Primo de Rivera, and the English twentieth century writer Wyndham Lewis. Gottfried Feder, a pivotal early member of the Nazi party, and even Hitler himself have similarly been praised. Benjamin Raymond has stated "As a teenager, *Mein Kampf* changed my life. I am not ashamed to say that I love Hitler" (Porter 2014). Likewise, he has lauded Anders Breivik as "the hero Norway deserves" (James 2014). Another NA member told the *Huffington Post* "What has been a successful nationalist movement?...[the Nazis]…that's why we're using [the Nazis]…they used it and they were able to gain power" (Sheriff 2014).

In an interview with *BBC* journalist Catrin Nye, Raymond elaborated on his views, which tick many of the boxes for typical extreme-right stances. There are conspiracy theories—"[t]hey collaborate with the global banking system to bring masses of third world people to replace, rape, murder our people. I wonder if one day they're just going to come together and say 'We've had enough of you. This is our country now.' And they get to make the rules" (Raymond quoted in Nye 2015). A "global economic system" has traditionally been used to signify Jewish influence but here it could also be read to symbolise the establishment and by establishment, those who were raised on the left-wing ideals of the 1960s and 1970s and who are currently in power, or white race traitors as many in the extreme-right regard them. Raymond clarifies the notion by stating "[w]e will form an institution and we will take back our country…[Nye: From who?] "The white traitors" (Raymond in Nye 2015).

For Raymond, "[i]t should be a white Britain" because everything can be brought back to race—

> The source of all conflict in society is the fact that all of these racial groups have been brought here to create a people who are deracinated and therefore more easy to control...[Nye: what does deracinated mean?]...deracinated means you have no sense of roots and no sense of identity." (Raymond in Nye 2015)

Similarly, Jack Renshaw—who was also involved with the EDL and the BNP—stated at a demonstration of the extreme-right North-West Infidels that Britain had taken the wrong side in the Second World War and should have backed Nazi Germany, "who were there to remove Jewry from Europe once and for all" (*The Times* 2018). To the nationalist Yorkshire Forum, he has stated that Jews are "Nature's financial parasite and nature's social vermin" (*The Times* 2018). Further, "Hitler was right in many senses but you know where he was wrong? He showed mercy to people who did not deserve mercy...as nationalists we need to learn from the mistakes of the national socialists and we need to realise that, no, you do not show the Jew mercy" (Hamilton 2016).

Again in the language of traditional biological racism, Renshaw described "[w]orld Jewry" as

> [A] disease, while its product ideologies are just the symptoms. Beat the symptoms and they'll return or be replaced—but—beat the disease and you'll eradicate the symptoms. The Jew aims to bastardise and mongrelise our race through Multiracialism and Multiculturalism...[t]he Jew has declared war on our people and we should—and in time we will—return the favour. (Renshaw 2014)

The connection of Judaism with disease has a lengthy ideological continuum, having been used by Paul de Lagarde and Nazi 'philosopher' Alfred Rosenberg. As with Anders Behring Breivik and other proponents of the ills of Cultural Marxism, Renshaw also levels grave charges at non-Jewish (or non-Muslim) 'enablers'—"When our time comes, the Jewish elites and the Judeophile traitors who were used as their puppets will be put on trial—if found guilty they will get the sentence that is deemed appropriate—and for me, that is hanging" (Renshaw 2015). In June 2018, Renshaw and five others went on trial for being members of the proscribed terrorist group National Action. Renshaw was further charged with planning to murder an MP [initially, the then Home Secretary Amber Rudd, but the plan was dropped in favour of murdering a different MP] and a police officer who was investigating him on separate charges of child sex offences and stirring up racial hatred (Hamilton 2018b; Hamilton and Gardham 2018). Christopher Lythgoe was also charged with complicity in the planning of the MP's murder. On June 12, 2018, Renshaw pleaded guilty to planning terrorist acts, namely plotting the murder of the MP and threatening to murder the police officer. At the time of writing, the trial of Renshaw and four others had not concluded.

In November 2018, Mikko Vehvilainen and Alex Deakin were each jailed for 8 years for being NA members and for an array of related terrorist offences, and a further six members who either pleaded guilty or were convicted of similar offences were awaiting sentence at the time of writing (Home Office 2018).

Since their proscription, NA have splintered into other groups—Scottish Dawn and NS 131 (131 refers to ACA or Anti-Capitalist Action). These two groups were banned as aliases of NA in September 2017. NS 131 is of particular note, given its self-description as a "visual blog of the NS revolt" and documenting banner drops, campaigns to put up propaganda stickers and posters throughout British towns and the painting of graffiti. One banner is emblazoned with the word 'love' but in the place of the 'o' is the *sonnenrad* or sun wheel, a symbol with a long history but notably adopted by the SS. In another image, extreme rightists hold up a banner marking the birth and death of Rudolf Hess, long a hero of neo-Nazis.

The stickers and posters also employ the sun wheel, the phrase 'Europa bleeds' and the statue of the goddess of Victory, Victoria, and her horses from atop Berlin's Brandenburg Gate in one image. 'Dailystormer.com', a prominent American neo-Nazi website, is also advertised on this poster. Another image shows a classical sculpture, the symbol of Italian Fascism, the fasces, and the words 'Defend the West'. A Molotov cocktail is featured in another image, along with the typically extreme-right Odin's Cross or the Sun Cross and the words 'Destroy Capitalism'. Each of these images succinctly depicts the message of NA and its offshoots—they are disseminating traditional Nazi and Fascist ideas—white supremacy, the decline of the West, the need to destroy the establishment—using the popular mediums of today—the Internet, graffiti and other forms of public urban art—in order to attract a wide, youthful audience. They are fashioning themselves as 'Nipsters'—Nazi hipsters (Rogers 2014). These methods are also being employed by very similar 'brother' groups elsewhere—Atomwaffen Division in the United States and Australia's Antipodean Resistance. In December 2018, alleged members of an extreme-right group System Resistance Network, apparently affiliated to NA, were identified in a *BBC Wales* undercover investigation (*BBC News* 2018). Also, three alleged members of the Sonnenkrieg Division, a small neo-Nazi group with connections to Atomwaffen Division, were arrested in the UK on terrorism charges (Gibbons 2018).

Europe, Youth, Reconquista!: Generation Identity

It is compelling to note that while NA and its splinter groups have been proscribed, other groups of a strikingly like stamp continue to spread their message in both actual and virtual reality. Those groups noted above share much with the Nordic Resistance Movement, for example, and Generation Identity (GI). The latter especially has mastered using today's media as a propaganda tool across all social media platforms, as well as through a myriad of demonstrations, banner drops and torchlight processions with the chant of "Europe! Youth! Reconquista!" ('reconquista' translates as 'reconquered' and has particular historical significance) throughout Europe and, increasingly, in the British Isles (there was a banner drop from Hastings Castle in late April). Describing GI as a "pan-European youth movement", Martin Sellner, an Austrian far/extreme right activist and leader of GI in Austria, has declared he is fighting an "infowar" on the Internet given that viewers of GI material are "just one mouse click away from our point of view" (Williams 2017). GI's *modus operandi* is to undertake a well-planned political (often publicity rich) action, film it and then immediately post it on social media. The Internet thus gives their activities an enormous immediacy. Sellner is also launching the 'Patriot Peer' app, which connects like-minded rightists with similar people in their area, thus enabling virtual connections to become real ones.

European GI members have dropped a banner from the top of the Brandenburg Gate reading "secure borders—secure future". In Vienna, the enormous statue of Empress Maria Theresa in the City's museum quarter was covered in a burka to bring attention to the supposed Islamisation of Austria. GI also attempted to charter a ferry on the Mediterranean to take any African refugees found in its waters back to Libya (Warren 2017) and they have recently been patrolling part of the French-Italian border as a further leg of their 'Defend Europe' campaign (Defend Europe 2018). As Paul Jackson pointed out, it can certainly be seen that GI has a "more serious, radical tenor" than groups such as the EDL (Jackson 2013). However, while the leading GI figures Sellner and American Brittany Pettibone have been banned from the UK, there have been no noticeable sanctions placed upon GI's web presence and their message is thus still loudly discernible.

With the "urbane charisma and clever phrasing" of such figures as Sellner (Williams 2017), GI are able to gain more widespread support. The Antifa (anti-fascists) argue that they are simply old Nazis in new clothes. "They want to make Nazis trendy and hip again" Austrian left-wing activist Natalie Goldman posits (Williams 2017). GI suggest that they are "for the people…[*but*]…they're really far-right", suggests Anna Müller, another figure in the Austrian Antifa (Williams 2017). Andreas Peham, a researcher into the extreme-right in Austria states that GI identify as New Right to try and get away from Hitler and the shadows of the past (Williams 2017).

Conclusions

Each of the cases considered here shows the long history of cultural despair in the ideological composition of the British extreme-right. From the anti-Semitism of the pre- and immediately post-World War Two period, through to the increasingly virulent and violent Islamophobia of the current period, there has always been a notion of a society or a component of society that needs to be swept away in order for the 'right' societal structure to be put in place.

This doom-laden and often apocalyptic vision is of particular concern as Europe and the western world more generally takes a step to the right. As the ideas of the extreme-right are now (often superficially) modified or repackaged for a wider general consumption, they are becoming increasingly subsumed into the mainstream. In turn, the Internet provides a forum for the dissemination of ideas the likes of which have not previously been known.

While proscription is an important measure to take in order to draw a heavy societal line in the sand, it may only serve to push dangerous groups underground and into less monitorable positions. As Jamie Bartlett from the UK think tank Demos has stated, "there is a danger that groups or individuals that are arrested or are prevented from speaking their minds in whatever way end up feeling like they are justified, that they are vindicated in some ways because they're anti-establishment many of these groups and whenever they're shut down by that establishment it's something of a badge of honour…but for them it...demonstrates that they are speaking truth to power and the fact that people tried to close them down it proves to them that they're right because they have the establishment scared" (Bartlett in Nye 2015).

So too, while the most obviously dangerous of these groups are proscribed, others which are more able to successfully hide their core beliefs and promote a more acceptable image continue on in the public domain. "[N]ormalization makes it even more difficult to pin the 'fascist' or 'Nazi' label on the well-groomed bespoke suits of Britain's latest generation of neo-fascist extremists" (Copsey 2007, 81).

It should be borne in mind that, despite the high profile of many of these groups, involving protests and Internet and social media campaigns, their numbers are far smaller than their profiles suggest. If one takes the combined core members of the largest groups [UKIP as 21,000 (ONS 2018); Britain First estimated as 50,000; and EDL estimated as 20,000], and generously multiplies the number of followers as being 20 times the core numbers, the total who might be expected to vote for a populist-, far-, or extreme-right candidate is 1.82 million, or 3.8% of the total UK electorate of 47.93 million. With such a tiny presence, there is little likelihood of their ever having a significant electoral impact under the present UK electoral system. Nevertheless, it is likely that they will continue to seek to infiltrate their ideology into the mainstream parties while maintaining their vigorous public messaging. The more extreme elements are also unlikely to forsake their violent proclivities in pursuing their agendas and, of course, as recent history has shown, even a lone extremist could murder or maim a large number of people in a single attack.

Risks arising may be summarised as follows (and further analysed in chapter 12):

Risk 1. Cultural despair leading to more extreme re-alignments

Cultural despair and alienation among British far- and extreme-right groups, and a frustration with their political failure, may spur a re-alignment of support among them towards more extremist views in which Britain First and National Action become the dominant face of the British far-right.

Risk 2. Cultural despair leading to more extreme right-wing actions

Cultural despair and alienation among British far- and extreme-right groups, and their fanatical supremacist ideology, may lead them to try to act out a 'cultural war' to 'save the nation' through any means, including violence and other hate crimes.

Risk 3. Proscription and punishment as perverse validation

Proscription of far-right groups and punishment of offenders by the authorities for hate crimes may, in the minds of extremists and their followers, validate their ideology and confer heroic status among them.

Risk 4. Political normalisation of far-right ideas

Far- and extreme-right ideology may, for a variety of reasons, become increasingly normalised and subsumed within mainstream political discourse and policies in Britain, thereby leading to potential human rights abuses and crimes against sectors of the population.

Risk 5. Internet as far-right weapon in asymmetric cultural war

The Internet and social media may increasingly provide a difficult-to-control vector for promulgation of far- and extreme-right views and propaganda.

References

BBC. 2014. "Britain First's Leader Paul Golding on BNP Breakaway". *BBC.* May 15, 2014, http://www.bbc.com/news/av/uk-politics-27427023/britain-first-s-leader-paul-golding-on-bnp-breakaway.

BBC News. 2014. "Jo Cox MP Dead After Shooting Attack", *BBC News,* June 16, 2016.

BBC News. 2018. "System Resistance Network: Neo-Nazi Group 'Should be Illegal'". *BBC Wales* investigation. *BBC News.* December 3, 2018. https://www.bbc.co.uk/news/uk-wales-46292599.

Blayden-Ryal, Miles. 2015. "We Want Our Country Back". https://www.youtube.com/watch?v=byRGsYJAPPA.

Bloom, Clive 2010. *Violent London: 2000 Years of Riots, Rebels and Revolts.* Basingstoke UK: Palgrave Macmillan.

Boyle, Danny. 2016. "Britain First Party Leader 'Just as Shocked as Everyone Else'". *The Telegraph,* June 16, 2016.

Britain First. Swanley UK. https://www.britainfirst.org/.

Britain First. 2015. "Is Britain First Against All Muslims or Just Extremists?" Swanley UK: Britain First.

Britain First. 2018. Principles of the British First Movement. Swanley UK: Britain First. https://www.britainfirst.org/principles.

British National Party. Wigton UK: BNP. https://bnp.org.uk/.

Brown, Jonathan 2014. "Far-Right Activists Hand Out Bibles Outside Mosques in Bradford". *The Independent*, May 11, 2014. https://www.independent.co.uk/news/uk/home-news/far-right-activists-hand-out-bibles-outside-mosques-in-bradford-9352271.html.

Copsey, Nigel. 2007. "Changing Course or Changing Clothes?: Reflections on the Ideological Evolution of the British National Party 1999–2006". *Patterns of Prejudice*, 41 (1), 61–82.

Copsey, Nigel and Richardson, John E. 2015. *Cultures of Post-War British Fascism*. Routledge Studies in Fascism and the Far-Right. Abingdon Oxon UK: Routledge.

Dearden, Lizzie. 2014. "Britain First Founder Jim Dowson Quits Over Mosque Invasions and Racists and Extremists". *The Independent*, July 28, 2014. https://www.independent.co.uk/news/uk/home-news/britain-first-founder-jim-dowson-quits-over-mosque-invasions-and-racists-and-extremists-9632770.html.

Defend Europe. 2018, http://defendeurope.net/.

De Simone, Daniel. 2016. "National Action Ban Highlights Concern Over Far Right". *BBC News*, December 12, 2016. http://www.bbc.com/news/uk-38293314.

English Defence League. http://www.englishdefenceleague.org.uk/.

Faridi, Hasan. 2015. "Veteran Reports Britain First for Defamation Over Fake Photo". *Yorkshire Standard*, March 6, 2015.

Filfilan, Karam. 2015. "Hateful and Here: German Anti-Islam Extremists Rally in Glasgow in Bid to Recruit Scots" *The Daily Record*, January 18, 2015. https://www.dailyrecord.co.uk/news/scottish-news/hateful-here-german-anti-islam-extremists-4998372.

Forster, Katie. 2016. "Jo Cox Dead: Britain First Denies Involvement in Attack on Labour MP". *The Independent*, June 16, 2016.

Gable, Gerry. 2016. "Britain First Extremist Filmed Joining Hate-Filled Vigilante Group Hunting Down Asylum Seekers in Bulgaria. *Searchlight*, October 29, 2016. http://www.searchlightmagazine.com/2016/10/britain-first-extremist-filmed-joining-hate-filled-vigilante-group-hunting-down-asylum-seekers-in-bulgaria/.

Garland, Jon and Treadwell, James. 2010. "'No Surrender to the Taliban': Football Hooliganism, Islamophobia and the Rise of the English Defence League". British Society of Criminology conference panel paper, 10, 19–35.

Generation Identity UK. https://www.generation-identity.org.uk/.

Gibbons, K. 2018. "Three Arrested by Anti-Terror Police Investigating Neo-Nazis". *The Times.* December 12, 2018. Page 12.

Griffin, Roger (ed). 1995. *Fascism.* Oxford: Oxford University Press.

Hamilton, Fiona. 2016. "Hitler's Only Fault Showing Mercy to Jews, Youth Leader Told Secret Meeting". *The Times*, November 28, 2016.

Hamilton, Fiona. 2018a. "EDL Founder Jailed for Court Rant". *The Times.* May 30, 2018. Page 7.

Hamilton, F. 2018b. "'Neo-Nazis' on Trial Over Plot to Murder MP". *The Times.* June 13, 2018. Page 5.

Hamilton, Fiona and Gardham, Duncan. 2018. "Far-Right Plotter Wanted Police to Kill Him". *The Times.* June 14, 2018. Page 19.

Hern, Alex and Rawlinson, Kevin. 2018. "Facebook Bans Britain First and Its Leaders". *The Guardian*, March 14, 2018. https://www.theguardian.com/world/2018/mar/14/facebook-bans-britain-first-and-its-leaders.

Home Office (UK). 2017. *List of Proscribed Organisations*, December 22, 2017, https://assets.publishing.service.gov.uk/government/uploads/system/uploads/attachment_data/file/670599/20171222_Proscription.pdf.

Home Office (UK). 2018. *National Action Cases - Statement and Factsheet.* HO News Team. November 12, 2018. London: Home Office. https://homeofficemedia.blog.gov.uk.

Huffington Post. 2014. "Electoral Commission Issues Grovelling Apology After Extremist Party, Britain First, Uses Lee Rigby Slogan". *Huffington Post,* April 26, 2014.

Jackson, Paul. 2017. "Identity Parade". *Searchlight*, Winter 2017–18, 26–29.

James, Ben. 2014. "23 Year-Old Race Hate Group Leader Uncovered in Sussex". *The Argus*, June 9, 2014. http://www.theargus.co.uk/news/11264390.25_year_old_race_hate_group_leader_uncovered_in_Sussex/.

Lusher, A. 2017. "EDL Founder Tommy Robinson to Address One of America's Most Prestigious Universities". *The Independent.* October 9, 2017. www.theindependent.co.uk.

Meredith, Charlotte. 2014. "Britain First 'Desecrate' Image Of Fearless Afghan Heroine In 'Ban The Burka' Campaign". *Huffington Post*, September 21, 2014. https://www.huffingtonpost.co.uk/2014/09/21/britain-first-_n_5857250.html.

NS131. https://logr.org/ns131/.

Nye, Catrin. 2015. "Radicals: the Proud Racist". *BBC News*, September 1, 2015, https://www.youtube.com/watch?v=gjVE4J4mBRA.

ONS. 2018. *Electoral Statistics for the UK.* March 22, 2018. London: Office for National Statistics.

Porter, Tom. 2014. "New UK Far-Right Group National Action Led By Student and Former Double-Glazing Salesman". *International Business Times*, June 8, 2014. https://www.ibtimes.co.uk/new-uk-far-right-group-national-action-led-by-student-former-double-glazing-salesman-1451795.

Renshaw, Jack. 2014. Renshaw's Corner (blog), December 15, 2014.

Renshaw, Jack. 2015. Renshaw's Corner (blog), November 2015.

Rogers, Thomas. 2014. "Heil Hipster: The Young Neo-Nazis Trying to Put a Stylish Face on Hate". *Rolling Stone*, June 23, 2014. https://www.rollingstone.com/culture/news/heil-hipster-the-young-neo-nazis-trying-to-put-a-stylish-face-on-hate-20140623.

Sellner, Martin. https://martin-sellner.at/.

Sheriff, Lucy 2014. "Meet New Neo-Nazi Group National Action Which Just Wants To 'Piss People Off'". *Huffington Post*, March 6, 2014. https://www.huffingtonpost.co.uk/2014/03/06/new-neo-nazi-group-national-action_n_4910260.html.

Stern, Fritz. 1974. *The Politics of Cultural Despair: a Study in the Rise of the Germanic Ideology*. Berkeley: University of California Press.

Sykes, Alan. 2005. *The Radical Right in Britain: Social Imperialism to the BNP*. Basingstoke UK: Palgrave Macmillan.

The Times. 2018. "Neo-Nazi Called for Eradication of Jews at Far-Right Rally". *The Times*, January 9, 2018. https://www.thetimes.co.uk/article/neo-nazi-called-for-eradication-of-jews-at-far-right-rally-mbt9n8nlx.

Warren, Rossalyn. 2017. "Europe's Far-Right Pirates of the Mediterranean are Targeting Refugee Rescue Missions. *Washington Post*, July 28, 2017. https://www.washingtonpost.com/news/global-opinions/wp/2017/07/28/europes-far-right-pirates-of-the-mediterranean-are-targeting-refugee-rescue-missions/?noredirect=on&utm_term=.2eb1f565a907.

Williams, Evan, Tozer, Joel and Anna-Lena Janzen. 2017. "Young, Hip and Far Right". *Dateline*, April 25, 2017, https://www.youtube.com/watch?v=f5eq-4xEAKk.

Zand, Benjamin. 2015. "Britain First: the "Most Dangerous Far-Right Party?" *BBC*. https://www.youtube.com/watch?v=e6LZt8BWqbE.

Further Reading

Fekete, Liz. 2018. *Europe's Fault Lines: Racism and the Rise of the Right*. London: Verso.

Trilling, Daniel. 2012. *Bloody Nasty People: The Rise of Britain's Far Right*. London: Verso.

Walker, Martin. 1977. *The National Front*. London: HarperCollins.

Wright, Simon, Glaze, Ben and Cortbus, Colin. 2014. "Exposed: Rise of Hitler-loving National Action Group Who Want to 'Ethnically Cleanse' the UK". *Daily Mirror*, June 7, 2014.

Chapter 5: The Murder of Jo Cox MP: a Case Study in Lone Actor Terrorism

By Paul Jackson

Abstract

The characteristics of lone actor extremism, radicalisation, and political violence are examined in relation to the particular case of Thomas Mair and his fatal attack on Jo Cox MP. Prominent factors that emerge are analysed, namely his far-right ideology (e.g. his long-term white supremacist and neo-Nazi beliefs), his apparent mental health issues, his relationship with the far-right community, his access to extreme right-wing literature, and his social isolation. The difficulties in identifying such individuals in advance and formulating an effective preventive risk management regime are discussed.

Key words: lone actor, far-right, extremism, violence, Jo Cox, risk management

Jo Cox's Murder

On the afternoon June 16, 2016, Thomas Mair drove to the centre of Birstall, a small town in West Yorkshire in England, and shot the Labour Party Member of Parliament Jo Cox twice in the head and once in the chest, using a sawn off .22 rifle. He also stabbed her fifteen times. A 77-year-old man, Bernard Kenny, intervened and was himself stabbed in the incident and was later awarded a George Medal for his bravery (Slawson 2017).

Mair was later arrested around a mile from the murder scene, and at this time described himself as a 'political activist'. The attack came just days before the British electorate voted in a major referendum on whether the United Kingdom should stay or leave the European Union (see chapter 3). During the attack, Mair was reported to have said "Britain first", "Keep Britain independent", "Britain always comes first" and "this is for Britain", thereby giving some indication of his political motivation. Jo Cox died of her wounds, while Mair was charged with murder. On November 23, 2016, after a short trial, Mair was convicted of murder, and given a whole life sentence due to the seriousness of his crime. The Crown Prosecution Service stated afterwards that, despite Mair not being prosecuted under specific terrorism legislation, they considered him to be a terrorist (CPS 2017).

In the wake of Mair's conviction, press attention shone a light into the ideological world that Mair inhabited, and this allows for a fuller understanding of this case of extreme-right lone actor terrorism. For press examples, see *BBC News* (2016), Burgis (2016), Corbin et al (2016), Evans and Millward (2016), and Higgens and Murphy (2016). However, many elements of the story remain unclear, and Mair himself has continued to be largely silent about his activities. Despite this, investigative journalists have drawn out more details about Mair's own life history, including his issues with mental health, and also offer details on how he engaged with extreme-right groups, both in the UK and internationally, and constructed his ideology. These aspects present a case that typifies the phenomenon of lone actor terrorism from the extreme-right. Largely disconnected from a wider culture of activism, Mair appears to have self-radicalised over a long period of time, engaging with a range of neo-Nazi materials, before deciding to take action stemming from a complex set of long- and short-term issues. This chapter explores the case in the light of a wider academic literature on lone actor terrorism, and concludes with a short discussion on how the case helps reflection on how to manage the risks posed by extreme-right lone actors.

A number of key points emerge from the case. Firstly, it shows that ideology is important, as it frames expression of a grievance, and offers lone actors a sense of purpose as well as ability to imagine a wider community supportive of their actions. However, ideology alone does not explain why a lone actor terrorist decides on political violence. Aside from ideology, a number of long- and short-term factors combine as lone actors go on a journey of radicalisation (Porter and LaFree 2012), which helps to make a violent solution appear desirable to someone. These factors may involve a mental health issue of some description, as was the case with Mair, though this too should be seen as merely one part of understanding a specific incident of terrorism. Finally, there is a range of relationships a lone actor may have with a wider ideological community, and exploring this issue helps reveal the ways figures such as Mair engaged with this wider milieu as part of their radicalisation. This also draws out the role of online activism, and how it is becoming increasingly simple to connect with international cultures promoting extreme perspectives. The online space also offered Mair a more practical knowledge on how to carry out an attack.

Lone Actor Terrorism and the Extreme-Right

Ideological violence from the extreme-right takes many forms, and has received growing interest from analysts such as Bale (2018). Analysts such as Daniel Koehler have argued that the issue has been neglected in recent years, especially by government agendas focused on tackling Islamist terrorism. Koehler (2017) has written on the major terrorist cell in Germany, the National Socialist Underground, and elsewhere explained that new networks, and militant extremist groups, were now engaging in a new type of spontaneous extreme-right violence, fuelled by factors spanning the growth of the Internet to fears regarding Muslim communities in Europe (Koehler 2016). This is certainly important, but while Koehler talked of a new wave of 'hives', or small groups, of extreme-right violence, the examples of those who act alone is also important to recognise. While extreme-right violence is a diverse and ever-changing phenomenon, figures like Mair can be located in an older tradition, one steeped in a long-lasting Anglo-America culture of extreme-right activity (Jackson and Shekhovtsov 2014).

In particular, a culture specifically focused on the romanticised idea of the 'lone wolf' was developed by American extreme-right ideologues, such as Tom Metzger and Alex Curtis. It was their writings that helped to popularise the term 'lone wolf' within extreme-right cultures presenting such activists as a freedom fighters, though purposefully disconnected from wider extreme-right organizations who shared the same ideology (Curtis 2017). As their idealised culture promoting the lone wolf activist developed in America, it also drew on existing elements of American neo-Nazi and white supremacist culture that was also steeped in a language that licensed violence. This included texts such as William Pierce's novel *The Turner Diaries* (Michael 2010) and Louis Beam's notorious essay on 'Leaderless Resistance' (Kaplan 1997). Framed around anti-Semitic conspiracy theory, this mythology presented the lone wolf as a revolutionary warrior fighting a moral battle in defence of white interests that were under attack from alleged Jewish controlled governments imposing immigration as a way to destroy white identity (Jackson 2011). Lone wolves would play a crucial role in liberating the world from such forces, and their actions would be inspirational to others, and would later be joined by fellow activists who were also sympathetic to defending white interests. As Moskalenko and McCauley (2011) pointed out, lone actor terrorists are inspired by the belief that the acts of the individual are for the benefit of a larger imagined community. Since the 1990s, such lone wolf mythology has been disseminated widely on the Internet, and is now easily accessible across the globe. In recent times, academic analysis has itself steered away from using the term 'lone wolf', while the more neutral, less romanticised, term 'lone actor' has become more typical.

Historian and theorist of fascism, Roger Griffin, has also commented on the ways ideology offers a sense of the 'higher' for such extreme-right lone actors. Such narratives are framed around what he calls a 'palingenetic' vision of a future society reborn, one that is purged of forces of corruption and decay. Ideological terrorists may imagine their own activities as part of an unfolding revolutionary crusade to purify the future (Griffin 2012). Griffin asserted that identifying as 'revolutionary', and developing an ultimately delusional perspective on how important one act of violence is going to be for redeeming an entire community, are a common features of terrorist ideologies, whether carried out by individuals or groups.

Meanwhile, the specialist literature on lone actors also stresses that ideological causes can take on peculiarly personal qualities, what Ramon Spaaij calls 'personalisation' of ideology. While a shared ideology is crucial, how each lone actor develops their understating of a wider ideology varies quite considerably. While some, such as Anders Breivik (see chapter 10), feel the need to develop a vast compendium to justify such political violence (Gardell 2014), others seem far less concerned with generating a detailed understanding of their ideological concerns. Spaaij has explained that, while ideological sophistication varies, lone actors use a shared ideology to develop belief in an underlying moral justification for their violence, combining elements of their own world-view, and individual frustrations, with wider elements drawn from a more general ideological context. As they do not need to act with others, lone actors are far freer to customise ideology, and develop unique perspectives. The example of David Copeland, who detonated three nail bombs in Britain in 1999, is instructive here. His first two targets were chosen as they represented multicultural communities that he felt clashed with his ideological vision of a white Britain. However, his third target was a pub popular among London's gay community, and Copeland was clear that his targeting of the venue was personal rather than ideological (McLagen and Lowles 2000). His homophobic outlook, Spaaij stresses, although certainly reinforced through his neo-Nazi ideology, was something that developed during his childhood (Spaaij 2011).

Mair was certainly sympathetic towards a wider white supremacist and neo-Nazi milieu, and also developed his own variations on these ideological themes. In general terms, Mair's ideological perspective became clear very quickly after the attack. In the hours that followed, the US watchdog the Southern Poverty Law Center released receipts that showed that he had purchased materials from the American neo-Nazi organisation the National Alliance over a number of years (SPLC 2016). The National Alliance was a leading US neo-Nazi group from the 1970s to the 2000s (Durham 2007). In 1999, Mair purchased editions of the National Alliance's magazines *National Vanguard* and *Free Speech*, as well as a book written by leading figures from the Nazi regime in the early 1940s, *Ich Kämpfe*. He also purchased several books on constructing making weapons, such as *Improvised Munitions Handbook* and *Chemistry of Powder and Explosives*. It was also revealed at this time that Mair's interests in other strands of white supremacist ideology could be dated to at least 1991. In 1991, he had a letter printed in the pro-Apartheid magazine *South African Patriot in Exile* where he explained: "I still have faith that the White Race will prevail, both in Britain and South Africa, but I fear that it's going to be a very long and very bloody struggle" (Sommers 2016). Clearly, Mair's ideological sympathies were developed through long-held racist beliefs and interest in extremist literature.

After his trial, more details emerged. In particular, images were released showing Mair's book collection, which helped to give a clearer picture of the unique range of Mair's interests. On the top of this bookshelf was a Third Reich-style eagle ornament, indicative of his fetish about Nazism. Book topics were dominated by interest in the history of the Nazi regime, as well as a wide collection of neo-Nazi produced literature (Wheatstone and Lion 2016). He was clearly very interested in the lives of leading Nazis, as his books included biographies on Herman Goering and Heinrich Himmler, while other typical titles included *Uniforms and Traditions of the Luftwaffe Volume Two*, and *SS Race Theory*. Some of these books were academic texts, including volumes by Michael Burleigh and Ron Rosenbaum, whereas others were reproductions of Nazi-era material created by neo-Nazi groups. Academic books also included Richard Thurlow's *Fascism in Britain*, and Mair was also clearly interested in volumes created by those with links to British fascism. In particular, he possessed a copy of Arthur Kemp's book *March of the Titans*, which presents itself as a 'history of the white race', yet in reality is steeped in pseudo-scientific claims and misleading interpretations of a 'white' history. Kemp himself was an activist in the British National Party in the 2000s, and before then had links to South African extremist groups. *March of the Titans* is a typical product of British neo-Nazism, synthesizing Holocaust denial and spurious claims about white racial superiority. Underscoring Griffin's theme of palingenesis, its final chapter on the future of the white race predicted the rise of a new era for white people once they had overcome the struggles of fighting against the rise of contemporary multicultural society, and drew on Norse mythology to articulate ideals of racial rebirth (Kemp 2006). These more clearly faith-based tropes in his reading can also be seen elsewhere in neo-Nazi contexts. For example, the culture promoted by the National Alliance and the group's founder, William Pierce, included promotion of a type of pagan neo-Nazi faith that Pierce called Cosmotheism (Durham 2004). Mair himself also showed interest in elements of neo-Nazi neo-paganism. For example, he purchased a book called *Secret of the Runes* from the National Alliance in 1999, while police evidence released after the trial also showed that Mair had a bag of runes in his possession.

While these data suggest there are elements of engagement with a wider far-right community, and some components of personalisation, since his arrest Mair has given few details on how he conceived his ideology. In his first court appearance after the attack, on the June 18, 2016, he gave his name simply as "death to traitors, freedom for Britain" (Slawson 2016). Clearly this was a political message, and probably related in some manner to the on-going referendum campaign. However, more details on his justifications for the murder are lacking. While being questioned by the police, Mair chose not to answer interrogators, and so gave no further details on his world-view. Mair did offer to address the court during his trial, but the judge refused this request, stating that he had been given earlier chances to explain his actions, but had rejected them (Cobain and Taylor 2016). While understandable, allowing him to talk could have led to a deeper appreciation of how he conceptualised his attack, and its purpose.

In terms of explaining Mair's ideology, it is clear that he developed a type of neo-Nazism, and probably combined this with elements of neo-pagan faith. He is likely to have linked American neo-Nazi themes to issues affecting him in his locality, and is also likely to have connected his own ideological position to the particular mood in Britain during the run up to the EU referendum. Examining his ideology certainly helps establish his broad political identity, and helps demonstrate that he was focused on Nazi and neo-Nazi cultures. However, ideology alone does not tell us why Mair engaged in political violence.

Long- and Short-term Factors Explaining Mair's Radicalisation

Another central figure in the study of lone actor terrorism is Paul Gill (2015), whose impact on the topic has been highly significant, and has helped to draw out a more complex picture of the non-ideological as well as ideological factors in radicalisation. Gill has developed a number of key observations that are crucial to the scrutiny of any individual case of lone actor terrorism. He is clear that each case is highly individualised, and so developing any sort of 'profile' of lone actors is not possible. He also explains that a range of factors, often individually seemingly quite banal, combine in lone actors in important ways—although these issues only really become apparent after an incident has occurred. In particular, Gill has identified how long-term, or distal, factors combine with short-term, or proximate, factors. A discussion around how these factors combine may help analysts piece together why an act of terrorism became desirable for a protagonist.

For Gill, typical distal factors help to foster a longer-term sense of disconnection, and help us understand how a person is somehow not fitting in with wider society. They can include mental health issues, previous incidents of criminality, and on-going social isolation, among other factors. Mair's case presented two of these issues, and the issue of mental health is worth developing further. A recent report by the Royal United Services Institute (RUSI) on European lone actors problematized the notion that all lone actors suffered from mental health issues, a common media explanation for extreme-right lone actor terrorists that moves attention away from their engagement with wider groups. RUSI's analysis concluded with the striking observation that "35% of the perpetrators reportedly suffered from some kind of mental health disorder [while] the estimated percentage [of such disorders] for the general population is 27%" (van Zuijdewijn and Bakker 2016). In other words, mental health is found in around one third of all cases of lone actors, but care should be taken when discussing this issue, as it is not an essential element found in all lone actor narratives. Spaaij has also identified that, aside from mental health issues being a regularly occurring element, there are few patterns to be found regarding typical types of mental health disorder, or how they actually cause the planning and carrying out of an attack. Gill, meanwhile, suggested mental health issues should be seen commonly acting as a 'cause of a cause', rather than a factor that directly explains an attack. For example, a mental health issue may be part of the reason why a lone actor feels socially isolated, or struggles to keep a job, rather than mental health condition being a factor that somehow removes culpability for their violence because they are do not have full control over their actions (Gill and Corner 2017).

While identifying such distal issues may help to explain how a lone actor starts to develop deep antagonism with the wider world, ahead of an attack, this needs to be intensified by more proximate factors, ranging from an escalation of a stressful situation, losing a job, a breakdown in a personal relationship, or even changing address. Again, individual proximate factors are in themselves relatively common issues, but help to trigger a sense of needing to do something extreme. For Gill, when distal and proximate factors combine, and when a potential lone actor turns to an ideology as an ostensible solution to these issues, this can then lead to radicalisation and political violence. He stresses that a typical narrative of radicalisation for a lone actor would start with experiencing long-term reasons for disconnecting with wider society, followed by one or a number of triggers intensifying an ideological view. From this, they will then find particular elements of an ideological milieu important, decide on the need to act violently, and develop an attack. Lone actor violence emerges over time, though often there is little scope for detecting whether someone is becoming susceptible to carrying out political violence, unless they disclose this information in some way.

A variation of this generic narrative unfolded with Mair. While it is clear he had sympathies with an extremist ideological milieu for around 25 years before the attack, before 2016 he was not a violent man. When he was arrested, Mair had no prior convictions and was unknown to the police. Mair was born in 1963 in Scotland, though the relationship between Mair's parents, James and Mary, broke down, and Mary moved to Birstall, along with her two sons Thomas and James. She had another son of mixed race by a different father. Mair then lived in the family home for the rest of his life, until he murdered Jo Cox in 2016. He shared the house with his maternal grandmother until she died in 1996, after which he then lived alone. According to Gill, living alone is another common feature of lone actor terrorists, though not present in all cases. The police confirmed his high degree of social isolation, and described him as a man who was not able to hold down a job, and who had neither girlfriends nor friends. Neighbours claimed that Mair was never able to secure full-time employment, and also noted he studied at a local college as a mature student. Mair sometimes worked as a volunteer gardener, and those who knew him have described how he would help maintain the gardens of elderly neighbours. While some who knew him described him as friendly, and gave no clues regarding his extremist political views, others who engaged with him felt differently. In particular, taxi drivers described how he would often say racist remarks when he was paying for fares, and was well known for making racist comments.

Media reports on the case demonstrate that Mair also suffered from long-term issues of depression and low self-esteem. While working as a volunteer gardener in 2010, Mair was interviewed for a local newspaper, the *Huddersfield Examiner*, and he explained that "many people who suffer from mental illness are socially isolated and disconnected from society ... Feelings of worthlessness are also common, mainly caused by long-term unemployment" (Corbin et al 2016). His brother also noted that Mair suffered from on-going mental health issues, and that he did seek help for these problems before the attack. After his first court appearance, Mair was analysed by psychiatrists, but they concluded that his mental health state did not mean that he was insane. In this way, his profile again fits the theme of mental health being an important framing factor in radicalisation. It helps to explain Mair's social isolation and ability to foster a grievance, but does not absolve him of responsibility for his actions. It is also likely his mental health had an influence on the way he personalised his engagement with neo-Nazi ideology, and saw it as a profound solution to deeply held grievances.

While longer-term factors are relatively easy to identify from Mair's case, what is less clear are the key 'triggers' that made him decide that political violence was necessary. Piecing this together is difficult, not least because of Mair's unwillingness to explain his actions. From what can be inferred, the political climate generated by the referendum campaign is likely to have been significant. Images released by the police show that his Internet searches on June 10, 2016 included Jo Cox's website, www.jocox.org.uk, and then at his first court appearance he implied that he considered Cox a 'traitor'. In the period the attack was carried out, the EU Referendum campaign was at its height, and Cox was a vocal MP campaigning for 'remain'. Given Mair's statements during the attack, he seems to have understood his actions as linked to promoting Britain's freedom, and saw the Remain campaigners as traitorous. Internet data suggests that it was the idea of attacking the political elite that was crucial. He showed interest in other parliamentarians, and also researched another prominent Yorkshire-based 'remainer', the MP William Hague. In general, extreme-right ideologies are replete with descriptions of mainstream politicians as essentially corrupt and contemptible figures manipulated by conspiratorial forces, which would have likely reinforced his distaste for the political class. The broader extreme-right community with which he identified was campaigning forcefully at this time, almost universally for 'leave'. Some groups, such as Britain First, were even issuing powerful statements that activists needed to take "militant direct action" against elected officials (Gable 2016). There is no evidence of a direct link to suggest Mair was himself acting on such pronouncements, and Britain First focused this call on Muslim elected representatives at this time, such as Sadiq Khan, the Mayor of London, and Conservative MP Sajid Javid. Nevertheless, the tenor of the extreme-right milieu around the time of the attack was increasingly provocative, and emotive.

While identifying triggers remains problematic, what emerges is a narrative typical of lone actors: Mair was someone whose long-term factors reveal a disturbed and isolated man, while more immediate issues demonstrate the role of a particularly stressful climate. He also plotted his actions, and adopted a rational, planned approach to committing an act of terrorism. Such details help demonstrate that Mair developed the attack ahead of the murder, and certainly this was not a spontaneous act of violence.

Mair's Relationship with a Wider Milieu

By focusing on ideology, as well as distal and proximal factors, a clearer picture emerges of a troubled man who sympathised with extremist views. However, this also raises the question of how engaged Mair was with other groups, and the wider extreme-right milieu. Raffaello Pantucci has also contributed to debates defining lone actors, and offers a useful model for reflecting on the types of relationship a lone actor might have with a wider ideological community, several of which apply to extreme-right contexts (Pantucci 2011). Pantucci identified firstly the 'loner' terrorists, or those who have a one-way relationship with larger groups, and so are not members of wider organisations. Ukrainian national Pavlo Lapshyn, who travelled to the UK in 2013 and had no links to groups in either country, is a clear example of this category (Shekhovtsov 2017). Lapshyn was sentenced in the UK in 2013 to at least 40 years' imprisonment for a racist murder and plotting explosions. A second category is 'lone actor', or those who have a more complex, two-way relationship with extreme-right groups, but decide to act alone. There is a greater likelihood of detecting figures in this category, as they have a wider range of conversations with likeminded militants. David Copeland, active in the British National Party and the National Socialist Movement, would be a good example here. Finally, Pantucci described small cells, lone actors who want to act violently with others and do find one or two associates to conspire with. Timothy McVeigh, Terry Nichols and others linked to the Oklahoma City bombing in 1995 would be a good example. Here it is worth noting that Metzger too, in his writings on the 'lone wolf', talked up the idea of small cells working together (Metzger 2017). Again, greater interaction between figures in such a cell makes their detection, in theory, more likely.

While influenced by wider extreme-right cultures, Mair was clearly someone who acted alone. As far as we know, Mair's relationship with extreme-right cultures was primarily indirect, and he did not regularly attend meetings of right-wing groups. Therefore, with the data so far at least, Mair appears to fit Pantucci's 'loner' category: he only had a one-way relationship with wider groups. This is despite one report of him being present at a key meeting of the extreme-right in 2000 (Potok 2016), which without wider verification remains speculative. Though he was not a figure well known to others in this milieu, Mair clearly engaged in complex ways with a wider extremist culture that, as noted already, regularly idealises political violence. As well as a profound interest in literature produced by US cultures fostered by the National Alliance, and South African white supremacism, Mair was interested in other terrorists as well. For example, police evidence shows that he kept press clippings related to Anders Breivik, whose attack in June 2011 led to the deaths of 77 people (see chapter 10). Breivik would be another who would fit Pantucci's 'loner' category.

It is important to stress that Mair also had many opportunities to become more involved in extremist groups, but seems to have rejected this type of engagement. Journalist enquiries painted a picture of a man who was disassociated from organisations, though it remains open to question whether those interviewed would want to admit publicly whether they had a more sustained engagement with Mair. Alan Harvey of the Springbok Club, which published a letter by Mair in 1991, claimed that Mair sent the group a small amount of money, but that they had never met (Corbin et al 2016). Similarly, Mair's purchasing of materials form the National Alliance in 1999 suggests a one-way relationship with a larger group. There were a number of extreme-right organisations active in the West Yorkshire region from the early 1990s to 2016. It was an area where the British National Party had a strong support base in the 2000s, and was where the English Defence League and its more extreme, overtly neo-Nazi offshoot the Infidels, had been present since 2009. Moreover, various openly neo-Nazi groups, such as the British Movement, the National Front and National Action, had all been active in the area. Other extreme-right lone actors had even been based in the locality. For example, in

2010, Terence Gavan, a former member of the BNP, was given an 11-year sentence for making improvised explosive devices (*BBC News* 2010). Also, in the 1990s, Paul Jeffries ran a British outpost of the National Alliance, and lived about a mile away from Mair. Questions have been raised as to whether Mair had any links with this group. As Nick Lowles, of the anti-fascist activist group HOPE Not Hate put it, "It is difficult to believe that he wrote off to the American organisation without having contact with its UK leader who lived just down the road" (Lowles 2016). Yet despite such speculation, little clear evidence points to Mair being linked in a sustained way with other groups.

Raffaello Pantucci also helped to lead the major RUSI research project on European lone actors, mentioned above, and his analysis included commentary on the role of online radicalisation. The extreme-right has been a prolific innovator in the use of online spaces. Other experts on the extreme-right have also been increasingly concerned with this arena. Chip Berlet has highlighted how activists such as Tom Metzger pioneered the use of bulletin boards from the mid-1980s, using his Commodore 64 computer (Berlet and Mason 2015), while Don Black created the widely used message board site Stormfront as early as 1995 (Beirich 2014). RUSI's analysis highlighted that extreme-right lone actors often posted details of their attacks online before an incident, which underscored how the online space had been crucial to their radicalisation. Others, including Michael Whine (2013), have also highlighted the crucial role now played by online environments for extreme-right political violence and terrorist radicalisation, while Gill has also stressed the on-going relevance of offline learning (Gill et al 2017). Reflecting on this issue also helps in thinking about the extent to which Mair created relationships with others.

Mair seems to have constructed his ideology without using the Internet, during the 1990s, though in recent years he did also use a computer. He was not a user of social media sites, and so again his online footprint suggests a one-way relationship with online material. He did not own his own computer either, and only used one at a public library. Here, Mair browsed a number of websites that underscore his interests of neo-Nazi and white supremacist themes, alongside political violence. His Internet history in the months before the attack included searches on the British Nationalist Party website, and in the days leading up to the attack he also searched for details on the Waffen

SS, the Ku Klux Klan and the murder of Ian Gow, who prior to Jo Cox was the last British Member of Parliament to be assassinated—in an IRA bomb attack in 1990. As well as researching his target online, and even the topic of matricide, Mair's Internet activity shows that he used the Internet to find out how to use his weapon, a .22 sawn off rifle. Unlike some lone actors who have had previous military experience, Mair was not expert in handling weapons. To help him, he watched a short online film giving instructions on how to use his chosen weapon (Wheatstone and Lion 2016).

This issue of the weapon links to a final element of the case that remains unclear: how Mair actually acquired the gun he used in the attack. The weapon had been stolen in August 2015 from the back of a vehicle, though West Yorkshire Police are still unclear on how Mair was able to lay his hands on the gun. Speaking on behalf of the police, Detective Superintendent David Wallen suggested it was likely to have circulated among criminal networks before falling into Mair's possession. He added that no forensic evidence established previous criminal owners, and so there remained no details on how Mair came into possession of the weapon. Investigation also included examination of Mair's mobile phone records, which also offered no answers and again pointed to a highly solitary man (Myall 2017).

Based on the evidence available, Mair appeared as a 'loner'. If he had closer relations with others or groups, as yet undocumented, perhaps in order to acquire the weapon, he could then be classified as a 'lone actor', according to Pantucci's model. What this categorisation as a 'loner' tells reveals is that, despite acting alone and in a self-directed way, many crucial contributing elements of his violence still came from a much broader extremist milieu. This is a culture that may not always be talking openly about terrorist attacks, but is one that often reinforces the grievances, deep distrust of wider society, and gives licence to a sense of urgency that 'something needs to be done', all of which helped to radicalise Mair. In his writings romanticising the idea of the 'lone wolf', Metzger explained he liked the term as it suggested a clear distinction between isolated figures acting independently, and ideologically similar organisations that needed to appear legitimate in order to develop sustained activity. Whichever of Pantucci's categories best describes Mair in the light of new evidence, it is important to explain that Metzger's mythology around the lone wolf as a truly isolated figure is not correct. Despite Mair's relationship with the wider extreme-right milieu being primarily one-way, he was powerfully influenced by this culture and his relationship to it played a central role in shaping his act of terrorism.

Conclusion

Thomas Mair exemplifies many typical elements of extreme-right lone actor terrorism, yet he remains a unique example of the phenomenon. This chapter has examined how such acts of terrorism may be analysed, and offers some general conclusions on issues of managing ongoing risks presented by such figures. This discussion is necessarily tentative, pointing to avenues that need further research. Clearly, there are no simple solutions to detecting, or preventing, such acts of lone actor terrorism. Moreover, as highlighted by figures who specialise in CVE (Countering Violent Extremism) work, tackling issues of extreme political violence from the extreme-right also relates to wider challenges of managing other forms of criminality, such as hate crimes, that emerge from this milieu (Ramalingam 2014). Relevant risks may be examined through three key areas, namely the ideological milieu of a lone actor, the long- and short-term factors feeding into the process of radicalisation, and also their relationships with a wider network of likeminded activists.

Regarding the role of ideology, although the types of material Mair used to develop his world-view were esoteric, they were also relatively easy to acquire via mail order. Some of this material even consisted of legitimate academic texts, while other elements were produced by groups steeped in the promotion of violence, such as the US-based National Alliance. Mair was also able to acquire such materials with limited access to the Internet, demonstrating online environments are only one way to find ideological material. While clearly impossible to prevent people from accessing all the material Mair found relevant, some possibilities emerge for controlling availability and access. The acceptability for mainstream media organisations to disseminate material is one example (see Internet, Social Media, and Related Strategies in chapter 14). In a pre-Internet age, a high street newsagent would not sell far-right publications, yet mainstream Internet companies do disseminate such material. However, attitudes are slowly changing. For example, after the Charlottesville far-right violence in August 2017, Internet service providers are becoming more reluctant to host such websites as the *Daily Stormer*, while social media companies such as *Twitter* ended 2017 by removing accounts of vocal extreme-right activists. Similarly, greater social and political pressures are being put on social media companies to stop disseminating extreme-right material. Online bookshops selling extremist literature, such as Holocaust denial texts, are also now under similar pressure. Narrowing of access to mainstream online spaces may well force more extreme-right activity to be conducted on the dark net, which is not what extremist groups want. They want their material to be as accessible and as normalised as possible.

However, strategies such as restricting online dissemination, and better education to develop in society critical skills to reject extremist propaganda, are unlikely to eliminate extreme-right ideology. It will still appeal to some people who are vulnerable to such polarised messages, and Mair's case shows that people are still able to access extremist materials regardless of the Internet.

Moreover, exposure to ideology alone does not explain radicalisation. Non-ideological factors that feed into a process of radicalisation, both long-term and short-term, suggest additional ways to manage risks posed by lone actors. As Mair's case highlights, lone actors are real, complex people. Their grievances, which become articulated in the language of an extremist ideology, are often rooted in non-ideological issues relating to much wider social issues such as housing, rehabilitating offenders, and managing chronic mental health issues. Potentially, Mair's long-term mental health conditions, and on-going sense of social isolation, could have been addressed differently, and this might have stopped him becoming so frustrated with the world around him that he turned to terrorism.

Potential solutions emerge, such as giving professionals who are likely to encounter people on a potential pathway to radicalisation greater training and awareness of extreme-right cultures. Professionals may then be able to better identify and help such individuals before they veer into criminality. Such territory is potentially fraught with controversy, and those working with vulnerable people, such as doctors or social workers engaging with people with mental health conditions or longstanding distrust of authorities, need to engage with such interventions with great care. The key point is to recognise that those drawn to lone actor terrorism are often vulnerable people before they become terrorists. Interventions might involve e.g. more supportive treatment of an underlying mental health condition, or finding ways of making someone's life more stable and less socially isolated. The Prevent agenda in the UK (Thomas 2012) or other strategies may also be relevant. However, one issue in Britain that also applies elsewhere is that more is needed to raise the skills of relevant professionals to better understand the nature of extreme-right cultures, to a level comparable with the efforts for fostering a deeper understanding of Islamist terrorist violence—a point made forcefully by Koehler (2016) and others.

Finally, good monitoring and intelligence about extreme-right networks, and criminal prosecution where warranted, remain important. In Mair's case, although he only developed one-way relationships with extreme-right groups, he was still able to acquire their extremist material so instrumental in his radicalisation. Some members of extreme-right groups such as National Action (proscribed under British terrorism legislation, in part for celebrating Mair's own terrorism) have been prosecuted for plotting other political assassinations, as well as for celebrating Mair himself (Allen 2017 and see chapter 4).

While unique, Mair's case should be seen as instructive more generally about threats posed by the extreme-right in fostering terrorism. In summary, risks relating to lone actor Alt-Right terrorism are identified as:

Risk 1. Exposure to right-wing extremist material

Ready availability of and access to inflammatory material (on-line, printed, mail order, video etc) promoting extremist right-wing ideology.

Risk 2. Vulnerable individuals susceptible to radicalisation

Vulnerable individuals characterised by social isolation, grievances, blaming classes of others, personality disorders, and mental ill-health who are potentially susceptible to right-wing radicalisation and extremism.

Risk 3. Poor preparation for professionals to detect and deter vulnerable individuals early

Inadequate monitoring and intelligence systems for professionals (e.g. doctors, health workers, social workers, police) to recognize risks early and deflect vulnerable individuals away from right-wing radicalisation and extremism.

References

Allen, C. 2017. "Proscribing National Action: Considering the Impact of Banning the British Far-Right Group". *The Political Quarterly* 88/4, 652–659.

Bale, J. 2018. *The Darkest Side of Politics, I: Postwar Fascism, Covert Operations and Terrorism*. Abingdon: Routledge.

BBC News. 2016. "Thomas Mair: Extremist loner who targeted Jo Cox", November 23, 2016. http://www.bbc.co.uk/news/uk-38071894 (accessed December 18, 2017).

BBC News. 2010. "Bomb Cache Bus Driver Gavan 'Obsessed with Weapons'", January 15, 2010. http://news.bbc.co.uk/1/hi/uk/8462205.stm (accessed December 18, 2017).

Beirich, H. 2014. *White Homicide Worldwide*. Montgomery, Al: Southern Poverty Law Centre. https://www.splcenter.org/sites/default/files/d6_legacy_files/downloads/publication/white-homicide-worldwide.pdf (accessed December 18, 2017).

Berlet, C. and Mason, C. 2015. "Swastikas in Cyberspace". In *Digital Media Strategies of the Far Right in Europe and the United States*, edited by Patricia Anne Simpson and Helga Druxes. Maryland: Lexington Books.

Burgis, T. 2016. "Thomas Mair: The Making of a Neo-Nazi Killer". *Financial Times*, November 23, 2016. https://www.ft.com/mair (accessed December 18, 2017).

Cobain, I. and Taylor, M. 2016. "Far-right Terrorist Thomas Mair Jailed for Life for Jo Cox Murder". *The Guardian*, November 23, 2016, available at: https://www.theguardian.com/uk-news/2016/nov/23/thomas-mair-found-guilty-of-jo-cox-murder (accessed December 18, 2017).

Corbin, I., Parveen, N. and Taylor, M. 2016. "The Slow-Burning Hatred that Led Thomas Mair to Murder Jo Cox". *The Guardian*, November 23, 2016, available at: https://www.theguardian.com/uk-news/2016/nov/23/thomas-mair-slow-burning-hatred-led-to-jo-cox-murder (accessed December 18, 2017).

CPS. 2017. "Thomas Mair Convicted of the Murder of Jo Cox MP". Crown Prosecution Service, available at: https://www.cps.gov.uk/news/thomas-mair-convicted-murder-jo-cox-mp (accessed December 18, 2017).

Curtis, A. 2017. *"Lone Wolf" of Hate Prowls the Internet*. Anti-Defamation League. https://www.adl.org/sites/default/files/documents/assets/pdf/combating-hate/Alex-Curtis-Report.pdf. (accessed August 11, 2017).

Durham, M. 2004. "The Upward Path: Palingenesis, Political Religion and the National Alliance". *Totalitarian Movements and Political Religions*, 5/3, 454–468.

Durham, M. 2007. *White Rage: The Extreme Right and American Politics*. Abingdon: Routledge.

Evans, M. and Millward, D. 2016. "Thomas Mair: Jo Cox's Nazi-Obsessed Killer who Hid His Extreme Far-Right Views for Decades". *Daily Telegraph*, November 23, 2016. http://www.telegraph.co.uk/news/2016/11/23/thomas-mair-jo-coxs-nazi-obsessed-killer-hid-extreme-far-right/ (accessed December 18, 2017).

Gable, G. 2016. "More Questions than Answers: a Searchlight Investigation". *Searchlight Magazine*. available at: http://www.searchlightmagazine.com/2016/12/more-questions-than-answers-a-searchlight-investigation/ (accessed December 18, 2017).

Gardell, M. 2014. "Crusader Dreams: Oslo 22/7, Islamophobia, and the Quest for a Monocultural Europe". *Terrorism and Political Violence*, 26/1, 129–155.

Gill, P. 2015. *Lone-Actor Terrorism: A Behavioural Analysis*. Abingdon: Routledge.

Gill, P. and Corner, E. 2017."There and Back Again: The Study of Mental Disorder and Terrorist Involvement". *American Psychologist*, vol. 72 no. 3, 231–241.

Gill, P., Corner, E., Conway, M. et al. 2017. "Terrorist Use of the Internet by Numbers". *Criminology and Public Policy*, 16/1, 99–117.

Griffin, R. 2012. *Terrorist Creed: Fanatical Violence and the Human Need for Meaning*. Basingstoke: Palgrave.

Higgens, D. and Murphy, A. 2016. "Thomas Mair: the Far-Right Extremist who Murdered MP Jo Cox". *The Independent*, November 23, 2016. http://www.independent.co.uk/news/uk/crime/thomas-mair-guilty-tommy-verdict-jo-cox-mp-murder-trial-court-latest-quiet-neighbour-a7434011.html (accessed December 18, 2017).

Jackson, P. 2011. "Solo Actor Terrorism and the Mythology of the Lone Wolf". In *Lone Wolves: Myth or Reality?* edited by Gerry Gable and Paul Jackson. 79–88. Ilford: Searchlight.

Jackson, P. and Shekhovtsov, A. (eds). 2014. *The Post-War Anglo-American Far Right: A Special Relationship of Hate*. Basingstoke: Palgrave.

Kaplan, J. 1997. "Leaderless Resistance", pages 80–95 in *Terrorism and Political Violence*, 9/3.

Kemp, A. 2006. "Ragnarök—the Coming Fall of the West", in *March of the Titans: The History of the White Race*. Burlington, Iowa: Ostara.

Koehler, D. 2016. "Right-Wing Extremism and Terrorism in Europe: Current Developments and Issues for the Future". *Prism* vol. 6, no. 2, 84–104.

Koehler, D. 2017. *Right-Wing Terrorism in the 21st Century: The "National Socialist Underground" and the History of Terror from the Far Right in Germany.* Abingdon: Routledge.

Lowles, N. 2016. "Thomas Mair: Far Right Terrorist". *Huffington Post,* November 24, 2016, available at: http://www.huffingtonpost.co.uk/nick-lowles/thomas-mair-jo-cox_b_13199436.html (accessed December 18, 2017).

McLagen, G. and Lowles, N. 2000. *Mr Evil.* London: Blake Publishing.

Metzger, T. 2017. *Laws of the Lone Wolf,* available at https://www.stormfront.org/forum/t454864/ (accessed December 18, 2017).

Michael, G. 2010. "Blueprint Fantasies: a Review and Analysis of Extremist Fiction". *Studies in Conflict and Terrorism,* 33/2 , 149–170.

Moskalenko, S. and McCauley, C. 2011. "The Psychology of Lone-Wolf Terrorism". *Counselling Psychology Quarterly,* 24/2, 115–126.

Myall, S. 2017. "Mystery of How MP Jo Cox's Killer Got His Gun Still Not Solved One Year On from Murder that Shocked Nation". *Daily Mirror,* June 12, 2017, available at: http://www.mirror.co.uk/news/uk-news/mystery-how-mp-jo-coxs-10586393 (accessed December 18, 2017).

Pantucci, R. 2011. *A Typology of Lone Wolves: Preliminary Analysis of Lone Islamist Terrorists.* London: International Centre for the Study of Radicalisation and Political Violence. http://icsr.info/wpcontent/uploads/2012/10/1302002992ICSRPaper_ATypologyofLoneWolves_Pantucci.pdf. (accessed August 11, 2017).

Porter, D.D. and LaFree, G. 2012. "Guest Editorial: Processes of Radicalization and De-radicalization". *International Journal of Conflict and Violence,* vol. 6 no. 1, 4–10.

Potok, M. 2016. "Accused British Assassin Thomas Mair Attended Racists' 2000 Meeting", available at: https://www.splcenter.org/hatewatch/2016/06/19/accused-british-assassin-thomas-mair-attended-racists-2000-meeting (accessed December 18, 2017).

Ramalingam, V. 2014. *Old Threat New Approach: Tackling the Far Right Across Europe: Guide for Policy Makers.* London: Institute for Strategic Dialogue. https://www.isdglobal.org/ISD_New_Approach_Far_Right_Report.pdf (accessed December 18, 2017).

Shekhovtsov, A. 2017. *The Transnational Lone-Wolf Terrorist,* available at: https://www.opendemocracy.net/od-russia/anton-shekhovtsov/transnational-lone-wolf-terrorist (accessed December 18, 2017).

Slawson, N. 2016. "Jo Cox Murder Accused Gives Name as 'Death to Traitors, Freedom for Britain'". *The Guardian,* June 18, 2016, available at: https://www.theguardian.com/uk-news/2016/jun/18/jo-cox-murder-suspect-thomas-mair-told-police-he-was-political-activist (accessed December 18, 2017).

Slawson, N. 2017. " 'A True Hero': Bernard Kenny, Stabbed Trying to Protect Jo Cox, Dies Aged 79". *The Guardian.* August 15, 2017, available at: https://www.theguardian.com/politics/2017/aug/15/a-true-hero-bernard-kenny-stabbed-trying-protect-jo-cox-dies-aged-79 (accessed December 18, 2017).

Sommers, J. 2016. "Jo Cox Murderer Thomas Mair: How Nazi Propaganda Turned a Loner into a White Supremacist". *Huffington Post* November 23, 2016, available at: http://www.huffingtonpost.co.uk/entry/jo-cox-murderer-thomas-mair-how-nazi-propaganda-inspired-a-quiet-solitary-man-to-kill-her_uk_58357f47e4b0ddedcf5b92ee (accessed December 18, 2017).

Spaaij, R. 2011. *Understanding Lone Wolf Terrorism: Global Patterns, Motivations and Prevention.* London: Springer.

SPLC. 2016. "Alleged Killer of British MP Was a Long-Time Supporter of the Neo-Nazi National Alliance", June 16, 2016, available at: https://www.splcenter.org/hatewatch/2016/06/16/alleged-killer-british-mp-was-longtime-supporter-neo-nazi-national-alliance (accessed December 18, 2017).

SPLC. 2017. *Tom Metzger.* Southern Poverty Law Center., https://www.splcenter.org/fighting-hate/extremist-files/individual/tom-metzger. (accessed August 11, 2017).

Thomas, P. 2012. *Responding to the Threat of Violent Extremism: Failing to Prevent.* London: Bloomsbury.

van Zuijdewijn, JdR. and Bakker, E. 2016. *Personal Characteristics of Lone-Actor Terrorists.* London: Royal United Services Institute., http://www.strategicdialogue.org/wp-content/uploads/2016/03/CLAT-Series-5-Policy-Paper-1-ICCT.pdf. (accessed August 11, 2017).

Wheatstone, R. and Lion, P. 2016. "Jo Cox 'killer' Thomas Mair Collected Nazi Memorabilia and Kept Third Reich Eagle Swastika Ornament on Bookcase", *Daily Mirror,* November 21, 2016, available at: http://www.mirror.co.uk/news/uk-news/jo-cox-killer-thomas-mair-9304223 (accessed December 18, 2017).

Whine, M. 2013."Trans-European Trends in Right-Wing Extremism". In *Varieties of Right-Wing Extremism in Europe,* edited by Andrea Mammone, Emmanuelle Godin and Brian Jenkins. London: Routledge.

Chapter 6: The Austrian Freedom Party

By Ruth Wodak and Markus Rheindorf

Abstract

This chapter traces the history of the Austrian extreme-right since 1945 and the rise of the *Freiheitliche Partei Österreichs (FPÖ)*, especially its conversion to an extreme-right ethno-nationalist party since 2008. While the party's misogynist, anti-intellectual, anti-modern, and anti-cosmopolitan character has been partly masked, its openly anti-Semitic, anti-Muslim and anti-immigrant ideology has remained. FPÖ's lack of success within previous coalition governments has been tempered by the larger Austrian People's Party (ÖVP) currently absorbing many FPÖ policies, thereby normalising them within the political mainstream. The adverse impacts of FPÖ ideology on freedom of speech, press freedom, immigrants, and other minorities are discussed. Risks are systematically identified.

Key words: FPÖ, Austria, ethno-nationalism, extreme-right, normalisation, risks

Right-Wing Ethno-Nationalism

The Austrian 'Freedom Party' (*Freiheitliche Partei Österreichs* or *FPÖ*) must be distinguished from other populist far-right parties, not only in some of its ideological positions but in terms of its history and continuous ties to National Socialism, as well as its fascist, racist and anti-Semitic, white-supremacist ideology.[1] Indeed, one might consider labelling the party nowadays as extreme-right, owing to some of its ide-

1 Amongst the vast literature on the FPÖ, see, for example, Forchtner et al. (2013); Wodak (2013a; 2013b; 2015; 2016; 2017); Scharsach (2017); Köhler and Wodak (2012); Wodak and Köhler (2010); Pelinka and Wodak (2002); Wodak and Pelinka (2002); Wodak and Reisigl (2002); Ötsch (2000); Ötsch and Horaczek (2017); Reisigl (2002); Reisigl and Wodak (2000; 2001); Ottomeyer (2000); Krzyżanowski and Wodak (2009) and Lehner (2018).

ological characteristics as well as specific members who belong to extreme-right duelling fraternities (see below). Although this chapter is not the place to discuss issues of terminology in detail, the authors would argue that there is a continuum reaching from right-wing populist one-issue parties, such as the Dutch PVV (see chapter 9), to extreme-right parties which continue to endorse fascist beliefs and symbols. Hence, other labels such as far-right or Alt-Right might also be applied.

Among these relevant terms, the concept of "ethno-nationalism" put forward by Jens Rydgren in his preface to the *Handbook of the Radical Right* captures some core elements of the FPÖ. Indeed, Rydgren contended that the term "right-wing populism" is obsolete; instead, parties labelled as such should be seen as "ethno-nationalist" parties that *also* feature a populist element:

> "Radical right parties and movements share an emphasis on ethno-nationalism rooted in myths about the past. Their programs are directed toward strengthening the nation by making it more ethnically homogenous and—for most radical right-wing parties and movements—by returning to traditional values. They also tend to be populists, accusing elites of putting internationalism ahead of the nation and of putting their own narrow self-interest and various special interests ahead of the interests of the people". (Rydgren 2017, 1–3)

Rydgren went on to argue that in contrast to such ethno-nationalist parties, extreme-right parties are characterized by their rejection of democracy and its institutions. However, Rydgren conceded, the boundaries between ethno-nationalist and extreme-right parties sometimes blur (for a similar argument, see de Cleen 2017, 8).

All far-right parties that also fall into the ethno-nationalist category propagate a particular imaginary of the *Volk*. This they share with the extreme-right, imagining the *Volk* as ideal male and female bodies whose roles and clearly delineated relationship constitute the foundation of the nation state and should therefore be protected at all costs. This conviction was once part and parcel of fascist (and National-Socialist) discourses in the imaginary of the *Volkskörper*, a national body constructed as a threatened and, indeed, compromised body that must be protected and restored. In the FPÖ, this body is further ethnicized by linking Austrian identity to a pan-German nationalist identity that goes back to National-Socialist ideology and before (e.g. Bailer 2013).

This chapter begins by tracing the history of the extreme-right in the Second Republic of Austria, i.e. post-WWII, to provide some relevant historical context. Continuities and recent permutations of extreme-right ideologies in the intertextual and interdiscursive relationships across genres and publics are then revealed through analyzing some of the utterances and performances of the FPÖ and their historical continuities with National Socialist rhetoric and imaginaries.

The Extreme-Right in Austria Since 1945: Tracing the History of the FPÖ

The history of the 'Freedom Party of Austria' or FPÖ dates back to the early years after World War II and the political situation created and maintained by the four post-war Allied Powers that liberated Austria from Nazi-occupation in 1945. The temporary occupation and partition of Austria enabled them to retain control until 1955, when the '*Staatsvertrag*' (State Treaty) marked the so-called 'rebirth of the Austrian Republic' and the withdrawal of Allied Forces from Austria. Between 1945 and 1955, the Allies supported the development of a bipolar political scene by encouraging (a) the cooperation of socialist-democratic movements on the left and the formation of what would evolve into today's Social Democratic Party of Austria (*Sozialdemokratische Partei Österreichs* or *SPÖ*), and (b) the merging of various right-wing, conservative and pro-clerical movements into the Austrian People's Party (*Österreichische Volkspartei* or *ÖVP*). Simultaneously, the forerunner of the FPÖ, the Association of Independents (*Verband der Unabhängigen* or *VdU*) was formed by incorporating now marginalized political movements: a vast array of "old Nazis, German nationalists, and a fair number of liberals" (Schiedel and Neugebauer 2002, 16), many if not all of whom were deliberately prevented from joining either of the two mainstream parties of the left and right. Interestingly, the VdU was created with the active support of both the SPÖ and the Austrian Communist Party (*Kommunistische Partei Österreichs* or *KPÖ*) in the hope that the new movement, i.e. "688,000 previously disenfranchised former members of the NSDAP who were allowed to vote for the first time in the 1949 parliamentary elections", would divide the bourgeois vote and thus diminish support for the conservative People's Party and thereby enhance the chances for the left (Manoschek 2002, 5).

In the 1949 parliamentary elections, the VdU won 12 percent of the national vote and soon issued the call for its main objective, i.e. "the abolition of all laws governing de-Nazification procedures" (Manoschek 2002, 7).

Following an internal crisis of the VdU, the FPÖ as its successor was established in 1955/56 "as a German nationalist party of the far right, in which former, seriously incriminated National Socialists took the leading functions" (Manoschek 2002, 6). Indeed, its first leader, Anton Reinthaller, had been a high-ranking member of the Austrian NSDAP and the SS, but had also held the position of Minister of Agriculture in the treacherous Austrian government of Seyss-Inquart in 1938. All this made the FPÖ the "successor to the Austrian NSDAP" in all but name (Manoschek 2002, 6–7).

When Friedrich Peter, another former Waffen-SS member, took over the FPÖ in 1958, the party's agenda did not change significantly. However, throughout the 1960s, the drive to moderate the FPÖ could be observed when liberal views were given voice alongside nationalist ideologies. In 1970, the newly elected Chancellor Bruno Kreisky (SPÖ) formed a minority government with the support of the FPÖ and appointed "four former NSDAP members to ministerial posts" (Schiedel and Neugebauer 2002, 17). At this juncture, the FPÖ's participation in mainstream Austrian politics was explicitly confirmed, signalling to the FPÖ "that the SPÖ, to gain power, could do business with former Nazis in a pragmatic way", which has since been frequently labelled as "necessary *Realpolitik*" in the political struggle to gain power (e.g., Wodak et al. 1990). These developments, however, did not occur without resistance from parts of the SPÖ who opposed a coalition with the FPÖ. Specifically, the disclosure of Friedrich Peter's Nazi past by Simon Wiesenthal led to an enormous mediatized scandal that was met with typical, overbearing rhetoric of justification: Kreisky defended his decision and tried to appease anti-fascist resistance in his own party, simultaneously denouncing Wiesenthal and thus playing into the hands of the FPÖ. This specific discourse of justification paved the way for explicit anti-Semitic rhetoric and related insinuations, prominently in the so-called Waldheim Affair of 1986 (Wodak et al. 1990).

In September 1986, the FPÖ's national convention witnessed an internal coup led by the leader of the Carinthian chapter of the FPÖ—Jörg Haider—who became the new federal chairman of the party. Haider's rise to FPÖ leader marked the turn of the majority of the FPÖ to radical and nationalist/nativist views. Employing strongly anti-Semitic, anti-foreigner, and revisionist slogans, Haider was a talented populist who managed to lead the FPÖ to successful elections at both federal and regional levels. In 1989, the FPÖ came second (after the ÖVP) in regional elections in Carinthia, and Haider was elected as regional governor. With the FPÖ managing for the first time to leave its seemingly perpetual third spot behind the two mainstream parties of the left and the right, the party's subsequent rise to power gained considerable momentum.

Throughout the late 1980s and the early 1990s, the nationwide anti-foreigner petitions championed by Haider's FPÖ, such as the 1989 "Declaration of St. Lorenzen", the 1992 "Austria First Petition" and the 1997 "FPÖ Party Platform", significantly increased its electoral support (Reisigl and Wodak 2002; Matouschek et al. 1995). In the parliamentary elections of October 1999, the FPÖ received an unprecedented 26.91 percent of the national vote and, for the first time in the party's history, took second place in the federal parliamentary election. After a short period of negotiations, the FPÖ signed a coalition agreement with the ÖVP and entered the federal government in early 2000. This was the first time that an extreme-right party, which had frequently expressed both coded and explicit praise for the actual National Socialist regime, its policies and ideologies, came to power in an EU member state (Wodak 2015; 2016).

Although sanctions against the Austrian government were eventually introduced by the 14 other EU member states at the time, it was not this external pressure but the controversial performance of the ÖVP-FPÖ government which pushed the FPÖ into gradual decline in the following years.[2] When the FPÖ suffered a severe defeat in elections to the European Parliament in 2004 (down to 6.3 from 23.4 percent in 1999) and then-leader Herbert Haupt was forced to resign, Haider began yet another comeback and established a new party called the Union for the Future of Austria (*Bündnis Zukunft Österreichs* or *BZÖ*). The national parliamentary elections of October 2006 marked a considerable defeat for both FPÖ-originated political group-

---

2 Indeed, such external pressure seemed to rally support behind the government, whose leading figures called for a "*nationaler Schulterschluss*", i.e. national closing of ranks, casting the EU sanctions as foreign attempts to influence or even dictate Austria's internal affairs.

ings. The FPÖ (now headed by Heinz-Christian Strache, a former confidante of Haider) and the BZÖ (headed by Haider himself) only managed to gain a combined 15.1 percent of the national vote.

Following a (typically) long period of negotiations, neither far-right movement became part of the new Austrian government, formed in early 2007 and headed by the SPÖ. And thus, after eight years in government, the far-right of Austria returned to its oppositional role, in which it remained until 2017 when—for a second time—a coalition between the ÖVP and the FPÖ was established, after the national election October 15, 2017. In this election, the ÖVP under its new leader Sebastian Kurz received 31.5 percent of the votes and came first, while the FPÖ came third, with 26 percent of the votes, the SPÖ having won 26.9 percent (Bundesministerium für Inneres 2017).

After Haider's sudden death in October 2008[3], the BZÖ gradually dwindled into electoral insignificance; the FPÖ, on the other hand, now led by H.-C. Strache, successfully used a vast array of populist performative strategies, some of them well-established rhetorical moves associated with Haider and some new strategies shared by populist parties across Europe and beyond. Significantly, the re-branded FPÖ worked very hard to present itself as a non-ideological common-sense movement, seeking to obscure both that it had been long part of the political establishment in Austria and that it continued to follow a clear xenophobic, anti-EU and anti-immigration agenda (Wodak 2015). The misogynist, anti-intellectual, anti-modern, and anti-urban or anti-cosmopolitan aspects of its agenda were pushed even more to the background in most public performances, while continuing to inform their underlying ideology in unadulterated form.

However, after a new government formed on December 18, 2017, frequent scandals related to anti-Semitic and revisionist documents disrupted the everyday agenda of the government. This included *Facebook* postings, as well as songbooks of extreme-right duelling fraternities from which the FPÖ recruited not just members but also leading figures of the party who became government ministers or their aides (critical and investigative journalists played a key role in this; see, e.g., *Der Falter* 4/18, January 23, 2018). It seems as if the ÖVP

---

3 Haider had a fatal car accident after having sped through a village, during the night and drunk, after leaving a gay club. After his death, conspiracy theories abounded, claiming that oppositional parties, Mossad, the Slovenes, or other alleged enemies of Haider had caused his death.

in its streamlined, strategically planned trajectory to power in the form of leading the new government had either ignored or quietly accepted the kind of ideologues they had aligned themselves with. For the purposes of this chapter, it should be noted that the FPÖ had certainly changed since 2007; it became obvious (Scharsach 2017; Bailer 2013) that the programmatic elites in the FPÖ were stemming increasingly from the extreme-right and were overwhelmingly based in German-nationalist duelling fraternities. This conclusion is also substantiated by the ideological orientation of the FPÖ's party program and other publications analyzed below.

This brief history of the far-right, as established in political organizations in the Second Austrian Republic, clearly indicates that radical right-wing parties were not successful when part of the government; their success in opposition seems to be deeply rooted in their "campaign habitus".[4] However, this might change with the current black-blue government, even if the first few months of the new government in 2018 revealed the same and thus predictable problems as before: On the one hand, today's FPÖ attempts to act "softer" while frontstage, but these discursive shifts are continuously disrupted by scandals related to extreme-right, anti-Semitic and xenophobic agenda and statements. The ÖVP, on the other hand, has appropriated many policies formerly suggested by the FPÖ (e.g., FPÖ-Bildungsinstitut 2013), thus arguably reducing tensions between the government coalition partners at least on the level of actual policy. In this way, the overt agenda of the FPÖ have become normalized into the political mainstream and, simultaneously if less clearly delineated, into popular culture at large (Wodak 2015b; 2017; 2018; Krzyżanowski 2013; Krzyżanowski and Ledin 2017; Rheindorf and Wodak 2018).

The Contemporary Extreme-Right in Austria

In the following, salient examples of the FPÖ's backstage (covert) and frontstage (overt) performances are presented across a range of different genres. Firstly, looking behind closed doors, some utterances

---

4 Of course, contemporary Polish, Turkish, US, and Hungarian governments illustrate that once such parties gain majorities, they will systematically attempt to discredit, curtail or even dismantle democratic institutions; authoritarian tendencies become manifest, particularly in attempts to censor media and independent courts.

by Johann Gudenus, vice-mayor of Vienna and currently party whip of the FPÖ in parliament are analyzed. Then, close attention is paid to key dimensions of the FPÖ's recent programmatic publications and, finally, illustrative analyses of slogans and posters from recent election campaigns are provided.

Recontextualising Extreme-Right Ideology: from Closed-Door Meetings to Handbooks

Arguably, no public figure represents extreme-right ideology within the FPÖ better than Johann Gudenus, head of the FPÖ's Vienna chapter and, since 2015, also non-acting Deputy Mayor of Vienna. Gudenus is prominent among the academically educated figures in the FPÖ, having studied law in Vienna and Russian in Moscow, and also completed an MA at the Diplomatic Academy of Vienna. He has maintained excellent relations with Russia, has vocally opposed EU's sanctions against Russia, and has endorsed an extremely sceptical stance towards the EU. Gudenus, whose father was convicted of Holocaust denial, is well-known as one of the authors of the FPÖ's programmatic agenda; moreover, his explicitly racist, nativist, anti-Semitic, and homophobic utterances at the party's more private meetings and activities have frequently been leaked to the press, causing scandals.

Addressing closed publics, Gudenus has often voiced ideological positions in no uncertain terms. This has included the call for racial purity policies for Europe such as the following: "Europe is the cradle of the white race. We demand a Europe-wide, coordinated policy for the family and reproduction, including a commitment to the fact that Europe is white." It has included defamation of political opponents with anti-Semitic slurs: "If you mix red and green together, you get yellow. And yellow is the colour of Judas, it is the colour of treachery." It has also included a blatant denial of basic human rights ("Asylum is not a human right") as well as homophobic, conspiracy theory-based evocations of a threatened or, alternatively, doomed nation: "The powerful European lobby of homosexuals wants absolute equality for homosexuals and lesbians. It is hard to imagine where all this will lead." Due to his high-ranking position in Austrian politics, Gudenus' more public appearances directly re-contextualize backstage agenda into frontstage performances and policies. Should the FPÖ win the next Viennese election in 2019 (opinion polls in early 2018 put the party at 32%), Gudenus may become the next Mayor of Vienna (see Pollak 2015 for more details and the specific references of the quoted utterances).

Gudenus' utterances bear a strong resemblance to the party-affiliated publication "*Für ein freies Österreich*" [For a Free Austria], written by local FPÖ politician Michael Howanietz in 2013. Albeit not officially party doctrine, the book closely mirrors the "*Handbuch freiheitlicher Politik*", the "handbook" of FPÖ politics drafted by the party leadership to serve as a guideline for party functionaries regarding key policy areas, containing many talking points and arguments related to key positions. Our focus here is on the former publication as it constitutes a less constrained articulation of extreme-right ideologies, free of the rhetorical limitations that even the FPÖ, as an established party, must follow in its frontstage politics.

"For a Free Austria" is elevated to representative status by endorsing forewords from the FPÖ's chairman, Strache, and vice-chairman and presidential candidate in 2016, Norbert Hofer. The text defines itself as a call for "an autonomous, independent country" (Howanietz 2013, 54), which the book frankly elaborates as meaning independent of international law, transnational organizations, the international economy at large, and specifically the international exchange of goods (both export and import). These aspects are all identified and discussed as pernicious ways in which Austria is being controlled by others, especially foreign elites, keying into a strong populist element in the FPÖ. Significantly, the various argumentative strands of the book—all ultimately intended to help save Austria from imminent doom—are linked to the extreme-right's constructions of the national body, for the book calls for "an independent country that depends on its many existent strengths, its Nature, its infrastructure, and the productive power of its people" (Howanietz 2013, 7). The compound terms "*fremdbestimmt*" [determined by others] and "*fremdverfügt*" [decided by others], like so many others in the book, incorporate the "Other" or "Foreign" ("*Fremde*") as a perceived controlling agency external to and inimical to "the people" ("*Volk*") of Austria. This "Other" is largely identified as the EU and metonymized as "Brussels", but a closer look reveals that in specific instances a wide range of actors are identified as enemies of the people: the international food, clothes and pharma industries, the Austrian government, the left, the mainstream, the media, feminists, and non-government organizations. The book thus seeks to link a wide variety of criticism—which, in the concrete instance, may indeed be justified—to an overall international conspiracy against the Austrian nation and its people. The actual corporations, for instance, are never named, and thus the scapegoat remains vague except for the EU, the supposed political establishment and elite, as well as the mainstream media.

Significantly, the book relates this conspiracy to the national body as "state territory" and its "borders", to the national body as "landscape and Nature", and to the national body as "the core family" and "procreation". Indeed, the call for "liberation" from foreign dependency is presented as a duty to "our children", especially of men to their families: "We owe it to those who come after us, our children" (Howanietz 2013, 7). The book is also abundantly clear about the relationship between identity and the nation: "The nation, once the main carrier of identity, has been replaced by societies and clubs and brands, weak prosthetics for the true belonging of national identity" (Howanietz 2013, 15). Such true belonging or "*Heimat*" supposedly still exists in the country and rural areas, the "heartland" of many right-wing populist movements, where it is assumed to be ostensibly recognizable in higher birth rates, working with one's hands as in centuries past, hardy craftsmen and "timeless values" (Howanietz 2013, 77). In this context, the book's author emphasized the spiritual and biological link of a people to the soil, the "most sacred property of the community", i.e. the nation (Howanietz 2013, 77). Equating soil and blood, to protect this "eternal *Heimat*" is thus to protect one's true self (Howanietz 2013, 141). Moreover, the reference to "blood and soil" clearly draws on Nazi ideology (Rheindorf and Wodak 2018).

In the extreme-right world-view informing Howanietz's book, which casts the modern, urban and intellectual as weak as opposed to the archaic, migrants are a threat precisely because they have stronger identities: Their "assault" or slow invasion to "demographically dis-place" the Austrian people makes the latter "a species on the brink of extinction" (Howanietz 2013, 19–20). To be modern, to include women in the workforce etc. is thus seen as a form of "self-demotion" and "self-destruction" (Howanietz 2013, 21), echoing Thilo Sarrazin's (2010) book *Deutschland schafft sich ab* [Germany Is Doing Away with Itself]. The battlefronts of this struggle are many: "It starts with a few English terms, inappropriate concessions to culturally foreign [*kulturfremde*] 'neo-Austrians' and years with a low birth-rate.

Every unborn potential mother and father of the future accelerates the process of self-annihilation" (Honwanietz 2013, 22). This, of course, links directly to attacks on legal abortion (see below) and is elaborated in the FPÖ's handbook.

Here, the argument is presented in the form of statistics: With alleged "estimates of over 50,000 abortions per year" as opposed to "76,344 births in 2009, that would mean that 4 out of 10 children are killed in their mother's womb. This would make the uterus the place with highest likelihood of death in our country" (FPÖ-Bildungsinstitut 2013, 160). This effectively attacks women's legal right to seek an abortion—until three months after conception and, beyond, only under grave threat to the physical or mental health of the pregnant woman or a serious risk that the child will be severely handicapped or if the pregnant woman was under the age of 14 at the time of conception (§ 74 of the Austrian Criminal Code)—it also constructs any such woman as "killing a child".

The gravest threat to the nation, however, is identified in decaying national pride: Honour and loyalty to the community of the nation are seen as the foundation for loyalty and faithfulness in the heterosexual relationship (Howanietz 2013, 31).[5] This makes those who would weaken nationalism also conspirators against the family: "*die Familienzerstörer*", destroyers of families. This, ultimately, defines the core of the FPÖ's current gender politics as a deeply conservative biopolitics:

> "The child needs the safety of the family. Its pillars are father and mother as positive male and female example. Both have been made deeply insecure in this self-understanding by the deliberate demolishing of the nature-given roles. Their disorientation leads to temporary relationships, because the image corresponding to the inner longing of the respective counterpart is not found. Man, who has been cast from the throne of the head of the family, still longs for a female partner who, in spite of the girls-own-the-world magazines, is still able to think in home-making categories, whose brood care drive exceeds the imposed ambitions for personal fulfilment. Woman, re-defined by feminist deconstructivist ambitions as a birth-certificate mother under the obligation to personal fulfilment still longs for a real man, who gives her all the emotional and economic securities that a young mother needs to devote herself almost without worries to her offspring". (Howanietz 2013, 32)

5 "*Ehre*" and "*Treue*", i.e. honor and loyalty, the two concepts the book praises in this context, formed the core of the SS motto "*Meine Ehre heißt Treue*", which is banned under Austrian law for its association with Nazism.

The book shamelessly uses hyperbole and strawman fallacies to drive home this point: "Because we are still permitted, without official permission, to have children and raise them as best we can. Independent of ideological approaches that want to tear away children from their parents immediately after birth" (Howanietz 2013, 34). The purported "conspiracy to brainwash children and abolish natural genders" (Howanietz 2013, 118) is seen as the cause for women wanting a career and financial independence, which in turn is seen as the cause for "many young women misrepresenting the initially desired impregnation as sexist harassment" and ignoring their "motherly brood care instincts" (Howanietz 2013, 119).

The other side of this gender politics is to denounce "effeminate" and "feminized" modern man, biologically destined to be "provider and protector of the family" (Howanietz 2013, 119). Alternative gender constructions are cast as a leftist conspiracy to undermine masculine ideals and thereby the nation's strength: "Sportsmen are the last remaining idols who may still be regarded as 'heroes', since all other traditional ideals, such as the embodiment of soldierly virtues, the ideals of chivalry, had to be sacrificed to the Zeitgeist" (Howanietz 2013, 35). Blame for this decay of traditional gender roles is placed on the left, feminists, civil society, NGOs, international organizations, corporations and, most of all, the media, which the book described as "weapons of mass destruction" when it comes to destroying the "*Volk*" (Howanietz 2013, 36–37). Finally, comparing this inner weakness to the external threat identified as migrants, the book offers two alternative prognoses for the future: The true Austrian "*Volk*" will either slowly degenerate and die off, "eaten from the inside like wasp larvae eat maggots" (Howanietz 2013, 117) or current developments will lead to a violent "civil war" (Howanietz 2013, 121). The book's author clearly preferred the latter, arguing that like any conflict it would be "productive" and "awaken potential"; either way, he concludes, "Europe will burn" (Howanietz 2013, 133–134).

The book also perpetuates attacks on the official state-media and quality press. So-called "Fake media" (while employing the German terms *"Lügenpresse"* or *"Systempresse"*, terms heavily used in Nazi propaganda to discredit first the Weimar and then international press, see Schmitz-Berning 1998, 327) is a core notion of the contemporary extreme-right in Austria.[6] It is also part of the current government's program to "reform" the media—which seems to be a euphemism for the continuous and vicious attacks on established journalists and moderators. Figure 6.1 below exemplifies such attacks by the FPÖ via social media, using the rhetorical strategy of "calculated ambivalence", which seeks to convey distinct messages to multiple audiences (e.g. the party's extreme-right base and the general public) while maintaining plausible deniability through ambiguity (Engel and Wodak 2013). In this case, the meme posted by Strache (as party leader and Vice-Chancellor of Austria) was headed by the label "satire!" and a smiling emoticon: Showing the well-known and internationally renowned journalist and moderator of the main news show of the Austrian public broadcaster *ORF* in the background to the right, the text reads "There is a place where lies become news. That is the *ORF*. The best of Fake News, lies and propaganda, pseudo-culture and involuntary fees. Regional and international. On television, radio and the *Facebook* profile of Armin Wolf."

6 For the current use of the term, see Frindte and Dietrich (2017).

Figure 6.1: ***Facebook* posting by Heinz-Christian Strache on February 13, 2018**

At the time of writing, both Armin Wolf and the *ORF* have sued Vice-Chancellor Strache and a court of law has given a preliminary cease-and-desist order. Meanwhile, the FPÖ has continued to publicly campaign for the downsizing or privatization of the *ORF*, while in the background pressure on editors and journalists has been increased.

The Extreme-Right in Election Campaigns

After Heinz-Christian Strache took control of the FPÖ in 2005, frontstage activities of the party—particularly in election campaigns and social media—saw a softening of extreme-right positions and an increase of salient mobilization of the symbols of banal nationalism (Billig 1995): displaying the Austrian flag, singing the national anthem, and showing an abundance of other symbols of national pride.

In terms of national identity, these symbols are linked to deeply conservative constructions of the national body, e.g. pristine landscapes, snow-covered mountain tops, skiing, traditional agriculture and farmers, religious symbols of Christianity. In many instances, the respective texts and performances feature Strache himself wielding these symbols (see Figure 6.2), portraying the FPÖ politicians dressed as brave, strong and skilled mountain climbers who have been able to climb to the very mountain top.

Figure 6.2: Vilimsky (Party Secretary), Strache, Gudenus and Kickl (former Party Secretary) brandishing the Austrian flag at the Grossglockner peak, Austria's highest mountain (Strache 2017)

Figure 6.3: Still from the FPÖ's alternative anthem and campaign song during the presidential election 2016 (FPÖ 2016)

Since these are all symbols of the state rather than any particular political party, their re-contextualization and re-semiotization by the FPÖ constitutes a provocative appropriation linked to the FPÖ's claim to be the only party to represent 'the people' and the nation or 'Heimat'. Indeed, with Strache's leadership came a re-branding of the FPÖ as the "*Soziale Heimatpartei*", the Social Homeland Party (a label it shares with the extreme-right NPD of Germany). Two such provocations relate to Austria's national anthem: (1) publicly refusing to sing the amended national anthem (since 2011, the lyrics include "daughters" alongside "sons"), thus breaking the relevant law; (2) using an alternative anthem for their campaigns, titled "*Immer wieder Österreich*". The lyrics of this song incorporate the well-established chorus of soccer fans at games of Austria's national team—"*Immer wieder, immer wieder, immer wieder Österreich*" [Time and again, time and again, time and again Austria]—but also appeal to the "honesty, righteousness and loyalty" of all true Austrians and call on them to "pledge" their loyalty to "their country". The accompanying video also re-semiotizes the lyrics of the actual Austrian anthem and alludes to the aesthetics of infamous Nazi era films, e.g. Leni Riefenstahl's work, emphasizing mountains, streams, and other aspects of the national body: white men and women, industry in the form of hammers, agriculture in the form of fields, see Figure 6.3 above.[7] In this image, the traditional trope of a blonde female farmer dressed in a Dirndl, the Austrian folkloric dress which has been emphasized in many films and pictures by Austro-fascists and Nazis, walking over the fields to harvest corn, draws attention not only to the landscape but also to manual labour, and more specifically to the importance of farming and the "soil".

Further notable provocations pertaining to the national body concern the use of religious imagery and symbols as well as the redefinition of religious concepts, e.g. "*Nächstenliebe*" [neighborly love or charity]. The accompanying claims to represent and "defend" the Christian heritage of Austria in the face of an alleged Islamic invasion have been protested by the Catholic Church. Indeed, the Austrian far- and extreme-right's 'othering' has come to focus strongly on religion,

---

7 See Pages, Rhiel and Majer O'Sickey (2008) for discussion of Leni Riefenstahl's work and her aesthetics which is uniquely associated with National Socialist propaganda in film.

i.e. Islam. In this opposition, the self is largely culturalized ("Christian-Judean culture") and may even be secularized ("European Enlightenment") or Europeanized ("European values"), whereas the Other is cast as an ethnic other, medieval/pre-modern/barbaric, and religious zealot/fanatic or terrorist threat (Wodak 2017, 116–137; Wodak 2015, 125–190.). To provide two salient examples of the links constructed by the FPÖ between religious imagery and the national body: (1) At a rally for the 2015 Vienna elections, Gudenus described the ringing of the "Pummerin", the prominent church bell of Vienna's St. Stephen's Cathedral, as the "heartbeat of Austria" (October 8, 2015). (2) A poster shown at the Dutch right-wing populist Geert Wilders' visit to the FPÖ visualized this threat as the violated national body, coded in the flag colours red-white-red and wounded by the spear-like minarets of mosques (see Figure 6.4 below). This image must be recognized as the re-contextualisation of an infamous poster of the Swiss People's Party (Betz 2013; Kallis 2013).

Figure 6.4: The wounded national body: Geert Wilders visits the FPÖ [Europe's threat from Islamisation] (Ichner 2015)

Such discursive strategies of anthropomorphizing, culturalizing and ethnicizing the national body go back many years. Indeed, the frontstage politics of the extreme-right in Austria are eminently culturalist and biologist (Köhler and Wodak 2012). Such constructions depend on emphasizing the inner homogeneity of the Austrian people or '*Volk*' (we/ "*wir*" and you/ "*Ihr, Euch*"), while highlighting its difference to other nations and peoples. In contrast to recently more mitigated rhetoric, the posters in Figure 6.5 below show the aggressive tone of FPÖ campaigns in the past. Their slogans, using very simple rhymes, always pit a positively represented "we" against a negatively presented "them" (see Wodak and Köhler; Köhler and Wodak) and position the FPÖ on the side of "the people". In these specific cases, from left to right, the Other is variously internal (the SPÖ, rewarding laziness rather than "honest work") and external ("asylum fraud", and unnamed Other threatening "our children" and "us Austrians", "Islam" as a threat to "home", "traitors in the EU" and migrants speaking bad German). In all of them, the slogans "We for You" and "Because He believes in You" seek to position the FPÖ as the party of the true Volk.

Figure 6.5: Election campaign posters used by the FPÖ in 2008 and 2010

Despite the focus on "islamization"—and despite the fallacious claim that the FPÖ are "the new Jews" or being persecuted (part of an ongoing strategy to present the FPÖ as the victim of the political establishment and mainstream media, see Stögner 2016)—anti-Semitism remains part of extreme-right discourse. While this is usually coded (e.g. "the east coast" as code for a Jewish conspiracy[8]) on the frontstage, there are still prominent exceptions such as the '*Facebook* incident' of 2012 (Wodak 2015). An even more prominent case is Barbara Rosenkranz, former MP and FPÖ candidate for presidency in 2010, who implicitly denied the Holocaust during her campaign. Rosenkranz also published a book (Rosenkranz 2008) that lashes out against feminism and gender mainstreaming. She vocally opposes civil partnerships for homosexual couples because—she argues—the legal definition of marriage also includes the intention to have and raise children (for analyses, see Engel and Wodak 2013; Wodak 2015).

In the 2016 election campaign for presidency, the FPÖ candidate Norbert Hofer's public performances offered a toned-down version of such ideology. The campaign was organized around central notions connected to the national body and its protection: "*Heimat*" [homeland], "*Heimatliebe*" [love for the homeland], "*Sicherheit*" [security], "*Flagge zeigen*" [literally 'to show flag', German idiom for 'to show one's colors']. Indeed, the Austrian flag and its colours were dominant in his campaign (some posters showing as many as five Austrian flags in different shapes and sizes), but it also took recourse to religion and religious imagery (see Lehner 2018).

Despite notable moderation, the FPÖ's gender politics remain patriarchal: In several TV debates leading up to the presidential election in 2016, Hofer maintained that any marriage of gay or lesbian couples as well as related adoption rights would destroy 'natural family structures': "The life partnership of man and woman becomes a family only through the child. Those who raise a child on their own create a family with the children". He also voiced his rejection of gender mainstreaming: "The aim of 'gender mainstreaming' is nothing short of creating the 'new human being' that Marxists-Leninists al-

8 See the detailed analysis of the term „east coast" insinuating "the powerful Jews living in New York" in Pelinka and Wodak (2002) and Wodak et al. (1990).

ready aspired to." Like many fundamentalist US Tea Party Republicans, Hofer also rejected "pro-choice" policies for women, i.e. women's right to decide on abortion (Wodak 2015, 168).

In this context, Hofer also described "the womb as the place with the highest mortality rate in our country" (*ATV* 2016). This gendered discourse clearly attempts to govern and regulate women's bodies and minds, thus objectifying and disciplining women in a way that is characteristic of the extreme-right. In the gender politics of such ideologies, the 'national family' must preserve the traditional paternalistic order of the sexes and maintain the nation's body as white and pure (see Gudenus' statements above). This draws on conservative and fascist imaginaries as extensively investigated by Andreas Musolff (2010) and John Richardson (2017) in their research on the concept of the '*Volk*' and the '*Volkskörper*' across German and British nationalist and fascist writing since the 18th century. In summary, the Austrian extreme-right's salient construction of the national body and use of associated symbols shows a constant effort to mobilize feelings of national pride but equally of national emergency, of threat and of the need to defend, as well as to reassert gender relations as heterosexual and primarily reproductive.

Conclusion

The conceptual focus of this chapter on the FPÖ and its salient identity politics, as articulated in body and gender politics, and theorized through the notion of the national body, facilitates a clear view of the extreme-right's imaginary of a *Volkskörper* in its contemporary forms. This imaginary reveals National Socialist ideology to be in evidence not only superficially (e.g., in imagery or symbols, with the principal aim of provocation) but also as a politics of hetero-normative, procreational gender roles predicated on the ideal of national integrity as racial purity and white Christian supremacy. The *homo nationalis* is thus constructed by the Austrian far- and extreme-right as white, binary (male/female), heterosexual, (culturally) Christian and rooted (by blood) in the soil of the national body. This ideal is contrasted with a negative fantasy which constructs Austrians as compromised on all levels, colonized by "parasites" as well as ruled by (foreign, Jewish) elites, incapable of action or emancipation. From this chapter's analysis, the ideal subject of the extreme-right is constructed across many social fields and contexts, evidencing continuities from backstage politics to popular culture.

Based on such evidence, the FPÖ—as the only established party in Austria which has consistently provided a home for extreme-right, indeed even neo-Nazi, positions—is far from homogenous. The ideological positions articulated by its leading figures range from extreme-right and pan-German nationalism to toned-down positions, particularly in public. Indeed, the ability to alternate between 'strong' and 'soft' performances according to context and audience is a defining characteristic of the contemporary far-right in Austria. Both allusions to and encoded references to extreme-right and Nazi ideologies are thus part of the strategy of "calculated ambivalence" that ensures deniability (Engel and Wodak 2013; Wodak 2015; Wodak and Reisigl 2002; Klein 1971). Closely related to these strategic performances are processes of normalization, removing taboos through re-contextualization and re-semiotization as aspects of extreme-right fantasies move from backstage to frontstage and from party politics to popular culture, and back again, in a recursive dynamic.

The risks inherent in such parties coming to power, in particular governmental power, are manifold. In the Austrian context, the two governments including the FPÖ/BZÖ in the 2000s were characterized by wide-spread corruption and nepotism, some cases of which were still being prosecuted in 2018. However, the actual people who came to power through the FPÖ then were not part of the extreme-right wing of the party; this seemed to be different in the later FPÖ leadership and its members of the government heading towards the third decade of the 21st century (Scharsach 2017). The risks, as even the first few weeks after they took office showed, are rather different than 10–15 years previously. For example, there were numerous instances of them seeking to undermine high-quality media and investigative journalists, both frontstage (see above) and backstage. Policy announcements in 2018 included wide-ranging revisions of the entire code of law, cuts and restrictions for unemployment benefits and welfare (targeting EU-citizens from Eastern Europe and refugees), as well as proposals to establish camps to "concentrate refugees [sic!]" and curfews for asylum seekers. However, there continued to be risks for the FPÖ as well: The last time they were in government, the party imploded and split, eventually losing significant electoral support.

In summary, risks arising from far-right parties in general, and FPÖ in particular, gaining governmental power include:

Risks for Austrian Society and Governance

Risk 1. Divisive inequality policies

Increasing imposition of divisive inequality policies based on nationalist white supremacism, and anti-Muslim and anti-immigrant prejudices, all likely to result in multiple adverse effects for those discriminated against and a reduction in social cohesion for all.

Risk 2. Disaffection

Stirring up of discrimination, hatred, and hate crimes against ethnic, religious, and immigrant minorities in Austria, may lead to disaffection and potential backlash among those discriminated against.

Risk 3. Attacks on press freedom

Sustained attacks on the Austrian media, in particular public broadcasters, so as to reject and avoid scrutiny, may undermine press freedom and inhibit its fundamental role in ensuring public accountability in a democracy.

Risk 4: Increasing far-right support and extremism

Increasing normalisation in society of previously unacceptable far-right ideology and harsh policies, may lead to increasing support for FPÖ and other far- and extreme-right organisations, as well as acceptance of their methods. This may also lead to increased nepotism and corruption owing to lack of democratic and transparent procedures.

Risk 5: Compromised democracy in Austria

A long-term governing power bloc in Austria, comprising FPÖ and its allies, may enable them to gradually subvert the post-war consensus of liberal democracy into an 'illiberal democracy'. More specifically, the separation of powers (legislative, executive, and judicial branches) is likely to be undermined.

Risks for Individuals

Risk 1. Harm from discriminatory policies

Discriminatory far-right government policies (whether against immigrants, minorities of all kinds, the disabled, the poor, the unemployed, or any other group) are likely to violate human rights obligations, international treaties and agreements, as well as constitutional protections. Indeed, an illiberal democracy is likely to challenge these constraints on the perceived *vox populi.*

Risk 2. Freedom of expression

Increasing authoritarianism from a far-right government may result in curbs on press freedom, as well as curbs on individual freedom of expression and privacy rights.

Risks for the FPÖ

Risk 1. Hubris in government

FPÖ policies may not prove as popular in practice as in rhetoric, and the coalition between FPÖ and other nationalist-conservative parties may also prove fragile and vulnerable to fracture, thereby dissipating voter support and the FPÖ's electoral chances for a significant period.

References

ATV. 2016. Television debate hosted May 9, 2016.

Bailer, Brigitte. 2013. *Rechtsextremes im Handbuch Freiheitlicher Politik. Eine Analyse.* Wien: Dokumentationsarchiv des österreichischen Widerstandes.

Betz, Hans-Georg. 2013. "Mosques, Minarets, Burqas and Other Essential Threats: The Populist Right's Campaign against Islam in Western Europe." In *Right-wing Populism in Europe: Politics and Discourse*, edited by Ruth Wodak, Majid KhosraviNik and Brigitte Mral, 71–87. London: Bloomsbury.

Billig, Michael. 1995. *Banal Nationalism.* London: Sage

Bundesministerium für Inneres. 2017. "Nationalratswahl 2017." Accessed February 23, 2018. https://wahl17.bmi.gv.at/

de Cleen, Benjamin. 2017. "Populism and Nationalism." In *Handbook of Populism*, edited by Cristóbal Rovira Kaltwasser, Paul Taggart, Paulina Ochoa Espejo and Pierre Ostiguy, 342–362. Oxford: Oxford University Press.

Engel Jakob, and Wodak Ruth. 2013. "'Calculated Ambivalence' and Holocaust Denial in Austria." In *Analysing Fascist Discourse: European Fascism in Talk and Text*, edited by Ruth Wodak and John E. Richardson, 73–96. London: Routledge.

Forchtner, Bernhard, Michal Krzyżanowski, and Ruth Wodak. 2013. "Mediatisation, Right-Wing Populism and Political Campaigning: The Case of the Austrian Freedom Party (FPÖ)." In *Media Talk and Political Elections in Europe and America*, edited by Mats Ekström and Andrew Tolson, 205–228. Basingstoke: Palgrave.

FPÖ. 2016. "Immer wieder Österreich." *FPÖ YouTube channel*, April 8, 2016. Accessed July 1, 2017. www.youtube.com/watch?v=IcV6aUw4xhU.

FPÖ-Bildungsinstitut. 2013. *Handbuch Freiheitlicher Politik. Ein Leitfaden für Führungskräfte und Mandatsträger der Freiheitlichen Partei Österreichs.* Wien: FPÖ-Bildungsinstitut.

Frindte, Wolfgang, and Nico Dietrich, eds. 2017. *Muslime, Flüchtlinge und Pegida. Sozialpsychologische und Kommunikationswissenschaftliche Studien in Zeiten globaler Bedrohungen.* Wiesbaden: Springer VS.

Howanietz, Michael. 2013. *Für ein freies Österreich. Souveränität als Zukunftsmodell.* Wien: Freiheitlicher Parlamentsklub.

Ichner, Bernhard. 2015. "Staatsanwalt Ermittelt Gegen Rechtspopulist Geert Wilders." *Kurier*, July 27. kurier.at/chronik/wien/staatsanwalt-ermittelt-gegen-rechtspopulist-geert-wilders/143.733.765.

Kallis, Aristotle. 2013. "Breaking Taboos and 'Mainstreaming the Extreme': the Debates on Restricting Islamic Symbols in Contemporary Europe." In *Right-wing Populism in Europe: Politics and Discourse*, edited by Ruth Wodak, Majid KhosraviNik and Brigitte Mral, 55–70. London: Bloomsbury.

Klein, W. 1991. *Die Argumentation in den griechisch-christlichen timanichaica.* Wiesbaden: Harrassowitz.

Köhler, Katharina, and Ruth Wodak. 2012. "Mitbürger, Fremde und 'echte Wiener.' Ein- und Ausgrenzungen über Sprache. Diskursive Konstruktion von Macht und Ungleichheit am Beispiel des Wiener Wahlkampfes 2010." *Deutschunterricht* 6 (11): 64–74.

Krzyżanowski, Michał, and Per Ledin. 2017. "Uncivility on the Web. Populism in/and the Borderline Discourses of Exclusion." In *Right-Wing Populism in Europe & USA: Contesting Politics & Discourse Beyond 'Orbanism' and 'Trumpism'*, edited by Ruth Wodak and Michał Krzyżanowski. Special issue of *Journal of Language and Politics* 16 (4): 566–581.

Krzyżanowski, Michał, and Ruth Wodak. 2009. *The Politics of Exclusion: Debating Migration in Austria.* New Brunswick, NJ: Transaction Publishers.

Krzyżanowski, Michał. 2013. "From Anti-Immigration and Nationalist Revisionism to Islamophobia: Continuities and Shifts in Recent Discourses and Patterns of Political Communication of the Freedom Party of Austria (FPÖ)." In *Right-wing Populism in Europe: Politics and Discourse*, edited by Ruth Wodak, Majid KhosraviNik and Brigitte Mral, 135–148. London: Bloomsbury.

Lehner, Sabine. 2018 (in print). "Rechtspopulistische Rhetorik Revisited am Beispiel der FPÖ-Wahlkämpfe in den Jahren 2015 und 2016." In *Linguistik Online*.

Manoschek, Walter. 2002. "FPÖ, ÖVP and Austria's Nazi Past." In *The Haider Phenomenon in Austria*, edited by Ruth Wodak and Anton Pelinka, 3–16. New Orleans: Transaction Press.

Matouschek, Bernd, Ruth Wodak, and Franz Januschek. 1995. *Notwendige Maßnahmen gegen Fremde? Genese und Form von rassistischen Diskursen der Differenz*. Wien: Passagen.

Musolff, Andreas. 2010. *Metaphor, Nation, and the Holocaust. The Concept of the Body Politic*. London/New York: Routledge.

Ötsch, Walter, and Horaczek, Nina. 2017. *Populismus für Anfänger: Anleitung zur Volksverführung*. Frankfurt/Main: Westend.

Ötsch, Walter. 2000. *Haider light. Handbuch für Demagogie*. Wien: Czernin.

Ottomeyer, Klaus. 2000. *Die Haider-Show: zur Psychopolitik der FPÖ*. Klagenfurt: Drava.

Pages, Neil Christian, Mary Rhiel, and Ingeborg Majer O'Sickey, eds. 2008. *Riefenstahl Screened: an Anthology of New Criticism*. New York: Continuum.

Pelinka, Anton, and Ruth Wodak, eds. 2002. *Dreck am Stecken. Politik der Ausgrenzung*. Wien: Czernin.

Pollak, Alexander. 2015. *Der Hassprediger. Der aufhaltsame Aufstieg des Johann G.* Wien: epubli.

Reisigl, Martin, and Wodak Ruth 2001. *Discourse and Discrimination. Rhetorics of Racism and Antisemitism*. London: Routledge.

Reisigl, Martin, and Wodak, Ruth. 2000. "'Austria First'. A Discourse-Historical Analysis of the Austrian 'Anti-Foreigner Petition' in 1992 and 1993." In *The Semiotics of Racism: Approaches in Critical Discourse Analysis*, edited by Martin Reisigl and Ruth Wodak, 269–303. Wien: Passagen.

Reisigl, Martin. 2002. *Dem Volk aufs Maul schauen, nach dem Mund reden* und *Angst und Bange machen*. Von populistischen Anrufungen, Anbiederungen und Agitationsweisen in der Sprache österreichischer PolitikerInnen. In *Rechtspopulismus. Österreichische Krankheit oder europäische Normalität?*, edited by Wolfgang Eismann, 149–198.Wien: Czernin Verlag.

Rheindorf, Markus und Wodak, Ruth (in press) "Austria First" Revisited: A Diachronic Cross-Sectional Analysis of the Gender and Body Politics of the Extreme Right. *Patterns of Prejudice, Special Issue: Cultural Imaginaries of the Extreme Right.*

Richardson, John E. 2017. "Fascist Discourse." In *The Routledge Handbook of Critical Discourse Studies*, edited by John Flowerdew and John E. Richardson, 447–462. London: Routledge.

Rosenkranz, Barbara. 2008. *MenschInnen. Gender Mainstreaming – Auf dem Weg zum geschlechtslosen Menschen.* Graz: Ares.

Rydgren, Jens. 2017. "The Radical Right. An Introduction." In *The Oxford Handbook of the Radical Right*, edited by Jens Rydgren. Oxford: Oxford University Press.

Sarrazin, Thilo. 2010. *Deutschland schafft sich ab. Wie wir unser Land aufs Spiel setzen.* München: Deutsche Verlags-Anstalt.

Scharsach, Hans-Henning. 2017. *Die stille Machtergreifung: Hofer, Strache und die Burschenschaften.* Wien: Kremayr & Scheriau.

Schiedel, Heribert, and Neugebauer Wolfgang. 2002. "Jörg Haider, die FPÖ und der Antisemitismus. " In "*Dreck am Stecken*". *Politik der Ausgrenzung*, edited by Anton Pelinka and Ruth Wodak, 11–31. Wien: Czernin.

Schmitz-Berning, Cornelia. 1998. *Vokabular des Nationalsozialismus.* Berlin/New York: Walter de Gruyter.

Stögner, Karin. 2016. "Secondary Antisemitism, the Economic Crisis and the Construction of National Identity in the Austrian Print Media." *Critical Sociology*, published online 7 August, DOI: 10.1177/08969205166 62507.

Strache, Heinz-Christian. 2015. "HC Strache." *Facebook page*, August 27, 2015. Accessed July 1, 2017. www.facebook.com/HCStrache.

Wodak, Ruth. 2013a. "'Anything Goes!'—The Haiderization of Europe". In *Right-Wing Populism in Europe. Politics and Discourse* ,edited by Ruth Wodak, Majid KhosraviNik, Brigitte Mral. 23–37. London: Bloomsbury Publishing.

Wodak, Ruth. 2013b. "The Strategy of Discursive Provocation: A Discourse-Historical Analysis of the FPÖ's Discriminatory Rhetoric". In *Doublespeak. The Rhetoric of the Far Right Since 1945,* edited by M. Feldman & P. Jackson, 101–122. Stuttgart, Ibidem Verlag,

Wodak, Ruth. 2015a. *The Politics of Fear: What Right-wing Populist Discourses Mean.* London: Sage.

Wodak, Ruth. 2015b. Normalisierung nach rechts: Politischer Diskurs im Spannungsfeld von Neoliberalismus, Populismus und kritischer Öffentlichkeit. *Linguistik Online* 73(4): 27–44.

Wodak, Ruth. 2016. Politik mit der Angst. Zur Wirkung rechtspopulistischer Diskurse. Wien und Hamburg: Edition Konturen.

Wodak, Ruth. 2017. "The 'Establishment', the 'Élites', and the 'People'. Who's who?" *Journal of Language and Politics*, 16(4): 551–565.

Wodak, Ruth. 2018. "Antisemitism and The Radical Right", In *Handbook of the Radical Right*, edited by Jens Rydgren, Oxford: OUP.

Wodak, Ruth, and Anton Pelinka. (eds.) 2002. *The Haider Phenomenon in Austria.* New Brunswick: Transaction Press.

Wodak, Ruth, and Katharina Köhler. 2010. "Wer oder was ist 'fremd'? Diskurshistorische Analyse fremdenfeindlicher Rhetorik in Österreich." *Sozialwissenschaftliche Studiengesellschaft* 2010/1: 33–55.

Wodak, Ruth, and Martin Reisigl. 2002. „... Wenn einer Ariel heisst ..." Ein linguistisches Gutachten zur politischen Funktionalisierung antisemitischer Ressentiments in Österreich. In *Dreck am Stecken,* edited by Anton Pelinka & Ruth Wodak. 134–172. Vienna: Czernin Verlag.

Wodak, Ruth, Johanna Pelikan, Peter Nowak, Helmut Gruber, Rudolf de Cillia, and Richard Mitten. 1990. *„Wir sind alle unschuldige Täter!" Diskurshistorische Studien zum Nachkriegsantisemitismus.* Frankfurt/Main: Suhrkamp.

Chapter 7: The Far-Right *Alternative für Deutschland* in Germany: Towards a 'Happy Ending'?

By Özgür Özvatan and Bernhard Forchtner

Abstract

The history of the German far-right before and since the 2013 launch of the AfD is traced, and its subsequent rapid migration from neo-liberal beginnings to its far-right present is detailed. The AfD's contemporary openly anti-liberal, (neo-)racist, anti-Muslim and anti-immigrant rhetoric (e.g. its election posters) is revealed. The chapter addresses how the AfD succeeded in drawing on, popularising, and catalysing far-right ideology into success in the 2017 *Bundestag* elections, and normalising its agenda into mainstream politics. Applying narrative analysis and narrative genres, the AfD's 'comic plot' for saving a threatened German cultural identity and creating a re-born nation is examined. Risks are systematically identified.

Key words: AfD, far-right, racism, immigration, narrative analysis, risks

German Far-Right Attitudes in Populist Form

Risks associated with the far-right are nowhere more apparent than in Germany, with its 20th century history—and although far-right actors have been present since the birth of the Federal Republic of Germany, threats originating from it have become especially pronounced more recently. On the one hand, while neo-Nazis have long played a violent role, the neo-Nazi terrorism by the *Nationalsozialistischer Untergrund* (National Socialist Underground) has most obviously illustrated the risks such groups pose for immigrants and citizens of 'foreign origin' (Quendt 2016). On the other hand, the rise of the populist far-right party *Alternative für Deutschland* (Alternative for Germany or AfD) gives voice to far-right attitudes at the centre of German politics, the parliaments. Founded in 2013 in response to the so-called

Euro-crisis and Germany's involvement in 'bailing out' Greece, the party evolved through various stages (see below), increasingly campaigning on a nativist ticket, and entered the German federal parliament in 2017.

In this chapter, the authors focus on the AfD, a political party that does not threaten to overthrow the Federal Republic, but nevertheless challenges, with its anti-liberal, (neo-)racist stance, the relatively liberal post-war order (for the notion of neo-racism, see Balibar 1991). The chapter addresses how the party has succeeded in drawing on, revitalizing, and giving rise to far-right stances by focusing on the narrative genres of, primarily, comedy and romance, in which the party has articulated its position(s).

Indeed, the success of the AfD does not come out of thin air, as far-right thought and (party) actors are not a new phenomenon in Germany. Research repeatedly shows relatively strong anti-democratic, authoritarian attitudes (for example, 26 per cent of the population in 2016 were characterised by strong, manifest/latent prejudices, strong disposition towards authoritarian aggression, and a severe lack of trust in the democratic system) and xenophobia (20.4 per cent; see Decker et al. 2016). Furthermore, recent decades saw far-right parties periodically succeeding at the ballot box. For example, during the late 1980s and early 1990s, the far-right party *Die Republikaner* (REP) established itself by pursuing a racist, anti-immigration agenda. However, the party ultimately failed to enter the German *Bundestag* in 1994 after the traditional parties reached a consensus on asylum policies introduced by the conservative liberal coalition government (the Christian-Democratic Union/Christian-Social Union and the Free Democratic Party) in the context of the early 1990s' '*Asyldebatten*' (Lochocki 2018). Renewed identity debates continued following the first coalition between Social Democrats and Greens in 1998, and their ideas of a liberal citizenship reform. The Berlin Republic faced contentious debates among the two *Volksparteien*, the Christian-Democratic Union/Christian-Social Union and the Social Democrats, over the liberalisation of naturalisation, from *jus sanguinis* to *jus soli*, and it was in 2005 that the then newly formed grand coalition government allowed immigrants to acquire German or dual citizenship (see also Brubaker 2010). Beyond party politics, far-right themes within the mainstream have recently been circulated by Thilo Sarrazin, a Social Democrat and former Senator of Finance in Berlin. Based on (neo-)

racist claims concerning (less intelligent but more fertile) Muslim immigrants outbreeding ethnic Germans, he prominently claimed that "Germany abolishes itself". Related claims have been made, for example, by the Pegida movement (Patriotic Europeans Against the Islamisation of the Occident) and, even more recently, far-right uproar in the Saxon city of Chemnitz (AfD Dresden 2018).

While provocative statements by the AfD are neither new nor isolated, the party has forcefully contributed to the discourse about immigrants in Germany. For example, one of the two prime candidates of the party during the national elections, Alexander Gauland, claims that "one wants to take away this Germany from us" through "an invasion", a "creeping land grab", and that the German politician Aydan Özoğuz (also then serving Federal Commissioner for Immigration, Refugees and Integration) should be "disposed in Anatolia". One of the most infamous 2017 general election placards deployed by the party (showing the belly of a white, pregnant women below the claim "New Germans? We make them ourselves."), see image bottom left of Figure 7.1, below, also pushes (neo-)racism in general and the alleged threat of *Umvolkung* (ethnicity inversion) in particular to centre stage. Such statements by members of the AfD have become increasingly common. Moreover, they are rarely questioned from within the AfD, which seeks to legitimize them via reference to 'the people'.

Thus, the risks associated with an alleged 'invasion' by foreign 'others' are connected to the populist rallying cry that 'the pure people' stand in an antagonistic relation to 'the corrupt elite' which is betraying the 'general will' of 'the people' (Mudde 2007, 23). Indeed, if 'the people' do not rally around a saviour (the AfD), only catastrophe can follow. For example (see also Figure 7.1), the fundamental campaign slogan of the party (right next to the party's emblem) demands "Have courage, Germany!". This presupposes that taking the party's position requires courage, as the people are somehow silenced and in a subordinate position; a yoke (kept in place by 'the elite') which needs to be shaken off through siding with the party. Anti-elite sentiments in the AfD's campaigns thus position 'the people' in opposition to the supposedly corrupt, or at least deluded, political elite.

Owing to this amalgam of increasingly (neo-)racist positions and a populist posture, the AfD can now be described, in the words of Mudde (2007), a 'populist radical-right party'. As the AfD is a western

European party, a brief terminological clarification (vis-à-vis the notion of 'Alt-Right') is necessary. In the US context, the Alt-Right occupies a broad spectrum outside the mainstream conservatism of the Republican Party, ranging from frustrated moderate right-wing Republicans, populist anti-establishment rebels e.g. Tea Party, and Trump supporters, through increasingly harsher and more strident advocates of economic nationalism, nativism and white supremacy, up to and including neo-Nazis and extremists who advocate and are willing to engage in hate crimes and violence (e.g. KKK), and even terrorism (e.g. the proscribed terrorist groups Aryan Nations and National Alliance). The term Alt-Right, and the ideology and movement it denotes, is remarkably recent, attributed to Gottfried (2008) and then promulgated widely by the far-right publisher Richard Spencer, as discussed in chapter 1. However, as Paxton in chapter 3 of Vol 1 reveals, the Alt-Right in the United States did not arrive from nowhere and represents a resurgence of pre-existing US nationalism and nativism, which has been assisted greatly by the presidential ambitions of Donald Trump.

The US Alt-Right spectrum overall, including the so-called Alt-Lite (ADL 2018), as with counterparts in other countries, shares to varying degrees authoritarian attitudes, ultra-nationalism, as well as nativism, and a rejection of moving further towards 'racial' and cultural diversity as well as minority rights—in combination with a severe critique of the political establishment. Such an understanding of the Alt-Right is in line with what has been known in western Europe by the names 'right-wing', 'radical right', 'extreme right' and 'right-wing extremist', and sometimes even '(neo-)fascist' (see Salzborn 2014). Differences between these concepts are beyond discussion here, but core features include authoritarianism, ethnocentrism and ethnopluralism, (neo-)racism and *völkisch* thought (the community defined as an ethno-racial one, as an organic, collective subject; more specifically, see Kellershohn 1998: 27f.), anti-pluralism, anti-socialism, and, consequently, a proclivity for scapegoating and historical revisionism (see, for example, Holzer 1994 and Salzborn 2014, 19–22)—nowadays often coupled with populism (Mudde 2007; Müller 2016; see Häusler 2018 on 'völkisch-authoritarian populism'). These aspects will be present to varying degrees and, depending on the strength of their presence, actors range from anti-liberal but still democratic ones to unreservedly anti-democratic ones (the latter posing far greater risks not only to political culture, but also to institutional frameworks). In the following, the authors refer to this wide range of actors as 'far-right'.

Against this background, far-right actors in Germany, including the AfD, pose a risk to, for example, fundamentals as diverse as the country's traditional post-1945 foreign policy and the fight against climate-change. This chapter, however, focuses more specifically on the far-right's core agenda—the racial/cultural purity of 'the people'—and thematises the risk posed by the AfD to the liberal post-war order, manifest in, for example, widespread liberal-democratic attitudes, recognition of human rights and equality, a relatively clear-cut rejection of the National-Socialist past and its presence. Indeed, as Funke (2016, 23) in his analysis of the AfD said: those who vote for the far-right endanger "post-war Europe and thus the fundaments of our co-existence". The puzzle guiding this chapter, as already mentioned above, is thus: how has the AfD successfully managed to draw on, revitalise and give rise to far-right stances?

The authors argue that the narrative genre through which the party presents its agenda provides valuable insights into the AfD's successful campaigns (though socio-economic factors are undoubtedly relevant as well, for example, Lengfeld 2017 and Lux 2018). The power of primarily comically constructed narratives of 'the world' lies in the fact that here, events are selectively arranged (beginning, middle, end) so as to result, after a deep fall, in a romantic ending (Frye 1957). There is, however, an overlap with the romance genre in that 'good' and 'evil' are rather sharply separated; also, as narratives are developing constantly, to pinpoint a genre remains an empirical matter. In the case of the German far-right, the happy ending rests in the promising of overcoming a pollution threat to 'true' Germans, something to be realised by the AfD which defends 'the general will' of 'the people', following years of 'liberal rule' and immigration (most manifestly present, in the eyes of the AfD, in the opening of borders during the so-called refugee crisis in 2015). Eventually, this construction of the events, with its promise of national rebirth, succeeded in the 2017 general election which saw the AfD entering the federal parliament.

The next section presents basic elements of the German far-right political spectrum since 1945, followed by an overview of how the AfD has developed since it was founded in 2013, pointing out major steps in the party's evolution. The authors subsequently theorise this development by drawing on narrative theory, in particular the theory of narrative genres, claiming that the AfD creates its narrative primarily as comedy and romance which thus presents the prospect of a happy ending for the 'true German people'. Finally, the findings are summarised and connected to the broader agenda put forward in this book.

Setting the Stage: the German Far-Right from 1945 to the AfD

The long history of the far-right in Germany can be traced back to the Romantic period and to ardent nationalists such as Ernst Moritz Arndt. Neither the story of early racism nor National Socialism are within this chapter's scope, other than noting that driving attitudes include, as mentioned above, authoritarianism, nativism, ethnocentrism, anti-pluralism, anti-socialism, a proclivity for scapegoating.

While these attitudes were, and still are, present throughout German society (see Decker et al. 2016), their first significant party-political representation in West Germany after 1945 was the Socialist Reich Party (SRP). The SRP was viewed as the descendant of the Nazi party owing not only to personal continuity, but also because it openly perpetuated their ideology (Hansen 2007). However, the SRP only once managed to gather significant public support (11 per cent in 1951 in Lower Saxony) and was subsequently banned by the Federal Constitutional Court in 1952. As such, the German far-right remained fragmented until the foundation of the National Democratic Party of Germany (NPD) in 1964. The party rapidly entered five state parliaments. However, after the party failed in the national election in 1969, it disintegrated and returned to some significance (especially in former East Germany) only in the 1990s and 2000s, emphasizing social issues and anti-globalization positions. Owing to internal quarrels and further dramatic electoral failure, the party has become irrelevant again. It has thus repeated the journey of other parties occupying various positions in the far-right spectrum, such as *Die Republikaner* in the 1980s/90s and the *Deutsche Volksunion* in the 1990s/2000s, which, in 2011, merged with the NPD.

These parties operated, however, in a context very different from the SRP, a context influenced by the (German) New Right (*Neue*

Rechte; see Weiss 2017). Distancing itself from the 'old right' (Nazism), this network of proponents and ideas is linked to thinkers associated with the so-called 'conservative revolution' (for example, Arthur Moeller van den Bruck, Carl Schmitt and Ernst Jünger). This difference is marked by, for example, not outright denial of the Holocaust; instead, the New Right 'simply' rejects the resulting so-called *Schuldkult* (guilt-cult) allegedly characterising German political culture, as it does not justly represent the German nation. Authoritarian, anti-Enlightenment and *völkisch*/ethnopluralist threads too are central and have been reworked by these actors, attitudes which are currently represented by, for example, Götz Kubitschek who co-founded the far-right think tank *Institut für Staatspolitik*, edits the magazine *Sezession* and supported far-right positions within the AfD.

Within the group of non-party far-right actors, Pegida as well as the Identitarian Movement (which overlaps particularly strongly with the German New Right) are especially relevant here due to their relation to the still evolving AfD (for more detail see, for example, Funke 2016; in fact, the AfD has been referred to as the 'parliamentary arm' of these far-right movements, see Gebhardt 2018, 109). When Pegida flourished in winter 2014, Gauland, in an interview with the German news magazine *Spiegel Online*, provided justification for AfD members to join weekly Pegida rallies, while in January 2015, he defended their position paper. At the beginning of 2018, the party in fact revised an earlier resolution (in place since 2016) which forbade party members from appearing at Pegida events in Dresden. Similarly, the German Identitarian Movement, a group of self-proclaimed 'idealist patriotic activists', is not part of the AfD, but pursues largely intersecting goals and appreciates the party's recent development and success. The ideological overlap of the AfD and the Identitarian Movement has resulted in various connections between, for example, the latter and the AfD's youth wing.

Before looking more closely at how the party has evolved by narrating an increasingly neo-racist and *völkisch* comedy, this section is concluded by taking an analytical look at how the AfD has been conceptualized. This concerns, first, what the AfD delivers (the supply side), and, second, which voters it appeals to (the demand side). Founded in the aftermath of, and in reaction to, the European financial crisis, the AfD defined itself as 'Eurocritical' (for research on the party's Euroscepticism, see Grimm 2015; Pieper et al. 2014). Research has also scrutinized whether the AfD belongs to the 'populist radical right' party family. For instance, Lewandowsky et al. (2016) introduced a fine-grained measurement concept of right-wing populism to get to grips with the AfD party profile in the 2013 German federal election. With a similar focus, Berbuir et al. (2015) concluded that both the party and its supporters resemble a 'European right-wing populist movement in the making', that is: while the party lacked a clear nativist ticket in the period investigated (before 2015), it did draw on anti-immigration and anti-elite stances, and can ultimately be defined as 'right-wing populist'. In contrast to these authors, Arzheimer (2015) argued that the AfD lacked a populist agenda, but is located on the far-right due to its nationalism, illiberal stances towards sexual diversity, market liberalism, and opposition to gender mainstreaming. These studies deal with a period in which the AfD largely made (neo-)liberal claims, i.e. before the so-called national-conservative turn in summer 2015 (see below).

Regarding the demand side, Lengfeld (2017) contested a popular proposition made in western Europe, namely that 'populist radical-right parties' would mainly cater for those who have not benefited from modernization and globalization. His approach indicates that this does not apply to AfD voters, as the typical supporter appears to be a risk-free middle-class citizen. Others consider the AfD as the parliamentary branch of a broader 'nativist and racial nationalist movement' in Germany (Virchow 2017; Gebhardt 2018). In the same vein, Salzborn (2017) postulated what is key in political messages put forward by the AfD: Germany portrayed as a victim of foreign invasion, and in need of a 'reawakening'. These accounts speak to changes the party went through following its takeover by Frauke Petry in 2015. Hitherto present multi-vocal positions within the party vanished afterwards, and what were previously latent characteristics became more clearly identifiable. As such, mobilisation occurred increasingly along the lines of classical western European populist far-right parties, such as the French National Rally and the Freedom Party of Austria: against the elites and foreign 'invaders', for the nation.

Given that the AfD has become the focal point of the German far-right, the next section introduces how the primarily comic narrative told by the AfD evolved, starting with the beginnings of the Party under Lucke, illustrating the rise of (neo-)racist and *völkisch* rhetoric under Petry during the middle period, and ending with the 2017 election campaign and its aftermath in 2018.

Saving 'the People': the AfD from 2013 to 2018

The Beginning: Greek Debt and the EURO

The AfD was officially founded in March 2013 by a group of conservatives and liberals under the lead of Bernd Lucke, a professor of economics, in reaction to the so-called Euro Crisis, which started in 2009 and triggered latent anti-Greek stereotypes. Whereas established German parties, the two German *Volksparteien* in particular, largely accepted the path of 'rescuing' European nation-states hit by the crisis, discussions over Greek debt caused some conservatives and neo-liberals to lament the plight of 'the German taxpayer' who had to pay for 'lazy Greeks', a story widely present in the German mainstream and tabloid media. The subsequently formed AfD was positioned right from its inception as not in line with the political establishment. While the '(neo-)liberal wing' led the party during this initial period, there was also a 'national-conservative wing' consolidating itself and, ultimately, coming to the fore during the party's public infighting of June 2015.

Initially, however, dominant stances within the party were twofold: the first one conceived of the AfD as a centrist, bourgeois party not connected to the far-right margins of society. For instance, Lucke stated that "[w]e really do not have any right-wing extremism in the AfD" (*Frankfurter Allgemeine Zeitung* November 24, 2014). The second dominant position was rooted in a rhetoric in opposition to political elites while positioning the AfD as the only political party protecting 'German interests'. This was, however, initially uttered in the context of debating the state of European integration; for example, when Lucke claimed that "the solution to the European crisis lies not in 'more Europe', but in more democracy, more responsibility, and more subsidiarity. Germany shall have the courage to also emphatically pursue its own legitimate interests" (*Frankfurter Allgemeine Zeitung* January 27, 2014).

In the beginning, the (neo-)liberal spirit of the party was thus articulated as 'German interest', framed in economic terms, and was related to a rejection of the elite-driven European project, calling for a politics of subsidiarity, in the name of 'the German people'. The latter remained relatively open, i.e. not yet determined by (neo-)racism, positioning the party simply as the only political alternative that speaks out for 'us' against past and present wrongdoing, mainly in economic questions, by a morally inferior political elite.

The Middle: Rescuing 'the German People'

Following Frauke Petry's ascension to leadership of the party at an extraordinary federal party congress in May 2015, Lucke and his (neo-)liberal fellows left the party. Petry's success should be viewed in the context of broader changes in the political landscape in Germany, Europe and beyond. While the European financial crisis and other economic issues were considered previously the most important public concern (Politbarometer 2014)—and thus internal party cohesion was based on Germany's financial interest—the so-called 'refugee crisis' since late 2014, and the 'welcome culture' inaugurated in late summer 2015, led to increasing migration-related public concerns and hefty debates over cultural issues in the wider public and party. Prominent (neo-)liberals felt the need to distance themselves from the 'new' AfD, due to ever more present (neo-)racist claims, concentrated in the increasingly influential internal organization '*Der Flügel*' and build around people like Björn Höcke and André Poggenburg, and their *Erfurter Resolution* (Resolution of Erfurt) in 2015. For example, the former IBM Germany CEO Hans-Olaf Henkel announced his resignation as vice-chairman by referring to far-right, anti-democratic tendencies he witnessed at a party congress.

During the pre-withdrawal period in 2015, the liberal pole was torn between the will to challenge the European integration project, and the actual political agenda that was debating migration-related public concerns. For instance, both the fatal Islamist attack on the French magazine *Charlie Hebdo* and the rise of Pegida prompted debates concerning the role of (political) Islam in 'the west'. It was during this period that scapegoating 'Islam' or 'Muslims' as a threat to 'our home' became increasingly mainstream within the AfD. For example, Gauland stated that he rejects any further immigration from a 'cultural tradition' which is 'at home in the Middle East' as this group would establish 'parallel societies' ['*Parallelgesellschaften*'] due to their 'difficulties to integrate here' (*Frankfurter Allgemeine Zeitung* January 28, 2015). From this perspective, 'true Germans' need to be protected from a 'Middle Eastern culture', which allegedly impedes social cohesion. Allegedly, the German political elite failed, consciously or unconsciously, to prevent the rise of Islam in 'the west', now threatening white native Germans. It was owing to this story that the need to save Germans arose.

(Neo-)Racist concerns were, however, also distributed in other ways. For example, at a symposium organized by the *Institut für Staatspolitik* the party's far-right 'poster boy' Höcke spoke about the different mating behaviours of Africans and Europeans, claiming that:

> "...as long as Germany eagerly welcomes those people, the reproduction strategy of Africans will not change (...) The nations of Africa, they need the German border, they need the European border in order to find a way to a sustainable population development". (*Süddeutsche Zeitung* December 12, 2015)

Höcke even questioned the state's raison d'être, the relatively self-critical remembrance of the Holocaust, in January 2017 during a speech at a meeting of the party's youth wing. Referring to the Holocaust memorial in Berlin, he stated: "We Germans, also our people, are the only people in the world which planted a memorial of shame in the heart of its capital", and further demanded "a memory-political 180 degrees turn" (already in 1998, the internationally renowned novelist and hitherto leftish political activist Martin Walser had similarly called it a 'memorial of shame'). Both speeches, on 'African reproduction strategies' and the 'memorial of shame', caused contentious debates and, ultimately, the AfD's federal board started exclusion proceedings against Höcke. However, by ultimately refraining from excluding Höcke illustrates the significance of *völkisch* forces in the party, illustrating how far the AfD had been drifting to the far-right. Another incident occurred in 2016 when Gauland admitted that German football fans would appreciate German national team defender Jerome Boateng's (whose father is black and whose mother is white) sporting performances, but "they don't want a Boateng as their neighbour". Further evidence is visible in then chairwoman Petry's reference to German law in order to raise the possibility of defending the national borders against 'illegal border crossers' via the use of firearms (*Spiegel Online* January 30, 2016). It is worth noting that Petry left the party the day after the successful federal election in 2017, justifying her departure through reference to the increasingly far-right drift of the party.

Hence, the middle period covers the shift within the AfD from a largely (neo-)liberal to an increasingly populist radical-right party, from May 2015 to the federal election campaign which began in 2017. This drift, and respective electoral triumphs in state elections, paved the way for the AfD to dig further into the far-right agenda by drawing on (neo-)racist narratives to save 'the German people'.

The (Preliminary) Ending: Election Campaign, Triumph and Beyond

The party's 2017 national election campaign followed successful local elections in 2016, which had already, and successfully, given much space to (neo-)racism (before the 2017 general election, the AfD had entered 13 state parliaments). Against the background of this rise, the campaign was characterized by an emphasis on (neo-)racist boundary-making combined with a doomsday scenario for Germany—but increasingly added the promise of a happy ending for native white Germans to its storyline, highlighting the party's role as a rescuer of an endangered (ethno-)nation. That is, the party narrated a story that included a bright future for 'true Germans' (national rebirth) which would happen only if the German electorate opted in favour of the AfD, thus giving finally a voice back to 'the German people'.

The parties' main way of communicating with the electorate is telling: its on- and off-line campaign posters (Figure 7.1). A (neo-)racist rhetoric marked the overarching theme of the narrative presented via these posters; ranging from preventing new (Arab/Muslim or African) immigrants from entering Germany, to preventing 'established immigrants' from symbolically polluting (Douglas 1966) German identity. This campaign was thus built around the attempt to induce or (re-)shape the nation's boundaries.

Figure 7.1: Selection of AfD Election Campaign Posters

The first main boundary concerns saving German cultural identity by strengthening protection of German borders from Middle East and North Africa region immigrants. Immigration has long been problematized by mainstream parties via the theme of 'criminal foreigners', but this locus was left wide open when Merkel moved towards a liberal 'Welcome Culture' in 2015. One campaign poster regarded the topic of sea rescue wherein Arab and African refugees are portrayed as entering Europe and, supposedly, ending up as criminals in Germany. Here, the far-right challenged the notion of people seeking refuge by claiming that Arab and African criminals take advantage of a window of opportunity to immigrate to Europe, and to Germany in particular. The aforementioned Identitarian Movement forcefully made this argument in its campaign to hinder the work of NGO rescue boats in the Mediterranean in 2017 (their self-styled 'Mission: Defend Europe'), but it is also found in AfD statements. In AfD online press releases, AfD spokespersons gave particular weight to the topic of 'illegal sea rescue of economic migrants' which they asserted, in consequence, demanded legal prosecution of those NGOs.

The second main boundary concerns immigrant 'integration', i.e. the belonging of those who had arrived at an earlier point, and how they affect Germany and its 21st century cultural identity. Influential immigrant groups such as *Neue Deutsche Organisationen* persistently endorse a pluralist understanding of belonging. Thus, they coined '*Neue Deutsche*' ('New Germans') to express their belonging to Germany, narrating a notion of 'us' that moves beyond *jus sanguinis*. The AfD engaged with the discourse on 'New Germans' by attaching an entirely different, racial and ethno-cultural, meaning to it. As such, one poster proclaimed "'New Germans?' We make them ourselves" (Figure 7.1). The whiteness of the woman (the focus on the belly furthermore stresses a female's apparent function in the nation; for an account of gender and the far right, see Köttig et al. 2016) indicates that 'New Germans' are those to be 'produced' by ethnic Germans. In the same vein, another poster opposes increased cultural diversity (i.e. difference which might, rightly or wrongly, cause discomfort) as '[w]e' supposedly already 'have it'. Thus, regional folklore, displayed by traditional clothing (and, importantly, represented as being the task of women), is emphasized in order to oppose actual ethnic, racial, and religious diversity. Opposition to immigration from ethnic and religious cultures (allegedly) incompatible with the western cultural tradition lies thus at the heart of the AfD's anti-immigration and anti-diversity stances. Here, Islam marks the prime 'other', whose 'cultural incompatibility' is most tellingly highlighted in four of the above campaign posters: German women drink Burgunder (wine), instead of wearing the burka (top left); they will continue topless sun-bathing, even during Ramadan (top right); their liberty is not up for negotiation, so they will not be oppressed by males to veil their faces (mid-left); and, finally, Germans will not abandon eating pork (mid-right).

Ultimately, the AfD election campaign posters boil down to a simple story: in order to protect 'us', someone has to stop pollution by 'others', for example Islam and/or non-white immigrants from North Africa.

The centrality of this dimension to the AfD's election campaign was, unsurprisingly, also present in the party manifesto and in public speeches. In the former, it is stated that "Islam does not belong to Germany", a reference to what, for example, then president of Germany Christian Wulff and chancellor Merkel had claimed in 2010 and 2015 respectively: "Islam belongs to Germany" (a claim which, to this day, causes controversies). In fact, Islam "spread[s] and the presence of over five million Muslims, a number which steadily grows" is viewed by the AfD "as a great threat for our state, our society and our value order" (AfD 2017, 34). Ending immigration is furthermore present in the party's programme which rejects the "ideology of multiculturalism" as a "serious threat to social peace and the survival of *the nation as a cultural unit*" (AfD 2016, 46, *italics* added). Again, such scepticism is not unprecedented; even chancellor Merkel had stated in 2010 that "multiculturalism has failed" (*Süddeutsche Zeitung* October 16, 2010). However, Poggenburg, then Saxony-Anhalt state chairman of the AfD, escalated similar themes when he gave a supposedly satirical speech, calling the Turkish community in Germany "caraway traders" ('caraway Turks' is a derogative term) and "camel jockeys". Referring to the Armenian genocide, he added that the Turks should come to terms with their own past before giving lessons to Germans on history and homeland. The 'Turkish issue' has been a longstanding concern for the German far-right, but was pushed to the fore recently, primarily because of increased tensions in German-Turkish relations (Özvatan 2017).

Following the successful 2017 election campaign, in which the party finished third and received 12.6 per cent of the votes, Petry left the party which had, according to her, drifted too far to the right. Her departure, however, has not changed the party's trajectory. Notably, Gauland stated in June 2018 that Germany's twelve-year period of National Socialism [under Hitler] resembled only "bird shit" when seen against more than 1,000 years of German history (*Frankfurter Allgemeine Zeitung* June 02, 2018). Some weeks later, Gauland defended far-right riots in Chemnitz as "normal" (*Zeit Online* June 02, 2018), when protesters marched through the town shouting 'foreigners out!'

and attacked people they identified as Muslims or refugees. Similarly, Markus Frohnmaier, an AfD member of the *Bundestag*, tweeted on August 26, 2018 that if the State is not able to guarantee the safety of the people, the latter have to "take to the street and protect themselves"......[so to stop] "knife migration". Höcke also called for a silent march to remember "all those who died because of forced multiculturalization in Germany", claiming that "Our country is at stake. We do not forget".

Looking back at the development of the AfD, it is striking how quickly, and relatively smoothly, the party moved from a (neo-)liberal, and in part national-conservative position, to a straightforwardly far-right one. Indeed, the party has not only shifted its focus, making it unsurprising that even neo-Nazi elements hope for the party's success, and have supported it at the ballot box, but has also aligned itself with e.g. the Freedom Party of Austria. All this has happened through pushing worries over perceived risks connected with (ethno-)cultural and racial 'others' and allegedly disengaged elites towards the centre of the political debate. Having outlined the content-related dimension of this risk performance, a way to understand the success of this push is suggested below.

Narrating Risk—Narrative Modes

Perceiving the AfD as a risk to the political culture of post-war Germany (either in the sense in which this volume understands the risk posed by far-right actors, or in the sense in which the party presents itself vis-à-vis the status quo) requires us to think about the notion of risk itself. As chapter 12 discusses, since its character, form, qualities, and scale are the product of a cerebral judgement, a particular risk is always subjective and its perception is subject to numerous variables and mediations, including possibly cultural and social construction (Burgess 2015; Johnson and Covello 1987). Following Ulrich Beck's (1992; 2007) work, risks are not simply objectively present and subsequently perceived as such through a common, standard, objective lens and epistemology. Rather, he suggests that risks are interpreted by actors through the variety of actions and performances of others. However, what Beck does not discuss in detail is the narrative embeddedness of such performances; the following focuses on the main form through which the world, including risks, is made meaningful: the narrative form.

Narrative is an ever-present condition of human life. It is, in short, "the principal way in which our species organizes its understanding of time" (Abbott 2002, 3). In other words, reality is always constituted through narrative. This approach to the social world has resulted in a 'narrative turn' in the social sciences and humanities (Czarniawska 2004) and unites scholars interested in the 'textuality of social life' (Alexander and Smith 2001). Accordingly, narratives mark humans' path to lend meaning to their experiences over time, to embed these experiences in a meaningful structure, and to interpret them meaningfully. What this implies is the *construction* of significant wholes, i.e. narratives, through the selective arrangement of events, characters and other elements. What Toolan (1988, 6) refers to as "a perceived sequence of non-randomly connected events" is the active work of narrators—of us—within particular contexts and against particular backgrounds. It concerns the different ways in which different actors, from their perspectives and with their strategic aims, will interplay foreground/background elements of events, and will even invent/ignore such events. It is through such emplotment, the act of grasping together diverse events, that meaning arises (Ricoeur 1984, 66). Thus, narratives are constructed (emplotted) not from the beginning, but rather from the end, and consequently, "the desire to control the ending (of a social drama)" (Wagner-Pacifici 1986, 282) is a desire to control meaning (and its political-cultural effects).

As such, narratives are key in the cultural (re)production of symbolic boundaries (Lamont and Molnar 2002; Bail 2008), as collective identity is constituted through stories about 'us' and 'them', stories which circulate within a particular web of 'we' (Somers 1994). Thus, private as well as public actors perpetuate a 'we' by (re-)telling stories about particular collectivities that inscribe a symbolic boundary into the web of social relations which bonds those belonging to 'us' and distinguishes them from 'others' not, or less fully, belonging to the in-group (Yuval-Davis 2011; Korteweg and Yurdakul 2014; Eder 2006).

Here, however, the authors neither want to focus primarily on the arrangement of actual events, nor on the particular content of these stories (see the previous sections), but rather on the wider, formal aspects of such arrangement. After all, emplotment of individual stories is structured on a deeper level, following certain patterns which are, though culturally specific, recognizable within such cultural formations as 'the west'. This points to the theory of narrative genres, which is a perspective through which the emergence of feelings the party was able to mobilise can be explained, and through which it ultimately succeeded (see Forchtner 2016a for this type of argument). This theory draws on the idea of four 'archetypical genres'—romance, comedy, tragedy, and irony (satire)—introduced by Northrop Frye (1957), as in Table 7.1.

Table 7.1: Narrative Genres

	Romance	**Comedy**	**Tragedy**	**Irony**
Sphere	Innocence, the ideal	Innocence, the ideal	Realism, the actual	Realism, the actual
Plot Line	Ascends within the sphere of innocence	Descends from innocence to realism, then finally ascends from realism to innocence	Descends from innocence to realism	Remains within the sphere of realism
End	*Agon*; 'Good' triumphs over 'evil' in an-ever-present conflict	*Anognorisis*; Happy ending, 'good' triumphs over 'evil' festively	*Pathos*; Cathartic doomsday	*Sparagmos;* No ending, confusion reigns over the world
Human vs. Nature	Human triumphs over nature	Human triumphs festively over nature	Nature causes despair ('shaking of the world'), but epiphany of the survivors	Human concedes the natural human condition to live with ambiguity and doubt
Symbolic Boundary	Fixing	Fixing	Renegotiation: Either fixing or blurring	Blurring
Feeling	Strong emotional attachment to the society of 'us'; self-righteousness and clarity	Strong emotional release of the society of 'us'; festivity, rebirth and reconciliation	Emotional detachment from the society of 'us'; despair, uncertainty and little hope	Strong emotional detachment from the society of 'us'; ambivalence, contingency and doubt

Table 7.1 illustrates the main characteristics of narrative genres. In the social world, these genres rarely occur in pure form; rather they adopt sequences from each other. According to Frye (1957, 162f), they are located in two vertically ordered spheres: the ideal and the actual. Through an ascending plot line e.g. the 'good' overcomes the 'evil' (romance), or a sharp decline being followed by ascendance and festive end (comedy), positive self-affirmation is secured. As representatives of the ideal sphere, romance and comedy thus tend to fix symbolic boundaries which anchor idealized manifestations of 'good us' and 'evil them' in their endings (see also Wagner-Pacifici 1986 above). This facilitates feelings of self-righteousness and certainty amongst those who identify with the 'good' in such stories (Forchtner 2016a). Tragedy and irony, in turn, enable the blurring of symbolic boundaries. Tragedy (a descending plot line) reflects a rather moderate and ambivalent type of boundary-blurring. The uncertain and desperate condition of the hero/heroine facilitates the emotional detachment from what was previously the most dominant notion of 'us'. Irony, however, mirrors the counterfactual of romance, "the sense that heroism and effective action are absent, disorganized or foredoomed to defeat, and that confusion and anarchy reign over the world" (ibid., 192; thus, no clear plot line can be assigned to irony, see Forchtner and Eder 2017). Consequently, irony blurs pre-existing, idealized definitions of 'us', dissolves respective collective feelings, and thus facilitates the engagement with ambivalence and doubt.

Looking at our empirical case, it becomes apparent that the AfD narrated itself and the world around the ideal sphere, primarily framed in terms of a comic plot (though romantic elements, such as the strong emotional attachment to the ethnically defined German society, are present too). This is the story of German cultural identity under a threat emanating from either Muslim or African immigrants. Allegedly, these will violently harm (terrorism and criminality), outbreed (immigration and reproduction), or pollute 'us'. Not all is lost, however: while Germany once had control over its national and ethno-cultural boundaries, but lost it due to a corrupt political establishment, the AfD will be able to see control greatly tightened. This arrangement of events mirrors Frye's (1957, 192) point about "the newborn society rising in triumph" and, in the context of far-right (neo-)racist nationalism, this echoes the far-right desire to celebrate the 'rebirth' or 'reawakening' of the nation.

This narrative facilitates the audiences' entrance into a feeling of certainty and self-assurance, based on a festive return to the nation proper—if the AfD succeeds. The rebirth implicitly promised in this story can be easily connected to what Roger Griffin (1993) has identified as being central to fascist actors: the palingenetic myth, i.e. fascism conceptualised as being based on a vision of, ultimately, a nation's rebirth from decadence. Of course, the authors do not claim that the AfD is a fascist party, but this myth is also of significance for the entire far-right, not just its utmost right and truly revolutionary fringe. To capture this aspect, one might draw on what Griffin (ibid, 50f) called 'proto-fascist' actors—that is, actors who are not actually breaking with parliamentary democracy (and do not even necessarily precede the emergence of a proper fascist subject), but still share the desire for rebirth. Within the comic/romantic form, the 'evil' opponent is not simply the African or Muslim non-white immigrant, but, in 'good' populist fashion, the political establishment, which is responsible for allowing ethno-cultural pollution to happen. Pollution will, however, not happen if the AfD is allowed to empower the homogeneous German body (*Volkskörper*) to stand up against the 'corrupt elite' [in the struggle against this 'other', a romantic element might well be present as genres are never present in pure form]. This will preserve 'German cultural identity' and rescue the nation vis-à-vis the prospect of an alleged Muslim or North African pollution of 'the German body'.

Conclusion

This chapter summarised the development of a European Alt-Right party, or in the authors' terms, a far-right party, the AfD. This party has become the most successful far-right party in Germany since 1945, and is affecting the country's political culture and politics. The rise of the party is illustrated through narrating its three stages thus far—from a rather neo-liberal beginning, to a turn towards the far-right and, ultimately, an astonishing success in the federal elections in 2017 owing to this very turn. Furthermore, theoretical sense of this success is made by drawing on narrative theory, especially the theory of narrative genres, which suggests that the party's success is built on a comic/romantic narrative that ends in the sphere of the ideal, promising a happy ending and the delights of self-affirmation. Thus, the AfD transformed its narrative from economic concerns to a 'cultural doom facing Germany' which requires 'the people', represented by the AfD, to struggle for cultural/racial purity as well as national rebirth.

Three points raised in the Introduction to this book are connected to the above analysis: first, the editor noted that the Alt-Right lays claim to offering 'true democracy', 'true security', 'true protection' etc. and this is exemplified in the AfD's communications. In line with an interest in elements of narrative analysis, the notion of 'true saviour' can also be added. This is not simply because it fits well with populism, but also because it is linked to comic/romantic storylines in which the putative hero—here, the AfD—is viewed as the legitimate authority coming to rescue the community. Second, the editor spoke of 'post-truth'. This is of obvious significance in the case of Donald Trump, and of some of the promises made during the Brexit referendum campaign. Within the German context, 'fake news' is also present, though the extent of such 'news' in AfD material is beyond this chapter's scope. Anyway, many of the events to which the AfD refers did happen, though they are emplotted in a particular way (however, some events have turned out to be fake, as in the prominent fake-news case of the 13-year old Russian girl allegedly raped by refugees). For example, criminal refugees certainly exist, but the way such cases are narratively arranged and foregrounded inflates their prevalence and conveniently fits into the AfD's story. Finally, the editor noted that some Alt-Right actors draw on Nazi ideology for inspiration. In Germany's case, the country's past is visible not in straightforward NS-propaganda, although some continuities in the vocabulary used do exist, but in the attempt to reaffirm the nation's history instead of, allegedly, reducing it to a period of 12 years. This also includes the notion that 'we' should be able to be proud of the Wehrmacht (Gauland), and transcend a culture of shame (Höcke).

As previously indicated, this development gives rise to risks such as, first and foremost, an ultimate end to Germany's comparably self-critical way of 'coming to terms with the past' and an increased liberalisation of society. This might well affect the issue of diversity and immigration, including the possible disaffection of affected minorities. The festively celebrated rebirth of the culturally/racially pure nation not only dissatisfies supposedly non-belonging minorities, but also fulfills the function of bonding among 'pure natives'. This is likely to result in the exclusion of minorities, a development undermining liberal democracy's key ingredient: the protection of minority rights.

These aspects have been at the centre of this chapter. In addition, the AfD has continuously sought to delegitimise 'mainstream' media, has provided a platform for climate-sceptic voices (see chapter 9 in Vol 1) and has created uncertainties concerning the future of the European project. Here, the AfD's vision of an assertive Germany is at odds with current arrangements—as is a potential proximity vis-à-vis Russia (like many far-right actors, the AfD too is relatively pro-Russian, see Shekhovtsov 2018) which would affect global politics. Such a stance would contradict the consensus-based approach to foreign policy characterising domestic German politics ever since the early 2000s—even the European financial crisis rarely led to competing stances among mainstream parties. In times of pressing global issues, the far-right AfD will challenge that approach, opposing the political establishment in the name of 'the German people', and this will introduce risk not only in the area of domestic politics, but also in the domain of foreign policy and international security policy.

Overall, given the historical context, the rise of the AfD is perhaps as striking as the successful presidential campaign of Donald Trump and the British exit from the European Union. Arguments, needs, and resentment visible across 'the west' materialised in Germany too—though standing next to and being 'hybridizised' by local aspects. As the party has now successfully established itself at the centre of German politics, the story will continue.

In summary, the risks arising from the growth of the AfD may be expressed as follows (which are further assessed in chapter 12):

Risk 1. A Potential Reversal of Present-Day Liberal Democracy in Germany

AfD encourages an end to a relatively self-critical engagement with the Nazi era. In line with this, the AfD is furthermore giving voice to, amplifies and mainstreams far-right stances, thus undermining diversity (for example, ethnic, religious and gender diversity), potentially leading to repression of minorities.

Risk 2. A Resistance to Certain Kinds of Multilateral and Multinational Cooperation

AfD may encourage in German society scepticism if not resistance to multilateral and multinational consensus and cooperation which is perceived as hampering Germany's influence, for example the EU and international agreements on climate change.

Risk 3. A Potential for a More Ambivalent Position towards Russia

AfD might affect Germany's position within western security policy; for example, adopting an accommodating attitude towards anti-liberal and anti-democratic policies in Russia, as well as ambivalence towards its aggressive foreign policy.

Risk 4. Disaffection

Stirring up of discrimination, hatred, and hate crimes against ethnic, religious, and immigrant minorities in Germany, may lead to disaffection among those affected.

Risk 5. Attacks on press freedom

Sustained attacks on and delegitimisation of the German 'mainstream' media, in particular public broadcasters, so as to reject and avoid scrutiny, may undermine press freedom and inhibit the media's fundamental role in ensuring public accountability in a democracy.

References

Abbott, H. P. 2002. *The Cambridge Introduction to Narrative.* Cambridge: Cambridge University Press.

ADL. 2018. *From Alt Right to Alt Lite: Naming the Hate.* Anti-Defamation League. New York: ADL. https:/www.adl.org'. (accessed January 31, 2018).

AfD. 2016. *Manifesto for Germany. The Political Programme of the Alternative for Germany.* Online at: https://www.afd.de/wp-content/uploads/sites/111/2017/04/2017-04-12_afd-grundsatzprogramm-englisch_web.pdf (accessed March 13, 2018).

AfD. 2017. *Programm für Deutschland. Wahlprogramm der Alternative für Deutschland für die Wahl zum Deutschen Bundestag am 24. September 2017.* Online at: https://www.afd.de/wp-content/uploads/sites/111/2017/06/2017-06-01_AfD-Bundestagswahlprogramm_Onlinefassung.pdf (accessed March 13, 2018).

AfD Dresden. 2018. Höcke, Kalbitz, Urban: *Aufruf zum Schweigemarsch in Chemnitz.* Online at: https://www.zeit.de/gesellschaft/zeitgeschehen (accessed October 30, 2018).

Alexander, J., and Smith, P. 2001. "The Strong Program in Cultural Theory: Elements of a Structural Hermeneutics". In *Handbook of Sociological Theory,* edited by J. H. Turner. 135–150. Boston: Springer US.

Arzheimer, K. 2015. "The AfD: Finally a Successful Right-Wing Populist Eurosceptic Party for Germany?". *West European Politics*, 38(3), 535–56.

Bail, C. A. 2008. "The Configuration of Symbolic Boundaries Against Immigrants in Europe". *American Sociological Review*, 73(1), 37–59.

Balibar, E. 1991. "Is There a Neo-Racism?" In *Race, Nation, Class: Ambiguous Identities*, edited by E. Balibar and I. Wallerstein. 17–28. New York: Verso.

Beck, U. 1992. *Risk Society—Towards a New Modernity*. London: Sage Publications.

Beck, U. 2007. „Einleitung: Die Inszenierung des Weltrisikos". Pages 13–54. In: U. Beck. *Weltrisikogesellschaft*. Frankfurt/Main: Suhrkamp.

Berbuir, N., Lewandowsky, M. and Siri, J. 2015. "The AfD and its Sympathisers: Finally a Right-Wing Populist Movement in Germany?" *German Politics*, 24(2), 154–78.

Burgess, A. 2015. "The Social Construction of Risk". In *Sage Handbook of Risk Communication*, edited by H. Cho, T. Reimer and K. McComas, 121–139. London: Sage.

Brubaker, R. 2001. "The Return of Assimilation? Changing Perspectives on Immigration and its Sequels in France, Germany, and the United States". *Ethnic and Racial Studies*, 24(4), 531–48.

Chin, R., et al. 2009. *After the Nazi Racial State: Difference and Democracy in Germany and Europe*. Ann Arbor: University of Michigan Press.

Czarniawska, B. 2004. *Narratives in Social Science Research*. London: Sage.

Decker, O., Kiess, J. and Brähler, E. (eds). 2016. *Die enthemmte Mitte. Autoritare und rechtsextreme Einstellung in Deutschland*. Giessen: Psychosozial-Verlag.

Douglas, M. 1966. *Purity and Danger*. London: Routledge.

Eder, K. 2006. "Europe's Borders: The Narrative Construction of the Boundaries of Europe". *European Journal of Social Theory*, 9(2), 255–271.

Forchtner, B. 2016a. *Lessons from the Past? Memory, Narrativity and Subjectivity*. London: Palgrave.

Forchtner, B. 2016b. "Longing for Communal Purity: Countryside, (Far-Right) Nationalism and the (Im)possibility of Progressive Politics of Nostalgia". In *The Commonalities of Global Crises: Markets, Communities and Nostalgia*, edited by C. Karner and B. Weicht. 271–294. London: Palgrave.

Forchtner, B. and Eder, K. 2017. „Europa Erzählen: Optionen Europäischer Identität". In *Europäische Identität in der Krise?* edited by K. Nottbohm and H.-W. Platzer. 179–200. Wiesbaden: VS.

Frankfurter Allgemeine Zeitung. 2014. „Im Gespräch: Der AfD-Bundesvorsitzende Bernd Lucke" (November 24, 2014).

Frankfurter Allgemeine Zeitung. 2014. „Die AfD will die EU schrumpfen. Parteichef Lucke: Die EU steht für Zentralismus, Bürokratie und weniger Freiheit" (January 27, 2014).

Frankfurter Allgemeine Zeitung. 2015. „AfD. Gauland will Einwanderung aus Nahost stoppen". Online at: https://www.faz.net/aktuell/politik/inland/afd-gauland-will-einwanderung-aus-nahost-stoppen-13394774.html (accessed at October 30, 2018).

Frankfurter Allgemeine Zeitung. 2018. *Bei AfD-Jugendorganisation. Gauland: Hitler nur „Vogelschiss" in deutscher Geschichte*. Online at: http://www.faz.net/aktuell/politik/inland/gauland-hitler-nur-vogelschiss-in-deutscher-geschichte-15619502.html (accessed October 30, 2018).

Frye, N. 1957. *Anatomy of Criticism: Four Essays*. Princeton: Princeton University Press.

Funke, H. 2016. *Von Wutbürgern und Brandstiftern. AfD – Pegida – Gewaltnetze*. Berlin: vbb.

Gebhardt, R. 2018. „>Mut zur Warheit<? Compact, Sezession und Junge Freiheit – das publizistische Netzwerk der AfD. In *Völkisch-autoritärer Populismus. Der Rechtsruck in Deutschland und die AfD* edited by Häusler, A. 109–116. Hamburg: VSA.

Gottfried, P. 2008. "The Decline and Rise of the Alternative Right". Address to H.L. Mencken Club AGM, November 21–23, 2008. Reproduced December 1, 2008 by *Taki's Magazine*. www.tkimag.com.

Griffin, R. 1993. *The Nature of Fascism*. London: Routledge.

Grimm, R. 2015. "The Rise of the German Eurosceptic Party Alternative für Deutschland, Between Ordoliberal Critique and Popular Anxiety". *International Political Science Review*, 36(3): 264–78.

Hansen, H. 2007. *Die Sozialistische Reichspartei (SRP): Aufstieg Und Scheitern Einer Rechtsextremen Partei*. Düsseldorf: Droste.

Häusler, A. (ed). 2016. *Die Alternative Für Deutschland: Programmatik, Entwicklung Und Politische Verortung*. Wiesbaden: Springer VS.

Häusler, A. 2018. "Die AfD: Partei des völkisch-autoritären Populismus" In *Völkisch-autoritärer Populismus: der Rechtsruck in Deutschland und die AfD* edited by Häusler, A. Hamburg: VSA. 9–20.

Holzer, W. I. 1994. *Rechtsextremismus: Konturen, Definitionsmerkmale und Erklärungsansätze: Sonderdruck aus Handbuch des österreichischen Rechtsextremismus*. Wien: Deuticke.

Johnson, B.B. and Covello, V.T. (eds). 1987. *The Social and Cultural Construction of Risk: Essays on Risk Selection and Perception*. New York: Springer.

Kellershohn, H. 1998. „Völkischer Nationalismus und seine Kernideologeme. Eine knappe Begriffserklärung". In *Der Spuk ist nicht vorbei. Völkisch-nationalistische Ideologeme im öffentlichen Diskurs der Gegenwart* edited by Jäger, S. et al. Duisburg: DISS.

Korteweg, A. C. and Yurdakul, G. 2014. *The Headscarf Debates: Conflicts of National Belonging*. Stanford: Stanford University Press.

Köttig, M., Bitzan, R. and Petö, A. (eds). 2017. *Gender and Far Right Politics in Europe*. Cham: Palgrave.

Lamont, M. and Molnár, V. 2002. "The Study of Boundaries in the Social Sciences". *Annual Review of Sociology*, 28(1): 167–195.

Lengfeld, H. 2017. „Die ‚Alternative Für Deutschland': Eine Partei für Modernisierungsverlierer?" *KZfSS Kölner Zeitschrift für Soziologie und Sozialpsychologie*, 69(2): 209–32.

Lewandowsky, M., Giebler, H. and Wagner, A. 2016. „Rechtspopulismus in Deutschland. Eine empirische Einordnung der Parteien zur Bundestagswahl 2013 unter besonderer Berücksichtigung der AfD". *Politische Vierteljahresschrift*, 57(2): 247–75.

Lochocki, T. 2018. *The Rise of Populism in Western Europe: A Media Analysis on Failed Political Messaging*. Cham, Switzerland: Springer.

Lux, T. 2018. „Die AfD und die unteren Statuslagen. Eine Forschungsnotiz zu Holger Lengfelds Studie Die ‚Alternative für Deutschland': eine Partei fur Modernisierungsverlierer?" *KZfSS Kölner Zeitschrift für Soziologie und Sozialpsychologie*, 70(2), 255–273.

Mudde, C. 2007. *Populist Radical Right Parties in Europe*. Cambridge: Cambridge University Press.

Müller, Jan-Werner. 2016. *What Is Populism?* Philadelphia: University of Pennsylvania Press.

Özvatan, Ö. 2017. "German-Turkish Tensions in a Collapsing Jamaica Coalition". *openDemocracy*. Online at: https://www.opendemocracy.net/can-europe-make-it/zg-r-zvatan/german-turkish-tensions-in-collapsing-jamaica-coalition (accessed February 18, 2018).

Pieper, M., Haussner, S. and Kaeding, M. 2015. „Die Vermessung des Euroskeptizismus der Alternative für Deutschland (AfD) im Frühjahr 2014". In *Die Europawahl 2014: Spitzenkandidaten, Protestparteien, Nichtwähler*, edited by M. Kaeding and N. Switek. 149–160 Wiesbaden: Springer.

Pirro, A.L. and van Kessel, S. 2017. "United in Opposition? The Populist Radical Right's EU-Pessimism in Time of Crisis". *Journal of European Integration*, 39(4), 405-420.

Politbarometer. 2014. Langzeitentwicklung Politik II: *„Wichtige Probleme in Deutschland"*. Forschungsgruppe Wahlen.

Quendt, M. 2016. *Rassismus, Radikalisierung, Rechtsterrorismus: Wie der NSU Entstand und was er über die Gesellschaft verrät*. Weinheim: Beltz Juventa.

Ricoeur, P. 1984. *Time and Narrative*, Vol 1. Chicago, Ill: University of Chicago Press.

Salzborn, S. 2014. *Rechtsextremismus: Erscheinungsformen und Erklärungsansätze*. Baden-Baden: Nomos.

Salzborn, S. 2017. „Von der offenen zur geschlossenen Gesellschaft. Die AfD und die Renaissance des deutschen Opfermythos im rechten Diskurs". In *AfD & FPÖ: Antisemitismus, völkischer Nationalismus und Geschlechterbilder*, edited by S. Grigat. 27–40. Baden-Baden: Nomos.

Shekhovtsov, A. 2018. *Russia and the Western Far Right. Tango Noir.* Oxon: Routledge.

Somers, M. R. 1994. "The Narrative Constitution of Identity: a Relational and Network Approach". *Theory and Society*, 23(5), 605–649.

Spiegel Online. 2016. „AfD-Chefin über Grenzkontrollen: „Notfalls auch von der Schusswaffe Gebrauch machen"". Online at: http://www.spiegel.de/politik/deutschland/petry-fordert-notfalls-schusswaffen-einsatz-gegen-fluechtlinge-an-der-grenze-a-1074816.html (accessed October 30, 2018).

Süddeutsche Zeitung. 2010. „Merkel: „Multikulti ist absolut gescheitert"". Online at: https://www.sueddeutsche.de/politik/integration-seehofer-sieben-punkte-plan-gegen-zuwanderung-1.1012736 (accessed October 30, 2018).

Süddeutsche Zeitung. 2015. „'Blanker Rassismus': Höcke und die Fortpflanzung der Afrikaner". Online at: https://www.sueddeutsche.de/politik/afd-thueringen-blanker-rassismus-hoecke-und-die-fortpflanzung-der-afrikaner-1.2780159 (accessed October 30, 2018).

Toolan, M. J. 1988. *Narrative: A Critical Linguistic Introduction.* London: Routledge.

Twitter. 2018. Tweet by Markus Frohnmaier online at: https://www.zeit.de/gesellschaft/zeitgeschehen/2018-08/chemnitz-alexander-gauland-ausschreitungen (accessed October 30, 2018).

Virchow, F. 2017. „Entgrenzung und Ordnung. Entstehung und Artikulation einer völkisch-nationalistischen Massenbewegung in Deutschland". *Neue Kriminalpolitik*, 29(1): 36–48.

Wagner-Pacifici, R. E. 1986. *The Moro Morality play: Terrorism as Social Drama.* Chicago: University of Chicago Press.

Weiss, V. 2017. *Die Autoritäre Revolte: Die Neue Rechte Und Der Untergang Des Abendlandes.* Stuttgart: Klett-Cotta.

Yuval-Davis, N. 2011. *The Politics of Belonging: Intersectional Contestations.* London: Sage.

Zeit Online. 2018. „Chemnitz. Alexander Gauland bezeichnet Übergriffe in Chemnitz als Normal". Online at: https://www.zeit.de/gesellschaft/zeitgeschehen/2018-08/chemnitz-alexander-gauland-ausschreitungen (accessed October 30, 2018).

Chapter 8: Marine Le Pen and the Front National in France: Between Populisms in the 2017 Elections and Beyond

By Gabriel Goodliffe

Abstract

This chapter traces recent history of Front National under Marine Le Pen's leadership. From a period in which FN was dominated by statist sovereignist policies, deep-seated ideological and strategic divisions arose whereby earlier far-right nativist authoritarian ideology eventually returned and took over the party. The in-fighting led to a muddled and erratic FN electoral campaign in 2017 and a fall in electoral appeal. Bitter rivalry between the two factions eventually split the party, with the Philippot (FN deputy leader) faction quitting in 2017. The populist anti-immigrant nationalist tone of the emergent FN may have mixed appeal for the changing character of the electorate and voter groups. The chapter also considers the viability of Marine Le Pen's continuing leadership of a far-right authoritarian FN.

Key words: Front National, Marine Le Pen, France, far-right, authoritarianism, risks

Marine Le Pen and the FN

Within the Front National (FN), Marine Le Pen's performance in the 2017 French presidential race, followed by that of the party's candidates in the ensuing parliamentary elections, was cause for disappointment if not despair. Numerous FN activists felt that Le Pen and the party had dramatically underperformed in these elections, some going so far as to judge that they had squandered an unprecedented electoral chance to win power.[1] The disaffection among the party

1 Such was the opinion of former party number two Bruno Mégret who observed that, despite "the collapse of the traditional political parties [which] had put the FN in an ideal ideological and electoral position to ensure [the nation´s] renewal,"

faithful was so great that Le Pen's leadership was even called into question, with a poll taken prior to the FN's March 2018 congress revealing that 55% of voters did not wish her to be the party's presidential candidate in 2022, and that less than one in five believed that she inspired confidence as a potential president (Willsher 2018). Taking stock of this appraisal, on the night of her defeat in the second-round presidential run-off Marine Le Pen called for a "profound transformation" and "renewal" of the FN so that it could "rise to the historic occasion and meet the expectations of the French" (AFP 2017).

On the face of it, such an assessment of Le Pen and her party's performance in the 2017 elections seems harsh. In both the first and second rounds of the presidential election, Le Pen smashed the FN's previous records, exceeding her 2012 performance by 1.2 million votes in the first round and then winning over 10.6 million votes (33.9%) in the second round, nearly doubling the score attained by her father in the run-off of the 2002 election. Considered in historical perspective, the 2017 presidential race yielded the party's best result since its founding in 1972, representing the seventh consecutive electoral cycle in which the party had exceeded its previous score in the same type of election since Marine Le Pen had assumed the party's leadership in January 2011. In turn, in the subsequent parliamentary elections, the FN returned its highest tally of eight deputies to the National Assembly since the abrogation of proportional representation in 1988, quadrupling the number of seats it won in 2012.

This chapter seeks to make sense of this contradiction between Marine Le Pen's and the FN's progress in the 2017 national elections and the negative reading of them by its leaders and members and to assess what it bodes for the party's development. Moving beyond the conjunctural explanations that focus on Le Pen's campaign (Perrineau 2017a; Lebourg 2017), the chapter argues that the latter reflected deep-seated ideological and strategic divisions which ultimately diminished its thematic coherence and electoral appeal. In turn, far from reconciling these internal divisions, the 2017 elections served instead to exacerbate them, pitting two leadership factions, sets of activists, and groups of voters against one another under the increasingly shaky auspices of Marine Le Pen's leadership. The chapter considers what

---

the party, "on account of an ill-adapted program and contradictory strategy…, had missed this historic opportunity." (Domenach 2017)

these divisions spell for Le Pen's leadership of the FN and, more broadly, for the party's post-2017 direction and prospects within an increasingly fractured and fluid partisan landscape.

Beyond a Conjunctural Account

Most explanations for Marine Le Pen's and the FN's underperformance in the 2017 national elections highlight the contrast between the favorable socio-structural and political context for the campaign, and its lack of focus and ineffectiveness (Perrineau 2017a, 252–53). From this perspective, despite the country's lacklustre economic performance and the climate of anxiety spawned by the 2015–16 terrorist attacks which lent resonance to the FN's criticisms of the Hollande administration's pro-EU economic agenda and security and immigration policies, a number of conjunctural factors of the party's and Marine Le Pen's own making overtook the campaign to squander these initial advantages and yield an unsatisfactory outcome for the party. At one level, its lack of thematic clarity—shifting from an initially reassuring line that sought to affirm Le Pen's presidential aura through the end of 2016 and start of 2017 to an affirmation of the party's anti-immigration, anti-Islamic repressive credentials in the run-up to the first round before finally giving way to an anti-EU economically and socially protectionist program during the two weeks preceding the run-off—created the impression of a reactive and poorly organized campaign that lacked direction and purpose. This impression of confusion was reinforced by the multiple judicial investigations in which Le Pen and her party found themselves embroiled as the campaign progressed.[2] Finally, growing doubts emerged regarding Marine Le

---

2 Thus, in October 2016 a case involving alleged campaign financing irregularities in the context of the 2012 campaign was deemed to be important enough to be transferred to a criminal court for judgement. In turn, in December 2016, following up on an internal investigation by the European Parliament into the illicit use of financial supports provided to the FN's European MP's to finance domestic party activities, the Paris Prosecutor's Office opened a judicial enquiry into these claims of abuse (Perrineau 2017a, 255). Among other things, these inquiries into the FN's alleged financial improprieties threw a light onto the more obscure aspects of the FN's finances, and notably its ties to Putin's Russia, which was responsible for lending the party 11 million euros in 2014 and a further three million euros in June 2016 in order to help underwrite its campaigns (Turchi 2018). Finally, these financial cases materialized on the backdrop of the protracted judicial proceeding opposing Marine Le Pen to her father following her expulsion of Jean-Marie Le Pen from the party presidium in April 2015 in response to TV and press interviews in

Pen's leadership competence and presidential calibre as the campaign progressed. In particular, her disastrous performance in the one-on-one debate against Emmanuel Macron just days before the second round vote, underscoring her ignorance of vital issues, such as her stated intention to withdraw from the euro currency, on which she had predicated her campaign as well as her serial aggressiveness and lack of decorum more generally, turned undecided voters against her while bringing FN members to question her candidacy and even leadership of the party.[3]

Thus, Le Pen saw her initial lead evaporate from 29% of voting intentions in September 2016 to 21.3% in the first round (23 April 2017), with a 6% erosion occurring in the single month preceding the vote. Likewise, largely as result of her debate performance which was estimated to have cost her 3.1% of the vote while affording a 3.5% boost to her opponent in the second round run-off,[4] she fell well shy of the 40% that had been projected after the first round (Vedel 2015, 112; Jaffré 2015, 279). In turn, this result started a negative spiral that carried over into the succeeding legislative elections in which the FN fell short of the fifteen seats required to form a parliamentary group, let alone the fifty or sixty seats predicted at the start of the campaign (Legrand 2016).

Yet, it could be argued that Marine Le Pen's muddled and erratic campaign was not simply attributable to poor logistics and organization, or even to her own failings as a candidate. Indeed, rather than

---

which he had repeated his incendiary claim—first made in 1987—that "the gas chambers were a mere detail in the history of the Second World War." By reminding voters of the party's radical right-wing pedigree and its historical associations with the country's collaborationist past, the ensuing scandal, sustained by the legal battle surrounding Le Pen *père*'s subsequent eviction from the FN, undermined his daughter's strategy to normalize the latter as a precondition for assuming the responsibilities of power (Lepelletier 2018).

3 Capturing this point, one FN insider observed: "Before the debate, Marine was '*présidentiable*,' she had put in some good appearances during the week following the first round. Whirlpool and the fishing boat [at the port of Grau-du-Roi], that was well-played, the [electoral] alliance with [Nicolas] Dupont-Aignan as well, and people on the right were only waiting for the damned debate to be persuaded [to vote for her.] Everywhere I heard guys on the right saying 'I don't care, I'm voting for Marine.' After the debate, in our party branch we received letters containing [FN membership] cards... that had been cut in two" (Turchi 2017).

4 In particular, it is estimated that roughly a million Fillon voters from the first round who had planned to vote for Le Pen in the run-off either changed their vote to Macron or abstained as a result of the debate (Jaffré 2015, 280).

representing actual causes of the problem, the above factors may instead have been symptomatic of deeper programmatic and strategic divisions within the party hierarchy, which in turn derived from the FN's ideologically conflicted, if not contradictory, development. From this perspective, the inconstancy of Le Pen's campaign was not only or even primarily the result of poor campaign stewardship or her own incompetence, but the product of a dialectical struggle for ideological and strategic primacy between two distinct and ultimately contrary conceptions of the FN's political purpose and of the optimal means by which to achieve it. In a strongly centralized anti-system niche party in which the attribution of politically remunerative posts within the upper echelons of the party hierarchy or as elected officials are exclusively decided by the party president, these ideological divisions in turn translated into increasingly personalized contests for programmatic and organizational supremacy within the party (Lebourg 2015, 125–26).

Nativist Authoritarianism

Ideological, and by extension institutional, struggles have been the hallmark of the FN's development since the party's foundation in 1972, the latter having been conceived as the organizational embodiment of a 'nationalist compromise' between the various branches and sensibilities composing the postwar French radical right (Milza 1986, 341–47, 437–39). As the factional components comprising the FN changed and the programs they advanced evolved, by the mid-1990s and especially from 2011 onwards the outlines of two distinct factions could be distinguished.

The first and oldest of these, the FN's nativist authoritarian faction, placed the ideological onus on cultural and identity-based issues, asserting the organic, essentialist, and exclusionary conception of the nation and society developed historically by the French national populist right as a basis for its political program (Goodliffe 2012, Ch. 2). Accordingly, since the late 1970s, this faction has campaigned on the triptych of 'immigration-insecurity-Islam', linking the principal social problems—notably rising unemployment and crime—plaguing late twentieth-century French society to the country's non-European immigrant population. Muslim immigrants, particularly those harkening from France's former colonies in the Maghreb, are especially targeted and portrayed as culturally refractory to authentic French traditions and values as initially identified with the country's Roman Catholic heritage and more recently, the secular republican ideal of *laïcité*. Since 9/11, this argument has assumed increasingly conspiratorial form, with Muslim immigrants imputedly seeking to demographically supplant the 'autochthonous' French population and impose a theocratic Islamic state within the country on the basis of Sharia Law (Camus 2011). Markedly absent was an economic or social critique of the prevailing national, and by extension European, economic policy consensus that emerged in France from the mid-1980s around the classical liberal tenets of market deregulation, fiscal consolidation and welfare retrenchment. If the European political concept was to be attacked, it was not so much on the basis of the neoliberal economic policies advanced by the EU as the portrayal of the latter as a cosmopolitan agent of immigration that weakened the primordial organic identities of its member states (Reungoat 2015, 231).

The nativist authoritarian faction can trace its influence within the party back to 1978, when the FN campaigned for the first time on an explicitly anti-immigrant platform rather than the primal anti-communism that had served as a rallying point for the otherwise antagonistic conservative and revolutionary factions present at the party's inception (Lebourg and Beauregard 2012, 99–101). In turn, this current came to reflect the influences of various subgroups that have flocked to the FN over the years, two of which remain significant today. The first is the Catholic nationalist sub-current that, professing the ideas of 'nationalisme intégral' inherited from the Action Française, integrated the FN in 1980–81, making it the oldest continuous sub-current within the party (Camus and Lebourg 2017, 164–65; Milza 1986, 348–50). Spearheaded through the 1980s by *intégriste* Catholic activists such as Romain Marie and Jean Madiran, this sub-current was dominated by Carl Lang and Bruno Gollnisch in the 1990s and 2000s before being symbolically taken over, from 2012 until her political retirement in May 2017, by Marion Maréchal-Le Pen (Lebourg and Beauregard 2012, Chs. 5–6; Mestre and Monnot 2015, 52). After a period of relative decline following Marine Le Pen's attempts to marginalize it within the party from 2004 onwards, culminating in her victory over Gollnisch to succeed her father as FN president at the 2011 party congress, this sub-current has recently seen its influence within the FN wax again, notably through its orchestration of the demonstrations against the Taubira Law of May 2013 which legalized gay marriage and the adoption of children by gay couples (Camus and Lebourg 2017, 162).

Despite its increasing sociopolitical visibility, however, Catholic nationalism remains secondary in importance to the mégrétiste subcurrent on the FN's nativist authoritarian right, particularly within the party's upper echelons. Composed of former followers of Bruno Mégret who broke with Jean-Marie Le Pen's FN in 1998 before being accepted back into it by Marine Le Pen since the mid-2000s, this cadre—notably Le Pen's brother-in-law Philippe Olivier, Nicolas Bay, Emmanuel Leroy, Steeve Briois, and Bruno Bilde—have sought to advance a nativist authoritarian program by euphemizing its xenophobic underpinnings whilst professionalizing the party by trying to build up a reservoir of local candidates in order to boost its appeal among conservative voters (Mestre and Monnot 2015, 56, 59).

As a result of these various civil society and grassroots initiatives, the FN's nativist authoritarian faction became particularly entrenched with party activists and remains dominant among party members. By the same token, the leading figures of this faction, such as Maréchal-Le Pen among the Catholic nationalists or Steeve Briois among the mégrétistes, built up substantial local power bases that counterbalanced the party's centralized Parisian executive (Crépon and Lebourg 2015, 450).

Strategically speaking, the proponents of nativist authoritarianism have historically alternated between a line of partisan differentiation through radicalization as a means of claiming an electoral monopoly on the anti-immigrant vote, versus that of contemplating electoral alliances with the mainstream right in order to help normalize the party.[5] Accordingly, the FN first broke onto the French political scene by winning representation on the municipal council of the town

5 Reflecting the party's initial dispensation as an alliance of revolutionary and conservative elements of the French radical right in the 1970s, nativist authoritarians within the FN have periodically entertained relations with and incorporated elements drawn from groups of the neo-fascist right, such as l'Œuvre Française or the Bloc Identitaire, who have made the struggle against Islam and the recreation of a preternatural 'white' France key pillars of their political struggle. However, since Marine Le Pen's embrace of *dédiabolisation* in 2011, these elements have either been expelled from the party or forced to soften their openly racialist and anti-Semitic discourses as part of the FN's strategy of partisan normalization (Lebourg 2015, 127-37).

of Dreux in September 1983, after backing the candidate of the mainstream right so the latter could win the mayoralty in the run-off (Milza 1986, 398–99). In turn, in the 1998 regional elections, the mainstream right won control of five of the country's 22 metropolitan regions by entering into electoral alliances with the FN in return for offering the latter a governing role within these regional councils (Lebourg and Beauregard 2012, 189–90). In short, the strategic orientation envisioning an alliance with the governmental right on the basis of an increasingly culturally authoritarian anti-immigrant program, though it really became preponderant following Nicolas Sarkozy's election in 2007, has been present within the FN for some time.

Statist Sovereignism

However, this program and strategy became a source of contention with the second principal current discernible within the FN, the statist sovereignist faction that emerged from the mid-1990s on. As the party made electoral inroads among lower, particularly working, class voters during this period, certain FN leaders, starting with Mégret himself, began to develop an economically nationalist orientation as a complement to its traditional nativist authoritarianism in order to solidify its attraction among this electorate (Lebourg and Beauregard 2012, 178–80). This orientation broadened the FN's critique of late-twentieth century French society and addressed the economic and social realms so as to appeal to the growing segment of the population which, under the twin processes of market deregulation and welfare state retrenchment engaged by the French state since the 1980s (Goodliffe 2012, 266–71, 327–28), had seen their jobs increasingly threatened and living standards progressively deteriorate. Posing the FN as the foremost critic of neoliberal globalization and European integration, this current sought to meld the party's traditional culturally authoritarian and identity-based politics with progressive economic and social policy proposals under the guise of an externally protectionist and internally statist and welfare chauvinist program (Ivaldi 2015, 171–72). Proclaiming itself the herald of a syncretic "neither right nor left" orientation that combined the right's cultural authoritarianism and nativism with the left's economic and social interventionism[6], the political aim of this faction was to achieve a synthesis between the traditional petit bourgeois electorate that had gravitated to the party during the 1980s with the new working class electorate that flocked to it from the 1990s on. Thus, it sought to resurrect the alliance between *l'atelier* (the workshop) and *la boutique* (the small shop) first envisioned by interwar fascist theorists.

However, it was really following Marine Le Pen's accession to the FN's leadership in January 2011 and her subsequent recruitment of figures, such as Florian Philippot and Paul-Marie Couteaux, issuing from anti-EU—principally Chevènementiste and Gaullist—formations that this line was programmatically systematized and the statist sovereignist faction grew ascendant within the party (Mestre and Monnot 2015, 58). Under Philippot, who became party number two after running Le Pen's 2012 campaign, the FN embraced a strategy of *dédiabolisation* (un-demonization) which sought to go beyond merely professionalizing the party and euphemizing its racially differentialist discourse by explicitly discarding the latter. Instead, the opposition to immigration was folded into a broader, pseudo-humanist critique of globalization and the repudiation of Islam into a generalized defense of *laïcité* (Crépon 2015, 178, 213–14). Thus, while shifting the content of its program increasingly onto the terrain of economic and social policy[7], the party also appeared to abandon Jean-Marie Le Pen's traditionalist social conservativism to embrace increasingly socially liberal positions in the name of the republican ideals of tolerance and equality. Thus, while Marion Maréchal-Le Pen appeared at the forefront of the movement against the Taubira Law, her aunt—a divorced mother of two living out of wedlock with her partner—was

---

6 Coined by the interwar fascist leader Jacques Doriot during the 1930s, this phrase was adopted by the head of the party's youth wing, Samuel Maréchal, in the run-up to the 1995 presidential election before being recycled by Florian Philippot upon his elevation to FN vice-president following the 2012 elections (Lebourg and Beauregard 2012, 178; Mestre and Monnot 2015, 52).

7 Socioeconomic policy proposals accounted for 56% (80 of 144 proposals) of the 2017 presidential campaign program, compared to 37% in 2012 and only 16% at the end of the 1990s. Of these policies, in 2017 80% (64 out of 80) could be situated on the left or anti-liberal end of the economic spectrum versus 68% in 2012, 46% in 1997 and only 18% in 1986. Conversely, cultural or identity-driven policies saw their proportion decline from 44% in the 1997 parliamentary campaign program to 28% in 2012 to only 22% (32 of 144 proposals) in 2017 (Front National 2017; Ivaldi 2015, 166-68).

conspicuous by her non-participation in the latter. By the same token, since 2011 the party has been trying to appeal to gays and Jews as a means of reinforcing its culturally tolerant credentials in contradistinction to the homophobia and anti-Semitism it identifies with Islam. In marked contrast to the days when the party was led by her father, who notoriously termed homosexuality a "biological and social anomaly" and whose anti-Semitic sallies were legion, the FN has made significant inroads among these groups (Crépon 2012, Ch. 5; Fourquet 2015, 379–84).

In institutional terms, since Philippot's accession to the post of FN number two the statist sovereignist faction became dominant within the party executive and especially the organs responsible for policy analysis and program formation. In particular, Philippot, himself a graduate of the École Normale d'Administration, surrounded himself with educationally and professionally accomplished technocrats who, sharing his statist and sovereignist convictions, occupied the party's top administrative and policy posts and were often nominated to the party's candidate lists. Unsurprisingly, the latter were often resented by career activists who aspired to parlay their service on behalf of the party into promotion to its executive or nomination to a candidate list. As Crépon and Lebourg noted, *la bande de Philippot* were thus widely viewed at the grassroots as "carpetbaggers who had appropriated to themselves the lion's share of the political dividends and media exposure resulting from the party's electoral ascendancy… a process begun long before their arrival" (2015, 446). Moreover, since the nativist authoritarian faction remained dominant among the FN's activist base, the division between the latter and its newly minted technocratic elite came to reflect not just an ideological but also a cultural conflict.

Finally, strategically speaking, whereas the FN's nativist authoritarian wing had more or less openly argued since the late 1980s for entering into political alliances with the mainstream right, its statist sovereignist wing sought to stake out the party's own space within the French party system by espousing an economically as well as culturally anti-systemic nationalism. Thus hoping to secure the support of malcontents deriving from both the left and the right of the political spectrum, this faction sought to introduce a new cleavage into the French partisan debate between the advocates of economic and cultural globalization on the one hand versus the defenders of the nation state, defined in economically sovereign and culturally specific terms, on the other (Perrineau 2017c, 129–30).

Diverging Electorates

The ideological and programmatic factionalism at the heart of Marine Le Pen's FN, translating into opposing strategic orientations and clashing cultural sensibilities, extends to the party's voters. One can distinguish between two temporally, geographically, and sociologically distinct electorates. The first, reflecting the historical dominance of the FN's nativist authoritarian current, appeared in the country's largest cities and its south eastern quadrant, in particular the Mediterranean basin and the Provence, during the 1980s (Milza 1986, 403, 404). Constituted principally of wealthier, petit bourgeois or bourgeois voters who had abandoned the mainstream right on the grounds of its cultural laxity and economic passivity in the face of the first Mitterrand administration's reforms, it is no accident that this primordial FN electorate arose in areas presenting the highest concentrations of non-European—primarily North African—immigration (Milza 1986, 407, 411–14).

Today, while the FN's nativist authoritarian appeal in the cities has largely dissipated, this vote remains dominant in the party's southern strongholds. Of the twelve departments of metropolitan France in which Le Pen won 30% of the first round vote or more in the 2017 presidential election, three (25%) were situated in the south: the Vaucluse (30.53%), the Var (30.43%) and the Pyrénées-Orientales (30.05%). Likewise, in the second round, in the ten metropolitan departments in which she received her highest scores, four were located in the south: the Corse-du-Sud (49.41%), the Var (49.15%), the Haute-Corse (47.72%) and the Pyrénées-Orientales (47.16%) (Perrineau 2017b, 360–73).

The second electorate, which first materialized in the 1995 presidential elections, is concentrated in the country's northern and northeastern industrial heartlands. Primarily composed of blue- and white-collar voters, many of them issuing from a political culture formerly situated on the left (Perrineau 2017c, Ch. 2), these voters represent the 'losers' of globalization who have been worst impacted by deindustrialization, outsourcing and the blights of unemployment and immiseration (Goodliffe 2012, Ch. 8). Contrary to the first set of FN voters, this working class electorate has been drawn primarily to the protectionist and welfarist discourse cultivated by the party's statist sovereignist wing (Perrineau 2017c, 66–9).

Since the 1990s and through the 2000s, it was primarily among this electorate that the FN expanded its support. This was again the case in 2017 when the FN consolidated its more affluent voter base in the south while continuing to progress in its working class bastions of the North and Northeast[8] (Perrineau 2017a, 261–62). Not only did these regions account for the greatest proportion of the FN vote in the presidential election, featuring 75% of the departments in which Le Pen received over 30% of the vote in the first round and 57% of those in which she won over 40% in the second, but they also contained those departments in which the vote for her was strongest. In the first round, the five departments in which she obtained her highest scores—the Aisne (35.67%), Pas-de-Calais (34.35%), Haute-Marne (33.22%), Ardennes (32.41%) and Meuse (32.32%)—were situated in the country's northern and northeastern quadrants. Likewise, these areas accounted for four of the five departments in which Le Pen achieved her best scores in the second round, including the two where she won an outright majority: the Aisne (52.91%), Pas-de-Calais (52.06%), Haute-Marne (49.52%) and Ardennes (49.27%). This electoral dynamic was confirmed in the June 2017 parliamentary elections in which five of the eight deputies returned by the party, including Le Pen herself, represented northern districts—four from the Pas-de-Calais and one from the Nord—versus three from the south (Hullot-Guiot 2017).

The relative preponderance of these distinct southern and northern electorates necessarily influenced the internal balance of power between the nativist authoritarian and statist sovereignist factions in defining the FN's program and strategy during the 2017 campaign. Accordingly, it remains an important factor to consider as the

---

8 Testifying to this lower-class profile, in the first round Marine Le Pen won 37% of industrial workers and 32% of service sector employees (ahead of the far-left candidate Jean-Luc Mélenchon, who came second amongst these categories with 32% and 22%), thereby exceeding her scores of 33% and 28% in 2012. Meanwhile, in the second round she won 56% of the blue-collar vote against Macron (the only socio-professional category amongst which she won a majority) and 46% of *employés*, far outdoing the percentages achieved by her father among these categories—24% and 21%--in the second round of the 2002 presidential election (Ipsos 2017a,5; 2017b, 7; Ifop 2012,10; Mayer 2002,507).

party reassesses its political position in the aftermath of the election and adjusts its future orientation and approach.

Beyond 2017

From the above, it could be argued that it was the fundamental ideological division between the nativist authoritarian and statist sovereignist currents in the party, and the strategic, organizational and electoral tensions it expressed, which accounted for Marine Le Pen's erratic and wayward campaign. In this light, the abrupt shift to emphasizing the traditional triptych of immigration-insecurity-Islam just prior to the first round of presidential voting, followed by the sudden affirmation of welfarist and protectionist themes in preparation for the second round, can as much be read as attempts to placate these rival factions and the cadres, activists and voters who identified with them as the product of a strategic calculus imposed by France's two-round majoritarian presidential electoral system. Reflecting this fundamental intraparty divide, even Le Pen's electoral program for 2017 attempted to square the circle of reconciling these ideologically, strategically, and organizationally antinomic factions by pledging to hold separate referenda in order to placate each of them: the first to write the principle of *la priorité nationale* into the constitution to address nativist authoritarian concerns; the second to restore the country's 'four sovereignties'—fiscal, legislative, territorial, and monetary—to propitiate the statist sovereignists (Perrineau 2017a, 256).

This fundamental struggle between native authoritarians and statist sovereignists continued to play out even following the elections, with representatives of each camp advocating contrary programs and strategies for the period ahead. Thus, in an interview given to *Le Figaro* in July 2017, Florian Philippot, after remarking that "restricting [the FN's] interventions to certain 'fundamental' subjects such as immigration, insecurity and Islamism… would be a fundamental error," called for the FN to situate itself on a broader range of political issues including "primary education, health care, the environment, *francophonie*, higher education, the *banlieues* and animal rights…" The very next day in the same newspaper, the party's ex-mégrétiste general secretary Nicolas Bay unveiled a strategy that ran diametrically counter to that outlined by Philippot, which called for a "frontal struggle against the global ideology of cultural liberalism," a return to an "identitarian" line, stepping up the fight against immigration and Islamism, the defense of the family, and a reversion to liberal economic principles to benefit small-and-medium enterprises (Espargliѐre 2017a). The party's positioning on the euro remained a particular source of conflict among statist sovereignists and nativist authoritarians, with Le Pen trying to propitiate both groups in October 2017 by somewhat contradictorily declaring her determination to quit the common currency unless a fundamental revision of the terms of EU economic governance occurred while assuring that such a departure would not be automatic but the fruit of deliberation with party members and voters (Espargliѐre 2017b).

From this perspective, one could view the intraparty discord manifested during the campaign and in its aftermath as less of a gambit by the FN's leading cadre to contest Marine Le Pen's authority and more as an attempt on the part of the nativist authoritarian faction to reassert the ideological, strategic, and organizational primacy that it had relinquished to the statist sovereignist faction following Le Pen's assumption of the leadership in 2011. By heightening expectations among party activists regarding the outcome of the 2017 elections and then attacking the statist sovereignist faction when Le Pen failed to win 40% of the vote in the second round or the FN failed to form a parliamentary group following the legislative elections, the nativist authoritarian faction was able to turn the tables on its internal rival and reassert its dominance within the party. This shift was consummated with Marine Le Pen's effective expulsion of Philippot from the FN in September 2017 when, in the face of widespread discontent within the party over the election results, she stripped him of his attributions as party vice-president in charge of strategy and communications. Faced with this demotion, Philippot resigned, taking much of his entourage with him to found a new party, Les Patriotes, leaving the statist sovereignist faction within the FN in tatters (Le Monde 2017).

This shift in the party's internal balance-of-power was officially consummated at the FN's 're-foundation' congress in March 2018. Ideologically, the congress heralded a return to the party's nativist and authoritarian fundamentals and a watering down of the statist and welfarist aspects of its program. With the American Alt-Right radical

Steve Bannon (see chapter 5 in Vol 1) looking on,[9] Marine Le Pen elevated the fight against immigration, Islamism and even "nomadism" as the recast party's new priority, while the vexed question of the euro was kicked indefinitely into the long grass to be resolved at an unspecified time (anon 2018; Delaporte 2018). In turn, strategically, the party ditched the 'neither right nor left' line it had espoused since 2012 and retrained its focus on forming alliances around identity and cultural issues with like-minded formations of the right[10]. This strategic shift is signaled by the new name the FN selected for itself, Rassemblement National (National Rally), which, pending membership approval, will replace the party's historic moniker[11].

Last but not least, from an organizational perspective, the 2018 congress saw the leaders of the party's nativist authoritarian wing elected to the first ten places of the FN's central committee. Comprising either *historiques* such as Louis Aliot and Bruno Gollnisch or former mégrétistes such as Steeve Briois and Nicolas Bay, none of this cadre issued from the statist-sovereignist current (anon 2018). Confirming this evolution, Philippe Olivier, Mégret's former lieutenant during the 1990s, replaced Philippot as Marine Le Pen's 'grey eminence' with a mandate to oversee the FN's return to its nativist, culturally authoritarian, and economically liberal fundamentals as well as to make common cause with the post-Sarkozy right (Delaporte 2018). In this sense, despite her absence from the proceedings, the

---

9 Bannon's appearance at the FN's party conference, where he delivered a barnstorming speech in which he exhorted his audience to openly endorse racism and nativism, was part of a broader European tour in which he also expressed support for and promulgated advice to radical right populist parties in Hungary, Germany and Italy, that he was seeking to place himself, following his eviction from the Trump Administration and *Breitbart News*, at the forefront of a global "alt-right" movement spanning the Atlantic (Horowitz 2018). Yet, such an international has already been in evidence in Europe for some time, with the constitution at the FN's initiative in June 2015 of a European parliamentary group of MPs representing European radical right-wing populist parties, the Europe of Nations and Freedom, which, in addition to FN, included members of the Dutch PVV, Austrian FPÖ, Italian Lega Nord, the Flemish Vlaams Belang, Polish KPN, and British UKIP (Le Tallec 2015).

10 In this sense, the FN's electoral alliance with Nicolas Dupont-Aignan's gaullist Debout la France prior to the second round of the presidential election might be seen as heralding this strategic reorientation that was ratified at its 2018 congress.

11 Calling to mind Marcel Déat's collaborationist Rassemblement National Populaire during World War II, this choice may not be totally innocent but signal instead a return to the party's radical right-wing roots (anon 2018).

2018 congress effectively consecrated the political line formerly enshrined by Marion Maréchal-Le Pen within the FN. It is difficult to imagine her not returning to politics in the near future, with her speech at the Conservative Political Action Conference in Washington DC in February 2018 conjoined with her ambition to launch a right-wing Academy of Political Sciences to counter the 'leftism' of *Sciences Po* suggesting as much (Huertas 2018).

In short, at the 2018 party congress, Marine Le Pen returned full circle to the nativist and authoritarian line that had been promulgated by her father and which she had formerly eschewed in favour of a statist sovereignist program and correlative strategy of *dédiabolisation* upon acceding to the FN's leadership in 2011. In the words of a close collaborator, Le Pen "has been reduced to defending a [political] line, essentially one of allying with the right, which is not at all hers [and] which she always fought during the period of Florian Philippot. The paradox," he concluded, "is that she is now surrounded by people who have never followed her line" and finds herself "very much alone" at the party's helm (Delaporte 2018).

Conclusion

Pierre Bourdieu observed that in a democracy any political party—and especially a niche party like the FN—is confronted by two potentially contradictory imperatives. The first, which is defended by the party leadership and cadre, is the institutional objective of winning power by electoral means. The second imperative, which drives the activist base, is to fulfill the party's vocation to transform society in conformity with its ideals (Crépon and Lebourg 2015, 435–36). Thus, whereas the first objective corresponds to a strategy of normalization whereby the party seeks to reassure the electorate by indicating that it is ready to play by the rules of the democratic game, the second fits with a strategy of radicalization through which the party tries to win support by underscoring its anti-systemic authenticity (Dézé 2015, 32–3). From this standpoint, one could argue that the factional struggle within the FN reflects these divergent 'normalizing' versus 'radicalizing' imperatives respectively evinced at the cadre and activist levels. For the former, the abandonment of the statist sovereignist line in favour of returning to the party's nativist authoritarian fundamentals, accompanied by a more or less explicit reassertion of economic liberalism, strategically lays the basis for governing alliances with the 'right of the right', thereby achieving Marine Le Pen's averred goal of participating in the exercise power. Simultaneously, at the level of the party activists, this return to a nativist authoritarian program heralds a reaffirmation of the FN's ideological purity and of its transformative intent, which many believed had been lost with the adoption of Philippot's statist sovereignist line (Crépon and Lebourg 2015, 450). Accordingly, this change in programmatic and strategic orientation has both the external function of endowing the FN with a credible political project by which it can realistically aspire to power[12] while internally reconciling the party leadership with its activist base—a division that ultimately proved fatal to the Philippot statist sovereignism.

That said, this rightward legitimist shift in the wake of the 2017 elections carries its own risks. First, at an intraparty level, there is an electoral risk involved in abandoning wholesale the statist sovereignist line. By reverting to an economically liberal program little different from that professed by the mainstream right, or indeed the new centrist government of Emmanuel Macron, the party could jeopardize its appeal among its newly won working class electorate. This point is especially worth remembering given that, as noted above, the greatest electoral gains registered by the FN since the 1990s have been precisely among such voters from the country's depressed former industrial heartlands. By placing the programmatic onus on cultural and identity-based issues while reverting to its preternatural economic liberalism, the FN thus risks losing the working class electorate it had won through its defense of a statist sovereignist line.

In turn, the FN's reversion to a nativist authoritarian line on cultural issues and a liberal one on economics also carries risks from an external partisan perspective, as its program proves increasingly indistinguishable from that of a mainstream right moving to occupy the same space on the political spectrum. Indeed, under the stewardship of Laurent Wauquiez, Les Républicains (LR), shorn of more centrist elements that chose to rally to the new president's party, have dou-

---

12 It is this line, combining cultural authoritarianism and nativism with economic liberalism, which has enabled radical right populist parties to enter governments in Austria, the Netherlands and Scandinavia (Camus and Lebourg 2017, 185, 188–189, 191–192, 199–200).

bled down on the strategy of *droitisation* first adopted by Nicolas Sarkozy during the 2007 election campaign (Delaporte 2017; Gougou and Labouret 2013; 294–96). Consequently, their discourse and proposals regarding immigration and Islam are now virtually identical to those advanced by the FN. Although the leaders of the 're-founded' FN will be betting that voters will continue 'to prefer the original to the copy', its proximity to LR on both cultural and economic issues could end up damaging the party's brand by diluting the anti-systemic appeal that formerly distinguished it from the mainstream right. Thus, it risks following in the footsteps of the Movimento Soziale Italiano in Italy which, by renouncing its radical nationalist roots and changing its name in order to pursue an alliance strategy with the mainstream right in the mid-1990s, effectively jettisoned its electoral specificity, condemning it to political extinction a little more than a decade later (Camus and Lebourg 2017, 181–83). More broadly, the FN's rightward shift on economics would leave it poorly placed to capitalize on the potential failure of the Macron government's liberalizing agenda or a recrudescence of the Eurozone debt crisis. In this sense, in terms of the political and structural contexts in which it has been undertaken, only time will tell whether the FN's abandonment of statist sovereignism in favour of nativist authoritarianism proved judicious.

Despite this uncertainty over its change of direction, however, the party will doubtless continue to play a key if not defining role in French politics in the years to come. The prospects for Marine Le Pen are much less clear. Not only has she had trouble regaining voters' and activists' confidence in the wake of her poorly managed campaign and disastrous debate against Macron, but one could legitimately ask whether she can now credibly assume the new nativist authoritarian line adopted at the March 2018 party congress—a line that she herself has never previously espoused and which, following her elevation of Philippot as party number two from 2012 to 2017, she even actively combatted. Thus, though her institutional position as FN president remains secure, it is not clear that, from an electoral perspective, she is ideologically and strategically best equipped to lead the party as it embarks on this new phase in its political-institutional development.

Therefore, despite attaining the highest electoral score in a presidential election and winning the most parliamentary seats in its history under the Fifth Republic's two-round majoritarian voting system, the FN is paradoxically embarking upon its greatest period of uncertainty since the mégrétiste scission of 1998–99. How effectively its leadership, starting with Marine Le Pen, is able to cope and, under a new name, restore the party's upward trajectory will be seen over the coming year with a preliminary answer to be provided in the 2019 European elections.

Of course, these risks impacting the Front National as a party and Marine Le Pen as its leader cannot simply be identified and assessed in isolation. The FN's success or failure will also have significant impacts on French society, its governance, and possibly even democracy itself. For example, should the FN continue to be successful in altering the terms of political debate and persuading the governing parties of the centre right and even left to 'correct' their stance and adopt policies that are increasingly exclusionary on immigration or Islam on the one hand, and assertive of national sovereignty (notably regarding the EU) on the other, or indeed should the party ever win national elections outright, such an outcome is likely to carry adverse effects that would impact society as a whole or important sections of it with respect to human rights, discrimination, hate crime etc. In such a case, representative democracy itself might well find itself at risk, with moderate centrist policies growing increasingly compromised or corrupted as a result of such pressure or even being discarded by an elected authoritarian FN government.

Accordingly, the risks arising in relation to the Front National may be summarized as follows (and assessed further in chapter 12):

Risks for the Front National

Risk 1. Policy swings and changes damage broad electoral appeal

The blurring of FN economic policies with mainstream centre-right parties may result in a loss of electoral support from working class voters, especially in the country's northern industrial belt.

Risk 2. Factional rivalries may cause a fragmented FN and dissipation of votes

Power struggles between ideological factions within the FN may lead to new rival parties splitting off (e.g. Les Patriotes) and a resulting fragmentation of the FN's populist vote.

Risks for Marine Le Pen

Risk 1. Personal dissonance with FN's nativist renewed authoritarian emphasis

Marine Le Pen's poor affinity with the newly predominant nativist authoritarian FN culture may result in her incapacity to remain as FN president and her eventual withdrawal or even removal from active involvement. In this respect, the 2022 presidential and parliamentary elections are likely to be determinative.

Risks for French Society, Governance, and Democracy

Risk 1. FN successes leading to greater authoritarianism and potentially harsh social and cultural policies from government

The FN's success in persuading the mainstream parties to adopt exclusionary and chauvinistic policies, or an outright FN victory in future national elections, could result in adverse effects on human rights, discrimination, hate crimes, as well as France's withdrawal from the EU.

Risk 2. Continued FN successes leading to threats to representative democracy

FN successes may result in moderate policies of mainstream centre-right and even centre-left parties becoming increasingly compromised, corrupted or even swept away by an elected authoritarian FN government, thereby threatening representative democracy itself.

References

Agence France Presse. 2017. "Malgré un Score Historique, Crise en Perspective au Front National." *France 24*. May 8, 2017. http://www.france24.com/fr/20170507-battue-marine-le-pen-pas-tout-perdu-presidentielle-fn-front-national-philippot-marechal.

anon. 2017. "FN: les Règlements de Comptes ont Commencé." *Médiapart*. May 8. https://www.mediapart.fr/journal/france/070517/fn-les-reglements-de-comptes-ont-commence.

anon. 2018. "Le FN Tourne la Page de la 'Dédiabolisation.'" *Médiapart*. March 11, 2018. https://www.mediapart.fr/journal/france/110318/le-fn-tourne-la-page-de-la-dediabolisation?

Camus, Jean-Yves and Nicolas Lebourg. 2017. *Far Right Politics in Europe*. trans. J.M. Todd. Cambridge, MA: Belknap Press.

Camus, Renaud. 2011. *Le Grand Remplacement.* Paris: David Reinharc.

Crépon, Sylvain. 2012. *Enquête au Cœur du Nouveau Front National.* Paris: Nouveau Monde.

Crépon, Sylvain and Nicolas Lebourg. 2015. "Le Renouvellement du Militantisme Frontiste" in *Les Faux-Semblants du Front National. Sociologie d'un Parti Politique*, edited by S. Crépon, A. Dézé and N. Mayer. 435–451. Paris: Presses de Sciences Po.

Delaporte, Lucie. 2017. "Derrière Wauquiez, l'Offensive des Nouveaux Conservateurs." *Médiapart.* September 7, 2017. https://www.mediapart.fr/journal/france/070917/derriere-wauquiez-l-offensive-des-nouveaux-conservateurs.

Delaporte, Lucie. 2018. "Le FN Fragilisé à la Veille de Son Congrès." *Médiapart.* March 10, 2018. https://www.mediapart.fr/journal/france/090318/le-fn-fragilise-la-veille-de-son-congres.

Dézé, Alexandre. 2015. "La 'Dédiabolisation.' Une Nouvelle Stratégie?". In *Les Faux-Semblants du Front National,* edited by S. Crépon, A. Dézé, and N. Mayer. 27–50. Paris: Presses de Sciences Po.

Domenach, Hervé. 2017. "Bruno Mégret: "Le Débat Sera le Point de Détail de Marine Le Pen." *Le Point.* June 29, 2017. http://www.lepoint.fr/politique/bruno-megret-le-debat-sera-le-point-de-detail-de-marine-le-pen-29-06-2017-2139196_20.php#xtor=CS2-282.

Espargliére, Loup. 2017a. "Après Son Séminaire, le FN à l'Épreuve de la Refondation," *Médiapart.* July 26, 2017. https://www.mediapart.fr/journal/france/250717/apres-son-seminaire-le-fn-l-epreuve-de-la-refondation.

Espargliére, Loup. 2017b. "Le FN Étale Ses Divisions sur l'Europe," *Médiapart.* October 10, 2017. https://www.mediapart.fr/journal/france/201017/au-front-national-pas-de-revolution-copernicienne-sur-leurope-le-fn-confirme-un-changement-de-methode-sur.

Fourquet, Jérôme. 2015. "Le Vote Front National dans les Électorats Musulmans et Juifs". In *Les Faux-Semblants du Front National,* edited by S. Crépon, A. Dézé, and N. Mayer. 375–393. Paris: Presses de Sciences Po.

Front National. 2017. *144 Engagements Présidentiels Marine 2017.* March. http://www.frontnational.com/le-projet-de-marine-le-pen/.

Goodliffe, Gabriel. 2012. *The Resurgence of the Radical Right in France: From Boulangisme to the Front National.* New York: Cambridge University Press.

Gougou, Florent and Simon Labouret. 2013. "La Fin de la Tripartition? Les Recompositions de la Droite et la Transformation du Système Partisan." *Revue Française de Science Politique.* 63(2), 279–302.

Horowitz, Jason. 2018. "Steve Bannon Is Done Wrecking the American Establishment. Now He Wants to Destroy Europe's." *New York Times.* March 9, 2018. https://www.nytimes.com/2018/03/09/world/europe/horowitz-europe-populism.html.

Huertas, Hubert. 2018. "Marion Maréchal-Le Pen: une Primaire à l'Extrême Droite." *Médiapart*. February 26, 2018. https://www.mediapart.fr/journal/france/260218/marion-marechal-le-pen-une-primaire-l-extreme-droite.

Hullot-Guiot, Kim. 2017. "Qui Sont les Huit Députés FN Élus à l'Assemblée?" *Libération*. June 18, 2017. http://www.liberation.fr/politiques/2017/06/18/qui-sont-les-huit-deputes-fn-elus-a-l-assemblee_1577726.

Ifop. 2012. "Premier Tour de l'Élection Présidentielle 2012: Profil des Électeurs et Clés du Scrutin." *Élection Présidentielle 2012*. April 22, 2012. Page 73.

Ipsos. 2017a. "1er Tour: Sociologie des Électorats et Profils des Abstentionnistes." *Élection Présidentielle 2017*. April 19–22, 2017. Page 31.

Ipsos. 2017b. "2nd Tour: Sociologie des Électorats et Profils des Abstentionnistes." *Élection Présidentielle 2017*. May 4–6, 2017. Page 16.

Ivaldi, Gilles. 2015. "Du Néolibéralisme au Social-Populisme? La Transformation du Programme Économique du Front National 1986–2012". In *Les Faux-Semblants du Front National*, edited by S. Crépon, A. Dézé, and N. Mayer. 163–183. Paris: Presses de Sciences Po.

Jaffré, Jerôme. 2017. "Un Second Tour de Présidentielle Si Différent du Duel Chirac-Le Pen de 2002". In *Le Vote Disruptif. Les Élections Présidentielle et Législatives de 2017*, edited by P. Perrineau. 269–284. Paris: Presses de Sciences Po.

Le Monde. 2017. "Florian Philippot Annonce qu'il Quitte le Front National." *Le Monde*. September 21, 2017. http://www.lemonde.fr/politique/article/2017/09/21/florian-philippot-annonce-qu-il-quitte-le-front-national_5188871_823448.html.

Lebourg, Nicolas. 2015. "Le Front National et la Galaxie des Extrêmes Droites Radicales". In *Les Faux-Semblants du Front National*, edited by S. Crépon, A. Dézé and N. Mayer. 121–39. Paris: Presses de Sciences Po.

Lebourg, Nicolas. 2017. "Comment Marine Le Pen a Mené une Campagne Médiocre." *Médiapart*. May 3, 2017. https://www.mediapart.fr/journal/france/220417/comment-marine-le-pen-mene-une-campagne-mediocre.

Lebourg, Nicolas and Joseph Beauregard. 2012. *Dans l'Ombre des Le Pen. Une Histoire des Numéros 2 du FN*. Paris: Nouveau Monde.

Legrand, Baptiste. 2016. "60 Députés FN à l'Assemblée en 2017?" *L'Obs*. June 22, 2016. https://www.nouvelobs.com/politique/20160622.OBS3143/60-deputes-fn-a-l-assemblee-en-2017.html.

Lepelletier, Pierre. 2018. "Comment Jean-Marie Le Pen a Résisté a Toutes les Attaques du FN en Justice." *Le Figaro*. February 9, 2018. http://www.lefigaro.fr/politique/le-scan/2018/02/09/25001-20180209ARTFIG00246-comment-jean-marie-le-pen-a-resiste-a-toutes-les-attaques-du-fn-en-justice.php.

Le Tallec, Camille. 2015. "Le Front National Forme un Groupe au Parlement Européen." *La Croix*. June 16, 2015. https://www.la-croix.com/Actualite/Europe/Le-Front-national-forme-un-groupe-au-Parlement-europeen-2015-06-16-1324240.

Mayer, Nonna. 2002. "Les Hauts et les Bas du Vote Le Pen 2002." *Revue Française de Science Politique*. 52(2), 505–520.

Mestre, Abel and Caroline Monnot. 2015. "Les Réseaux du Front National". In *Les Faux-Semblants du Front National*, edited by S. Crépon, A. Dézé, and N. Mayer. 51–76. Paris: Presses de Sciences Po.

Milza, Pierre. 1986. *Fascisme Français, Passé et Present*. Paris: Champs-Flammarion.

Perrineau, Pascal. 2017a. "Marine Le Pen au Premier Tour: la puissance d'une Dynamique, l'Échec d'une Ambition". In *Le Vote Disruptif. Les Élections Présidentielle et Législatives de 2017*, edited by P. Perrineau. 251–268. Paris: Presses de Sciences Po.

Perrineau, Pascal. 2017b. "Annexe 2". In *Le Vote Disruptif. Les Élections Présidentielle et Législatives de 2017*, edited by P. Perrineau. 357–416. Paris: Presses de Sciences Po.

Perrineau, Pascal. 2017c. *Cette France de Gauche qui Vote FN*. Paris: Seuil.

Reungoat, Emmanuelle. 2015. "Le Front National et l'Union Européenne. La Radicalization Comme Continuité". In *Les Faux-Semblants du Front National*, edited by S. Crépon, A. Dézé, and N. Mayer. 225–245. Paris: Presses de Sciences Po.

Turchi, Marine. 2018. "Marine Le Pen Signe à Nouveau Pour de l'Argent Russe." *Médiapart*. April 1, 2018. https://www.mediapart.fr/journal/international/300317/marine-le-pen-signe-nouveau-pour-de-l-argent-russe.

Vedel, Thierry. 2017. "La Télévision, un Vieux Média qui Ne Meurt Pas" in *Le Vote Disruptif. Les Élections Présidentielle et Législatives de 2017*, edited by P. Perrineau. 101–113. Paris: Presses de Sciences Po.

Willsher, Kim. 2018. "Bannon to Address Front National as French Far-Right Leaders Seek Unity." *The Guardian*. March 9, 2018. https://www.theguardian.com/world/2018/mar/09/marine-le-pen-under-pressure-to-unite-front-national.

Chapter 9: Wilders' Party for Freedom and the Dutch Alt-Right

By Ineke van der Valk[1]

Abstract

This chapter discusses the Party for Freedom (PVV) and its leader Geert Wilders, as well as the far-right groups Erkenbrand and Forum for Democracy. The impact of the 'poldering' principle within the Dutch brand of populism is discussed in terms of its enabling far-right political influence on mainstream party politics such as from the Christian Democrat party CDA, the liberal VVD, and the Christian SGP, so as to normalize anti-immigrant, anti-Muslim and anti-minority policies. Risks arising are identified.

Key words: Netherlands, Alt-Right, PVV, Wilders, poldering, risks.

PVV History

The Party for Freedom (PVV) was created in 2006 by Geert Wilders, a former MP of the Liberal party VVD and political assistant to its leader, Frits Bolkestein, who later became an EU Commissioner. Unlike other political parties in the Netherlands that are formally democratic associations having members and applying democratic procedures, the PVV is not an association and has only one 'member' i.e. Geert Wilders himself. The Dutch Constitution guarantees passive voting rights for all citizens and allows this construct. It implies that Geert Wilders, unlike all other elected PVV representatives in Parliament and civil servants employed by the party, has sole authority over decisions taken by the PVV.

Wilders' leadership is authoritarian and only allows limited voice to a small group of loyal individuals around him. It is generally

1 This research was conducted as part of the EU DARE (Dialogue About Radicalization and Equality) project Horizon 2020/ number 725349.

assumed that the driving motive for this model, which is widely considered undemocratic, is the wish of its leader to avoid destructive power struggles and infighting. Such problems were among the causes of decline of populist predecessors of the PVV party, such as the LPF (see later). The picture that emerges from media interviews and academic studies among former adherents, civil servants, and representatives (see e.g. Vossen 2013; Akkerman 2016) is that the PVV is weak in its internal structure and organization. Despite eschewing the normal association membership of political parties and having officially only one member, nevertheless PVV does have supporters and elected representatives. The party organization is not only characterized by hierarchy and arbitrariness but also by lack of true leadership and a controversially extreme media focus. Many of those PVV representatives in positions of responsibility, such as members of local councils and parliament, are driven by fear of the authoritarian leader. Over a number of years, dozens of them have left the party, publicly criticizing its functioning and Wilders' role as a leader. After Wilders' discriminatory statements against Moroccans in spring 2014, even more of them left the party, including main election candidates. Other PVV representatives frequently fall into disrepute because of a lack of integrity for a variety of reasons such as fraud, crime or membership of right-wing extremist groups. Nevertheless, and despite the political isolation of the party from 2014 onwards, the PVV ranked second in the 2017 elections.

Who Votes for the PVV and Why?

Wilders is known nationally and internationally for his anti-Islam and anti-Muslim attitudes. Although these are main ideological components of his world-view and an important dimension of his electoral achievements, the rise of Wilders and his success in the politics should be seen in a broader context than only his anti-Muslims/Islam stances. However, a minority of his followers either fully or mainly support him and vote for him because of his strategically inspired stance against austerity measures, in particular concerning the elderly, and (rhetorically) in favour of the preservation of the welfare state, a strategy that he chose to follow from 2010 onwards. A minority are also attracted by his anti-European, anti-establishment politics. Moreover, his more general anti-immigration attitude and criticism of the lack of integration of immigrants appeals to the public, and not only his specific views on Islam/Muslims. For many of his followers, he is too extreme in this respect. Vossens' (2013) portrait of his followers in the elections of 2010—15.5% of the electorate showed that these voters mainly live in the western part of the country, on the outskirts of cities and municipalities that are still white but are becoming more ethnically diverse. They are generally poorly educated, have a low or middle income and are not religious. De Koster et al. (2014, 584–604) investigated the motives of PVV followers and concluded that rejection of cultural and ethnic diversity remains the main motivation for voters to join the PVV. Aalberts (2012), based on interviews and focus group discussions with PVV followers, identified that the PVV is mainly popular because of its wake-up call for mainstream politics. Followers do not necessarily agree with the points of view of the PVV, or may even disagree with them, but nonetheless want mainstream politics to move in the direction of Wilders PVV, in particular concerning questions of social security, law-and-order and the problems of a multicultural society. They oppose unemployment, the lack of social cohesion, oppression of women, and criminality amongst young people.

Research on the attractiveness of a populist vote, carried out by the Open Society Foundation (OSF 2014) in various European cities, has shown that seeking a voice for extreme-right and populist parties is related to feelings of powerlessness and critical attitudes towards mainstream politicians who do not keep their promises. The immigration theme is another topic that shows respondents feeling that they had little control over the democratic process. Their struggle was not so much with immigrants but with 'the system' in the first place. Nevertheless, daily experience of annoyance and irritation in relation to diversity of neighbourhoods may create tensions and feelings of discontent. Increasing diversity is considered by them as a threat to social cohesion. In such studies, respondents held not only immigrants but also 'the elites' accountable for this situation. Such people want to be heard and taken seriously. In various studies (Welschen 2014; Broekhuizen and van Wonderen 2012; Smits et al. 2010), it was found that anger about the multicultural society results in sympathy for Wilders and his PVV. Increasingly, however, not only poorly educated and vulnerable people experience feelings of loss, fear and insecurity that accounts for their orientation towards populist parties. Increasingly, this is also the case for middle income groups and urban professionals who fear loss of wealth and power. The evaporation of belief in progress, once a source of optimism, and belief in and hope for a better future, is an important factor in populist support, as sociologist Koen Abts argued (ten Hooven 2016). The late Zygmunt Bauman (2006; 2007) pointed to the pitiful but nevertheless threatening image of the needy refugee who, in their own country, once knew prosperity and well-being comparable to western middle and higher income groups. The fear is, he argues, that the experience of the refugee might also be ours one day!

Looking at more objective factors, the role of the media in the rise and prospering of populism in general, and the PVV in particular, cannot be denied (see chapter 11 in Vol 1). Nowadays, the media put a lot of emphasis on emotions and sensationalism. Often the news is not put into a broader social and historical context and lacks profound analysis. In Baumans' vision, this creates feelings of powerlessness, passivity and lack of commitment among media consumers. It creates despair about the world's future. Without doubt, Wilders and his PVV would not have reached the fame, reputation and support he now has in the Netherlands if the media had not paid him so much attention. Since its creation, both PVV and Wilders have obtained more media coverage than any other party, even though Wilders and his party avoid debate and discussion. The same holds for mainstream politics. The parties that formed the 2010–2012 government, the Liberal VVD and the Christian Democrats CDA, while 'agreeing to disagree' on Islam, even made an agreement with the PVV to gain its support in exchange for concessions to his political wishes. The PVV at that time functioned as a de facto third governmental party. However, this coalition did not last long, and parties changed their attitudes towards the PVV after the collapse of the government.

Historical Legacy

Wilders built on the legacy of the late Pim Fortuyn who was murdered in 2002 for political reasons, just as he built on the legacy of Bolkestein, former leader of the Liberal Party, whose assistant he once was, and on the legacy of Ayaan Hirsi Ali, a former notorious member of the Liberal Party, with whom he also closely cooperated. Both Bolkestein and Hirsi Ali later distanced themselves from him because of his increasingly extreme views and further radicalization on Islam. In search for an explanation of his radicalization, some point to the effects of the 24-hour protection that he is subjected to. The literature reports effects of a permanent presence of guards such as a heightened stress level, a lack of sense of reality, and an increase in sensitivity to conspiracy theories. Wilders built upon the experience of a country traumatized by two political murders—the politician Pim Fortuyn in 2002 and filmmaker Theo van Gogh in 2004—and he learnt from the experience, mistakes, and errors made by the political party LPF (Lijst Pim Fortuyn) founded by Fortuyn. He became popular because of, among other things, his critical stance on Muslims/Islam and multicultural society in general, his rejection of cultural relativism, and his critical attitude towards the neglect of historical and cultural awareness of the Dutch (Fortuyn 1997). In addition the success of Fortuyn was also due to his direct emotional appeal to ordinary people. These attitudes were informed by his underlying libertarian values (Vossen 2013, 275). The LPF gained a lot of support in the elections, just after the death of Fortuyn in 2002, but it quickly disappeared because of political mistakes and internal dissent and infighting.

PVV Ideology

Characterizing parties and movements as 'populist' has become fashionable in recent decades. The PVV is among them. But what is populism? Jan-Werner Müller (2016) called it "the permanent shadow of representative politics". Populist politicians insist that they are the exclusive legitimate representatives of 'the people'. However, 'the people' ultimately is an abstract, rhetorical entity. While pretending to be anti-elitist, populists are essentially and intrinsically anti-pluralist, argued Müller: they know what is good for the people and what the people want. What they want is what the people want. This claim to exclusive representation makes populist parties appear immune to criticism of other political and civil society actors. That is why populism may be considered as a real danger not only to democracy, but also to the rule of law of the constitutional state.

The Dutch senator and philosopher of law, Schaap (2016) elaborated on this in his discussion of the on-going decline of the constitutional state and the crucial and catalysing role of populism in this process. He pointed to the populist political strategy seeking to prepare people for authoritarian leadership by raising various emotions, such as insecurity, fear, rancour, and hate. Under authoritarian leadership, relations formerly based on recognized and widely accepted authority would, he said, be replaced by relations based purely on power. This populism does make use of democracy and the constitutional state but without loyalty and with the exclusive objective of undermining these institutional constructs. Schaap argued that current populism is both a symptom and a catalyst of an insidious but acute process of decline of the democratic constitutional state and the institutional order on which it is based. Not only are the *trias politica* (separation of powers) at stake, the law making, executive and judicial powers, but also the totality of socio-cultural and political institutions of society, including the media and academia. That order has been developed throughout a long historical process. It structurally protects individuals against arbitrariness, inequality, and authoritarian abuse of power. In this ideological battle that Schaap called a 'cold civil war', stigmatization, accusation, and incitement are current instruments that are given more salience and importance than the facts. Negative profiling of ethnic others may be used to create and strengthen discontent and resentment when the discontent is projected unto the threatening 'Other'. Populism is not a corrective to democracy, Muller argued, in the sense of bringing politics closer to the people. However, it may function as a warning that politicians had better listen to 'the people' because parts of them feel, or are in fact, insufficiently represented.

Where does Muller's strategy of listening to the people end and where does Schaaps' emphasis on countering the undermining of democracy and the rule of law begin? Are these compatible strategies? To gain more insight, this chapter later looks at how mainstream politics in the Netherlands has reacted when confronted with populism. First, some other major ideological elements of the PVV will be examined.

Obviously, the most salient aspect of Wilders' world view is the anti-Islam/Muslim dimension. Over a period of several years, the PVV stood out on account of its clear Islamophobic statements. His remarks about Islam were the subject of criminal proceedings in 2010–2011, when he faced investigations into whether he had made deliberately insulting statements towards Muslims as a group because of their religion (Art. 137c of the Criminal Code), or whether he had incited discrimination and hatred (Art. 137d of the Criminal Code/ Art. 90 *quater*), or both, against Muslims on account of their religion. Although the court took the view that some of his comments were discriminatory in themselves, or offensive and insulting, and that one was of an inflammatory nature that went to the very limit of what was lawful, Wilders was acquitted in the light of the overall context of his arguments and the wider social context, the hard-line debate about the multicultural society in the Netherlands, and the freedom of expression granted to politicians. An additional factor in the acquittal was that many of the statements concerned the religion itself rather than its adherents. The court also took the view that the degree to which utterances are allowed is greater, the fiercer the general level of public debate. The court considered that statements are only unlawful if they represent a threat to public order.[2] Wilders has indeed not sought to make any distinction between Islam and extremist Islamism, which misuses the religion for political ends. In his view, Islam is not a world religion but a totalitarian political ideology that should be forbidden.

In 2012, Wilders published his book *'Marked for Death, Islam's war against the West and me.'* This book throws more light upon his views of Islam and Muslims. The Eurabia-ideology that he adheres to in his book is also of importance for many of his followers who may be found on various populist and extremist websites in the Netherlands, and those who inspire him nationally and internationally such as Hirsi Ali, Bat Ye'or, Oriana Fallaci, Pamela Geller and Robert Spencer. The right-wing extremist Norwegian terrorist Anders Breivik (see chapter 10) also found inspiration in the Eurabia-ideology (Bangsted 2014). Breivik's manifesto extensively referred to Wilders and his film *Fitna.*

The approach of Wilders' book is alarmist and may be summarized as follows: We are engaged in warfare, a World War that we did not unleash ourselves but is imposed on us by 'Islam'. We are now hit by a third Islamic invasion using immigration and procreation as weapons to obtain a majority.[3] If we lose, we shall be enslaved. Islam

---

2 Amsterdam Criminal Court, June 23, 2011, LJN BQ9001.

3 The first one was in the eighth century and was stopped in Poitiers, the second ended with the Turks at the gates of Vienna in the 17th century.

is a political ideology, a totalitarian system in disguise comparable to fascism or communism whose objective is to dominate the entire world. In the Islamophobic theories of the PVV, old images of an Islamic threat and theories about the primordial roots of European civilization are mixed with Huntington's (1997) theory of a clash of civilizations and a vision of Islam as totalitarian and fascist, with the political left as allies, the Koran as a 'fascist book' and Israel as avant-garde of the frontline defending the free western world.

Wilders' attitude towards Islam is fixatedly hostile. Investigating the background of such hostile attitudes towards Islam, Schaap (2012, 201–209) pointed to socio-psychological mechanisms in which social unease produces resentment (see also chapter 2). The bearer of this sentiment experiences himself as a victim and looks for a perpetrator. This kind of resentment is poisonous and may infect society as a whole, he argued. The members of society that are targeted by, and become victims of, such resentful emotions are exclusively viewed as manifest exemplars of the kind they so hate.

In Mid-March 2014 during a local election meeting in The Hague, Wilders asked his followers if they wanted more or less Moroccans in the city. The followers exclaimed "Less, less, less", and Wilders answered "We will arrange that". The result was that polls indicated a loss of 5–7 seats for the PVV (from 27 to 20–22) and a rejection of his statements by almost three quarters of the Dutch population. Within the PVV, a quarter of his followers rejected his statements, and many PVV representatives in public bodies such as the Provincial and Municipal councils, the national and European Parliaments left the party. The government and political parties at all levels of politics in public bodies officially declared their refusal to cooperate with the PVV, in general or at least as long as Wilders did not withdraw his statements. On a political level, the party therefor got into an isolated position. The Public Prosecutor decided to prosecute Wilders because of these statements. After a trial that lasted almost a year, the court of Amsterdam took a decision on December 9, 2016, on the eve of the International Day of Human Rights. Geert Wilders was sentenced for group defamation and inciting racial discrimination because of his call for "fewer, fewer, fewer Moroccans". He was found not guilty of the charge of inciting racial hatred. A punishment was not imposed because the court considered the conviction for defaming a group and inciting racial discrimination as sufficient punishment for a politician and democratically elected lawmaker.

Alongside Islamophobia and other major ideological elements of Wilders' PVV, such as populism, nationalism and law-and-order, it became increasingly apparent that racism in general should be included as a substantial dimension of the PVV ideology, in particular after his conviction for inciting racial discrimination. The party should therefore be characterized as populist, chauvinist and ('modern') contemporary racist, rather than as merely right-wing extremist as it has previously been done (Davidovic et al 2008,167–90). However, the PVV's alliances with European right-wing extremist parties may have effects in this respect and move the party even more to the extreme right wing of politics, in particular if it gains more electoral support.

Given his strategy on home affairs of not wanting to be associated with right-wing extremism, it came as a surprising change of course that at the European level Wilders allied with far-right extremist parties in Europe, such as the Front National of Marine le Pen in France, the FPÖ of Heinz-Christian Strache in Austria, Lega Nord in Italy and Vlaams Belang of Philip de Winter in Belgium, parties that are known for their anti-Semitic and/or racist background. This dynamic of increasing association with right-wing extremist groups can also be observed in the political situation in the Netherlands. Geert Wilders is not anti-Semitic, however. His viewpoints in relevant matters are generally pro-Israel, a country that he has visited many times. He profiles himself as Israel's friend, a preserver of a Jewish-Christian heritage that he considers the main building blocks of Europe at the expense of Islam. However, this viewpoint does little to prevent him seeking alliances in neo-Nazi and anti-Semitic milieus, as far as these support his Islamophobic stances.

Anti-Constitutional Election Programme

In spring 2017, general elections took place in the Netherlands. Since 2013, various opinion polls had pointed to the PVV as the most popular party, if elections had taken place at the time of the opinion polls. This did not change after Wilders was sentenced for insulting Moroccans and inciting discrimination. Wilders' programme for the last elections was only a page long. Measures against Muslims and immigration continued to be number one in PVV politics: closing the borders to immigrants from Islamic countries, withdrawing the temporary residence permit of asylum seekers, and closing reception centres. These proposals were contrary to international and European law and to the prohibition against discrimination, as a Commission examining if election programs were in line with the constitutional state identified (Commissie Rechtstatelijkheid in verkiezingsprogramma's 2017). In addition, the party wanted to close down all the mosques and Islamic schools, prohibit the Koran, and incarcerate radical Muslims for preventative reasons. This is a case of infringement of the freedom of education, the freedom of religion, the freedom of opinion, the right to a fair trial, and the non-discrimination provision. Women were also to be prohibited from wearing headscarves in public functions, such as in education and the courts. Again, the principles of freedom of religion and non-discrimination were at stake in this PVV proposed prohibition.

Mainstreaming: Election Programmes of Political Parties

Compared to the elections of 2012, many more mainstream political parties had integrated programme items for the 2017 elections that were barely, or not at all, compatible with the provisions of the constitutional state, in particular in relations to the principle of equality and the freedom of religion. The same committee of academics specialised in law also analysed the programmes of 13 of the most important mainstream parties that were represented in Parliament in December 2016 with two or more seats (Commissie Rechtstatelijkheid in verkiezingsprogramma's 2017). The following briefly discusses the outcomes, which illustrate the pressure that populism exerts on mainstream parties.

The CDA, VVD, and Other Parties

The CDA, the Christian-Democrats, now want a prohibition of funding by foreign states of mosques and Islamic organisations. This is an example of direct discrimination because this prohibition exclusively targets the Muslim religion and no other denominations. Various parties such as the Liberal VVD and the CDA also have programme items that do not respect the provisions of international and European law concerning the reception of refugees. Regarding tension between security measures and freedom of religion, various left wing and right wing parties want to take protective measures against so-called hate preachers and Salafist organisations. It would depend on cautious implementation whether these program items would be compatible or in conflict with the principles of the constitutional state, such as article one on the equality of all citizens. Moreover parties have not always clarified how they want to protect human rights and whether judiciary power would be involved.

Christian SGP

A special case is the right-wing, quasi-fundamentalist Christian SGP, a party that does not grant equal rights to women vis-à-vis positions of responsibility in politics. The SGP wants the authorities to be wary to grant permission for the construction of new mosques. In its election programme, the SGP emphasised that the authorities should remain vigilant as to the differences between religions, with Christians deserving a preferential position. Muslim festivities and holy days should not be recognized on equal footing with Christian feast days. The constitution should refer to Christian values. These programme items are contrary to constitutional law, in particular in relation to the freedom of religion and the non-discrimination principle.

Anti-Muslim Actions Prior to 2017 Election Campaigns

Even before the election campaigns, various anti-Muslim political initiatives were taken by various political parties. For example:

In 2015, the Party for Animals initiated a draft law against ritual slaughter. A previous draft law had been rejected by the Senate.[4] Following previous proposals and draft laws against the burqa and niqab, a majority of the House of Representatives accepted a prohibition of face-covering in education, public transport, hospitals and public administration buildings. There would be a fine of €405 for contravening this law. This draft law was against the advice of the Council of State who rejected the proposal (W04.15.0170/I).[5] The law was considered symbolic and not really aiming at a solution of a social problem, since such a problem does not exist: only 200 to 400 women in

---

4 https://www.partijvoordedieren.nl/kamerinitiatieven/initiatiefwet-onverdoofd-ritueel-slachten.

5 https://www.raadvanstate.nl/adviezen/samenvattingen/tekst-samenvatting.html?id=353&print=1&summary_only&print=1.

the Netherlands wear burqas or niqabs. Moreover, the Council is of the opinion that this prohibition is an infringement of the freedom of religion that is guaranteed by the European Convention on Human Rights.

In December 2015, a proposal by MPs, who had left the PVV to change provisions in penal law, was discussed in Parliament. The proposal was to eliminate articles in the law on group defamation and incitement to hatred and discrimination. The objective was to broaden the scope of freedom of expression. A majority in Parliament rejected the proposals as they would weaken the antidiscrimination provisions. The Liberal Party VVD, however, agreed with the elimination of the article on group defamation.[6]

The Liberal Party VVD

In the 2017 elections, Wilders did not obtain the number of seats that the polls had predicted. It was the Liberal party that got most seats. The Prime Minister, Marc Rutte, was praised nationally and internationally. He had said "halt to the wrong kind of populism", to use his own words. The facts are: in spite of the gains of the Greens and the Liberal Left of D66, the Left in general has declined, in particular because of the loss by the social-democrats. Wilders did not become the largest party but he did obtain five more seats than in the previous elections—in spite of being convicted in court, in spite of his anti-constitutional and discriminatory party programme, and in spite of his cooperation with EU right-wing extremist movements. This gain is probably related to the amount of media attention that he typically generates and as well as in the campaign for the general elections. However, his participation in the campaigns was minimal, with the exception of his regular tweets, i.e. imitating Trump. He seldom gave interviews and was hardly ever willing to debate with other candidates. Altogether, Wilders obtained 20 seats (out of 150) and became the second largest political party. Nevertheless, other parties were still no more willing to cooperate with this party in forming the new government. Moreover, the new party Forum for Democracy, a politer Islamophobic version of PVV, obtained 2 seats.

---

6 VNL did not obtain enough votes in the last elections and did not come back in the Parliament.

The Poldering Principle

The voter intention polls proved inaccurate. However, was it a victory for democracy and the constitutional state over populism, or was that wishful thinking? The Netherlands, with its traditional diversity of religious groups, has a long history of what is called 'poldering', i.e. pacification by bringing together contradictory opinions and perspectives, repressive tolerance, and incorporation of movements of resistance. A process of accommodation around Wilders' PVV and increasing populism that mutually reinforce each other has been going on for some time. At first, a formula of cooperation in the 2010–2012 government, which was supported by Wilders based on an agreement to disagree on Islam, failed at the instigation of Wilders. Subsequently, emphasis in the relationship moved from form to content: mainstream parties became unwilling to cooperate, in particular after Wilders call for fewer Moroccans, but nonetheless his visions were increasingly incorporated.

In the campaign of the general election, the media and politicians in an effort to accommodate discontent—a Dutch political habit—gave a voice to angry white men and women and tried to meet their concerns. Major themes in the campaigns, however, were not about the economy or problems in social welfare provisions, let alone about foreign policy and international relations. Rather, the discussion was about Dutch identity, about 'behaving normally'. Norms and values were central issues. In January 2017, during the election campaign, Prime minister Rutte wrote an open letter to all Dutch people asking them to "behave normally". The word 'normal' was repeated eleven times in this short text: "Sometimes it is as if nobody behaves normally any more", he said and "behave normally or leave". He seemed to address in particular people with a migrant background. For the Christian Democrats, 'values and traditions' were the number one topic of the election program, including a proposal to introduce the singing of the national anthem in schools. Party leader Buma argued that immigration "threatens Dutch norms and values". The party was rapidly moving to the conservative, nationalist right of the political spectrum. Leader Asscher of the social democrats, in an effort to integrate a nationalistic appeal in his campaign, pleaded for "progressive patriotism". The new party Forum for Democracy even advocated introducing a law for Protection of Dutch Values, a symbolic move because most of the values mentioned are already in the constitution. Not only the PVV but also the new Forum voor Democratie tried to instrumentalize different, but often futile, issues in their Islamophobic and anti-immigrant agenda, which subsequently went viral in the online and offline public domain. When supermarkets for various reasons change the names of certain products related to traditional Dutch or Christian festivities such as Christmas or Easter, these parties and their followers frame them as signs of submission to Islam. When the public broadcaster and Dutch embassies abroad wished people 'Happy Holidays' instead of 'Happy Christmas' in December 2016, Forum voor Democratie attacked "the self-hating elites who collaborate enthusiastically to destroy our culture ... in the name of diversity and inclusivity"[7]. Surprisingly, the prime minister joined the complainers—obviously for electoral reasons. For prime minister Marc Rutte, all politicians should be populists, although he distinguishes between 'good' and 'bad' populism.

The Dutch Alt-Right Movement

A striking dimension of the process of globalisation of ideas is the speed in which American debates are leaking into public debates in Europe, or at least in the Netherlands. The same holds for topics of action of social movements and discursive lexical items such as 'Alt-Right'. A European Alt-Right movement developed parallel to its counterpart in the US, where Paul Gottfried (2008) coined the concept and Richard Spencer in 2011 promoted it with the creation of the website alternativeright.com (later altright.com)—see chapter 1. In Europe, as in the US, the Alt-Right developed as a movement composed of different strands such as libertarians, white nationalists and supremacists ('white pride'), anti-Islam campaigners and neo-Nazis. Identitarians and anti- Social Justice Warriors (SJW's) are also a significant group. Some groups and sympathizers reject racism and violence whereas others promote it. In its style and vocabulary, the European Alt-Right largely imitates the US Alt-Right discourse with terms like 'red pill' (the moment of revelation of the truth—after the film the Matrix),

7 Forum Voor Democratie, "Stop de zelfhaat! Behoud het Kerstfeest," *forumvoordemocratie.nl*, (December 16, 2016), retrieved December 29, 2016, from https://forumvoordemocratie.nl/actueel/kerstmis.

'pol'(politically correct), 'normies', 'snowflakes' (people who supposedly melt when insulted or feeling pressured), and 'social justice warriors' for political opponents, 'Cultural Marxism' for important dimensions of the latter's ideology, and not to forget the use of online culture symbols and memes such as the now iconic frog Pepe. At first, Pepe was a joke to trick journalists and academics but later its use became serious. Irony, trolling, and straightforward provocative ideas and insulting language are mixed up so making it hard to know what is meant as an argument and what is a joke.

Erkenbrand

One of the major representatives of the Alt-Right movement in the Netherlands is without doubt the group 'Erkenbrand' (since spring 2016), which defines itself as a study society. The name Erkenbrand is an old Dutch word for 'holy sword' or 'pure flame' and taken from a figure in the famous Tolkien novels. Surrounding the sword/ flame in the logo of the group is an old Germanic expression meaning 'fidelity creates power'. Its core group consists of around 25–30, mainly young highly educated males. For the first time in decades, the Netherlands has witnessed the rise of a right-wing extremist group whose sympathisers are in large parts highly educated. Members of Erkenbrand, with some exceptions, use pseudonyms and disguises in order to prevent identification. For the same (security) reason, it is not easy to access the media that the group uses. These media consist of chat channels—such as *European Right*—, or discussion platforms—such as *4chan*, as well as the highly protected platform *Discord*. Off-line meetings are equally difficult to access without being approved beforehand. Some of the core members are classical neo-Nazis and distribute anti-Semitic statements. Despite Erkenbrand's closed character, two research journalists from the mainstream newspaper *de Volkskrant* (Kranenburg 2017) managed to penetrate the group and published a feature article based on interviews. After publication of the article, one of the leading members, who had openly spoken with the journalists including about the use of violence, was expelled from the organisation, evidently for damage control and face keeping. The argument used was that his "texts and expressions are in conflict with the core values of our society" and "it is evident that he is further radicalised than we assumed before"[8].

Erkenbrand distributes podcasts and articles, organizes local and national discussion events, nature walks, training in martial arts, parties and festivities, and annual conferences. Notorious representatives of the international Alt-Right movement such as so-styled Millenial Woes, or of right-wing extremist groups such as Alexandros Lyris from Golden Dawn, are regularly invited to speak and participate. The second national conference was held on October 14, 2017 under the title "Towards a new Golden Age". Around 240 people attended, including around forty from abroad. Among them was Alt-Right activist Jared Taylor from the site *American Renaissance,* who embraces theories about racial hierarchy and white superiority. Erkenband is obviously well embedded in international networks of the Alt-Right. The various European alternative right strands share some similar viewpoints. They are in favour of a white, racially pure, homogenous Europe (from a cultural or racial point of view) that preserves its own identity and culture, a Europe without ethnic minorities, Muslims in particular. In line with similar movements in other European countries, Erkenbrand opposes immigration, Islam, 'cultural Marxism', homosexuality, and feminism. The emphasis on anti-feminism is a relatively new characteristic as far as right-wing extremist perspectives are concerned, at least in the Netherlands. A focus on masculinity, physical culture, and training in fighting and the use of violence have long been hallmarks of Nazism and various right-wing extremist milieus. The new dimension is that the Alt-Right movement opposes a more general 'feminisation of the western man.' Together with homosexuality and immigration, feminism is considered a main threat to Erkenbrands' central idea of a superior white race. Violence is a recurrent topic, the discourse is war-like—'a war against white people is ongoing'—and various core members openly advocate the use of violence, and organize or follow training in the use of violence. Fighting is considered a natural, biologically given tendency, and is presented as an important instrument to reach the objective of a racially pure ethno state. Violence is not advocated in words alone, however.

8 www.Erkenbrand.nl

Erkenbrand organizes training in martial arts, as a way to prepare members for an expected civil war, as a member has argued.[9]

Erkenbrand emphasizes the differences that distinguish the group from those right-wing extremist groups that are more action-oriented street groups, given Erkenbrand's primary function as a meeting place for study and debate for more educated young people. This did not, however, hamper Erkenbrand members from participating in rallies of Pegida and the group increasingly cooperates with likeminded members of the right-wing extremist group Voorpost.[10] As far as official parliamentary politics is concerned, more than supporting Wilder's PVV, Erkenbrand members rather support and promote the relatively new party on the New Right spectrum in Dutch Parliament, Forum for Democracy and its leader, the young (aged 34) and highly educated Thierry Baudet. The Israel-friendly attitude of Wilders is among Erkenbrand's arguments to keep its distance from PVV. Wilders is considered too Zionist. Many members of Erkenbrand claim membership of Forum for Democracy (Kranenburg 2017). In April 2017, Erkenbrand members tweeted a photo(shopped) picture of Baudet lying on a piano with the head of Pepe, the green frog, the Alt-Right mascot. The picture was retweeted by Baudet. The racial purity advocated by Erkenbrand also implies that there is no place for Jews in the imagined ideal society of this group. While refraining from profiling the movement too much on this issue, given its sensitive character, members of Erkenbrand rather hold and sometimes express anti-Semitic opinions. At a reception meeting for the New Year 2018, in a speech called "Past and Present of Radical-Nationalist Netherlands", the speaker extensively discussed the pre-war fascist movement in the Netherlands and its failure. At the end, he expressed his wish for an organisation based on classical fascism. He also advocated collaboration with more action-oriented groups such as Identitair Verzet (Identitarian Resistance), Voorpost and Falanx Nederland: "Together they must form the bundle, or should I say the *fascio,* that saves the Netherlands from the upcoming watery grave. We have to get rid of these thuggish groups with at most 25 members among their

---

9 Elsevier, Nikki Sterkenburg, December 15, 2017. https://www.elsevierweekblad.nl/nederland/achtergrond/2017/12/alt-right-in-nederland-verlangen-naar-een-etnostaat-2965829W/

10 See Kafka.nl/erkenbrand-alt-right in Nederland

ranks.(...) It is up to us to finally succeed where our predecessors failed".[11]

Forum for Democracy

At the political level, the young party Forum for Democracy (FvD) may be considered an Alt-Right political faction. The mostly young constituency of Forum for Democracy is sharply increasing. In January 2018, the party claimed to have more than 20,000 members, while having had only 1,863 members in January 2017.[12] Seventeen thousand people are estimated to have attended its congress in the fall of 2017. By winter 2018, the party was expected to have 12–16 (out of 150) seats in Parliament, if elections were to take place at that time, while the PVV would lose 1–5 seats (of 20 obtained in the last elections in 2017). Forum for Democracy has been noticeably outpacing Wilders.

Baudet, the leader of Forum for Democracy, used to openly support Alt-Right view points, including those expressed by Erkenbrand. Indications of mutual sympathy and contacts are numerous, as the research group Kafka showed.[13] In October 2017, when Jared Taylor was in the Netherlands at the occasion of the Erkenbrand congress, a five hours long discussion between Taylor and Baudet took place. The event was held secret until the online platform *De Correspondent* reported it several months later. Confronted with the large press coverage, and in accordance with his much employed general tactics of evasion, denial, and creating confusion when confronted with manifestations of extremism in relation to his party, Baudet neither denied nor confirmed the meeting and said: "Every day we have discussions with tens of people. Sometimes we agree and sometimes we disagree with them". However, his sympathy for theories about racial hierarchy and white superiority as expressed by Taylor were evident, for example when he spoke of "homeopathic dilution" of the population resulting in the disappearance of Dutch people as a result of immigration. This terminology resembles his use of the concept of 'replacement of populations' that is equally used by Jean-Marie le Pen, whom he met on several occasions, and other representatives of rightwing extremism

11 Erkenbrand.eu / artikelen posted January 1, 2018. accessed January 23, 2018, author's translation.

12 Except the two largest parties the five other major parties that are represented in Parliament have between 25,000 and 30,000 members.

13 Kafka.nl /erkenbrand-alt-right in Nederland

in France. [14] Both these terminologies refer to the conspiracy theory of 'white genocide'. This theory holds that influential Jews and/or Muslims aim to destroy the white race by intermingling and immigration. When challenged, Baudet also refused to condemn and distance himself from the discourse of a candidate for the upcoming municipal elections in Amsterdam, who had argued in a radio interview in 2016 that "people with a dark skin are less intelligent than people from other races". Instead, Baudet merely said "It is a scientific discussion". This caused the Minister of the Interior, Kasja Ollongren, to observe in a public speech on fundamental rights that Baudet continues where Wilders stops and defends theories of racial hierarchies. For the first time in decades, the taboo against these kinds of theory has been broken by Baudet.[15] Also in line with his tactics of denial and evasion when confronted about racist and anti-Semitic expressions of Erkenbrand members, Baudet has formally distanced himself from this group. However, it is becoming increasingly difficult for him to hide his connections and sympathy for new and old right-wing extremism.[16]

Altrechts.com

Another Alt-Right manifestation in the Netherlands was the website Altrechts.com. This website quickly came into disrepute because it published lists of influential Jewish people and lists of people and organisations known for their antiracist stances. The site is now offline.

Conclusion

Dutch new right populist parties, PVV and Forum for Democracy, are on the rise. Taken together, they would gain a major percentage of seats in Parliament if elections were to take place today (late 2018), and this trend looks set to continue. Both parties tend to radicalise

---

14 https://decorrespondent.nl/7955/hoe-thierry-baudet-aan-de-lippen-hing-van-jean-marie-le-pen/811713530980-29774dcf

15 https://www.rijksoverheid.nl/documenten/toespraken/2018/02/02/burgemeester-dales-lezing-door-minister-ollongren

16 https://decorrespondent.nl/7955/hoe-thierry-baudet-aan-de-lippen-hing-van-jean-marie-le-pen/811713530980-29774dcf

people. In the shadow of this development, even more extreme, violence-prone action-oriented groups are also becoming more organized and their ideology regarded as more normalised.

Besides elections, populist parties and citizens adhering to them generally have a lot of influence on the socio-cultural and political institutions of society, including the media and academia. As Schaap has argued, current populism is both a symptom of and a catalyst for a process of decline of the democratic constitutional state and the institutional order on which it is based. The democratic functioning of Dutch society is at stake. At a socio-psychological level, mechanisms that produce resentment are at work in large sectors of society. Such resentment may infect society as a whole and favour the creation of outgroups for scapegoating. Mainstream parties increasingly tend to incorporate a populist agenda rather than taking a firm stance against its anti-constitutional and discriminatory content. Identity politics that are increasingly embraced by mainstream politics as a reaction to populist rhetoric rather tend to widen gaps in the social fabric than to add to social cohesion. Efforts, if any, by mainstream parties to listen to legitimate concerns of the people remain a symbolic gesture as their daily, in particular socio-economic, needs are generally not met. Conversely, neither PVV nor FvD show signs of mainstreaming. The headline risks may be summarised as:

Risk 1. Threats to democracy

Democratic functioning of society and the state under threat by excessive populist demands that are frequently unlawful, unconstitutional, and arguably pathological.

Risk 2. Propagation of resentment, scapegoating and hate crimes

Propagation of resentment in society about perceived economic, social and cultural damage allegedly caused by uncontrolled minority groups, leading to scapegoating and hate crimes against such outgroups.

Risk 3. Mainstream parties adopting Alt-Right policies to capture votes

Political opportunism among mainstream political parties to attract populist voters, whereby they are prepared to shift their policies rightwards to embrace Alt-Right demands, thus threatening a permanent Alt-Right character to national governance.

References

Aalberts, C. 2012. *Achter de PVV, Waarom Burgers op Geert Wilders Stemmen.* Delft: Eburon.

Akkerman, T. 2016. "The Party for Freedom: Balancing Between Mission, Votes and Office". In *Radical Right-Wing Populist Parties in Western Europe,* edited by T. Akkerman, S. de Lange, and M. Rooduijn. London: Routledge.

Bangsted, S. 2014. *Anders Breivik and the Rise of Islamophobia.* London: Zed Books.

Bauman, Z. 2006. *Liquid Fear.* Cambridge: Polity Press.

Bauman, Z. 2007. *Liquid Times, Living in an Age of Uncertainty.* Cambridge: Polity Press.

Broekhuizen, J. and van Wonderen, R. 2012. *Samenleven met Verschillen, Signaleren van Spanningen en Versterken van Vertrouwen in Amsterdamse Buurten.* Utrecht: Verweij-Jonker Instituut en O&S.

Commissie Rechtstatelijkheid in Verkiezingsprogramma's. 2017. *In De Rechtsstaat, een Quick Scan, de Partijprogramma's voor de Verkiezingen 2017 Rechtsstatelijk?* Den Haag.

Davidovic, M. et al. 2008. "Het Extreemrechtse en Discriminatoire Gehalte van de PVV". In *Monitor Racisme & Extremisme: Achtste Rapportage,* edited by J. van Donselaar and P. Rodrigues. Amsterdam: Anne Frank House/Leiden University.

Fortuyn, P. 1997. *Tegen de Islamisering van Onze Cultuur.* Utrecht: Bruna.

Gottfried, P. 2008. "The Decline and Rise of the Alternative Right". Address to H.L. Mencken Club AGM, 21-November 23, 2008. Reproduced December 1, 2008 by *Taki's Magazine.* www.tkimag.com.

de Gruyter, M., Smits van Waesberghe, E., and Boutellier, H. 2010. *Een Vreemde in Eigen Land, Boze Autochtone burgers over Nieuwe Nederlanders en de Overheid.* Amsterdam: Aksant/AUP.

ten Hooven, M. 2016. "Bang voor Terugval en Verlies, ook Rijken Stemmen Extreemrechts". *De Groene.* July 7, 2016.

Huntington, S. 1997. *Botsende Beschavingen, Cultuur en Conflict in de 21ste Eeuw.* Baarn: Anthos.

de Koster, W., Achterberg, W. P., Van der Waal, J. et al. 2014. "Progressiveness and the New Right: The Electoral Relevance of Culturally Progressive Values in the Netherlands". *West European Politics* 37(3): 584–604.

Kranenburg, Annieke. 2017. "Alt-right in Nederland: Hoe Erkenbrand zich Opmaakt voor de Strijd om een Blanke Natie". *De Volkskrant*, November 19, 2017. https://www.topics.nl/alt-right-in-nederland-hoe-erkenbrand-zich-opmaakt-voor-de-strijd-om-een-blanke-natie-apn4539593vk/6be38fb33ea969003473c2f1be1cc24ba6843c70b48fa30376839cd3950b1dbb/?context=playlist/m-onze-verslaggever-duikt-het-land-in-bdbd09/&referrerUserId=1f549012642a457c91936300110a9f4f

Müller, J.W. 2016. *What is Populism?* Philadelphia: University of Pennsylvania Press.

OSF. 2014. *Europe's White Working Class Communities, a Report on Six European Union Cities.* London: Open Society Foundations.

Schaap, S. 2012. *Het Rancuneuze Gif, de Opmars van het Onbehagen.* Budel: Damon.

Schaap, S. 2016. *Rechtsstaat in Verval, Over de Lange Mars door de Instituties.* Budel: Damon.

Vossen, K. 2013. *Rondom Wilders, Portret van de PVV.* Amsterdam: Boom.

Welschen, S. 2014. *Europe's White Working Class Communities, a Report on Six European Union Cities.* London: Open Society Foundations.

Wilders, G. 2012. *Marked for Death, Islam's War against the West and Me.* Washington: Regnery Publishing.

Chapter 10:
A Case Study of Anders Behring Breivik, Extreme-Right Terrorist

By Emily Turner-Graham

Abstract

This chapter examines the motivating extreme-right ideology and psychology of Anders Breivik, who carried out the lone-actor mass murder in Norway in July 2011. Breivik's infamous acts have inspired the far-right in general and unleashed other extreme-right lone terrorists. Such lone perpetrators act without the need for direct leadership or organisation, instead typically drawing on a vast well of incendiary far-right inspiration online. Breivik's narcissistic beliefs and detailed extreme-right manifesto, as revealed during his prosecution, are analysed. Difficulties in deterring such individuals are acknowledged. Risks arising are identified.

Key words: Breivik, terrorism, mass murder, Norway, extreme right, risks.

Breivik, the Extreme-Right Anti-Hero

In January 2018, Jordan Jereb, leader of the white supremacist group Republic of Florida, posted a photograph online of Norwegian extreme-right terrorist and murderer Anders Behring Breivik. He captioned the photo "This man is a hero. Period. He opened fire on a far-left summer camp...[t]he future of Norway is going to be brighter because of Breivik." (Anti-Defamation League 2017). On February 14, 2018, Nikolas Cruz opened fire on his fellow students at a Florida high school, killing seventeen people and injuring fifteen more, making it one of the deadliest school massacres. Cruz had connections to the Republic of Florida, training with their militia. He espoused anti-Muslim and anti-African-American ideas online. This chapter looks primarily at the case of Anders Behring Breivik. In particular, in an age marked by heightened levels of terrorism, a renewed and emboldened extreme-right throughout Europe and the United States, the infiltration of many extreme-right arguments into mainstream discourse and an increasingly powerful digital media, this chapter examines Breivik's motivating ideology and his psychological composition, as well as the new, disturbing trend within the extreme-right that he has played an enormous part in unleashing. Lone perpetrators who act without the need for leadership or organisation, who have a vast well of incendiary inspiration online at their disposal and who, within modern, western societies have fallen through the cracks, appear as "victims of nobody in particular and everybody in general" (Anspach 2013).

Breivik's Massacre

On July 22, 2011, Anders Behring Breivik detonated a bomb in Norway's capital, Oslo, and went on a shooting rampage on the nearby island of Utøya, killing a total of seventy-seven people. The crime committed by Breivik was "the first anti-Muslim massacre outside the Balkans in post-Holocaust Europe" (Gardell 2011). After months of single-minded planning, he parked a van loaded with a sizeable fertiliser bomb in Oslo's government quarter, outside of the building housing the office of then-Prime Minister Jens Stoltenberg. It detonated, killing eight people and injuring 209, twelve of them seriously. Amidst the ensuing chaos, he made his way to the island of Utøya, which lies in the Tyrifjorden Lake, thirty-eight kilometres north-west of Oslo. On Utøya, the annual Labour Party (*Arbeiderpartiet*) youth summer camp was in progress. In Breivik's view, the Labour Party had "betrayed the country and the people" by allowing non-white immigrants into the country. On the day of the massacre, in Breivik's view, they "paid the price of betrayal" (Breivik psychiatric report 2011, 2.4.2).

Breivik regarded the summer camp as "an elite training camp for young political leaders" (Breivik 2012), and, as such, felt he was quite within his rights as the self-appointed "Commander of the anti-communist resistance movement against the Islamisation of Europe and Norway" (Seierstad 2015, 340) to open fire unimpeded for over an hour on groups of terror-stricken young people with an array of assault weapons and cries of "I will kill you all, Marxists!" (Seierstad 2015, 320). He needed to "choke future recruitment" to the Labour Party (Breivik psychiatric report 2011, 2.4.2). Indeed, although he conceded it was difficult, it was a mission he was compelled to complete. It was a military "operation" (Seierstad 2015, 339) in a longstanding war against "Cultural Marxism". He was a "Caucasian hero who came to the rescue on behalf of a suppressed European people" (de Graaf et. al. 2013, 9). With a misguided belief in his own supposed altruism, he stated that he was "trying to prevent civil war in Norway in the future. I and others in Europe are convinced we can avert a major civil war. If we wait another 20–30 years, ethnic Europeans will be in the minority" (Breivik in de Graaf et. al. 2013, 9). Referring to the Norwegian Nazi collaborator of the 1940s, Vidkun Quisling, Breivik said "Today [*on July 22, 2011*] I'm the greatest monster [*in Norway*] since Quisling" (Borchgrevink 2013, 243). However, the massacre was also "an expression of my love for my own people and country" and in fact his "love, empathy and conscience were overdeveloped", allowing him to apparently overcome his personal feelings of repulsion in order to kill (Borchgrevink 2013, 243). Breivik killed eight people in Oslo, sixty-nine people on Utøya and injured many more, some of whom later died. Following his arrest on the island, he was prosecuted for the 77 murders as well as terrorism offences and convicted in 2012. He has since been imprisoned for Norway's maximum sentence of twenty-one years, but this is extendable by either five years or indefinitely for as long as Breivik is considered a risk to the public.

As well as the shocking physical violence perpetrated by Breivik on July 22, 2011, on the same day that Breivik launched his "revolutionary national conservati[ve]"campaign (Breivik 2011), he not only struck against Islam, but he also sought to land a strong blow against what he regarded as its western conduit—'Cultural Marxism'. A key part of Breivik's preparation for the horrific events of July 22 was the compilation of his 1,500-page 'manifesto' entitled (in homage to another prominent Norwegian counterjihadist, Fjordman) *2083—A European Declaration of Independence*. As much as it is a statement of his own views, it is also an ideological capsule of current, widely held extreme-right views. Breivik has in fact stated that the July 22 attacks were a sort of (appalling) advertisement for his manifesto—a violent *actual* means of bringing attention to his *virtual* message. This is no surprise from a terrorist "formed, dressed and armed on the Internet" (Borchgrevink 2013). Indeed Aage Borchgrevink, who has made a close study of Breivik and his crimes, referred to Breivik's electronic distribution of his manifesto as "the book launch" (Borchgrevink 2013, chapter 9).

Breivik's Ideology

While Breivik can certainly be identified and considered a 'lone wolf' in terms of his physical preparation for and the perpetration of his crimes, his driving ideology is very much representative of a number of key and broadly held extreme-right views. Anti-Muslim sentiment has now largely replaced the earlier biological racism of the extreme-right (von Brömssen 2013, 26) and the intellectual motivation for Breivik's attacks is the most profound expression of that prejudice to date. He can best be considered as "a loner from a flock" (Strømmen 2011, 32). Though the 'white revolution' he promised upon his arrest did not transpire, he can clearly be seen as a key cog in the virtual extreme-right network. As much as he has drawn inspiration from the Counter-jihadists of the 1990s and 2000s, now he inspires and is feted by elements within the extreme-right today, as has already been suggested. He is "both audience and participant, disciple and messiah" (Turner-Graham 2014, 417).

Of the founding Counter-jihadists, Breivik is clearly greatly influenced by many of the key writers. Fjordman (Peder Are Nøstvold Jensen), for example, features particularly heavily in Breivik's manifesto. Fjordman is also Norwegian and is characterised as 'far-right' and 'anti-Islamic'. As a Counter-jihadist, he argues that multiculturalism and Muslim immigration are posing a threat to western civilisation. His book, *Defeating Eurabia*, was of particular influence on Breivik. The concept of Eurabia was coined by the Egyptian-born British-Swiss writer Bat Ye'or (or 'Daughter of the Nile', the pen name of Gisele Littman) in the early 2000s in her book *Eurabia: the Euro-Arab Axis*. Eurabia refers to a supposed conspiracy to 'Islamise' Europe—thus creating 'Eurabia'—in order to destroy its existing culture and to break its traditional ties to Israel and the United States of America.

As Mattias Gardell has observed, anti-Muslim sentiment in Europe has a long history. It dates back to at least the Middle Ages when Muslims, like Jews, were cast by the Church as "enemies of God" (Gardell 2011). More recently, however, the terrorist attacks of September 11, 2001 gave Islamophobia huge new impetus. Fjordman and Ye'or, along with such key virtual voices as Pamela Geller's *Atlas*

Shrugs blog, the *Gates of Vienna*, Robert Spencer's *Jihad Watch* and *The Brussels Journal* have at once fanned the flames of Islamophobia and been emboldened by its renewed stance. The Internet has given Islamophobia an entirely new and vast forum for broadcast (see later section and chapter 14; also chapter 11 in Vol 1).

According to Ye'or, in order to undermine Israel and the US, the supposed Euro-Arab alliance compels the European powers to deny their own culture, stay silent on Muslim atrocities, accept Muslim immigration and provide economic aid to Islamic countries. Within Europe, this alleged conspiracy is aided and abetted by communists, the media, universities, Muslim cultural centres and mosques, European bureaucrats and politicians and the Euro-Arab Dialogue. Ye'or argues that a secret agreement was made between a number of European politicians and the Arab League after the 1973 oil crisis—publicly referred to as the Euro-Arabic Dialogue—that was in effect the "*deus ex machina* by means of which European politicians and civil servants willingly prepared for the subjugation of Europe" (Ye'or quoted in Carr 2006, 6). The argument follows that Europe continues to be transformed through immigration, outbreaks of jihad in European cities and the 'islamification' of textbooks and teaching at schools and universities.

Oriana Fallaci, an Italian writer also within the Counter-jihadist/Eurabian genre, expressed what many on the far- and extreme-right argue,

> "Don't you see that all these Ousama [sic] Bin Ladens consider themselves authorized to kill you and your children because you drink alcohol, because you don't grow the long beard and refuse the chador or the burkah [sic], because you go to the theatre or to the movies, because you love music and sing a song, because you dance and watch television, because you wear the miniskirt or the shorts..." (Fallaci 2002, 84–85)

What characterises almost all of these works is a profoundly dichotomous world-view, and this can be seen to be replicated by Breivik, and indeed many virtual extreme-right voices. Islam is "homogeneous, never changing, barbaric and violent" (von Brömssen 2013, 24). It is characterised as "the exact reverse of European democracy" (Taras 2012, 121). Europe, by contrast, is "old, tired, decadent, spiritually weakened, and slowly dying due to the apathy of its own native people" (von Brömssen 2013, 24).

Breivik did not officially belong to any political groups prior to the massacre, so in this sense, absorbing the ideological abyss of the Internet alone in his bedroom, he is a self-radicalised terrorist. Yet, as has been discussed, he drew on the work of and made electronic contact with others within the extreme-right scene and since the massacre, his work and actions have been drawn on by others (see, for example, the section on Breivik and the English Defence League in CST 2011—Breivik claimed to have made 'friends' with more than 600 EDL members on *Facebook*). As Mattias Gardell put it, Breivik's manifesto "reveals four distinct influences we need to understand: contemporary Islamophobic ideologies, cultural conservative/neo-Confederate traditions, elements of White Power thinking, and anti-feminist thought" (Gardell 2011). In short, Breivik brings together key ideological threads of the contemporary extreme-right. He is representative of a new brand of terrorist—attacking both in actual and virtual reality. A product of the Internet age, Breivik obviously understood that he needed to enact an "activism of the word" as well as an "activism of the deed" to make the greatest impact (Lievrouw 2011).

The now oft-referenced notional ideology of 'Cultural Marxism' is closely aligned to this idea that there are various indigenous agents being employed within Europe to Islamise its culture and ethnicity. Breivik, in keeping with his cut-and-paste pastiche manifesto and his position as an ideological "shopper" (von Brömssen 2013, 13), drew on both the theories of Eurabia and Cultural Marxism to explain his violent actions. The *YouTube* video, which he released six hours prior to the Oslo and Utøya attacks, clearly indicates this emphasis in synthesised, accessible Internet-friendly form.

Similarly, in a potent visual expression, Breivik's video charts the 'rise of Cultural Marxism' from the end of World War Two through to Europe's current "Islamic Colonization", brought about by the likes of "Marxists[...]Suicidal Humanists...[and]...Capitalist Globalists" (Breivik 2011). Islam is portrayed as a Trojan horse within the EU, bringing various means of waging Jihad (holy war) on the population. (Breivik 2011) "Violent Jihad" is the most obvious of strategies, followed by "demographic Jihad [*childbirth*], institutional... cultural... economic... educational... media/propaganda... criminal... [and]... drug distribution Jihad" (Breivik 2011).

The ultimate conclusion of such a strategy is what is widely known in extreme-right circles as 'white genocide'—that is, a conspiracy theory which suggests that the annihilation of the 'white race' is being brought about by mass immigration, racial integration, miscegenation, low fertility rates and abortion, encouraged by such western 'facilitators' as "Cultural Marxists", "Suicidal Humanists", "Capitalist Globalists" and, of course, the non-white ethnic groups themselves. To this end, Breivik quoted one such perceived 'facilitator', the Norwegian anthropologist Thomas Hylland Eriksen. Hylland Eriksen states that the current mission of western societies should be "to deconstruct the majority so thoroughly that it can never be called the majority again." (Hylland Eriksen quoted by Fjordman 2008).

In keeping with many voices on the extreme-right, Breivik argued that Europe's decline had been caused by its allegiance to the notions of 'Cultural Marxism' since the victory of the Allies and their Soviet partners in World War Two. The floodgates had been opened for such all-pervading social ills as feminism and multiculturalism. Feminism drew women away from the traditional family unit and therefore white European birth rates (and thus populations) went down. The 1950s was idealised by Breivik as a golden age, when "ladies devoted their time and effort to making good homes, rearing their children well and helping their communities through volunteer work" (Breivik 2011). With woman's departure from the domestic sphere, a torrent of social decay and degeneration had been let loose, in Breivik's view. Men had lost respect for women and women had lost respect for themselves. Popular culture had become infiltrated with pornography, drug use was rife, and homosexuality was regarded as "normal and good" Breivik (2011). Beset by a world in which sex was encouraged for pleasure's sake alone, non-child producing relationships flourished, and drugs encouraged greater degeneracy still, "[the ideal]1950s family would head back to the 1950s as fast as they could, with a gripping horror story to tell" (Breivik 2011).

Breivik can be seen as situated within a broad ideological network, but the brutal physical attacks on Oslo and Utøya saw him operate very much within the confines of the 'lone wolf', employing the notion of 'leaderless resistance'. The term 'leaderless resistance' was first used by an American intelligence officer, Colonel Ulius Louis Amoss, in the 1950s. The concept was picked up and developed by the American extreme-right figure, Louis Beam, in the 1980s. In an essay entitled "Leaderless resistance", Beam stated, the term means that "all individuals and groups operate independently of each other, and never report to a central headquarters or a single leader for direction and instruction" (Beam 1992). Beam was a new type of white supremacist in the 1980s—he was media savvy, ambitious and he recognised that the old-style, highly visible white robes and cross burnings of the Ku Klux Klan were no longer enough to make progress in a more security conscious world. Greater stealth would be needed—"[i]t will become necessary to consider other means of organization—or as the case may very well call for: non-organization" (Beam quoted in Smith 2017) The adoption of such a modus operandi is telling for Breivik. As Gardell observed, leaderless resistance is a means of "substituting unity of organization with unity of purpose" (Gardell 2003). Within the American context, notes Beam, "[t]he last thing federal snoops want...is a thousand different small phantom cells opposing them...[s]uch a situation is an intelligence nightmare". Along with Breivik's crime, the Oklahoma bombing in 1995 made clear the profound dangers of leaderless resistance. In 1999, the FBI stated,

> "The overwhelming majority of extremist groups in the United States have adopted a fragmented, leaderless structure where individuals or small groups act with autonomy. Clearly, the worst act of domestic terrorism in the United States historically was perpetrated by merely two individuals: Timothy McVeigh and Terry Nichols. In many cases, extremists of this sort are extremely difficult to identify until after the incident has occurred". (Gardell 2003, 200)

Some parallels can, of course, be drawn between Breivik and McVeigh and their stances of anti- government militancy. The idea of leaderless resistance was developed further by another prominent American white supremacist, Tom Metzger, in the 1990s. Active within far-right, extreme-right, white supremacist and neo-Nazi circles since the 1960s, Metzger founded White Aryan Resistance or WAR in 1983. In order to achieve "a violent white revolution to 'cleanse' the societal status quo", Metzger was of the belief that attempting to bring large numbers of the general population on-side with the extreme-right cause was futile. The majority, in Metzger's view, were sheep. What was needed were committed individuals who would isolate themselves from their personal ties and from society in general, focussing only on their white nationalist mission. They would act alone or in small groups, not relying on large organisations or leaders, which, within the extreme-right, tended to be weak or ineffectual. "[We are going to]...use whatever means necessary to further a White revolution", Metzger posited. "And if it takes violence and pure hate to get what we want, that's what we're gonna use" (Gardell 2003, 178). In Breivik's preparation for and enactment of his 2011 attacks, exactly such an approach was employed.

Therefore, Breivik can be seen to bring together an identifiable and accessible ideological base, along with the actual, violent expression of that ideology—the word and the deed. He is representative of today's Counter-jihadism, the conduit between Counter-jihadist ideology and practice. As *The Local* (2012) put it, he has played a large role in radicalising today's extreme-right politics. He is a part of the broader far-right and extreme-right milieu, which has seen the rise of various once fringe-dwelling parties such as France's *Front National* (National Front), Austria's *Freiheitliche Partei Österreichs* (Freedom Party of Austria), Germany's *Alternative für Deutschland* (Alternative for Germany) and numerous other groups at varying points on the right-wing spectrum to mainstream electoral success or, at least, prominence. With platforms of 'mono-culturalism, cultural conservatism, anti-intellectualism and anti-feminism' thus brought into general political dialogue, anti-Islamism has replaced anti-Semitism and captured popular sentiment reeling from the various Islamic terrorist attacks of the twenty-first century (Gardell 2011). The rise of Donald Trump and the predominantly American Alt-Right movement in the United States has similarly brought far-right voices into public discourse and a degree of mainstream acceptance or at least awareness. The far- and extreme-right is no longer "just speaking, they're marching" (Dixon 2018).

Thus, current violent and highly visible extreme-right organisations like Britain's National Action, Scandinavia's Nordic Resistance Movement and America's Atomwaffen Division, support Breivik, along with a plethora of individual, underground online voices. Breivik's radical heirs plan, applaud, and seek to normalise political violence online and enact it in reality. In a firmly twenty-first century version of leaderless resistance, the Internet has provided a worldwide stage that has thus far been denied to those on the extreme political fringe (Lievrouw 2011).

The Role of the Internet

The Internet has given all sorts of groups the opportunity to:

> ".....creat[e] unprecedented opportunities for expression and interaction, especially amongst activists, artists, and other political and cultural groups around the world who have found new media to be inexpensive, powerful tools for chal lenging the givens of mainstream or popular culture. Websites, mobile telephone, digital photography, video and audio, blogs, wikis, file-sharing systems, social media, and open-source software all permit social groups with diverse interests to build and sustain communities, gain visibility and voice, present alternative or marginal views, produce and share their own do-it-yourself...information sources, and resist, talk back, or otherwise confront dominant media culture, politics and power". (Lievrouw 2011)

Users are encouraged to 'like', share or re-blog what they see. They are no longer just absorbing the opinions of others but also creating and recreating their own opinions and so comparing themselves against others, allowing for self-validation, and offering up their own world-view for the critique of others. Even early in the Internet's development, the extreme-right recognised the "new possibilities for influencing people...arising in the area of communications networks" (Hooper 2002). David Duke, the well-known American extreme-right figure, has stated that the Internet will become "the tool of the White revolution" (Kaplan et al. 2003).

The Internet has allowed supporters of Breivik to build a virtual world in which their extraordinary views are validated and normalised. On the second-generation Counter-jihadist microblogging sites e.g. Tumblr, Breivik is lauded as a man of action, strong enough to complete his "atrocious but necessary" task. Just as Dietrich Eckhart sought out "a guy[...]who doesn't mind a machine-gun" in interwar Germany with Adolf Hitler in mind (Turner-Graham 2011, 95), so photographs of Breivik are captioned with such phrases as "Stop talking—start doing" and "Stop waiting for things to happen—Go out and make them happen". Such is their embrace of Breivik that his crimes are even the subject of jokes. With a photograph of Utøya, Breivik and a gun, the text reads:

> BREIVIK'S PRIVATE SWIM SCHOOL[...]Revolutionary teaching methods[...]A truly life-changing experience[...]No child left behind[...] "Swim or DIE!"—Anders Breivik, Coach & Manager. (variously cited).

Current web forums such as *4chan* underscore this, allowing for anonymous and unmoderated discussion. *4chan* boards such as 'Politically Incorrect' regularly air a range of extreme-right views. In late February 2018, several discussion threads were entitled "Andres [sic] Breivik is a hero[.] Prove me wrong", "Why aren't there more people going full Breivik?" and "Breivik did nothing wrong" (*4chan* 2018).

Violent Proclivities of Neo-Breivik Acolytes

Along with the shocking virtual sentiment revealed in the 'private swim school' joke, the second generation—Breivik's legacy, essentially—are seemingly also more prepared to enact actual violence. The Atomwaffen (atomic weapon) Division, an American paramilitary neo-Nazi group, is one example. Although associated loosely with the more populist Alt-Right factions, it has criticised them for not being radical enough. The aim of the Atomwaffen Division is the violent overthrow of the United States government by way of terrorism and guerrilla warfare and the implementation of a National Socialist (Nazi) state. Like the Republic of Florida group mentioned in this chapter's introduction, and to whom they have at the very least ideological connection, the Atomwaffen Division (AWD) have voiced their support for Breivik (Thompson et al. 2018).

AWD describes itself as a "very fanatical, ideological band of comrades" who participate in "activism and militant training. Hand to hand, arms training..." (AWD 2018). In short, they seek not only to 'talk the talk' of the Internet's 'keyboard warriors' but also 'walk the violent walk', just as Breivik did—and more so. "Keyboard warriorism [*sic*] is nothing to do with what we are or what we do", the Atomwaffen Division website states (AWD 2018). "If you don't want to meet up and get things done: don't bother" (AWD 2018). They have conducted campaigns on university campuses, as other Alt-Right groups have done, as well as more extreme, openly National Socialist groups like the UK's National Action and Australia's Antipodean Resistance. AWD's posters urge students to "Join your local Nazis!" and warn (or boast) "The Nazis are coming!". "Don't prepare for exams! Prepare for race war!", exhorts another. Their website leaves little doubt as to their brutal and actively violent message. "Marxists [,] Sodomites[,] Traitors[,] Bureaucrats[,] Niggers[,] Kikes[,] Race Mixers[-]Nowhere to run or hide[-]We are everywhere", one image reads. "The frail whites will serve as prey to the Aryan predator[.]Join the Atomwaffen Division", declares another; and "the only right is the right of lead". Calling for "White Jihad", they seek not to take over the world as it stands (or change its composition as Breivik did) but to destroy it and rebuild it—"Embrace Futurism! Honour Armageddon!" (AWD 2018). They are a new generation, built on Breivik's example, but they are also a step beyond their 'hero'.

In January 2018, AWD member Samuel Woodward was charged in California with murdering Blaze Bernstein, an openly gay Jewish teenager. Extraordinarily, one member of the AWD even supports ISIS (for detailed examination of such strange convergences, see e.g. Michael (2006) and also comment in chapter 14). Eighteen-year-old Devon Arthurs converted to the ultra-conservative Salafist Islam and proclaimed himself to be a 'Salafist National Socialist'. He stated that Omar Mateen, perpetrator of the 2016 Orlando (Florida) nightclub shooting to be a hero, and attended a vigil for victims of the shooting in a skull mask and carrying a sign stating "God hates fags". In 2017, he took the occupants of an Orlando shop hostage, angry about America bombing Muslim countries. When police arrived, he took them to his apartment, where he had killed two fellow AWD members (and flatmates). The motivation for the murders is still under investigation. Certainly Arthurs had been mocked within extreme-right circles for his conversion to Islam. He has claimed that he murdered Jeremy Himmelman and Andrew Oneschuk (his fellow AWD members) because they were planning a terrorist attack. "I prevented the deaths of a lot of people" Arthurs said in a police statement (Finn 2017).

A fourth flatmate and co-founder of AWD, Brandon Russell, has been charged regarding the explosive material, detonator components and ammonium nitrate found in their garage. Arthurs claims Russell was planning to bomb power lines, nuclear reactors and synagogues. Unsurprisingly, given the overall context, Arthurs now features on a AWD poster with the statement "Race traitors get the fucking knife!" (AWD 2018).

Breivik's Mental State

Although there has been much conjecture over Breivik's mental condition—and that of those who have followed him—one phrase which has consistently arisen is malignant narcissism. Narcissistic, antisocial, aggressive and paranoid with a drive for power and the respect they feel is their due that overshadows all else, including the rights of other people, malignant narcissism—understood either as a defined psychiatric condition or more loosely as a general description— can also be seen to colour what Breivik has sparked (see chapter 2 on the difficulties and dangers in ascribing mental disorders to egregious conduct). Malignant narcissism often operates in tandem with negative individuation—"psychic development which is hindered or goes radically wrong and which may then become destructive" (Virtanen 2013, 657). There is much—already well documented—in Breivik's childhood and youth which can be seen to have given rise to such an individuation. This, as a component of a narcissistic personality disorder, leads to black and white thinking—the notion that everyone can be seen as either "gods or assholes" (Virtanen 2013, 660).

So too, in Jungian typology, negative individuation can take the form of an over-identification with the shadow or "the inferior function...the dark side of the personality, which is the door into the unconscious" (Virtanen 2013, 667). That is, in a manner that can be correlated back to Breivik and many of his successors, "[a]n idea or image from the unconscious takes over the individual's ego and conscious identity and creates a psychotic inflation or depression." (Virtanen 2013, 667). Notably, giving thought to the social and psychological machinations of the Internet, such psychologies can also happen *en masse*. Indeed, Jung explained at least part of the German national adherence to National Socialism as "shadow identifications...on a collective level" (Virtanen 2013, 668).

The Norwegian psychiatrist Ingrid Melle has provided much detail on the sequence of Breivik's psychiatric evaluation over some six to nine months, contextual events and nuances that were involved, the diagnoses that were made, and how the court reached its judgement on his sanity (Melle 2013). As Melle described, psychiatric evidence presented in Breivik's trial was contradictory. Initially and following Norwegian judicial protocol, two psychiatrists were appointed by the court to evaluate his mental state, diagnose any diseases or disorders, and evaluate the relevance of these to his conduct at the time of the alleged offences. They concluded that he was psychotic and suffering from paranoid schizophrenia. Therefore, under Norwegian law, he could not be held accountable for his actions. After this diagnosis leaked out, there was much public disquiet and pressure on politicians to seek a second opinion. The court appointed a second pair of psychiatrists to conduct a second evaluation, and while they shared the first psychiatrists' observations on Breivik's grandiose delusions, paranoid elements, and pathological self-aggrandisement, Melle reported that they concluded that these were due to a severe narcissistic personality disorder combined with pathological lying, and not psychosis and paranoid schizophrenia. The court accepted the second psychiatrists' diagnosis—that is, that he was sane, with the legal implication that Breivik was fully accountable under criminal law for his actions.

Breivik had pleaded not guilty. Initially, the strategy of Breivik's legal defence team, with Breivik concurring, was to establish that he was not guilty by reason of mental illness. However, Breivik evidently had second thoughts, as such an assessment would deny him the opportunity to manipulate his trial to gain maximum publicity and exposure for his extremist manifesto. According to de Graaf et al (2013), Breivik had actually written in his manifesto (Breivik 2011) about the very eventuality he now faced following the kind of spectacular attack his manifesto recommended:

> "If for some reason you survive the operation, you will be apprehended and arrested. This is the point where most heroic Knights would call it a day. However, this is not the case for a Justiciar Knight. Your arrest will mark the initiation of the propaganda phase. Your trial offers you a stage to the world". (de Graaf et al. 2013, 7)

Similarly, Breivik wrote in a letter from prison "The process looks like a circus with 450 accredited journalists from all over the whole world. I cannot say I look forward to it, but it is certainly a unique opportunity to explain the idea of 2083 [*his manifesto*]" (de Graaf et al. 2013, 7). For Breivik, his murderous attacks were a stepping stone to a far more valuable 'propaganda phase' that a trial could afford him, and if he were declared insane much of his courtroom propaganda opportunity would disappear. His defence team now switched strategy by dropping an insanity defence, dismissing the first two psychiatric reports, and putting forward what amounted to a political self-defence justification (Melle 2013). Breivik's objective was to be seen as a political activist and his killing spree a political mission, so as to consolidate the existing support of the like-minded and bring new supporters on side—indeed the "maximum amount of sympathizers and supporters" (de Graaf et al. 2013, 8).

Breivik's attempt to get himself declared sane succeeded with the second two psychiatric reports, but not perhaps in the way he had intended. Breivik desperately sought to convince the court and the world that he was both sane and brilliant, that the genius of his manifesto was clear evidence of his sanity, and moreover that the pure logic of his hideous actions at Utøya and Oslo on July 22, 2011 based on his manifesto and his altered defence of 'politically justified self-defence' would result in his acquittal (Melle 2013). Instead, his various attempts at grandstanding oratory in court, and his request to wear a self-made military uniform complete with fake 'medals of honour', simply made him and his ideas appear preposterous and grotesque. Only perhaps the small number of already convinced neo-Breivik extreme-right followers referred to earlier were encouraged by his courtroom behaviour and rhetoric. Breivik was found guilty on all counts and jailed for the maximum 21 years, with a potential indefinite extension for as long as he is considered a risk to public safety. In 2017, following his failed appeal against his conviction, for reasons not revealed, Brevik legally changed his name to Fjotolf Hansen.

It is, perhaps, worth considering briefly how similar or dissimilar Breivik's antecedents were to those of other far- or extreme-right lone terrorists who have been convicted. On the one hand, there are obvious similarities between, for example, Breivik, Thomas Mair the murderer of British MP Jo Cox (see chapter 5), Darren Osborne who murdered one person and attempted to murder nine others outside a London mosque in June 2017 (Rawlinson 2018), and Ethan Stables who planned a massacre at an LGBT event in Cumbria, Britain (Swerling 2018a), in respect of their various severe personality disorders, their utter conviction that those they wished to kill or otherwise destroy represented pathological agencies of destruction to white culture which justified a pre-emptive strike against them, and their active engagement with sources of far- and extreme-right literature and propaganda. However, some differences do stand out. For example, neither Breivik nor Mair had any significant prior criminal convictions, in contrast to Stables and Osborne (over 100 in the case of the latter). Moreover, whereas Mair, Osborne, and Stables were all loners, socially isolated, and suffering from various forms of depression, which no doubt added to their inflated sense of grievance, despair and rage, Breivik was markedly different. He thrived on his loner existence and indeed seemed to regard this as a necessary right-of-passage for the saviour of a white Christian Europe. The narcissistic Breivik believed he had no need for friends on a regular face-to-face basis as he would soon have the adulation of the whole world, once they recognised the brilliance of his manifesto.

Thus, as chapters 5 and 14 discuss, looking for common characteristics that might alert professionals to potential lone terrorists is not simple or straightforward, nor is what can be done practically if they are identified, although some potential generic strategies are put forward.

Conclusion

In the dark corners of the Web and in the dark actions that they fuel, the negative individuation of the "victims of nobody in particular and everybody in general" allow for a vast and dangerous racial mythology to develop, petrified in the dichotomous imagery of macabre fairy-tales (Vitranen 2013, 669). In a world of "generalized indifference" (Anspach 2013), Breivik and his acolytes have found new and horrifying means to get themselves noticed. The stark constraints of the extreme-right *Weltanschauung* (see Introduction and Glossary) give them the structure and discipline they lack and its apparently justifiable violence gives them the means to violently grab the world's attention.

Although the avid hero worship Breivik enjoyed from some pockets of the extreme-right in the aftermath of the massacre has ebbed away, as was observed at the beginning of this chapter, a renewed interest has emerged in the Norwegian killer. A Russian neo-Nazi stated in 2016 "He is most definitely an authoritative figure. And I think the numbers of those who support and sympathize with him will only grow" (Seierstad 2016). It is worth noting that what markedly slowed down Breivik's capacity to build up a self-focussed cult of personality was the Norwegian State's increased control of his incoming and outgoing mail. While there were no restrictions on his lines of communication in the year following the massacre, as of August 2012, new controls were applied. His letters to the Aryan Brotherhood—an American white supremacist prison gang—didn't make it to their destination and a letter to Breivik from Nikolai Korolev, a Russian nationalist who bombed a marketplace in Moscow in 2006, killing mainly Central Asian traders, didn't make it to the Norwegian killer's cell. Specific legislation put in place to respond to particular individuals and groups may be one answer in controlling the amount of propaganda that extremists can disseminate. In recent times, several of Atomwaffen Division's online platforms have been closed to them (Thompson et al. 2018). Similar measures have been taken in the United Kingdom in relation to the extreme right neo-Nazi group National Action, as discussed in chapter 4. However, the vast information superhighway makes such control a difficult task.

Of course, some measures must be attempted to at least partially minimise the risks relating to lone actor terrorists such as Breivik. In conclusion, those risks are summarised as a means of opening up further discussion, as follows:

Risk 1. Popularisation

The popularisation of lone actor terrorists such as Breivik via the Internet and social media may encourage and embolden susceptible others to support or even emulate them.

Risk 2. Far and extreme right material and propaganda catalysing support

The continuing ubiquitous availability of far- and extreme-right material and propaganda via multiple channels may encourage and embolden susceptible others to support or even emulate them.

Risk 3. Practical difficulties in identifying and thwarting lone terrorists in advance

Lone actor terrorists may not be readily identifiable in advance and, even if identified, there may be little or no potential, practical follow-through to deter or thwart them.

References

4 chan. 2018. http://boards.4chan.org/pol/thread/161722254/anders-breivik-is-a-hero.

4 chan. 2018. http://boards.4chan.org/pol/thread/162244589/breivik-did-nothing-wrong.

4 chan. 2018. http://boards.4chan.org/pol/thread/162092718/why-arent-there-more-people-going-full-breivik.

Anspach Mark 2013. "Understanding Anders Breivik". *Imitatio*. 2013. http://www.imitatio.org/mimetic-theory/markanspach/understandingbreivik.html.

Beam, Louis, 1992. "Leaderless Resistance". *The Seditionist*. Issue February 12, 1992. http://www.louisbeam.com/leaderless.htm.

Borchgrevink, A. 2013. *A Norwegian Tragedy: Anders Behring Breivik and the Massacre on Utøya*. Cambridge. Polity Press.

Breivik, A. B. 2011. *2083—A European Declaration of Independence*. https://publicintelligence.net/anders-behring-breiviks-complete-manifesto-2083-a-european-declaration-of-independence/.

Breivik, A. B. 2012. "Letter to Angus". July 12, 2012. https://sites.google.com/site/breivikreport/letters/anders-behring-breivik-letter-12-07-02-to-angus.

The Breivik Report. 2011. *Anders Behring Breivik: Court Psychiatric Report*. Oslo. https://sites.google.com/site/breivikreport/documents/anders-breivik-psychiatric-report-of-2011.

CST 2011. "Anders Behring Breivik's Political Platform". *CST Blog*. July 26, 2011. Community Security Trust. London: CST. https://cst.org.uk/.

Fallaci, O. 2002. *The Rage and the Pride*. New York: Rizzoli International Publications.

Gardell, M. 2003. *Gods of the Blood: The Pagan Revival and White Separatism*. Durham NC: Duke University Press.

Gardell, M. 2011. "The Roots of Breivik's Ideology: Where Does the Romantic Male Warrior Ideal Come From Today?" *Open Democracy*. August 1, 2011. https://www.opendemocracy.net/mattias-gardell/roots-of-breiviks-ideology-where-does-romantic-male-warrior-ideal-come-from-today.

Gardell, M. 2011. "Terror in the Norwegian Woods". *Overland*. Summer 2011. https://overland.org.au/previous-issues/issue-205/feature-mattias-gardell/.

de Graaf, B., van der Heide, L., Wanmaker, S. et al. 2013. *The Anders Breivik Trial: Performing Justice, Defending Democracy*. ICCT Research Paper. June 2013. International Centre for Counter-Terrorism. The Hague: ICCT.

Jackson, P. 2016. "Behind the Lone Wolf". *Searchlight*. Autumn 2016. 18–21.

The Local. 2012. "Breivik 'Gets Love Letters from 16-Year-Old Girls'". *The Local*. June 18, 2012. https://www.thelocal.no/20120618/breivik-gets-love-letters-from-16-year-old-girls.

Melle, I. 2013. "The Breivik Case and What Psychiatrists Can Learn From It". *World Psychiatry*, 12, 16–21, February 2013. DOI: 10.1002/wps.20002.

Michael, G. 2006. *The Enemy of My Enemy: The Alarming Convergence of Militant Islam and the Extreme Right*. Lawrence KA: University Press of Kansas.

Nagle, A. 2017. *Kill all Normies: Online Culture Wars from 4chan and Tumblr to Trump and the Alt-Right*. 2017.

Phillips, P. J. 2011. "Lone Wolf Terrorism". *Peace Economics, Peace Science and Public Policy*. Vol. 17 Issue 1 2011. 1–29.

Rawlinson, K. 2018. "Darren Osborne Jailed for Life for Finsbury Park Attack". *The Guardian*. February 2, 2018. https://www.theguardian.com/.

Reid, J. M. and Yakeley, J. 2014. "The Violent True Believer as a "Lone Wolf"—Psychoanalytic Perspectives on Terrorism". *Behavioural Sciences and Law* 2014. DOI: 10.1002/bsl.2109 .

Seierstad, Å. 2016. "Is Norwegian Mass Murderer Anders Breivik Still a Threat to Europe?". *Newsweek*. April 13, 2016. http://www.newsweek.com/anders-breivik-neo-nazi-suing-norway-asne-seierstad-447247.

Seierstad, Å. 2015. *One of Us: The Story of Anders Breivik and the Massacre in Norway*. London: Virago Press.

Smith, L. 2017. "Armed Resistance, Lone Wolves, and Media Messaging: Meet the Godfather of the 'Alt-Right'". https://timeline.com/louis-beam-white-supremacy-history-20d028315d.

Spaaj, R. 2011. "Far-Right Terrorism". *La Trobe University News*. December 16, 2011. http://www.latrobe.edu.au/news/articles/2011/opinion/far-right-terrorism.

Swerling, G. 2018. "Nazi Spent Seven Months Plotting Gay Massacre". *The Times*. February 6, 2018.

Taras, R. 2012. *Xenophobia and Islamophobia in Europe*. Edinburgh: Edinburgh University Press.

Thompson, A.C. and Winston, A. 2018. "Atomwaffen, Extremist Group Whose Members have been Charged in Five Murders, Loses Some of Its Platforms". *ProPublica*. March 6, 2018. https://www.propublica.org/article/atomwaffen-extremist-group-whose-members-have-been-charged-in-five-murders-loses-some-of-its-platforms.

Thompson, A.C., Winston, A. and Hanrahan, J. 2018. "Inside Atomwaffen as it Allegedly Celebrates a Member Killing a Gay Jewish College Student". *ProPublica*. February 23, 2018.

Turner-Graham, E. 2014. "'Breivik is My Hero': the Dystopian World of Extreme Right Youth on the Internet". *Australian Journal of Politics and History*. Vol. 6 No. 3 2014. 416–430.

Turner-Graham, E. 2006. *"Never Forget That You are a German": Die Brücke, Deutschtum and National Socialism in Interwar Australia*. Frankfurt-am-Main: Peter Lang Verlag.

Virtanen, H. 2013. "The King of Norway: Negative Individuation, the Hero Myth and Psychopathic Narcissism in Extreme Violence and the Life of Anders Breivik". *Journal of Analytical Psychology*. 58, 657–676.

von Brömssen, K. 2013. "2083—A European Declaration of Independence"—An Analysis of Discourses from the Extreme". *Nordidactica—Journal of Humanities and Social Science Education*. 1 2013. 12–33. http://www.diva-portal.org/smash/get/diva2:623531/FULLTEXT03.

Chapter 11: The Alt-Right Ideology in Russia

By Antonis Klapsis

Abstract

The Alt-Right ideology as conceived by various political parties and groups in Russia is explored. Four main Alt-Right groupings are examined, the mainstream populist United Russia party of President Putin being the largest platform. Nationalist and nativist ideological underpinnings to the Russian Alt-Right, most notably provided by Alexander Dugin, are analysed. Recurrent themes suffusing the Russian Alt-Right, such as racism, anti-Semitism, anti-Muslimism, xenophobia, and Russian supremacist expansionism, are revealed. Risks arising are identified.

Key words: Russia, Alt-Right, Putin, nativism, expansionism, risks.

The Alt-Right, Russian Style

After the collapse of the Soviet Union, the Russian political system has been gradually dominated by political parties and political leaders who—no matter how they call themselves—are clearly identified with what in modern-day language is called an Alt-Right to Far-Right ideological background. Traditionalism, anti-liberalism, anti-westernism, aggressive nationalism, chauvinism, and in some cases even open racism and anti-Semitism, form the hard core of the beliefs of the Russian Alt-Right. This chapter explores in brief the various concepts of Alt-Right ideology in Russia. It distinguishes four different notions or subcategories (mainstream/populist Alt-Right, geopolitical Alt-Right, ultranationalist Alt-Right, and chauvinist Alt-Right) which, over the years, have formed the spectrum of the Russian Alt-Right. Apart from the internal Russian political landscape, this chapter also focuses on the international implications that the rise of the Russian Alt-Right has caused, especially in relation to the policies of Russian President Vladimir Putin.

Mainstream Alt-Right: Vladimir Putin

The appearance of Vladimir Putin in the political foreground of Russia marked the beginning of a new era in the country's modern history. Ever since 1999, the former KGB foreign intelligence officer has managed to dominate the political landscape in Russia in an absolute and undisputable way. Sometimes described as a 'new tsar' and by others as the most powerful leader in the country after Joseph Stalin (*Economist* 2017), by 2018 Putin had not only been the leader of Russia for almost two decades, but he had also imposed his ideological supremacy in the country. A mixture of authoritarianism, social conservatism, and nationalism, this ideology has transcended the borders of Russia and has become a sort of ideological beacon for Alt-Right political parties all over Europe—and even beyond it. Further, what is interesting in the case of Putin in comparison to other politicians, who can also be identified as Alt-Right, is that he has been in the unique position to actually put his ideology into action. This ideology constitutes the core of the platform of the political party United Russia which clearly dominates the Russian political system (e.g. in the legislative elections which took place in 2016, United Russia secured 54.2% of the popular vote).

The cornerstone of Putin's ultra-conservative/Alt-Right ideology was epitomized in his speech in September 2013, in which he referred to the need to establish a united national idea:

> "Today we need new strategies to preserve our identity in a rapidly changing world, a world that has become more open, transparent and interdependent ... For us, questions about who we are and who we want to be are increasingly prominent in our society ... It is evident that it is impossible to move forward without spiritual, cultural and national self-determination ... We can see how many of the Euro-Atlantic countries are actually rejecting their roots, including the Christian values that constitute the basis of western civilisation. They are denying moral principles and all traditional identities: national, cultural, religious and even sexual ... I am convinced that this opens a direct path to degradation and primitivism, resulting in a profound demographic and moral crisis". (*Russia Today* 2013)

In a nutshell, the west is depicted as decadent and forgetful of its own Christian origins. A return to 'traditional values' is coupled with references to national integrity. Multiculturalism is rejected and otherness is perceived more or less as a threat to a long-established way of living. Globalisation is seen as a force that undermines the authority of nation-states and their cultural inheritance. The need for action in order to save a world shaken by unprecedented and extremely rapid developments is now thought to be greater than ever. As a result, the need for a strong leader appears to be self-evident: a leader like Putin, who can decisively implement these policies.

Indeed, Putin has ruled Russia in an utterly authoritarian way. Elections are held, but his political opponents are routinely oppressed and freedom of speech is not at all guaranteed. Those who criticize Putin are in danger of finding themselves in prison or even losing their lives. Special laws provide the imposition of extremely heavy fines and other punishments to participants in 'unauthorized demonstrations', to such an extent that Amnesty International noted that "spontaneous protest has been virtually outlawed" (Boghani 2015). On top of that, Putin has imposed extremely tight controls on the media. In practice, almost all of the Russian media promote only official government views with no reference to opposing opinions. Journalists who dare to criticise his choices are very likely to be subjected to pressures of various kinds, including the risk of being attacked or even murdered (Heritage 2013; *BBC News* 2017). As part of his 'iron fist rule,' he has also imposed repressive measures against foreign non-governmental organisations operating on Russian soil, which have been accused of being spies and sponsors of foreign interests that undermine Russian sovereignty (Orttung 2013). Civil society is thus perceived and treated as a threat against state and national interests. The establishment of this autocratic regime is coupled with the cult of personality (Cassiday and Johnson 2010), which is cultivated systematically by the media in order to create the image of Putin as a strong and masculine leader—for example, frequently portrayed bare-chested riding a horse, or engaging in martial arts.

A crucial element of Putin's ideology and practical policies is the imposition of an economic system of state capitalism. Indeed, the Russian state owns about two-thirds of the market capitalization in the stock market of Russia, which is even greater in certain sectors, such as energy (mainly oil, gas and electricity), banks, and transportation (Dresen 2012). This tight control of the state over vital economic sectors gives Putin the opportunity to use them in order to promote his political aims, both in and outside Russia. Through this control, he gains access to money and consequently to economic power. Putin has thus been able to dominate a pyramid of political and economic patronage, a development that became clearly evident in the way that even privately owned media are manipulated by the Kremlin.

A key feature of Putin's Alt-Right ideological background is undoubtedly his ultraconservative approach to social issues. He has presented himself and Russia under his rule as the bastions of traditional values against the decay of these values in the western world. The constant reference to a pure, ethical, and morally unspoiled past is part of this approach and a deliverance of his promise to protect Russia from western decadence. Rejection of globalization and multiculturalism is one aspect, whereas in many cases, human rights are perceived as an obstacle in pursuing this moralistic vision. One of the most obvious examples of this trend is the homophobic campaign that has been launched in Russia in the last few years. Putin has repeatedly referred to the need to counter 'homosexual propaganda,' which threatens to undermine the foundations of a society based on heterosexual families. Lesbian, gay, bisexual and transgender (LGBT) rights, including gay marriage, have practically no place in this context. In June 2013, Russia adopted a law banning the distribution of 'propaganda of non-traditional sexual relationships' among minors (Article 19 2013; Wilkinson 2013). Western liberalism, which grants equal rights to all citizens irrespective of their sexual, religious or other preferences, is thought to be degenerate and is perceived as a social and national threat. This approach is associated with the belief that the west (most importantly Europe and the US) is in decay and that—as a result– its downfall is more or less inevitable.

Religion has also played a vital role in Putin's ideology and rhetoric. As the leader of the largest Christian Orthodox nation in the world, Putin likes to present his country as the international protector of Orthodoxy. This is not a new strategy, but one that goes back centuries to the time of the Russian tsars and that has traditionally been shared by the Patriarchate of Moscow. In the case of Putin's Russia, it is a way of boosting not only the religious, but equally the national, feelings of the Russian people, and at the same time providing a tool for promoting the Kremlin's international footholds, especially in other Orthodox countries such as Serbia, Bulgaria, and Greece. His visits to Mount Athos in 2005 (*BBC News* 2005) and 2016 (*BBC News* 2016) were huge advertisements of this cause: in fact, Putin was the first Russian leader ever to pay a visit to the world-famous Orthodox monastic community.

Another core element of Putin's ideology has been his aggressive nationalism. His initial aim of restoring Russia as a major power in the international system for the first time in the post-Soviet era was soon replaced by clear expansionist tendencies. His constant efforts to rebuild Russian national pride are only one side of the coin. The other is his resolve—even if he has to resort to the use of force—to protect alleged Russian national interests beyond Russia's international borders. The invasion of Georgia, the support provided by the Russian government to the secessionist movements in South Ossetia and Abkhazia, as well as the more recent Russo-Ukrainian conflict and the Russian annexation of Crimea, are the most striking examples. The concept of the 'Russian near abroad,' which sees most of Russia's neighbours as part of a wider Russian 'backyard,' provides the theoretical and ideological pretext for the establishment of spheres of tight influence beyond the national borders of Russia (Toal 2017).

Last but not least, what has made Putin a unique case is the great appeal of his ideology and policies to Alt-Right politicians, political parties, and other Alt-Right activists and movements outside Russia. Putin's Russia has cultivated strong and intimate relations with many Alt- or Far-Right political parties in Europe (including the Front National in France, Jobbik in Hungary, the Freedom Party of Austria, L'SNS in Slovakia, NDP in Germany, and Northern League in Italy). For Putin, this is an integral part of a wider strategy that aims at the destabilization of the European Union and NATO. For such foreign parties, Putin is seen as a model of a strong leader who does not hesitate to use authoritarian measures in order to achieve his goals. Moreover, Russia is thought to be the geopolitical alternative to both the European Union and NATO, whereas, for those who have expansionist tendencies against their neighbouring countries, Putin's disregard for international legality seems to open a window of opportunity for promoting their own aims. In the last few years, an unofficial, but in many cases quite effective, alliance has been forged between the Kremlin and the European Alt-Right parties which have become increasingly pro-Russian (Klapsis 2015). Similarly, many of the American Alt-Right find Putin's social conservatism very attractive: they admire and openly praise the Russian President and the policies that he has implemented in his country (Zimmerman 2017). These admirers include leading Alt-Right personalities in the United States, ranging from white supremacists such as Richard Spencer (who has described Putin's Russia as the "sole white power in the world") and Matthew Heimbach (who has attributed to Putin's Russia the title of "the leader of the free world") (Porter 2017), to anti-gay activists such as Scott Lively (who sees Putin as "an example of moral leadership that has shamed the governments of Western Europe and North America and inspired the peoples of the world") (Lively 2013).

Geopolitical Alt-Right: Alexander Dugin

In terms of the ideological background of the Alt-Right in Russia, Alexander Dugin is a key person. Dugin's works seem to provide the basis for Putin's geopolitical analysis and thus have affected the Russian president's strategy (Barbashin and Thoburn 2014). What is equally important is that Dugin's concepts of Eurasianism, national bolshevism and conservative revolution appear to be very appealing, not only within Russia but also to a great number of Alt-Right and far-right politicians across Europe, as well as in the United States. His nationalist, socially traditional, totalitarian, anti-liberal and generally anti-western ideology adds to his international success among far-right circles. For many Alt-Right politicians and activists, Dugin is considered to be an ideological guru, whose analysis epitomises an alternative way of thinking to that of western liberalism.

The basic principles of Dugin's ideological system are laid out in his well-known book *The Fourth Political Theory* (Dugin 2012). In it, Dugin identified three major political ideologies that had shaped all political systems of the modern age, i.e. liberal democracy, Marxism, and fascism. Out of these three, he maintained that the latter two had already failed and they belong more or less to history. On the contrary, liberal democracy is still operating, but not as an ideology, in the sense that it is not evolving but it is taken for granted: "When liberalism transforms from being an ideological arrangement to the only content of our extant social and technological existence, then it is no longer an 'ideology' but an existential facet, an objective order of things." Dugin rejected the liberal monopoly, which he perceived as a threat to cultural and national variety on a global scale. Therefore, he put forward his own ideological proposition, which he called the Fourth Political

Theory; it is an ideology that, allegedly, integrates parts of the previous three theories while at the same time superseding them.

Dugin openly called for a return to traditional values, such as religion, family, and hierarchy, which, in his view, had been overthrown with the dawn of modernity. At the same time, he rejected some of the foundations of the modern west, which he perceived as a menace. In doing so, he predicted more clearly and more profoundly than any other Alt-Right thinker or politician in Russia the end of the west and, alongside with it, the world order as we know it today:

> "... post-modernity (globalization, post-liberalism, the post-industrial society) is easily recognized as "the kingdom of the anti-Christ" (or its counterparts in other religions—'*Dajjal*' for the Muslims, '*Erev Rav*' for the Jews, the '*Kali-Yuga*' for Hindus, and so on). Now this is not simply a metaphor capable of mobilizing the masses but a religious fact—the fact of the Apocalypse ... Moving from crisis to crisis and from one bubble to the next (thousands of Americans held a demonstration at the time of crisis with the following slogan, "Give us a new bubble!" Can they be any more blunt?), globalist economy and the structures of the post-industrial society make mankind's night more and more black. It is so black, in fact, that we gradually forget that this is night time. "What is light" people ask themselves having never seen it". (Dugin 2012, 20 and 23)

In this context, the role of Russia is going to be pivotal; however, it is clear that for Dugin the Fourth Political Theory was not only valid in Russia but could also be implemented on a global scale—and that's what makes it appealing to Alt-Right enthusiasts in Europe and the United States.

Dugin's Fourth Political Theory is an integral part of his wider concept of Eurasianism. In his geopolitical analysis, Dugin identified a conflict between Russia and Atlanticism (represented primarily by the United States and NATO) for the control of Eurasia. He thus argued that it was imperative that the American influence in Eurasia should be diminished and that, at the same time, Russian influence in the same region should be restored to a level parallel to the tsarist and/or the Soviet era. In this context, he called for the annexation to Russia of certain areas belonging to neighbouring countries (such as Finland, Ukraine, Georgia, and the former Soviet republics in Central Asia), as well as for the creation of spheres of influence (e.g. in the Balkans) and the forge of alliances (e.g. with Iran) in the Russian periphery (Dugin 1997).

For Dugin, the geopolitical clash that he described between Russia and the United States (and its allies) in Eurasia was part of the long-established conflict between land-based civilizations and sea-based civilizations: the opposition between the two was inevitable. However, apart from geopolitical implications, today the conflict is also ideological: on the one hand, Russia represents and defends traditional values, the blossoming variety of cultures, as well as a multipolar world with no hegemony imposed by one country over the others; on the other hand, the Atlanticists stand for liberal values and the market-driven society, and promote the unipolar hegemony of the United States. Thus, Russia must follow its Eurasian destiny as a means of both securing its place in the world and opposing western liberalism (Dugin 2014; 2015). According to Dugin, the formation of a Russian-driven Eurasian state would gradually lead to a minimisation of US influence in Europe and eventually to the inclusion of most EU countries within the Russian sphere of influence.

Dugin's theoretical approaches influenced the creation of a nationalist ideological background which became very popular in the Russian Alt-Right community. They also exercised a profound influence on Russian political and military elites. His geopolitical analysis concerning the role of Russia in Eurasia can be seen as the ideological driving force behind Russian interventions in third countries (the Russian annexation of Crimea is the latest but not the only example) and the Kremlin's attempt to destabilize the west through various forms of activities (ranging from under-the-table economic support to pro-Russian political parties in Europe to cyber attacks in the United States). The creation of the Eurasian Economic Union with the participation of Russia, Belarus, Armenia, Kazakhstan, and Kyrgyzstan may also be included in the same pattern (Clover 2016).

At the same time, many prominent Alt-Right personalities outside Russia see Dugin as their ideological mentor. Dugin's theories offer inspiration to Alt-Right politicians and activists in Europe and in the United States. His anti-liberal and anti-western manifestos are treated with admiration by those who would like to see the downfall of both liberal democracy and the west and what it stands for. Dugin's concepts offer them an ideological and seemingly practical scheme of how a new, ultra- conservative world, founded on traditional values, could be brought about.

Ultranationalist Alt-Right: Liberal Democratic Party of Russia

In the constellation of Alt-Right political powers in Russia, the Liberal Democratic Party of Russia (LDPR) has an exceptional place. By 2018, LDPR was the third biggest political party in the Russian State Duma, and had achieved considerable electoral support in the previous two-and-a-half decades. It had been established as one of the most stable political parties in Russia in the post-Soviet era and, at the same time, the strongest ultra-nationalist party in Russia. Despite its official name, LDPR is definitely neither liberal nor exactly democratic; in fact, it is more accurate to describe it as anti-liberal and even more precisely as ultra-nationalist and inclined to authoritarianism.

LDPR's ideological background is a mixture of extreme-right populist rhetoric, ardent anti-westernism and anti-Americanism, homophobia, racism, and above all Russian nationalism. Its main aims are the 'revival of Russia as a great power' and it identifies the United States and NATO as the main enemies of Russia. In this context, it fosters the restoration of Russia in its 'natural borders,' which are identified with those of the former Soviet Union, through a closer economic and political union of the Russian state with all the former Soviet republics. It is also inclined to anti-Semitism (despite the fact that its leader is half-Jewish) and conspiracy theories. As far as the economy is concerned, it favours a strong intervention of the state and it supports the nationalization of certain sectors of industrial production (Rudakova, 2017). Not surprisingly, its base of electoral support consists primarily of young and middle-aged males of lower to lower-middle class background. From a geographic point of view, this base is located mostly in small- and medium-sized towns of Russia (Shekhovstov 2011).

The key figure of LDPR is undoubtedly Vladimir Zhirinovsky who has led the party ever since its creation in the early 1990s. In fact, LDPR is largely a reflection of his personal ideological beliefs. Quite often being described as a 'clown of Russian politics,' Zhirinovsky is a typical example of a populist Alt-Right leader. On several occasions, he has engaged in physical fights with political rivals even in the parliament; during the 2008 campaign for the Russian presidential elections, he released actual footage of himself shooting a rifle at targets representing his fellow candidates. Over time, his ultra-nationalist views expressed through public statements have called for the need for Russia to retake Alaska from the United States, the deployment of tactical nuclear weapons against targets in Chechnya, and the deportation of all Chinese migrant workers from Russia's Far East (*Al Jazeera* 2012).

Zhirinovsky's aggressive nationalism, as reflected in his book *The Last Break Southward* (1995), is based on the territorial expansion of Russia in order to reach "the shores of the Indian Ocean and the Mediterranean"—a goal almost identical to the one set by the tsarist Russia for acquiring access to the 'warm seas.' Similarly, most—if not all—of the former Soviet republics should be integrated, through peaceful means, in the geographically extended Russian state (Rudakova 2017). In his concept, Russia would become the dominant power from the Middle East to Central Asia, which would effectively fall within the direct sphere of Russian political, economic, cultural, and linguistic influence, even if this development brought Russia in direct confrontation with affected countries, and most importantly with Turkey, Iran, and Afghanistan: "Unfortunately some will die, since the South lacks medicine and a high level of culture. So there will be a process of survival of the fittest, assimilation and adaptation" (Zhirinovsky 1995; Koman 1996; Umland 2008).

All in all, LDPR and Zhirinovsky express the growing Russian Alt-Right nationalism. In some respects, their views are quite similar to and definitely compatible with those of Putin, as well as with the geopolitical doctrines of Dugin. As a result, they form part of a wider ideological and political trend which has deep roots in the Russian public opinion. As Andreas Umland put it:

> "The idea of a new, more or less substantial expansion of Russia's present territory finds reflection in the programs of most Russian right-wing extremists, and sometimes in the statements of nationalists with a reputation for moderation. What is special about Zhirinovsky's 'revolutionary expansionism' is that the LDPR leader ... has in mind not simply the restoration of the tsarist or Soviet empire but something more—the salvation of Russia and of the whole world from the subversive activity of 'southerners' and the all-encompassing new birth of a unitary and authoritarian Russian state within completely new borders, both to the south and to the west (where a new Russian-German border is to appear). Russia's subjugation of 'southerners' beyond the limits of the former borders of the Russian empire, and the conduct of military operations as such, will lay the foundation for a new era in Russian history, cleanse the Russian people, and make Russians happy ... Consequently, his plan is not an expression of revisionism or restorationism. Nor is his idea of occupying the 'South' based on a simple

> calculation of the costs and benefits of such action. Rather, Zhirinovsky's statements tell us that ... he believed that by pursuing an age-old strategy of the Russian state—solving domestic problems through external expansion—Russia will be revived in the new capacity of ruler of what Zhirinovsky calls the 'South'". (Umland 2008, 37)

In this context, it is definitely no coincidence that in the legislative elections held in September 2016, LDPR secured 13.14% of the popular vote, thus raising its percentage by almost 1.5% in comparison with the 2011 elections and losing second place to the Communist Party only by 0.2%.

Chauvinist Alt-Right: Pamyat and Russian National Unity

The analysis of the Alt-Right ideology in Russia would be incomplete without some reference to two small groupings: Pamyat and the Russian National Unity. Reference to these groupings is not based on their actual leverage in the political landscape of Russia, since their appeal to public opinion has been only marginal. However, they are mentioned here because of their extreme-right to neo-Nazi leanings, and thus complete the spectrum of the Alt-Right phenomenon in Russia.

Pamyat (in English: Memory) was created in Moscow in the early 1980s. Very soon, groups under the same name appeared in other major cities of the then Soviet Union. Its official goal was the protection and restoration of buildings of historical importance for the Russian nation. However, under this pretext, it soon evolved into the flagship organization of Russian nationalists in the late Soviet era. It embraced anti-Zionism and anti-Semitism as integral parts of its ideological background, with clear leanings to the adoption of conspiracy theories about the role of the Jews in modern and contemporary history. In this respect, Pamyat continued the long anti-Judaic tradition present in Russia ever since the tsarist era. Pamyat was also fiercely anti-communist and described the Soviet Union as a disaster for the Russian nation; the October Revolution of 1917 was described as a 'Zionist occupation.' Not surprisingly, in the post-Soviet era, Pamyat perceived the US dollar and transnational capital as the main weapons used by 'international Zionist-imperialism' against Russia (Garrard 1991; Midford 1991; Korey 1995; Sukhanin 2017).

From the very beginning, the members of Pamyat presented themselves as the defenders of traditional Russian values. One of these was, of course, the Orthodox faith which together with nationalism and anti-Semitism gave Pamyat its extreme-right ideological character. At a time when the Soviet regime was crumbling, Pamyat openly added a monarchist element to its ideological arsenal, in the sense that it was in favour of the restoration of the monarchy in post-Soviet Russia. At the same time, Pamyat expressed its desire to join forces with other anti-Semitic and chauvinist movements already existing in western European countries. As early as March 1990, one of the leading personalities of Pamyat summed up all these elements while talking at a press conference in Moscow:

> "Russia has always stood on three principles—Orthodoxy, Autocracy, and Nationality. Revival of this tradition is the basis of our movement. With the rebirth of the Orthodox spirit will begin the destruction of all evil in the world, i.e. Zionism. We appeal to all healthy forces in Europe to consolidate our activities. These healthy forces are Le Pen's National Front, La Rouche's European Party, the Republic Party (FRG) ... We need a German-Russian alliance which will finally put an end to Zionism. Marks left by Zionism in our land are the genocide against all peoples in Russia, the ritual murder of the Russian Royal Family, and the downtrodden personality of the Russian man. The destruction of both the Russian Orthodox faith, and the Aryan genotype and the disintegration of Russia, are the fundamental credo of Zionism. Liberalism, humanitarianism, Communism and democracy are the tools with which Judaism seeks to destroy and blacken the Aryan world. Anti-Semitism illegalized and the philo-Semitism of sections of the pseudo-intelligentsia are a plot against Russia. We demand a stop to the emigration of Soviet Jews until we can carry out an investigation into the part they have played in destroying the country. The Jews bear collective responsibility for the 73-year-old diabolical bacchanalia directed from the USA in our country. Zionism must be destroyed!". (Garrard 1991, 133)

However, Pamyat did not manage to become a significant political power in the post-Soviet era. Actually, it never became a real political party. Despite the fact that it had paved the way for the expression of aggressive chauvinism in Russia, it was surpassed by other far-right groupings which emerged after the collapse of the Soviet Union. One of those is the notorious Russian National Unity (RNU) party which in fact was founded in 1990 by dissatisfied members of Pamyat led by Alexander Barkashov—interestingly, after almost 30 years, Barkashov was still the leader of RNU in 2018. RNU differed from Pamyat in the sense that it was openly neo-Nazi: even its emblem resembles the Nazi swastika. Moreover, in contrast to Pamyat, from the outset RNU adopted the structure of a military unit: its members wear black uniforms, they attend some sort of military training and form paramilitary groups, whereas their favourite collective actions seem to be military-like marching and patrolling streets as volunteers. In some cases, some of its members were also involved in criminal activities, including murders (Simonsen 1996; Sokolov 2008).

RNU identifies itself as an "all-Russian public patriotic movement of the Russian Nation, based on the principles of the Orthodox tradition and the Russian national ideology." Its chauvinist and effectively racist background is depicted in reference to "common blood-related origin and ... common historical destiny, which determine the commonality of language and territory, the economic way of life, culture and the national-psychological type—that is, the national character." Its ultra-nationalist programme calls for the territorial expansion of Russia so that it effectively restores its borders of the late tsarist era; Ukraine and Belarus are thought to be integral parts of the Russian nation. Russian supremacy, and a special (i.e. dominant) international role for Russia, is of the essence. Anti-Semitism is also fundamental. As Barkashov put it, "The Jews as a religious community have shown their absolute disharmony with Russian culture, religion and statehood". As a result, there is no place for them in Russia: "We cannot get on. And this is our land, and therefore we have the right to live as we like ... Let them leave quietly, while they have such an opportunity." The democratic order is castigated as a tool in the hands of the Jewish international-financial oligarchy, which is used with the aim of crushing the Russian nation. Being utterly anti-liberal, RNU calls for the establishment of an authoritarian order in Russia in the form of a national dictatorship which will regenerate the Russian state and the Russian nation (Russian National Unity, Undated; Simonsen 1996; Jackson 1999; Romov 2001).

As in the case of Pamyat, RNU has not managed to secure significant public support. In fact, it has not even managed to retain its internal coherence, and has suffered repeated splits. Fragmentation has led to the gradual decrease of its influence, especially after 2000, and consequently to its further marginalization.

Conclusions

Russia is a country where Alt-Right ideology is definitely very appealing to a large audience. An amalgam of ultra-conservatism, anti-liberalism, anti-westernism, pro-authoritarianism, and—above all—aggressive nationalism, seems to dominate the Russian political landscape. This is particularly the case as Putin's ideological background includes all these elements and he has effectively used them as integral parts of his political programme and his style of government. The fact that these elements are common a wide range of political parties, politicians, and influential thinkers is associated with the perception that they are preconditions for the political, economic, social, and moral regeneration of Russia, as well as the restoration of its international status after the harsh experiences of the early post-Soviet years.

One might argue that this is an internal Russian issue and should not pose any worries to the rest of the world. However, this is not the case. Russia's size and international status is such that any internal development may have international implications. The dominance of Alt-Right ideology in Russia, especially to the extent that—through Putin's administration—it forms part of the governing policy, poses a triple threat, summarised as follows:

Risk 1: Russian regional hegemony and expansionism

The first kind of risk is associated with the expression of Russian regional hegemony and territorial expansionism which is, in turn, directly related to the domination by ultra-nationalist views in large parts of the Russian political, military, and even intellectual elites. Developments such as the Russian invasion of Georgia and the annexation of Crimea not only show complete disregard for international legality, but—to make matters worse– they pose direct threats to international security. It is quite possible that Moscow, under the leadership of Putin, might pursue similar endeavours in the not so distant future. In turn, these might lead to greater escalation of international tension than that experienced so far.

Risk 2: Russian role model for Western Alt-Right

Alt-Right parties and politicians in Europe and the United States will continue to see Putin's Russia as a semi-authoritarian and neo-conservative model of governance that they would most probably like to see in their own countries. This model fits their beliefs and is perceived as a dynamic response to the 'malice' of liberalism, openness and tolerance from which western democracies suffer. Apart from the ideological connection, European far-right politicians clearly see Russia as an ally in their desire to dismantle the EU and to diminish NATO's (and consequently the US's) role in European security issues. Moscow is thus held up as a geopolitical alternative to both the EU and NATO (Klapsis 2015, 55–56). The American Alt-Right has also found in Putin a sort of a natural ideological ally, who supports everything they stand for. The Kremlin stands as a beacon for Alt-Right nationalists of the western world. Interestingly enough, it appears that, to a certain extent, even Donald Trump and his hard core followers see rather positively Putin's anti-liberal and nationalist policies (Bertnard 2016; 2017).

Risk 3: Using Western Alt-Right as its Trojan horse proxy to destabilize Western democracies

Last but not least, for the Kremlin, the growing success of Alt-Right parties abroad is clearly an advantage, since it is thought that this will destabilise the west as a whole (Orenstein 2014). Putin's ambition to make Russia the dominant power in Eurasia and create a sort of a regional Russian hegemony (Aron 2013) has played, and will most probably continue to play, an important role in his attempt to establish closer ties with EU Alt-Right and far-right political parties that can facilitate the achievement of his goals. With this strategy, Russia seeks to create problems for NATO, as the pro-Russian Alt-Right and far-right political parties are equally Eurosceptic and anti-NATO. Similarly, American Alt-Right leaders have repeatedly been calling against US and NATO involvement in Russia's vicinity, a position which perfectly fits the Kremlin's strategic goals (Bertnard 2016). The old 'Trojan horse' tactic against enemies may well be how the Kremlin seeks to encourage and manipulate the Alt-Right in the west against the extant liberal democracies.

References

Al Jazeera. 2012. "Vladimir Zhirinovsky: an Aggressive Voice". February 26, 2012. http://www.aljazeera.com/indepth/spotlight/russianelections/2012/02/201221801731930183.html. accessed on December 11, 2017.

Aron, L. 2013. "The Putin Doctrine: Russia's Quest to Rebuild the Soviet State". *Foreign Affairs*, March 8, 2013. http://www.foreignaffairs.com/articles/139049/leon-aron/the-putin-doctrine. accessed on December 9, 2017.

Article 19. 2013. *Russia: Federal Laws Introducing Ban of Propaganda of Non-Traditional Sexual Relationships.* London: Article 19. https://www.article19.org/.

Barbashin, A. and Thoburn, H. 2014. "Putin's Brain: Alexander Dugin and the Philosophy Behind Putin's Invasion of Crimea". *Foreign Affairs*, March 31, 2014. https://www.foreignaffairs.com/articles/russia-fsu/2014-03-31/putins-brain. accessed on October 31, 2017.

BBC News. 2005. "Putin on Mount Athos Pilgrimage". *BBC News*, September 9, 2005. http://news.bbc.co.uk/2/hi/europe/4229342.stm accessed on December 10, 2017.

BBC News. 2016. "Vladimir Putin Visits Mount Athos, All-Male Orthodox Enclave". *BBC News,* May 28, 2016. http://www.bbc.com/news/world-europe-36405480. accessed on December 10, 2017.

BBC News. 2017. "Russia Profile". *BBC News*, April 25, 2017. http://www.bbc.com/news/world-europe-17840134. accessed on November 15, 2017.

Bertnard, Natasha. 2016. "'A Model for Civilization': Putin's Russia Has Emerged as 'A Beacon for Nationalists' and the American Alt-Right". *Business Insider*, December 10, 2016. http://www.businessinsider.com/russia-connections-to-the-alt-right-2016-11. accessed on December 10, 2017.

Bertnard, N. 2017. "Trump Won't Condemn White Supremacists or Vladimir Putin—and the 2 Are Closely Linked". *Business Insider*, August 14, 2017. http://www.businessinsider.com/trump-putin-connections-to-american-alt-right-and-white-nationalists-2017-8. accessed on December 10, 2017.

Boghani, P. 2015. "Putin's Legal Crackdown on Civil Society". *PBS*, January 13, 2015. https://www.pbs.org/wgbh/frontline/article/putins-legal-crackdown-on-civil-society/. accessed on November 15, 2017.

Cassiday, J. A. and Johnson, E. D. 2010. "Putin, Putiniana and the Question of a Post-Soviet Cult of Personality". *The Slavonic and East European Review*, 88:4, 681–707.

Clover, C. 2016. *Black Wind, White Snow: The Rise of Russia's New Nationalism.* New Haven/London: Yale University Press.

Dresen, F. J. 2012. *The Role of State Corporations in the Russian Economy.* Wilson Center, October 1, 2012. https://www.wilsoncenter.org/publication/the-role-state-corporations-the-russian-economy. accessed on December 12, 2017.

Dugin, A. 1997. *The Foundations of Geopolitics: The Geopolitical Future of Russia.* Moscow: Arktogeya [in Russian].

Dugin, Alexander. 2012. *The Fourth Political Theory.* London: Arktos Media.

Dugin, A. 2014. *Eurasian Mission: An Introduction to Neo-Eurasianism.* London: Arktos Media.

Dugin, A. 2015. *Last War of the World-Island: The Geopolitics of Contemporary Russia.* London: Arktos Media.

Economist. 2017. "Russia Under Vladimir Putin—A Tsar is Born". *The Economist.* October 26, 2017. https://www.theeconomist.com/.

Garrard, J. 1991. "A Pamyat Manifesto: Introductory Note and Translation". *Nationalities Papers,* 19:2, 134–145.

Heritage, T. 2013. "Putin Dissolves State News Agency, Tightens Grip on Russia Media". *Reuters,* December 9, 2013. http://www.reuters.com/article/2013/12/09/us-russia-media-idUSBRE9B80I120131209. accessed on November 15, 2017.

Jackson, W. D. 1999. "Fascism, Vigilantism, and the State: the Russian National Unity Movement". *Problems of Post-Communism,* 46:1, 34–42.

Klapsis, A. 2015. *An Unholy Alliance. The European Far Right and Putin's Russia.* Brussels: Wilfried Martens Centre for European Studies.

Koman, A. J. 1996. "The Last Surge to the South: the New Enemies of Russia in the Rhetoric of Zhirinovsky". *Studies in Conflict & Terrorism,* 19:3, 279–327.

Korey, W. 1995. *Russian Anti-Semitism, Pamyat, and the Demonology of Zionism.* London/New York: Routledge.

Lively, S. 2013. "An Open Letter to President Vladimir Putin". *Scott Lively Ministries,* August 30, 2013. http://www.scottlively.net/2013/08/30/an-open-letter-to-president-vladimir-putin/. accessed on December 10, 2017.

Midford, P. 1991. "Pamyat's Political Platform: Myth and Reality". *Nationalities Papers,* 19:2, 183–213.

Orenstein, M. A. 2014. "Putin's Western Allies". *Foreign Affairs,* March 25, 2014. http://www.foreignaffairs.com/articles/141067/mitchell-a-orenstein/putins-western-allies. accessed on December 9, 2017.

Orttung, R. 2013. „Kremlin Nationalism Versus Russia's NGOs". *Russian Analytical Digest,* 138, 8–11.

Porter, T. 2017. "Charlottesville's Alt-Right Leaders Have a Passion for Vladimir Putin". *Newsweek,* June 8, 2017. http://www.newsweek.com/leaders-charlottesvilles-alt-right-protest-all-have-ties-russian-fascist-651384. accessed on December 10, 2017.

Romov, R. 2001. "Russian National Unity and the 'Nation of Slaves': New Versions of an Old Myth". *Russian Politics & Law,* 39:3, 66–77.

Rudakova, D. 2017. "Interview with Russian Presidential Candidate Vladimir Zhirinovsky". *South Front,* December 30, 2017. https://southfront.org/interview-russian-presidential-candidate-vladimir-zhirinovsky/. accessed on December 30, 2017.

Russia Today (2013). "'It is Impossible to Move Forward Without Spiritual, Cultural and National Self-Determination'—Putin". *Russia Today*, September 20, 2013. https://www.rt.com/politics/official-word/putin-valdai-national-idea-142/. accessed on November 15, 2017.

Russian National Unity (undated). *Fundamentals of the Socio-Political Concept of RNU.* Russian National Unity. http://www.rusnation.org/org.shtml#1. accessed on December 20, 2017 [in Russian].

Shekhovstov, A. 2011. "Vladimir Zhirinovsky and the LDPR". *Foreign Policy Journal*, November 7, 2011. https://www.foreignpolicyjournal.com/2011/11/07/vladimir-zhirinovsky-and-the-ldpr/. accessed on December 12, 2017.

Simonsen, S. G. 1996. "Aleksandr Barkashov and Russian National Unity: Blackshirt Friends of the Nation". *Nationalities Papers*, 24:4, 625–639.

Sokolov, M. 2008. "Russian National Unity: an Analysis of the Political Style of a Radical-Nationalist Organization". *Russian Politics & Law*, 46:4, 66–79.

Sukhanin, S. 2017. "Anti-Semitism in the Late Soviet Union: the Rise and Fall of Pamyat Movement". *Tiempo Devorado. Revista de Historia Actual*, 1, 39–60.

The Economist. 2017. "Russia Under Vladimir Putin. A Tsar in Born". *The Economist*, October 26, 2017. https://www.economist.com/news/leaders/21730645-world-marks-centenary-october-revolution-russia-once-again-under-rule. accessed on October 30, 2017.

Toal, G. 2017. *Near Abroad: Putin, the West and the Contest over Ukraine and the Caucasus.* Oxford: Oxford University Press.

Umland, A. 2008. "Zhirinovsky's Last Thrust to the South and the Definition of Fascism". *Russian Politics & Law*, 46:4, 31–46.

Wilkinson, C. 2013. "Putting Traditional Values into Practice: Russia's Anti-Gay Laws". *Russian Analytical Digest*, 138, 5–7.

Zhirinovsky, V. 1995. *The Last Break Southward.* Moscow: Foliant [in Russian].

Zimmerman, J. 2017. "It's Not Just Trump Who's Fond of Putin: Why Social Conservatives Have a Thing for the Russian President". *New York Daily News*, March 6, 2017. http://www.nydailynews.com/opinion/social-conservatives-vladimir-putin-article-1.2989959. accessed on December 10, 2017.

Part 3:
Conclusion

Chapter 12: A Risk Analysis and Assessment of the European Alt-Right and its Effects

By Alan Waring

Abstract

The risk evidence and interpretations from preceding chapters are subjected to a systematic analysis and assessment. Such relevant factors as objective and subjective risk, pure and speculative risk, assessment methodology, and psychological factors affecting risk analysis and assessment are discussed. From the collated assessments, a number of key observations emerge, including six common themes among the identified risks concerning unchecked resurgent nationalism, nativism, and Alt-Right agendas.

Key words: Alt-Right, risk assessment, Delphi technique, heuristic, themes.

A Collated Risk Analysis and Assessment

The preceding chapters provided a detailed description and analysis of a wide range of topics and risk issues on which the Alt-Right worldview, agendas, and actions have significant impacts. In one direction, the Alt-Right presents threats and risks to a range of individuals, groups, entities, populations, and nations. In another direction, the Alt-Right attracts threats and risks to itself. Both sets of risks warrant attention.

This chapter provides a risk analysis based on the evidence and interpretations provided in Part 2. However, before addressing the particular risk exposures revealed in those chapters, it is worthwhile reconsidering a number of matters of relevance to any risk analysis of this kind. In particular, how each individual conceives of risk, and risks of different kinds in different contexts, is not uniform across a population or across humanity. There are wide variations. Even individuals may be inconsistent in their beliefs and attitudes e.g. an individual may be a heavy cigarette smoker or engage in highly dangerous sports, yet avoid vaccination against dangerous diseases.

Risk as a Cognitive Phenomenon: Objective and Subjective Risk

As noted in chapter 2, Table 2.1, the integrated multi-level conceptual framework for exploring risk (Glendon and Clarke 2016) incorporates cognitive perception of risk (thinking, awareness, appraisal etc including threat perception). However, problems arise from the notion of risk as a cognitive phenomenon. First, the terms used to describe and communicate risk are fluid and variable. The recursive and interchangeable nature in everyday speech of such terms as 'hazard', 'danger', and 'risk, as well as 'assessment', 'analysis', 'appraisal', 'estimation', and 'evaluation', even among risk specialists, creates fertile ground for ambiguity and confusion. Second, since its character, form, qualities, and scale are the product of a cerebral judgement, a particular risk is always subjective. Analogous to such concepts as love and power, a risk has no ontological, reified existence as a tangible object. Whereas many people may agree that a particular risk exists, and concur about its description and likely impact, that consensus cannot objectify the risk. Further, any individual who analyses or assesses a risk, whether risk specialist or lay person, comes to the task bearing the baggage of their individual life experiences, world-views, cognitive biases (Douglas 1992; 1994), and pre-conscious biasing (Dixon 1981). Such a statement counters the claims of some (e.g. Chicken 1996) that objective risks are those determined by experts, whereas subjective risks are determined by non-experts, one implication of such claims being that expert risk assessment is inherently more accurate, reliable, valuable and trustworthy than that of a non-expert. As Waring and Glendon (1998, 37) pointed out, "Because of its essentially judgemental nature, risk assessment cannot be neutral or value-free, whoever carries it out and however impartial they seek to be". Risk assessment techniques may be objective in the sense that they use validated methodologies consistently. However, the risk assessment process itself is always subjective, because the choice of which particular methodology to use involves personal judgement, even if this is expert judgement. Similarly, most individual determinations about probabilities, frequencies, projected outcomes and other aspects of risk assessment, although they may be based on good or even best available evidence, are nonetheless judgemental. For a detailed discussion of the subjective/objective issues, see Shrader-Frechette (1991).

However, as Durodié (2002; 2005a and b) warned, it may be unwise in general to give equal weight to expert and non-expert risk perception and assessment or, worse, automatically to give precedence to non-expert views. It should be recognized that, by definition, an expert in a particular topic is expected to possess enhanced knowledge and experience relating to it beyond that of a non-expert and, so far as humanly possible, impartiality in rendering judgements about it. An expert is required to focus on facts and substantiated evidence and to guard against emotionality, prejudice and wishful thinking, whereas a non-expert may have no such constraints. For these reasons, it is usual to rely on expert rather than non-expert opinion on a wide range of risk issues, for example, in medicine, public health, aviation safety, and nuclear safety. Nevertheless, every individual is fallible and therefore even an expert is capable of error, misperception and faulty judgement.

A prominent example of where expert judgement appears to have been faulty is the Grenfell Tower fire disaster in London on June 14, 2017, in which fire safety assessments and risk decisions had involved a variety of experts responsible for external cladding of high-rise residential blocks. Although the official public inquiry into the disaster did not start until August 15, 2017, early investigations revealed that apparently large numbers of Grenfell residents (i.e. non-experts) had raised concerns for several years about fire safety, including their doubts about the cladding, but allegedly these had been dismissed as exaggerated fears by the managing authority and its expert suppliers, executives, and advisers, both internal and external.

A recognition that experts are fallible is not, however, a valid argument for discrediting them or downplaying their vital role in risk analysis and assessment, as some critics (e.g. Trump) have done selectively when expert pronouncements have inconveniently challenged their prejudices. What is important is that expert risk analysis and assessment should take account of significant contexts and non-expert valuations, not to unduly influence their expert judgement but to ensure that pertinent matters of significance are not overlooked. This is not intended to patronise non-expert views but to ensure that they are accounted for, even if in a particular instance they may not be well substantiated by facts or evidence.

A further broad and related area of psychology is also relevant to this chapter, as summarised in Appendix 12.1: Factors Affecting Risk Perception and Therefore Risk Analysis.

Pure Risk and Speculative/Opportunity Risk

Two classes of risk are generally recognized (IRM 2010)—pure risks (sometimes referred to as 'downside risks') and speculative or opportunity risks (which may be either 'upside', 'downside' or more usually a combination of the two). The distinction is significant to risk analysis, since the two classes warrant different approaches.

A pure risk relates only to negative or undesirable events and impacts and is one that is characterized by (a) the probability or likelihood that the undesirable event will occur, and (b) the scale of the potential or likely undesirable event or impact. In common parlance, a pure risk is one where the best that can happen is that nothing bad happens. Thus, management of pure risks prioritizes the elimination and prevention of threats and hazards (i.e. sources of pure risk exposures) as well as risk reduction and control methods. Typical examples of pure risks are: hazards to environment, health and safety; product liability; disaster/crisis preparedness; natural hazards; IT systems failures; information and cyber security threats; piracy; fraud; intellectual property theft; trafficking (people, weapons, drugs); tax evasion; terrorism.

In terms of computation or estimation, a pure risk is measured as the product of the likely scale of impact/severity of the undesired event and the probability of occurrence:

Pure Risk = (Scale of Negative Impact/Severity) x (Probability of Occurrence).

An opportunity or speculative risk may result in either a desirable outcome (benefit, gain, advantage), or an undesirable outcome (detriment, loss, disadvantage), or a combination of desirable impacts in some aspects and undesirable impacts in others. Usually, opportunity risks involve a mixture of good and bad effects, although efforts may be made to maximize desirable outcomes and minimize undesirable ones. Typical examples of opportunity risks are: market credibility;

bargaining power; strategic alliances; sales growth; brand enhancement; mergers and acquisitions; political risks; economic risks; foreign policy; new technology; investments.

In terms of computation or estimation, an opportunity risk is measured as the product of the likely scale of impact (positive, neutral or negative) and the probability of occurrence:

Opportunity Risk = (Scale of Impact) x (Probability of Occurrence).

It should be noted that some risks may appear to be both pure and opportunity risks or exhibit ambiguous characteristics. In such cases, an analysis should enable sufficient deconstruction to clarify matters. For example, at first glance it may appear that environmental issues and global warming, addressed in chapter 9 of Vol 1, would be classified exclusively as pure risks. However, whereas environmental risks and global warming risk per se are best classified as pure risks, associated political, economic and social risks are really opportunity risks.

In this chapter, the author has chosen to approach all the identified risks for estimation as opportunity risks, as these overwhelmingly predominate in this book's context. Pure risk elements, such as environmental damage, are encompassed for this chapter's purposes as negative impacts within the opportunity risk estimation formula applied.

Risk Analysis and Assessment Methodology

Risk assessment may be defined (Waring and Glendon 1998, 45) as: "the process of estimating and evaluating a defined risk in order to determine whether current risk strategies are appropriate and adequate". The ultimate purpose of risk assessment, therefore, is to inform decision-making about whether the current level of a particular risk is acceptable, and whether further action is required to manage the risk more effectively. That principle applies regardless of whether the assessment is being done by a risk expert or non-expert. Clearly, processes of identification and analysis of any relevant hazard, threat or opportunity would need to precede any estimation or evaluation.

There is no single, 'standard' method for risk assessment and, for example, methodological differences exist between assessment of pure and speculative risks respectively. IRM (2010) has recognized the eclectic range of potential techniques in risk assessment methodology.

However, the basis of all risk assessment comprises this sequence of linked processes (Royal Society 1992):

- Identification of hazard/threat/opportunity (as in chapters 3 to 11)
- Analysis of hazard/threat/opportunity (as in chapters 3 to 11)
- Establishing risk acceptability/tolerability criteria
- Risk computation/estimation
- Evaluation of risk estimates against acceptability/tolerability criteria

As noted in Waring and Glendon (1998), two broad approaches to risk assessment technique have arisen—heuristic and scientific. A heuristic approach is primarily qualitative and relies on the judgement (mediated by knowledge and experience) either of the individual conducting the assessment, or of a number of individuals collectively. A heuristic approach is essentially 'rule-of-thumb', usable both by experts and non- experts, and may involve modest quantification, typically in the form of risk scores and ratings e.g. the Delphi technique—see later. Although some individuals may find the scoring and rating processes challenging, since they require the cerebral collapsing and merging (consciously and pre-consciously) of many ill-defined subcomponent variables into a single measure, in fact this process approximates systematically the 'how big?/how small?' judgements that humans make naturally, and often informally, in their daily lives when addressing the multitude of risk exposures they face. See Shrader-Frechette (1991) for further discussion on scientific and other approaches to risk assessment.

Glendon and Clarke (2016, 364) pointed out that increasingly the complexity of risk issues has been reflected in the plethora of sophisticated risk assessment methodologies, models, and statistical procedures that continue to emerge, and that a "considerable diversity, almost a profusion, of conceptual frameworks and methodologies is available for the study of risk. This reflects the complexity and multidimensional nature of risk concepts", as discussed further by Durodié (2017).

Some risk experts believe that a scientific approach, employing quantitative modelling and probabilistic computation, is inherently superior to that of heuristics. However, such an assertion suggests a structural/functionalist world-view (Burrell and Morgan 1979), which has been challenged in the risk assessment context by such authors as Burgess (2015); Douglas (1992; 1994); Durodié (2017); Mudu and Beck (2012); Toft (1996); Waring and Glendon (1998); and Waring (2013). As Glendon and Clarke (2016) noted, current trends in risk research involve increased adoption of multi-disciplinary approaches, as well as socially constructed and multi-scalar definitions of key risk terms across a range of dimensions. This book follows such trends, for example by acknowledging the well-established risk principles of redundancy (multiple analyses by different authors), diversity (range of different analyses reflecting different disciplines), and triangulation (fusion of analyses to highlight agreement and disagreement), as applied in a variety of risk contexts.

Appendix 12.2 provides a systematic narrative compilation of the risks identified in all the chapters in Part 2. This is followed by Appendix 12.3, a reference utility which adopts a relatively simple risk-rating heuristic approach, based loosely on the well-known Delphi technique originated in the 1950s by the Rand Corporation (Linstone and Turoff 1975; 2002). Appendix 12.4 summarises the rating and scoring heuristics used in Appendix 12.3.

Findings and Conclusion

This Volume's sub-title, 'A Risk Analysis of the European Alt-Right Phenomenon', clearly states its primary focus. This chapter has provided a risk evaluation in relation to the array of risks identified and analysed in chapters 3 to 11. A number of points that require comment emerge from this analysis and evaluation.

1. All the evaluated risks in Appendix 12.3 indicate negative impacts. The overwhelmingly negative evaluations reinforce the view that the Alt-Right phenomenon presents a multi-dimensional threat to society, human rights, and liberal democracy, as well as to itself.
2. All the evaluated risks in Appendix 12.3 fall within the range of medium-high-exceptional, and a majority fall within the

medium-high range. Only a handful has been evaluated as being exceptionally high. This evaluation should be a signal neither for alarm nor complacency, but for timely actions appropriate to eliminate, reduce, or control the threats and risk levels.

3. Although the risk evaluation covers Alt-Right risks relating to the individual countries examined, it does not address directly the higher order threat of the trans-national appeal of the phenomenon, and its internationalisation. Some symptoms of this threat include those relating to Putin's connections with foreign Alt-Right groups (chapter 11), US far-right groups' connections with those in Europe and Russia, and cross-border funding. This higher-order threat is addressed in chapter 13.
4. Common themes among risks identified across the chapters are that unchecked resurgent nationalism and Alt-Right agendas are leading to (1) polarisation in societies, discrimination against minorities of all kinds but especially immigrants and Muslims, hate crimes, and loss of social cohesion; (2) a variety of human rights abuses; (3) attacks on press freedom; (4) attempts to normalise both egregious government policies and conduct and acceptance of hate crimes and Internet and social media abuses by far-right elements; (5) threats to representative democracy; (6) threats to international peace and security.
5. Some of the identified risks are strategic in nature, while others are more operational. Some may respond to relatively quick controls whereas others will require longer-term action. Some will require multiple, different interventions by different agencies or parties, possibly in parallel or perhaps at different times. There is no 'quick fix' or 'single solution' to most of the risks identified, a message taken up in the final chapter.
6. Whereas the risks are those identified by the individual authors, the risk evaluations are those of this chapter's author in collaboration with them. They are not the absolute declarations of a 'Risk Oracle' applying universal laws of risk, since no such laws or certitudes exist. Others may disagree with some of the identified risks or the extent of them, and others may disagree with the risk evaluations or even many of them. Indeed, such differences of opinion are almost inevitable.

> However, hopefully the evaluations provide both a basis for discussion and debate i.e. a reference utility for development and pointers to the furtherance of attenuating harm associated with the Alt-Right.

The following chapter 13 considers, on the basis of the preceding analysis and risk evaluations, how the Alt-Right may develop in the short-to-medium term and various scenarios that might unfold.

Appendix 12.1: Factors Affecting Risk Perception and Therefore Risk Analysis

In addition to sensory defects and potential interferences with sensory perception, a range of psychological and social-psychological factors (e.g. the individual's world-view in relation to risk) potentially affects risk perception, and therefore risk analysis and assessment as well as risk decision-making. The considerable array of such factors, and the literature on these, is too extensive to examine closely in this chapter. For brevity, an illustrative list of factors prominent in the literature is summarised below, based on Waring (2015):

Failures of Hindsight, Foresight and Learning

The contribution of organizational learning, hindsight and foresight to understanding human-created risk failures has been addressed by Le Coze and Dechy (2005), Toft (1990), Toft and Reynolds (1997), Turner (1992), and Turner and Pidgeon (1997). The assumption that organizations are likely not only to seek to learn from risk failures (their own and those of other organizations) but also to seek to take actions that would help to avoid such failures has been challenged by Fischhoff (1975), Toft (1990), Turner and Pidgeon (1997), and Waring and Glendon (1998). In many organizations, despite multiple organizational and human failings having been identified as factors, there is frequently a prevailing culture of denial of failure and disasters being explained away as 'freak events'. For example, as discussed in chapter 9 of Vol 1, the various BP disaster cases over a period of decades (Deepwater Commission 2011; HSE 1989; 2003; Reader and O'Connor 2013; USCSHIB 2007), with often broadly similar causal factors, have suggested failures of hindsight and organizational learning. See also Kastenberg (2014) and Pidgeon (2012) on similar findings about the Fukushima Daiichi disaster. Financial disasters, such as the collapse of Barings Bank (BoBS 1995; Leeson 1996; Glendon and Waring 1997; Waring and Glendon 1998) and the failure of the Royal Bank of Scotland (FSA 2011) further exemplify the issues.

Ignorance and Bounded Rationality

Bounded rationality (Johnson 1987; Kahneman 2003; March and Simon 1958; Morgan 1986; Simon 1972) concerns the inherent limitations on what an individual or a group can know and understand about a particular matter and how this may influence their decision-making about it. However, recognition of such limitation does not justify neglectful ignorance. Corporate and elected political leaders, along with their various senior executives and advisers are expected to show due diligence in acquiring the necessary breadth and depth of knowledge about risks—economic, financial, political, and others—as well as the various risk management requirements that may affect their areas of responsibility. Johnson (1987) and Morgan (1986) have commented on the potential negative effects of bounded rationality whereby individuals, groups and organizations may settle for decisions that are 'good enough' based on simple routine procedures and limited information. Whereas such an approach may be generally acceptable to those responsible for risk decisions, it may prove inadequate for coping with significant risks. For example, in some cases laissez-faire directors, boards or administrations may be content to wait to receive periodic risk reports from subordinate units and accept them with minimal examination. In extreme cases, such reports may never be examined at all, e.g. the Buncefield Disaster (HSE et al 2011).

Confirmation bias (Dror and Fraser-Mackenzie 2008; Nickerson 1998, Zimmerman 2011), which relates to a self-bounding of knowledge, may be defined as the result of seeking out and/or interpreting information that tends to confirm the individual's preconceptions about a particular topic, while also avoiding, ignoring or rejecting information that tends to disconfirm those preconceptions. Although confirmation biasing is frequently a conscious process, a large degree of pre-conscious processing is likely to be involved (Dixon 1981). Such cognitive bias is likely to result in systematic error i.e. the individual's beliefs, while reinforced, may not born out by the facts. The Trump administration has provided numerous examples of confirmation bias.

Groupthink, Authority and Conformity

Groupthink (Janis (1972; 1982) describes a tendency for groups to form a consensus attitude and view on a particular topic. Typically, such a consensus forms around an authority figure, even when that figure's views may not always be supported by facts or be in the group's best interests. For example, Leeb (2006) attributed the 'herd behaviour' frequently exhibited by investors to a combination of authority, conformity, and groupthink. In contrast to recognizing risks and reacting rationally in response, for example by researching the risks and forming their own judgement, the groupthink principle asserts that investors tend to follow what trusted, respected or authority figures recommend or do. Groupthink is evident in the development of such high profile corporate investment collapses as Madoff (Kirtzman 2010), Enron (Maclean and Elkind 2004), and Stanford International (US Department of Justice 2012). The term 'groupthink' may also be applied to inappropriate risk decision-making and actions of people in organizations in the build-up to major hazard disasters, see for example: Dekker and Nyce (2014), Ferraris and Corveth (2003), Le Coze and Dechy (2005), Lunenburg (2010), NAIIC (2012), Toft and Reynolds (1997), and Vaughan (1996; 1999).

Authority and conformity are recognized as characteristics of power relations, whether obtrusive or unobtrusive (see, for example, Bacharach and Lawler 1980; Fincham 1992; Hardy 1985; Pettigrew 1973; Pfeffer 1981). Although power relations within organizations have frequently been examined within the topic of organizational culture (which encompasses shared characteristics), Waring and Glendon (1998) argued that power analysis tends to focus on differentials and resulting power relations and political processes. Power relations within boards, cabinets and their subordinate organizations (e.g. the White House and the President's administration) are likely to be relevant to risk decision-making, risk decisions and the general tone and culture of an organization. Power attributes, in the form of leadership and direction from authority figures, are likely to be significant in either promoting or downplaying risk management. However, sometimes power relations become 'toxic' (Walton 2007), which may have negative implications for a range of organizational matters (e.g., the evident power struggles in 2017 among President Trump's cabinet members, executives and advisers and between Trump and the Attorney-General and successive Directors of the FBI).

Perceptions or cognitions of risks are often coloured by the culture of a particular profession, department or 'silo' in which an individual works. Authority, conformity and groupthink of the particular sub-culture, plus the fear of being perceived as different and no longer trusted by one's peers, may create complacency towards particular risks within a sub-culture.

Risk Perception and Risk Attitudes

Risk perception or risk cognition is a comprehensive term applied to an individual's sensory, perception, and cognitive processes, including thinking, reasoning, evaluating, comparing, judging, learning and deciding (Glendon 1987; Glendon, Clarke and McKenna 2006; Glendon and Clarke 2016; Waring and Glendon 1998). Knowledge, and sense-making, of a risk topic, preferences an individual applies, conclusions that are drawn, and decisions that are made are all clearly significant to the individual's general behaviour towards that risk and any specific actions regarding it. Memory, learning, and experience are clearly relevant, as are moods, emotions and motivations.

A risk attitude is a predisposition, specifically acquired and influenced by learning and experience, whether towards risk in general, or to a particular class of risk, or to a particular risk topic. A risk attitude is significant to risk perception and may predict judgement, behaviour, and actions, whether in the White House, or the corporate boardroom, or elsewhere in an organization, or in the general population.

Risk Appetite

Risk appetite is relevant as an implicit (and, in some cases, explicit) attitude in risk decision-making. Risk appetite applies to individuals, and in its corporate form may be defined (IRM 2011) as "The amount of risk that an organization is willing to seek or accept in pursuit of its long-term objectives". Risk appetite relates primarily to speculative or opportunity risks in, for example, business, commerce, banking, and finance (see, for example, Aven 2012; Gai and Vause 2006; Hillson and Murray-Webster 2011; 2012), rather than to pure risks such as security, environment and safety. If a board makes a strategic decision to invest in a new capital project, for example, the underlying speculative risk decision assumes a healthy return on capital employed. A number of risk issues will be evaluated in reaching that decision, but if the board's risk appetite is large enough then it may over-ride these so that the project may proceed. An analogous application of the concept would be to risk issues affecting government policy decisions on such matters as defence, foreign relations, foreign trade, taxation, immigration, and health care.

Risk Tolerability

Risk tolerability or acceptability refers to a level of risk that is neither unacceptably high nor negligible but somewhere in between. A tolerable risk level is typically less than ideal but enables a trade-off of time, cost, and effort against risk reduction and control benefits up to a pre-set limit. Slovic et al (1982) discussed risk tolerability at the individual level, and Douglas and Wildavsky (1982) at group level, while corporately, IRM (2011) defined risk tolerability as "Boundaries of risk-taking outside of which the organization is not prepared to venture in the pursuit of its long-term objectives". The latter implies that risk tolerability is a strategic issue that is most likely to be applied to speculative risk evaluation at senior management levels. Risk tolerability may also be applied to pure risks and, for example, the principle is central to major hazard risk assessment such as EHS risks (Baybutt 2013; HSE 1988; Jonkman et al 2003; Kasperson and Pijawka 1985; Slovic et al 1982; Waring and Glendon 1998). As with risk appetite and other personal factors, risk tolerability varies between individuals and therefore risk tolerability on a particular topic will vary widely within the general population and between different interest groups.

Motivation and Expectancy

The expectancy theory of motivation (Campbell and Pritchard 1976; Lawler and Porter 1967; Vroom 1964) is generally taken to explain motivations in risk decisions. Expectancy theory asserts that the strength of a particular motivation attributed by an individual to an expected outcome of a relevant decision or choice is the product of valence (the value attributed to the desired outcome), instrumentality (the effectiveness of the proposed method of attainment) and expectancy (the expectation that the desired outcome will result). See also Glendon et al (2006) and Glendon and Clarke (2016). Strong motivations supported by strongly held beliefs may sometimes override caution and competent risk analysis so as to propel individuals, groups, or even organizations into taking precipitate action that may cause harm to many parties including the protagonists themselves, and this is especially so where ideological, political or religious convictions are involved. Examples include the Trump administration's withdrawal from the Paris Climate Accord, the unravelling of Obamacare, and the Mexican wall project.

Risk Decision-Making

Risk decision-making theories such as expected utility theory (EUT), originated by von Neumann and Morgenstern (1944), and examined by Mosher (2013) and Rabin (2000), and prospect theory (PT) (Kahneman and Tversky 1979; Tversky and Wakker 1995), are relevant to investment, financial and other speculative risk decision-making (see, for example, Barberis 2013). Glendon et al (2006) asserted that EUT assumes an essentially rational choice model devoid of complex influences likely to be found in reality. In certain contexts, EUT may therefore be regarded as an example of bounded rationality whereby speculative risk assumptions and criteria applicable to financial, economic, or political matters might be misapplied to risk decisions where different assumptions and criteria are salient. For example, a moral imperative implicit in decision-making relating to environmental risks may be absent from speculative risk evaluations and decisions. Whereas the probability of a major hazard accident may be low, moral and regulatory criteria should ensure that the consequences factor outweighs the low probability factor, a deliberate biasing that economic models such as EUT and PT may not recognize. See also Arai, Yamamoto and Makino (2005) and Jongejan and Vrijling (2009).

Cultural Effects

Various authors, such as Davies (1988), Deal and Kennedy (1986), Schein (1985), Smircich (1983), Westrum (2004), and Wilkins and Dyer (1988), have examined the nature of organizational culture. Waring and Glendon (1998) defined the phenomenon as: a set of unwritten, and relatively unobtrusive, attitudes, beliefs, values, rules of behaviour, ideologies, habitual responses, language expression, rituals, quirks and other features which characterize a particular organization or a defined part of it. According to Waring (2013), organizational culture provides a continuous psycho-social reference frame through which its members interpret their existence within that organization and enables them to consider what is good and bad, right and wrong, acceptable and unacceptable, imperative and taboo. An individual's sense of identity and what it means to be a member is strengthened by organizational culture, which also provides some unique characteristics that distinguish one organization from another. The purposive and unobtrusive 'identity protection' function of organizational culture may explain why organizational members may resist attempts to change it (see, for example, Beer et al 1990; Westley 1990). Organizational culture may be more predictive than official policy of what actually happens and how, within an organization, and this applies to risk and risk management as much as to any other aspect of an organization. See, for example, Douglas (1992); Douglas and Wildavsky (1982); Durodié (2017); Glendon (2008); Glendon et al (2006); Glendon and Clarke (2016); Le Coze (2005); Turner (1988; 1992; 1994); Waring and Glendon (1998); and Waring (2013).

Other cultural effects on risk perception are likely to arise from an individual's memberships of different sub-cultures, such as professions, peer groups, interest groups, and organizational units (see, for example, Douglas 1992; Douglas and Wildavsky 1982). For example, employment as a technical specialist within the EPA is likely to confer a perception of environmental and global warming risks that is significantly different to that of a political functionary employed in the White House administration of President Trump. See Vaughan (1996; 1999; 2004; 2006; 2014) on NASA and the Columbia disaster. Wider cultural effects on risk perception are also likely to operate, for example values and beliefs about particular risk issues shared by a particular community, religion, or regional populace that might not accord with government policy or mainstream scientific views (Douglas and Wildavsky 1982).

Socially Constructed Emergence

A social construction of reality (Berger and Luckmann 1967) is based on the theory that how individuals make sense of the real world is mainly determined by societal structures, relationships and processes that are largely unobtrusive and over which they have little control.

Cultural effects arising from shared ideas, beliefs and values among members of an identifiable group form part of a socially constructed view of reality, as do the effects of inequalities, power differentials, and power relations between different groups or parties.

Applied to risk perception and risk assessment (Burgess 2015; Johnson and Covello 1987), the theory predicts that, for example, particular threats will be viewed differently by different parties in society because their experiences, objectives, motivations, and expectations differ markedly as a result of their different societal loci. In a dystopian extension of this view, Beck (1992) separated society into risk 'perpetrators' (i.e. industry, government, and the 'Establishment') and risk 'victims' (i.e. powerless citizens). Less pejoratively, job security threats are likely to be perceived differently by blue collar workers in traditional industries, contract 'gig' workers, skilled IT workers, and qualified professional workers. Health care risks are likely to be perceived differently by care-home workers, hospital clinical staff, patients, hospital administrators, civil servants, private health insurers, and government ministers.

Language expression, as evidence of individuals' risk worldviews, is regarded by social constructionists as a determinant of an individual's reality rather than as describing risks as objective realities. Social amplification of risk (Kasperson et al 1988; Pidgeon et al 2003), for example as a result of repetitive communicated discourse across society, is relevant. The social constructionist view has led to an emphasis on grounded theory (Glaser and Strauss 1967), ethnographic and discourse analysis approaches to the study of risk contexts (for example, Perrow 1984; Vaughan 2004; 2006; 2014). Wodak (2015) and Wodak et al (2013) applied critical discourse analysis to the European Alt-Right. The interplays of language expression, and widely differing meanings and perceptions of risks, is evident in such concepts as 'Brexit', 'asylum seekers', 'Muslim', 'global warming', 'right-wing', 'globalisation', and 'national identity'.

Appendix 12.2: Qualitative Risk Analysis of the Alt-Right Phenomenon

The following sub-sections provide a collation of the risks identified in the preceding chapters of Part 2. This summary analysis is necessarily that of this chapter's author, although steps were taken to validate it with the other relevant authors and to highlight if and where significantly divergent opinions exist. The author takes into account all the caveats and cautions raised in the preceding appendices of this chapter and requests that the reader does likewise.

The Alt-Right in Selected European Countries

Alt-Right Brexit Agenda (chapter 3)

Risks from the Alt-Right's Stance on Brexit

1. Anti-immigrant rhetoric encouraging blame allocation and an insular, defensive world-view, leading to increased division and polarisation in society.
2. Pressure on government for Alt-Right orientated nationalist policies if Brexit negotiations with EU succeed (i.e. so-called 'soft Brexit') and harsher nationalist policies if Brexit negotiations fail (i.e. so-called 'hard Brexit').
3. Pressure on government for harsher immigration policy if post-Brexit economy declines (e.g. potential GDP fall, stagflation, higher living costs, higher unemployment, business closures, businesses relocate abroad).
4. Potential encouragement for extremist nationalist elements to engage in violence and other hate crimes against immigrants, ethnic and religious minorities, or political opponents of nationalism.

Brexit-related Risks for the UK Alt-Right

1. The Brexit goal having been achieved, electoral oblivion for UKIP as a result of its loss of relevance.
2. Post-Brexit withdrawal of major financial backers of UKIP, frustrated by the party's poor electoral showing and organisational and political incompetence.
3. Strident and inflammatory rhetoric from the Alt-Right post-Brexit against immigrants and minorities steadily losing its appeal to Eurosceptics, thereby ensuring the Alt-Right remain as fringe agitators.
4. Failure by Alt-Right to impose a permanent nationalist timbre on UK governance post-Brexit.

British Far- and Extreme-Right (chapter 4)

1. Cultural despair and alienation among British far- and extreme-right groups, and a frustration with their political failure, may spur a re-alignment of support among them towards more extremist views in which Britain First and National Action become the dominant face of the British far-right.
2. Cultural despair and alienation among British far- and extreme-right groups, and their fanatical supremacist ideology, may lead them to try to act out a 'cultural war' to 'save the nation' through any means, including violence and other hate crimes.
3. Proscription of far-right groups and punishment of offenders by the authorities for hate crimes may, in the minds of extremists and their followers, validate their ideology and confer heroic status among them.
4. Far- and extreme-right ideology may, for a variety of reasons, become increasingly normalised and subsumed within mainstream political discourse and policies in Britain, thereby leading to potential human rights abuses and crimes against sectors of the population.
5. The Internet and social media may increasingly provide a difficult-to-control vector for promulgation of far- and extreme-right views and propaganda.

Lone Actor Extremism in UK (chapter 5)

1. Ready availability of and access to inflammatory material (on-line, printed, mail order, video etc) promoting extremist right-wing ideology.
2. Vulnerable individuals characterised by social isolation, grievances, blaming classes of others, personality disorders, and mental ill-health who are potentially susceptible to right-wing radicalisation and extremism.
3. Inadequate monitoring and intelligence systems for professionals (e.g. doctors, health workers, social workers, police) to recognize risks early and deflect vulnerable individuals away from right-wing radicalisation and extremism.

FPÖ in Austria (chapter 6)

Risks for Austrian Society and Governance

1. Increasing imposition of divisive inequality policies based on nationalist white supremacism, and anti-Muslim and anti-immigrant prejudices, all likely to result in multiple adverse effects for those discriminated against and a reduction in social cohesion for all.
2. Stirring up of discrimination, hatred, and hate crimes against ethnic, religious, and immigrant minorities in Austria, may lead to disaffection and potential backlash among those discriminated against.
3. Sustained attacks on the Austrian media, in particular public broadcasters, so as to reject and avoid scrutiny, may undermine press freedom and inhibit its fundamental role in ensuring public accountability in a democracy.
4. Increasing normalisation in society of previously unacceptable far-right ideology and harsh policies, may lead to increasing support for FPÖ and other far- and extreme-right organisations, as well as acceptance of their methods. This may also lead to increased nepotism and corruption owing to lack of democratic and transparent procedures.
5. A long-term governing power bloc in Austria, comprising FPÖ and its allies, may enable them to gradually subvert the post-war consensus of liberal democracy into an 'illiberal democracy'. More specifically, the separation of powers (legislative, executive, and judicial branches) is likely to be undermined.

Risks for Individuals

1. Discriminatory far-right government policies (whether against immigrants, minorities of all kinds, the disabled, the poor, the unemployed, or any other group) are likely to violate human rights obligations, international treaties and agreements, as well as constitutional protections. Indeed, an illiberal democracy is likely to challenge these constraints on the perceived *vox populi*.
2. Increasing authoritarianism from a far-right government may result in curbs on press freedom, as well as curbs on individual freedom of expression and privacy rights.

Risks for the FPÖ

1. FPÖ policies may not prove as popular in practice as in rhetoric, and the coalition between FPÖ and other nationalist-conservative parties may also prove fragile and vulnerable to fracture, thereby dissipating voter support and the FPÖ's electoral chances for a significant period.

AfD in Germany (chapter 7)

1. AfD encourages an end to a relatively self-critical engagement with the Nazi era. In line with this, the AfD is furthermore giving voice to, amplifies and mainstreams far-right stances, thus undermining diversity (for example, ethnic, religious and gender diversity), potentially leading to repression of minorities.
2. AfD may encourage in German society scepticism if not resistance to multilateral and multinational consensus and cooperation which is perceived as hampering Germany's influence, for example the EU and international agreements on climate change.
3. AfD might affect Germany's position within western security policy; for example, adopting an accommodating attitude towards anti-liberal and anti-democratic policies in Russia, as well as ambivalence towards its aggressive foreign policy.
4. Stirring up of discrimination, hatred, and hate crimes against ethnic, religious, and immigrant minorities in Germany, may lead to disaffection among those affected.
5. Sustained attacks on and delegitimisation of the German 'mainstream' media, in particular public broadcasters, so as to reject and avoid scrutiny, may undermine press freedom and inhibit the media's fundamental role in ensuring public accountability in a democracy.

Front National in France (chapter 8)

Risks for the Front National

1. The blurring of FN economic policies with mainstream centre-right parties may result in a loss of electoral support from working class voters, especially in the country's northern industrial belt.

2. Power struggles between ideological factions within the FN may lead to new rival parties splitting off (e.g. Les Patriotes) and a resulting fragmentation of the FN's populist vote.

Risks for Marine Le Pen

1. Marine Le Pen's poor affinity with the newly predominant nativist authoritarian FN culture may result in her incapacity to remain as FN president and her eventual withdrawal or even removal from active involvement. In this respect, the 2022 presidential and parliamentary elections are likely to be determinative.

Risks for French Society, Governance, and Democracy

1. The FN's success in persuading the mainstream parties to adopt exclusionary and chauvinistic policies, or an outright FN victory in future national elections, could result in adverse effects on human rights, discrimination, hate crimes, as well as France's withdrawal from the EU.
2. FN successes may result in moderate policies of mainstream centre-right and even centre-left parties becoming increasingly compromised, corrupted or even swept away by an elected authoritarian FN government, thereby threatening representative democracy itself.

PVV in Netherlands (chapter 9)

1. Democratic functioning of society and the state under threat by excessive populist demands that are frequently unlawful, unconstitutional, and arguably pathological.
2. Propagation of resentment in society about perceived economic, social and cultural damage allegedly caused by uncontrolled minority groups, leading to scapegoating and hate crimes against such outgroups.
3. Political opportunism among mainstream political parties to attract populist voters, whereby they are prepared to shift their policies rightwards to embrace Alt-Right demands, thus threatening a permanent Alt-Right character to national governance.

Lone Actor Extremism in Norway (chapter 10)

1. The popularisation of lone actor terrorists such as Breivik via the Internet and social media may encourage and embolden susceptible others to support or even emulate them.
2. The continuing ubiquitous availability of far- and extreme-right material and propaganda via multiple channels may encourage and embolden susceptible others to support or even emulate them.
3. Lone actor terrorists may not be readily identifiable in advance and, even if identified, there may be little or no potential, practical follow-through to deter or thwart them.

The Alt-Right Ideology in Russia (chapter 11)

1. Russian regional hegemony and territorial expansion, encouraged by ultra-nationalist views dominating Russian political, military and intellectual elites, posing threats to international security and raising tensions.
2. Foreign Alt-Right regarding Putin's Russia as their role model in pursuing nationalist and anti-liberal policies and agendas.
3. Putin using the Alt-Right in Western countries as his Trojan horse proxy to destabilize Western democracies.

Appendix 12.3: Risk Assessment Summary Tables

Table 12.1: Risks Relating to the Alt-Right in Selected European Countries

The risk scores may be interpreted by reference to Table 12.4 in Appendix 12.4

Risk Exposure Country (as listed in Appendix 21.2)	Desirable/ Undesirable Score (+5 to -5)	Desirable/ Undesirable Rating	Probability Score (1 to 5)	Probability Rating	Risk Score (-25 to +25)
UK Alt-Right Brexit Agenda					
Risks from Alt-Right Stance					
Risk 1	-3	Moderate detriment	4	Likely/high	-12
Risk 2	-3	Moderate detriment	4	Likely/high	-12
Risk 3	-3	Moderate detriment	4	Likely/high	-12
Risk 4	-4	Major detriment	4	Likely/high	-16
Risks for Alt-Right					
Risk 1	-5	Exceptional detriment	4	Likely/high	-20
Risk 2	-4	Major detriment	4	Likely/high	-16
Risk 3	-4	Major detriment	4	Likely/high	-16
Risk 4	-5	Exceptional detriment	4	Likely/high	-20
British Far- and Extreme-Right					
Risk 1	-4	Major detriment	4	Likely/high	-16
Risk 2	-4	Major detriment	4	Likely/high	-16
Risk 3	-3	Moderate detriment	4	Likely/high	-12
Risk 4	-4	Major detriment	4	Likely/high	-16
Risk 5	-4	Major detriment	4	Likely/high	-16

UK Lone Actor Extremism					
Risk 1	-3	Moderate detriment	4	Likely/high	-12
Risk 2	-4	Major detriment	4	Likely/high	-16
Risk 3	-3	Moderate detriment	4	Likely/high	-12
FPÖ in Austria					
Risks for Austrian Society & Governance					
Risk 1	-4	Major detriment	5	Very likely	-20
Risk 2	-4	Major detriment	4	Likely/high	-16
Risk 3	-4	Major detriment	5	Very likely	-20
Risk 4	-4	Major detriment	4	Likely/high	-16
Risk 5	-4	Major detriment	3	Conceivable	-12
Risks for Individuals					
Risk 1	-4	Major detriment	4	Likely/high	-16
Risk 2	-3	Moderate detriment	4	Likely/high	-12
Risks for the FPÖ					
Risk 1	-4	Major detriment	3	Conceivable	-12
AfD in Germany					
Risk 1	-4	Major detriment	4	Likely/high	-16
Risk 2	-3	Moderate detriment	4	Likely/high	-12
Risk 3	-4	Major detriment	4	Likely/high	-16
Risk 4	-4	Major detriment	4	Likely/high	-16
Risk 5	-4	Major detriment	4	Likely/high	-16
FN in France					
Risks for FN					
Risk 1	-4	Major detriment	4	Likely/high	-16
Risk 2	-4	Major detriment	3	Conceivable	-12
Risks for Marine Le Pen					
Risk 1	-3	Moderate detriment	4	Likely/high	-12

Risks for French Society and Governance					
Risk 1	-4	Major detriment	4	Likely/high	-16
Risk 2	-4	Major detriment	3	Conceivable	-12
PVV in Netherlands					
Risk1	-4	Major detriment	3	Conceivable	-12
Risk 2	-4	Major detriment	3	Conceivable	-12
Risk 3	-4	Major detriment	3	Conceivable	-12
Norway and Lone Actor Extremism					
Risk 1	-4	Major detriment	4	Likely/high	-16
Risk 2	-4	Major detriment	4	Likely/high	-16
Risk 3	-4	Major detriment	4	Likely/high	-16
Alt-Right in Russia					
Risk 1	-5	Exceptional detriment	4	Likely/high	-20
Risk 2	-4	Major detriment	4	Likely/high	-16
Risk 3	-5	Exceptional detriment	4	Likely/high	-20

Appendix 12.4: Rating and Scoring Heuristics Used in this Chapter

The risks evaluated in this book are predominantly opportunity risks or may be viewed as such. For example, the pure risks of global warming may be viewed as negative opportunity risks. For opportunity risks, the rating and scoring schema in Table 12.2 reflects the fact that impacts may be positive, negative, or neutral, and that in some instances a combination of both positive and negative impacts.

Table 12.2: Rating and Scoring Heuristic for Estimation of Opportunity Risks

Desirable/Undesirable Rating	Desirable/Undesirable Score
Exceptional benefit	+5
Major benefit	+4
Moderate benefit	+3
Minor benefit	+2
Negligible benefit	+1
Neither benefit nor detriment	0
Negligible detriment	-1
Minor detriment	-2
Moderate detriment	-3
Major detriment	-4
Exceptional detriment	-5

Source: based on Waring and Glendon (1998)

Application of the scores from Table 12.2 in the formula Opportunity Risk = (Scale of Benefit/Detriment) x (Probability of Occurrence) will produce a risk level score in the range -25 to +25.

Table 12.3: Probability Heuristic for Estimation of Risks

Probability Rating*	Probability Score
Very unlikely	1
Unlikely/low	2
Conceivable	3
Likely/high	4
Very likely	5

*as presently controlled, unless a particular risk is a future or theoretical possibility.
Source: based on Waring and Glendon (1998).

Table 12.4: Rating Heuristic for Estimation of Risk Levels

Risk Level Scores	Risk Level Rating
- (20 to 25)	Exceptional negative
- (12 to 20)	High negative
- (8 to12)	Medium negative
- (4 to 8)	Low negative
- (1 to 4)	Insignificant negative
+ (1 to 4)	Insignificant positive
+ (4 to 8)	Low positive
+(8 to 12)	Medium positive
+ (12 to 20)	High positive
+ (20 to 25)	Exceptional positive

Source: based on Waring and Glendon (1998).

Negative risk level ratings imply a corresponding degree of urgency required in relation to threat/hazard elimination and risk reduction and control. It should be noted that with pure risks the impact/severity component should always take precedence over the probability component. Such deliberate biasing provides a means for a realistic evaluation of high impact/low probability events for risk management purposes. For example, the probability of a significant nuclear accident at a nuclear power station may be very low (the typical design standard being less than one significant accident in 10,000 operating years), but the negative impact would probably be catastrophic, as in the example of Chernobyl (IAEA 1992). For major hazard risk exposures (nuclear, chemical, oil and gas facilities, aircraft, and so on), a low probability factor should not be unrealistically or unreasonably emphasised, at the expense of safety prudence. A similar reasoning may be applied to negative opportunity risks that are rated high or exceptional.

References

Arai, T., Yamamoto, S. and Makino, K. et al (eds). 2005. *Systems and Human Science, for Safety, Security and Dependability.* Selected papers of the 1st International Symposium SSR 2003, Osaka, Japan, November. Amsterdam: Elsevier.

Aven, T. 2012. "On the Meaning and Use of the Risk Appetite Concept". *Risk Analysis*, Vol 33 Issue 3, 462–468.

Bacharach, S.B. and Lawler, E.J. 1980. *Power and Politics in Organizations: the Social Psychology of Conflict, Coalitions and Bargaining.* San Francisco: Jossey-Bass Inc.

Barberis, N.C. 2013. "Thirty Years of Prospect Theory in Economics: a Review and Assessment". *Journal of Economic Perspectives*, 27(1), 173–196.

Beck, U. 1992. *Risk Society—Towards a New Modernity*. London: Sage Publications.

Beer, M., Eisenstat, R. A. and Spector, B. 1990. "Why Change Programs Don't Produce Change". *Harvard Business Review*, 68(6): 158–166.

Berger, P. and Luckmann, T. 1967. *The Social Construction of Reality*. Garden City, NY: First Anchor Books.

BoBS. 1995. *Report of the Inquiry into the Circumstances of the Collapse of Barings*. Chairman E.H. George. July 18, 1995. Board of Banking Supervision. London: The Stationery Office.

Burgess, A. 2015. "The Social Construction of Risk". In *Sage Handbook of Risk Communication*, edited by H. Cho, T. Reimer and K. McComas, 121–139. London: Sage.

Burrell, G. and Morgan, G. 1979. *Sociological Paradigms and Organisational Analysis*. London: Heinemann.

Campbell, J.P. and Pritchard, R.D. 1976. "Motivation Theory in Industrial and Organizational Psychology". In *Handbook of Industrial and Organizational Psychology*, edited by M.D. Dunnette, 66–130. Chicago, Ill: Rand McNally.

Chicken, J. 1996. *Risk Handbook*. London: Thomson/Cengage.

Deal, T.E. and Kennedy, A.A. 1986. *Corporate Cultures: Rites and Rituals of Corporate Life*. Reading, MA: Addison-Wesley.

Dekker, S.W.A. 2011. *Drift into Failure—from Hunting Broken Components to Understanding Complex Systems*. Farnham, Surrey UK: Ashgate/Taylor & Francis.

Dekker, S.W.A. and Pruchnicki, S. 2014. "Drifting into Failure: Theorizing the Dynamics of Disaster Incubation". *Theoretical Issues in Ergonomics Science*, 14(6), 534–544.

Dixon, N.F. 1981. *Preconscious Processing*. Chichester: John Wiley & Sons.

Douglas, M. 1992. *Risk and Blame: Essays in Cultural Theory*. London: Routledge.

Douglas, M. 1994. "Who is the Public?" Pages 48–66, symposium proceedings. *Risks to the Public: The Rules, The Rulers and the Ruled*. December 14, 1994. London: The Hazards Forum.

Douglas, M. and Wildavsky, A. 1982. *Risk and Culture: an Essay on the Selection of Technological and Environmental Dangers*. London: University of California Press.

Dror, I.E. and Fraser-Mackenzie, P.A.F. 2008. "Cognitive Biases in Human Perception, Judgment, and Decision Making: Bridging Theory and the Real World". In *Criminal Investigative Failures*, edited by Kim Rossmo, 53–67. Abingdon Oxon UK: Taylor & Francis.

Durodié, B. 2002. "Trust Comes from Expertise". In *Science: Can We Trust the Experts?* edited by T. Gilland, 17–38. Abingdon, UK: Hodder & Stoughton.

Durodié, B. 2005a. *The Concept of Risk. Risk Case Studies.* Nuffield Trust Global Programme on Health, Foreign Policy and Security. London: Nuffield Trust.

Durodié, B. 2005b. "Limitations of Public Dialogue in Science and the Rise of 'New' Experts". In *The Changing Role of the Public Intellectual*, edited by D. Cummings, 82–92. Oxford: Routledge.

Durodié, B. 2017. "Theory Informed by Practice. Application Informed by Purpose. Why to Understand and Manage Risk, Cultural Context is the Key". *Safety Science,* 99 Part B, 244–254.

Ferraris, C. and Corveth, R. 2003. "NASA and the Columbia Disaster: Decision-Making by Groupthink?" *Proceedings of the 2003 Association for Business Communication Annual Convention.* Blacksburg, Va, USA: Association for Business Communication.

Fincham, R. 1992. "Perspectives on Power: Processual, Institutional and 'Internal' Forms of Organizational Power". *Journal of Management Studies,* Vol 29 No 6, 741–759.

Fischhoff, B. 1975. "Hindsight Does Not Equal Foresight: the Effect of Outcome Knowledge on Judgement in Uncertainty". *Journal of Experimental Psychology, Human Perception and Performance,* 1, 288–299.

FSA. 2011. *Report on the Failure of the Royal Bank of Scotland (RBS).* December 2011. FSA Board, chairman Adair Turner. London: Financial Services Authority.

Gai, P. and Vause, N. 2006. "Measuring Investors' Risk Appetite". *International Journal of Central Banking,* Vol 2 No 6, March, 167–188.

Glendon, A.I. 1987. "Risk Cognition". In *Risk and Decisions,* edited by W.T. Singleton and J. Hovden, 87–107. Chichester: John Wiley & Sons.

Glendon, A.I. and Clarke, S.G. 2016. *Human Safety and Risk Management: a Psychological Perspective.* 3rd edition. Boca Raton, Florida: CRC Press/Taylor & Francis.

Glendon, A.I. and Waring, A.E. 1997. *Barings: A Case of Human Resource Mismanagement?* Pages 31–40, in conference proceedings of ANZAM 97 Conference, Management Theory and Practice—Moving into a New Era. Monash University and Macmillan Australia.

Glendon, A.I., Clarke, S.G. and McKenna, E. 2006. *Human Safety and Risk Management.* 2nd edition. Boca Raton, Florida: CRC Press/Taylor & Francis.

Hardy, C. 1985. "The Nature of Unobtrusive Power". *Journal of Management Studies,* Vol 22 No 4, 384–399.

Hillson, D. and Murray-Webster, R. 2012. "Using Risk Appetite and Risk Attitudes to Support Appropriate Risk-Taking: a New Taxonomy and Model". *Journal of Project, Program and Portfolio Management*, Vol 2 No 1, 29–46.

HOCTC. 2009. *Banking Crisis: Dealing with the Failure of UK Banks*. Report HC416, May 1, 2009. 7th report of session 2008–9. House of Commons Treasury Committee. London: The Stationery Office.

IAEA. 1992. *Chernobyl Accident: Updating of INSAG-1 Report*. Safety Series No 75 – INSAG 7 Report. Vienna: International Atomic Energy Agency.

IRM. 2010. *A Structured Approach to Enterprise Risk Management (ERM) and the Requirements of ISO 31000*. London: Institute of Risk Management.

IRM. 2011. *Risk Appetite and Tolerance*. Guidance Paper. London: Institute of Risk Management.

Janis, I.L. 1982. *Groupthink: Psychological Studies of Policy Decisions and Fiascoes*. 2nd edition. New York: Houghton Mifflin.

Johnson, G. 1987. *Strategic Change and the Management Process*. Oxford: Basil Blackwell.

Johnson, B.B. and Covello, V.T. (eds). 1987. *The Social and Cultural Construction of Risk: Essays on Risk Selection and Perception*. New York: Springer.

Kahneman, D. 2003. "Maps of Bounded Rationality: Psychology for Behavioural Economics". *American Economics Review*, 93(5), 1449–1475.

Kahneman, D. and Tversky, A. 1979. "Prospect Theory: an Analysis of Decision Under Risk". *Econometrica*, Vol 47 No 2, March, 263–292.

Kasperson, R.E., Renn, O., Slovic, P. et al. 1988. "The Social Amplification of Risk: a Conceptual Framework". *Risk Analysis*, Vol 8 No 2, 177–187.

Kirtzman, A. 2010. *Betrayal: The Life and Lies of Bernie Madoff*. London: Harper Perennial.

Lawler, E.E. and Porter, L.W. 1967. "Antecedent Attitudes of Effective Managerial Performance". *Organizational Behaviour and Human Performance*, Vol 2 No 2, 122–142.

Le Coze, J-C. 2005. "Are Organizations Too Complex to be Integrated in Technical Risk Assessment and Current Safety Auditing?" *Safety Science*, Vol 43 No 8, 613–638.

Le Coze, J-C. and Dechy, N. 2005. "The Common System and Organizational Issues of Security and Safety: the 9/11 Case". *Proceedings of the ESRDA 29th Seminar*, October 25–26, 2005. JRC, IPSC, Ispra, Italy.

Leeb, S. 2006. *The Coming Economic Collapse—how you can thrive when oil costs $200 a barrel*. New York: Warner Business Books/Grand Central Publishing.

Leeson, N. 1996. *Rogue Trader*. London: Little Brown.

Linstone, H.A. and Turoff, M. (eds). 1975. *The Delphi Method: Techniques and Applications*. Reading Mass: Addison-Wesley Publishing Co.

Linstone, H.A. and Turoff, M. (eds). 2002. *The Delphi Method: Techniques and Applications*. New Jersey Institute of Technology. Newark, NJ: NJIT.

Lunenburg, F.C. 2010. "Group Decision-Making: the Potential for Groupthink". *International Journal of Management, Business and Administration*, Vol 13 No 1, 1–6.

Maclean, B. and Elkind, P. 2004. *The Smartest Guys in the Room: The Amazing Rise and Scandalous Fall of Enron*. New York: Portfolio Trade, Penguin Group (USA) Inc.

March, J.G. and Simon, H. 1958. *Organizations*. New York: John Wiley.

Morgan, G. 1986. *Images of Organization*. London: Sage.

Mosher, G.A. 2013. "Trust, Safety and Employee Decision-Making. A Review of Research and Discussion of Future Directions". *Journal of Technology, Management and Applied Engineering*, 29(1), 1–11.

Mudu, P. and Beck, E. 2012. "Navigating Scientific Routes to Risk Assessment: a Tortuous Path". *Journal of Risk Research*, 15(10), 1217–1222.

NAIIC. 2012. *The Official Report of the Fukushima Nuclear Accident Independent Investigation Committee*. Chairman Kiyoshi Kurokawa. National Diet of Japan. Tokyo.

Nickerson, R.S. 1998. "Confirmation Bias: a Ubiquitous Phenomenon in Many Guises". *Review of General Psychology*, 2, 175–220.

Perrow, C. 1984. *Normal Accidents: Living with High-Risk Technologies*. New York: Basic Books.

Perrow, C. 2011. "Fukushima and the Inevitability of Accidents". *Bulletin of Atomic Scientists*, 67(6), 44–52.

Perrow, C. 2013. "Nuclear Denial: from Hiroshima to Fukushima". *Bulletin of Atomic Scientists*, 69(5), 56–67.

Pettigrew, A. 1973. *The Politics of Organizational Decision-Making*. London: Tavistock.

Pfeffer, J. 1981. *Power in Organizations*. London: Pitman.

Pidgeon, N., Slovic, P. and Kasperson, R.E. (eds). 2003. *The Social Amplification of Risk*. Cambridge, UK: CUP.

Rabin, M. 2000. "Risk Aversion and Expected Utility Theory". *Econometrica*, Vol 68 No 5, September, 1281–1292.

Royal Society 1992. *Risk: Analysis, Perception, Management*. Report of a Royal Society Study Group. London: The Royal Society.

Shrader-Frechette, K.S. 1991. *Risk and Rationality: Philosophical Foundations for Populist Reforms*. Berkeley: University of California Press.

Simon, H.A. 1972. "Theories of Bounded Rationality". In *Decisions and Organization*, edited by C.B. MaGuire and R. Radner, 161–176. Amsterdam: North Holland Publishing Co.

Slovic, P., Fischhoff, B. and Lichtenstein, S. 1982. "Why Study Risk Perception?" *Risk Analysis*, Vol 2 No 2, 83–93.

Toft, B. 1990. *The Failure of Hindsight.* PhD Thesis. Department of Sociology, University of Exeter, UK.

Toft, B. and Reynolds, S. 1997. *Learning from Disasters: a Management Approach*, 2nd edition. Leicester: Perpetuity Press.

Turner, B. A. 1988. "Connoisseurship in the Study of Organizational Cultures". In *Doing Research in Organizations*, edited by A. Bryman, 108–122. London: Routledge.

Turner, B. A. 1992. *Organizational Learning and the Management of Risk.* Paper presented at the British Academy of Management 6th Annual Conference; 14–16 September, Bradford University, England.

Turner, B.A. and Pidgeon, N. 1997. *Man-Made Disaster: the Failure of Foresight.* 2nd edition. London: Butterworth Heinmann.

Tversky, A. and Wakker, P. 1995. "Risk Attitudes and Decision Weights". *Econometrica*, Vol 63 No 6, November, 1255–1280.

US Department of Justice. 2012. *Statement on Criminal Conviction and Sentencing of Allen Stanford of Stanford International Bank.* 14 June 2012. Washington DC: US Department of Justice.

Vaughan, D. 1996. *The Challenger Launch Decision: Risk, Technology, Culture and Deviance at NASA.* Chicago, Ill: University of Chicago Press.

Vaughan, D. 1999. "The Dark Side of Organizations: Mistake, Misconduct and Disaster". *Annual Review of Sociology*, 25, 271–305.

Vaughan, D. 2006. "NASA Revisited: Theory, Analogy and Public Sociology". *American Journal of Sociology*, 112(2), 353–393.

Vaughan, D. 2014. "Analogy, Cases, and Comparative Social Organization". In *Theorizing in Social Science: The Context of Discovery,* edited by R. Swedberg, 61–84. Redwood City CA: Stanford University Press.

von Neumann, J. and Morgernstern, O. 1944. *Theory of Games and Economic Behaviour.* Princeton New Jersey: Princeton University Press.

Vroom, V.H. 1964. *Work and Motivation.* Chichester: John Wiley & Sons.

Walton, M. 2007. "Toxic leadership". In *Leadership: The Key Concepts,* edited by J. Gosling and A. Marturano. Oxford: Routledge.

Waring, A.E. 2013. *Corporate Risk and Governance: an End to Mismanagement, Tunnel Vision, and Quackery.* Farnham UK: Gower/Routledge.

Waring, A.E. 2015. "Managerial and Non-Technical Factors in the Development of Human-Created Disasters: a Review and Research Agenda". *Safety Science*, 79, 254–267.

Waring, A.E. and Glendon, A.I. 1998. *Managing Risk: Critical Issues for Survival and Success into the 21st Century.* Aldershot, UK: Thompson/Cengage.

Westley, F. R. 1990. "The Eye of the Needle: Cultural and Personal Transformations in a Traditional Organization". *Human Relations* 43(3): 273–293.

Wodak, R. 2015. *The Politics of Fear: What Right-Wing Populist Discourses Mean*. London: Sage.

Wodak, R., Mral, B. and KhosraviNik, M. (eds). 2013. *Right-Wing Populism in Europe: Politics and Discourse.* London: Bloomsbury Academic.

Zimmerman, M. 2011. "Confirmatory Bias". Page 661. *Encyclopaedia of Clinical Neuropsychology*. New York: Springer.

Chapter 13: A Prognosis for the New Authoritarianism

By Alan Waring

Abstract

A SWOT analysis of the Alt-Right is used to examine its strengths, weaknesses, opportunities, and threats, and their implications. Five projected scenarios for an evolving Alt-Right are identified, ranging from maintenance of the current status quo of (typically) democratic order, to manipulation of democratic process, and increasingly authoritarian positions up to and including coups d'état. The chapter concludes that, whereas extreme scenarios are unlikely, manoeuvring by Alt-Right groups and parties to normalise their policies through mainstream parties, either through the latter copying them to attract votes or through coalition, is already on the increase.

Key words: Alt-Right, SWOT, political evolution, prognosis, US, Trump.

A Potential Alt-Right Future

The first two Parts of this Volume examined the spectrum of characteristics and issues relating to the new authoritarianism arising from Alt-Right ideology and nationalist activism in selected European countries including Russia. The preceding chapter also provided a summary of risk analyses and evaluations derived from the chapters in Part 2. This chapter draws together all the preceding content to consider potential scenarios for how the new authoritarianism may unfold, and makes a prognosis for the most likely outcomes, which may differ from country to country.

The following four sections present a conventional SWOT (Strengths, Weaknesses, Opportunities, Threats) analysis (Humphrey 2005; Learned et al 1965; Weirich 1982) of the Alt-Right before finally considering potential scenarios for what might happen in relation to the Alt-Right in the short-to-medium term.

Relative Strengths of the Alt-Right

In most countries, the Alt-Right has emerged from pre-existing disaffected elements within the conservative establishment, joining with equally disgruntled elements among the mass population and the far-right to express a common dissatisfaction with the ideology, tone, and product of traditional 'liberal' administrations. Despite asserting that they specifically reject mainstream conservatism and what they regard as the weak and corrupt liberalism of the conservative political establishment (e.g. the tired Republican Party in the US, the Washington 'swamp', the pandering to quasi-socialist ideas, the deals made by politicians to favour vested corporate or sectoral interests), the fact remains that the political backbone of the Alt-Right comprises individuals from that very milieu. One has only to consider the make-up of the Trump Cabinet and senior figures in the White House administration, which reveals a cast of characters each of whom has substantial experience working in 'the Establishment'—the Senate, state legislatures, state judiciaries, the military, big corporations. A similar picture emerges in other countries, where thus far Alt-Right politicians have been drawn largely from existing conservative political parties or backgrounds, and many of them even remain within the mainstream parties they so criticise while seeking to convert them into Alt-Right vehicles. As Burleigh put it: "One day, serious historians will have enough material to do more than a first-draft history of European (or US) populism. They may highlight the fact that many of the 'insurgencies' involve parties that have been around for a long time" (Burleigh 2018a).

The Alt-Right is seeking to create a new illiberal political Establishment, a new elite made up of leaders and senior and middle-ranking functionaries drawn from among self-imposed exiles from the traditional liberal establishment they claim to despise. They therefore bring to the task considerable knowledge and experience of how existing government works at different levels, as well as networks of personal contacts both within and beyond any political party they nominally espouse or represent, for example, the Republican Party in the US, the Conservative Party in the UK. All of this knowledge and experience is invaluable to the furtherance of the Alt-Right movement, and is a strength relative to that available to any new political movement or party starting from scratch without such resource to draw on.

The Alt-Right also enjoys considerable financial support and patronage from a cadre of wealthy business owners and professionals who espouse the nationalist authoritarian cause. In the US, these include William Regnery II (Roston and Anderson 2017) who finances the white supremacist National Policy Institute, alongside its wealthy director Richard Spencer, and Robert Mercer a successful hedge fund manager who has backed *Breitbart News* and other Alt-Right operations (Hermansson 2017). Mercer was among a group of billionaires who individually backed the Trump election campaign (Hackett 2016), most of whom previously had been backers of the mainstream Republican Party.

In the earlier stages of the Trump campaign in 2015, there had been conjecture that the brothers Charles and David Koch, owners of Koch Industries, might inject some of their $889 million donor fund into the Trump campaign. After all, they had previously helped the anti-establishment Tea Party in 2009 and 2010. However, the Tea Party had since evolved from a populist anti-'big government' movement into being part of the strident anti-immigrant nationalism of the Alt-Right, which was anathema to the Kochs (Vogel 2016). None of their funds went to the Trump campaign.

In the UK, the main financial backer of the populist UKIP has been Arron Banks, a millionaire insurance broker, who in 2014 alone pledged £1m to UKIP. For the 2016 unofficial Leave.EU Brexit referendum campaign, he donated £8m, for which he came under investigation by the Electoral Commission and the Major Crimes Agency as to whether the sources of his donations were outside the UK and therefore not permitted (Walker 2018; Watt 2017). Later allegations based on court documents (*C4 News* 2018) suggested that in 2015 Banks had sought Russian investment for his South African mines, at least some of which was alleged to have been diverted into the Brexit campaign. Banks denied this but the chair of the House of Commons Select Committee, to which Banks had previously testified about the sources of his Brexit campaign donations, suggested that Banks had seriously misled the Committee by omission. Other controversies involving Banks included his open calling via *Twitter* on July 16, 2017 for a Muslim immigration ban into the UK and "levelling all Saudi/Qatari funded mosques" (Cork 2017). In March 2017, Banks was suspended by UKIP for openly denigrating its leadership. It is unclear whether Banks has continued to fund UKIP.

The main political donor to the English Defence League (EDL) was reported to be computer engineer Alan Ayling, also known as Alan Lake, although information about the scale of his donations is not available.

In France, Front National (FN) (rebranding itself Rassemblement National in 2018) is a much larger party than all of the UK Alt-Right parties combined, and consequently its funding requirements are that much larger. Details of its funding sources remain hidden. However, a *BBC Panorama* investigation (Gatehouse 2017) concluded that FN had been securing multi-million Euro loans from Russian banks, after FN leader Marine Le Pen had shown Russia's Vladimir Putin political favours. Such bank loans became unavailable in France owing to Le Pen's anti-Semitic statements. In view of Putin's known mutual cooperation pacts with far-right parties in other European countries, such as the Austrian Freedom Party, and Northern League in Italy, it is reasonable to infer that Russia has also provided FN with financial assistance, however indirectly.

Depending on what kind of government is in power, a thriving economy may either attract or repel populist Alt-Right support. For example, a liberal regime in power during a period of a strong economy, with likely low unemployment and other indicators beneficial to the mass electorate, is less likely to witness an upsurge in populist Alt-Right support. Conversely, if a populist right-wing regime is in power (as during the Trump administration), and the economy is good and improving, then the regime's popularity will probably be enhanced. As the first year of the Trump administration progressed, there was some evidence of US economic recovery and growing business confidence, as well as Trump's core supporters reporting satisfaction with his policies. His major tax reforms heralded a potential boost to employers and the stock market, and also to a lesser extent to ordinary voters. Thus, at least in the short term, the Trump regime and other Alt-Right politicians in the US were likely to enjoy popularity among core supporters and also those less committed floating voters who were still feeling vindicated in their contemporary support. However, Trump's proposal in February 2018 for a $4.4 trillion budget that would increase spending massively, both on US military programs and on infrastructure renewal projects, effectively abandoned the Republican mantra of reducing federal deficit and instead signalled its enlargement to more than $7 trillion. Trump's assumption appeared to be that the US economy is 'too big to fail' and implied a calculated gamble. Notably, on assuming the presidency, Trump had promised to balance the books over ten years. This may happen, but there was a real risk that it would not. His stated determination in March 2018 to impose a 25% tariff on a range of imported goods, so as to support his 'America First' agenda, also threatened a global trade war that could badly damage the US economy. A heavily debt-driven economy is vulnerable to a myriad of unforeseen and unforeseeable factors and events that may create an unwelcome crisis, and one that may be difficult to grapple with. Sudden draconian austerity measures and job losses arising from such a crisis would immediately impact Trump's supporters.

Moreover, regardless of specific government policies, any national economy may take a serious downturn. This is a probable occurrence in any economy, given the cyclical nature of economic performance and the multiple variables that are difficult to control, even ignoring economic incompetence of an incumbent regime that may accentuate a downturn. The state of the global economy, and the national economy's inter-relationship with it, will also be a factor.

Up to the time of this book's publication, grassroots support for Trump remained high in the older industrial 'rust belt' areas historically dependent on such industries as coal mining and steel making e.g. Pennsylvania, West Virginia. Some early signs of economic revival became evident in such areas, but whether sufficient or sustained enough to turn the clock back to the golden days of the 1950s to 1980s is unlikely. If large numbers of voters are hit by renewed unemployment, reduced incomes, and other negative impacts, such support for Alt-Right policies is likely to wane, save, perhaps, for a minority of die-hard supporters who remain in denial that such policies have failed to be their saviour. While such hard core support is undoubtedly a strength, their numbers are not sufficient to ensure continued electoral success. Non-committed, floating, and frustrated protest voters determine election outcomes.

It could also be argued that trans-national inter-connections, amoral ideological support and encouragement, and financial support from abroad, together create a systemic strength for the Alt-Right that goes beyond what is identifiable in any single country. The activities and apparent gains by the Alt-Right in one country seem to energize and encourage their counterparts in other countries in a kind of social contagion (e.g. Germany, Austria, Hungary, Italy). Indeed, it is not simply a case of tacit acknowledgement among the Alt-Right in different countries of what the others are doing and their apparent successes. Evidence presented above and in earlier chapters demonstrates active trans-national collaboration between them, from which collaborating parties presumably derive synergetic benefit. Globalisation of the far-right has also certainly extended beyond the US, UK, Europe, and Russia to e.g. South Africa, Philippines, South Korea.

Nevertheless, as noted in chapter 1, there is evidence (e.g. Michael 2006) that far-right groups in the US have also sought to gain strength through conceptual and potential practical alliances with foreign terrorist organizations outside the far-right. More particularly, Michael highlighted the extraordinary ideological alliances apparently made with Islamist extremists overseas i.e. with groups whose ideology the far-right explicitly hates. While it would appear from statements made by far-right leaders that such paradoxical alignments arose from shared anti-Semitism and anti-US foreign policy positions, and a common desire to tear down the US power elites, nonetheless any potential strength gained through this by the Alt-Right also became a weakness once the fact of the alliances became public. Indeed, such alliances also became a threat to the Alt-Right, in terms of unfavourable public perceptions of them supporting IS terrorism.

Relative Weaknesses of the Alt-Right

The Alt-Right suffers from an inherently conflicted ideology, an observation not unique to the Alt-Right. On the one hand, its clarion call is that the Alt-Right represents individual freedom against alleged oppression by national and/or federal government and alleged abuses by large corporate interests. On the other hand, the Alt-Right is predicated on an absolute conviction of white, nationalist supremacy combined with supremacy of society's 'natural masters' i.e. the Alt-Right, with a concomitant relegation of the poor, the vulnerable, immigrants, ethnic and religious minorities, and political opponents to an underclass of victims/losers. Such Aristotelian primitivism necessarily denies freedoms to the underclass, as it reserves freedoms only for those whom the Alt-Right regards as the most deserving (i.e. themselves and favoured classes). While some of the populist Alt-Right may not hold this stark model *in extremis*, preferring to leave its more rigorous and strident pursuit to less squeamish far-right fellow travellers, the fact remains that the 'freedom' they all strive to obtain necessarily comes at the denial of freedoms (and, moreover, human rights) of other sectors of society.

The freedom whose threatened loss so energises the Alt-Right is not some abstract monolithic concept having an agreed meaning shared by them and their opponents, such as liberals and those adversely affected by the Alt-Right. They are not competing to grab the same freedom. The freedom the Alt-Right so desperately campaign for includes (in the US) the right for citizens to bear and use firearms without controls, regardless of the unwarranted threat of injury and death this poses to other citizens; (in the US) the right not to have universal health care, regardless of the consequential denial of health care to millions of vulnerable citizens without insurance; (in Austria and Germany) the right to limit women to the role of housewives and mothers; (generally) the right to treat immigrants, ethnic and religious minorities, the unemployed, poor people, and other vulnerable groups as an underclass who should be denied full citizens' rights, and who should be repressed and eliminated as far as possible e.g. the essence of Trump's six traits identified by Neiwert (2017)—see later section. The Alt-Right especially values 'freedom of speech', but only in the sense that they should be allowed to utter whatever racist, misogynist, anti-religion, or other hate-filled views or allegations they think fit, including intimidation and threats of violence. They extend this to claiming a right to curb or muzzle press freedom in order to suppress scrutiny or criticism of their views, policies and actions (e.g. Trump's assertion that the press are "enemies of the people", his campaign against *CNN* and national newspapers; also similar actions in Austria and Hungary). Such abuse of the freedom of speech represents a weakness in their case; if their case were strong, they would not need to resort to such egregious tactics.

Widening the inequalities gap in society, and the denial of freedoms and human rights to the underclass, are essential parts of Alt-Right ideology. The inherent authoritarianism further contradicts its claim to offer 'freedom'. Moreover, the Christian values oft-proclaimed by Alt-Right protagonists and supporters are at odds with the manifestly un-Christian rhetoric and behaviour of some of them e.g. Trump, Roy Moore (see chapter 10 in Vol 1; Sherman 2017; Sherwood 2017). Such contradiction, or hypocrisy in some people's view, is of course not unique to the Alt-Right. However, this contradiction has become publicly associated especially with Alt-Right predispositions because of (a) policy statements of far-right groups that explicitly boast of their Christian beliefs and motives (e.g. in Austria, Italy, Hungary, Russia, and US), and (b) similar public statements by high profile Alt-Right politicians.

A further weakness of the Alt-Right is the contradiction between its claim, on the one hand, to be the champion of 'the people', and especially the ordinary masses, against uncaring self-serving elites, and the reality on the other hand of renegade members of that class cynically having "adopted 'the people' in the way a regiment acquires a goat as a mascot" (Burleigh 2018a). Alt-Right leaders and supportive populist demagogues are liberally represented by members of the aristocracy (e.g. Duchess von Stork, deputy leader of AfD), wealthy oligarchs, financiers, newspaper proprietors, and business tycoons (e.g. Arron Banks, Robert Mercer, William Regnery II, Silvio Berlusconi, Ross Perot—and of course Donald J. Trump), the very Establishment that the same Alt-Right say they will overturn. Trump may have attacked pre-existing Establishment elites, only to create new ones that suit his interests; 'the people's' interests are unlikely to feature much in the latter.

In short, as with many other ideologies, a major theoretical if not practical weakness of the Alt-Right in terms of its attractiveness to non-committed voters is the incoherence of its ideology, which is riven with serious internal contradictions and invented 'facts' that seek to validate Alt-Right assertions and positions. While such obvious contradictions and alternative-reality falsehoods are unlikely to be of concern to committed Alt-Right supporters (Neiwert 2017), and indeed in the US, for example, they seem oblivious to the litany of scandalous statements and behaviour of Trump, they may well be of concern to undecided and floating voters who frequently decide the outcome of elections. The more extreme rhetorical assertions of the Alt-Right are likely to fail to match the reality of most people. The apparent strength of Trump's combative personality, and his 'sticking to his Alt-Right manifesto guns', may also be a weakness in many voters' eyes. The manifest anger, paranoia, and egregious policies of the Alt-Right will be objectionable to many. In the US, for example, while pursuing a nationalist populist agenda, the Trump administration has tacitly gone along with some of the much more strident and objectionable demands of far-right extremists. This may backfire eventually at the ballot box, although Frum (2018) has expressed concerns that it may not. The widespread exposure of Trump's capricious and often volatile personality, coupled with an equally exposed dysfunctional White House (e.g. Green 2017; Neiwert 2017; Wolff 2017), is a further weakness of the US Alt-Right.

In some countries e.g. Britain, membership numbers and supporters of right-wing political parties, whether populist or more extreme, are all miniscule compared to those of mainstream parties (see chapters 3 and 4). Funding for Alt-Right parties and groups is likely to remain a perennial problem for them.

Opportunities for the Alt-Right

The Alt-Right ideology lacks a 'first principles' attractiveness to the majority of voters, who may be anticipated to follow a Normal or Gaussian distribution on a range of attitudes towards related issues (political, economic, social, income, taxation etc) e.g. Rice (1928), Page and Goldstein (2016). Of the 50% of the population who range from politically neutral to extreme right-wing, 34.1% (i.e. two thirds of the 50%) would be expected to fit within the first standard deviation from the mean i.e. showing weak to moderate right-wing views more in keeping with mainstream conservative parties. However, higher concentrations of Alt-Right supporters may occur in particular locations where they have migrated to be with people like themselves e.g. Alabama. "And more of America is becoming like this and has been for decades. People move to the place where folk are like them and not like those others" (Aaronovitch 2017). Such 'tribal osmosis' raises the possibility of political secession (Blest 2017). Nevertheless, the further that Alt-Right principles stray towards authoritarian, nationalist harshness, the fewer the citizens who are prepared to vote for them. This predisposition in the population presents the Alt-Right with limited opportunities to acquire political power via normal democratic means, the success of e.g. Trump in the US, the FPÖ in Austria, Fidesz in Hungary, AfD in Germany, and 5 Star/Lega in Italy notwithstanding.

However, it is perfectly possible to manipulate the democratic process to create an authoritarian right-wing regime, even an elected dictatorship, using appropriate opportunities. This is the gist of Frum's book *Trumpocracy* (Frum 2018; Pavia 2018), going so far as to assert that we "are living through the most dangerous challenge to the free government of the United States that anyone alive has ever encountered". Democratic opportunities to achieve an Alt-Right takeover include sneak infiltration (or Trojan Horse), as applied by Steve Bannon in orchestrating an unelected Alt-Right control of the Trump White House and undue influence on Trump's policies, as discussed in chapter 5 of Vol 1 and Green (2017), Neiwert (2017), Sherman (2017), and Wolff (2017), and camouflage.

Whereas Trump, Bannon, Gorka, Moore and other high profile Alt-Right political operators in the US succeeded in using the Republican Party as a stepping stone to achieving an Alt-Right power base, different tactics have been used in Europe. Although sharing with their American counterparts the same ideology of imposed inequalities based on racial supremacy, nationalism, anti-immigration, anti-Semitic, and anti-Muslim beliefs, and promulgating fears that such topics raise, the various European populist Alt-Right political leaders have tended to adopt a 'mixed messages' camouflage approach. Some of them have tried to appear to be quite normal, rational and reasonable, for example UKIP's Nigel Farage, although it proved difficult to fully hide racist or religious hatreds among party members and supporters or indeed subsequent contenders for UKIP leadership (e.g. Anne Marie Waters) and the actual new leader Gerard Batten in 2018. Sebastian Kurz, charismatic leader of Austria's populist conservative Austrian People's Party, found no difficulty in forming a majority coalition with the smaller far-right Freedom Party and its leaders Haider and Strache (see chapter 6 and Atkins 2017), thus providing a cloak of public respectability for essentially far-right beliefs and policies. Even Marine Le Pen, leader of the Front National in France, attempted to adopt a more moderate tone following years of previous rants against immigrants and Muslims (see chapter 8). However, no matter how hard such leaders try to camouflage their own true Alt-Right beliefs and their party's ideology, it is usually their uncontrollable colleagues and supporters who spoil the deception e.g. UKIP (see chapter 3). Nevertheless, Viktor Orban, the far-right Hungarian Prime Minister, has not sought to hide his party's openly anti-Muslim, anti-multicultural and anti-immigrant policies and, indeed, heeding Bannon's exhortation to France's National Front, wears them "as a badge of honour" (Pasha-Robinson 2018; Waterfield 2018).

A second democratic opportunity arises from a chance confluence of a charismatic demagogue, a naïve but disgruntled and angry population, and a right-wing salvationist manifesto within a democratic system. The most obvious example is the rise of Hitler and the National Socialist German Workers' Party (Nazi Party) in the 1920s and early 30s. By convincing a major proportion of largely disaffected voters that his policies offered them salvation from post-WWI humiliations, unemployment, economic disaster and external threats (all symptomatic of an alleged global Jewish-communist conspiracy against Germany), Hitler manipulated the democratic process to make the Nazis the largest elected party in the Reichstag and himself appointed as Reichskanzler in 1933.

More recently, in Hungary its Prime Minister Viktor Orban, leader of the ruling populist right-wing Fidesz party, openly expounded his hard-line views on immigration and the need to protect Hungarian identity from foreigners having allegedly alien religions, such as Muslims and Jews (Gauriat 2017). He has led a particularly vicious propaganda campaign against the Hungarian-born global financier and philanthropist George Soros, who is Jewish, accusing him of supporting Muslim immigration to undermine Hungary's white Christian culture (Kington 2018a). The vilification of Soros has become part of the standard Alt-Right narrative around the world depicting the alleged evils of globalisation and financiers and the alleged 'Jewish-Cultural Marxist-Muslim' conspiracy to destroy white, Christian Europe. Orban is a populist demagogue who claimed that only his 'Hungary for Hungarians' policy would save the country. Although Fidesz and the smaller far-right Jobbik party run by Gabor Vona are right-wing competitors, Orban cultivated a close relationship with Jobbik to the extent that their respective policies and rhetoric became largely indistinguishable (Day 2015). If anything, by 2017 Jobbik had toned down its extreme rhetoric so as to appear more in line with Fidesz. The numerically dominant Fidesz-Jobbik axis in parliament ensured democratically that its nationalist, racist ideology could be implemented without realistic challenge. A difference between the Fidesz-Jobbik axis and the axis formed by the People's Party and Freedom Party in Austria is that, whereas the latter sought to appear rational and reasonable (even if that is debatable), the Hungarian axis was openly irrational in its assertions and aggressively hostile towards its opponents and policy targets, indeed against any form of dissent from the government's far-right positions (Kington 2018b). In July 2018, Orban openly boasted that his Christians-only nationalist policies were both democratic and inherently illiberal, and that he was vigorously supporting his far-right colleagues in other EU countries to create a far-right power bloc within the European Parliament (Waterfield 2018).

The febrile ultra-right climate in Hungary attracted a considerable number of disgruntled Alt-Right nationalists from the US and other European countries to visit or take up residency in Hungary. According to Schaeffer (2017), these included a coterie formed around the Swedish right-wing activist Daniel Friberg, a close associate of Richard Spencer, the radical American ultra-right champion and director of the National Policy Institute. The trans-national and international collaboration among Alt-Right leaders and activists has provided an ego-boosting show of mutual 'moral' support (or perhaps amoral support) between like-minded zealots, for example UKIP's Nigel Farage formed a cooperation pact with a far-right Polish party in 2014 (Mason and Syal 2014), attended foreign Alt-Right rallies in 2016, such as the AfD in Germany and the far-right Sweden Democrats, and praised Viktor Orban's regime in Hungary in 2017 (HT 2017). Such opportunities may strengthen the appeal of the parties involved. See also Michael (2006) on the surprising ideological convergence of US far-right groups and foreign Islamist extremists.

A third democratic opportunity arises from seeking to apply direct democracy in a setting where representative democracy is the constitutional requirement. In a representative democracy, a successful candidate is elected to the legislature as an individual who is meant to represent the interests of every member of the particular constituency i.e. for the overall public good and not biased towards partisan or sectoral interests. Even though probably being a member of a political party, and therefore favouring that party's policies, the elected member may exercise latitude according to his or her personal views or conscience when voting on a particular issue. The elected member is not sent by constituents or local party committee as a delegate to vote according to their instruction. In addition, in public referenda, the mere fact that voters may have clearly indicated a preference for a particular proposed outcome does not (or should not) bind the government to pursue that outcome or in a way that some voters want.

Binding governments by popular vote in a referendum is a form of direct democracy, and as such allows little scope for experiential wisdom or moderation. It is a recipe for grass roots 'inverted authoritarianism'.

A recent example of inverted authoritarianism is furnished by the Brexit referendum of 2016 in the UK. The populist Alt-Right party UKIP and many others in the Vote Leave camp gave every indication to voters that a Brexit win necessarily would have to be enacted by the government. This was not the case constitutionally, although clearly a Brexit majority vote would be an influential, if not compelling, factor in their eventual decision. In reality, following the referendum result of 52% for Brexit and 48% against, the government did decide to pursue Brexit (see chapter 3).

One could be forgiven for thinking that at that point the whole issue was over. However, UKIP leaders and other passionate Brexiteers continued to assert not only that Brexit must now be an absolute certainty, but also that all particular aspects of it as they had campaigned for in the referendum were equally guaranteed so as to fulfil 'the will of the people'. Such partisan aspects were not identified on the government's official referendum papers to voters. In the Brexiteers' determined authoritarian view, however, no aspect of the complex spectrum of legal, constitutional, inter-governmental, economic, and practical issues arising could be discussed or debated in Parliament, in case it resulted in a dilution of the Brexiteer 'shopping list' presented to the electorate in their referendum campaign. In their anxiety-laden view, the direct democracy of the referendum must take precedence over the representative democracy of Parliament, because 'the people have spoken'. Despite knowing that their 'cherry-picking' approach to democracy has no lawful or constitutional basis, UKIP and Brexiteers generally persisted in telling the public that their referendum decision was being subverted by parliamentary interference. However, the UK Supreme Court upheld the position that Parliament must have the prerogative to consider the Brexit process in detail (UKSC 2017).

Another example of inverted authoritarianism and demands for direct democracy is that of the Italian 5 Star populist Alt-Right movement which firmly believes in 'will of the people' direct democracy over-riding representative democracy and whose success alongside the far-right Lega Party in the 2018 general elections ensures a sharp move towards harsh right-wing authoritarian policies.

Beyond democratic opportunity always lies the possibility of a right-wing coup in which democracy is overturned by force. Violence and intimidation have always been a hallmark of the ultra-right but their relatively small numbers have usually kept violent conflicts localised (e.g. Charlottesville ultra-right attacks, August 2017) or confined to singular acts of terrorism (e.g. Oklahoma City bombing in 1995). However, in order to stage a political coup capable of withstanding the armed forces of the legitimate government, even at local state or regional level, would require substantial resources of trained personnel, military equipment, and communications facilities and these would be way beyond the combined financial resources of the far-right in any country. Although small self-styled armed militias have sprung up among the far-right, especially in the US, they are self-limiting fantasists who are never likely to be more than a noisy nuisance involved in isolated acts of violence. A similar picture emerges in the UK, where a small number of arrested members of the proscribed terrorist group National Action have been charged for being members and planning acts of violence against individual political targets. Some were convicted and sentenced to 8 years imprisonment, while others await verdicts (see chapter 4). Such groups are under close surveillance by state security services and it is unlikely that they would ever have a capacity to undertake an armed coup against the government, much less a successful one.

A bigger concern would be if Alt-Right politicians and fellow travellers within the 'Establishment', frustrated by what they regard as unacceptable liberal policies of the ruling government, joined up with rogue right-wing elements at senior level in the armed services to plan an armed coup. There are precedent coups, such as that by the right-wing military coup in Greece in 1967, followed by seven years of the Junta, and similarly the right-wing coup by General Pinochet in Chile in 1973, followed by seventeen years of authoritarian rule.

Threats to the Alt-Right

A robust, burgeoning economy with low unemployment takes away one of the main propaganda weapons of the Alt-Right, namely that tired economic policies of a corrupt status quo political system have brought hardship to the population, and all exacerbated by liberal policies opening the gates to a flood of immigrants who take away native citizens' jobs, block public services, and live parasitically off the taxpayer. However, whereas most politicians seek to achieve a robust and stable economy, in the real world it is rarely possible to both achieve and sustain one for very long periods. There are simply too many variables and factors that are difficult to control. Typically, economic success varies cyclically. Thus, whereas a robust economy tends to weaken Alt-Right propaganda, its perseverance cannot be relied upon. However, as noted above under Strengths, a lot depends on the character of the incumbent government. A robust economy under a liberal regime is an electoral threat to the Alt-Right, whereas under an illiberal, Alt-Right dominated regime (e.g. the Trump administration) a robust economy tends to validate and strengthen the Alt-Right.

The first eighteen months of the Trump administration saw the US economy strengthening, partly owing to the global economy but also owing to announcement of public infrastructure projects, major tax reforms, a gathering de-regulation programme, and a generally 'business friendly' administration. His 'America First' policy and trade protectionism, while welcomed by some sectors and their workforces, was not guaranteed to boost the economy and protect US jobs in the medium and long-terms, since it ignored the primary weakness of American companies and products becoming outdated and uncompetitive in global terms. Moreover, his trade protectionism was likely to have little impact on China's long-term strategy to become the next superpower—economically, politically and militarily. Trump's salvation manifesto was more likely than not to show signs of faltering within his first term, with a potential drop in his popularity and electoral support. Further, his cavalier approach to, and antagonistic Alt-Right rhetoric on, foreign policy appeared to raise regional and international tensions and threaten international peace and security.

Trump was a miraculous gift to the US Alt-Right in terms of exercising Alt-Right ideology and policies. However, there was no guarantee that he would survive a first four-year term as President, let alone get re-elected, although Frum stated his belief that Trump may well be a strong candidate in 2020 (Pavia 2018). Nevertheless, there will be increasing anxiety among the Alt-Right in America that Trump may be a presidential one-term wonder. Trump was unique in many respects, and certainly in his larger-than-life presence and populist persona and rhetoric. It is difficult to identify another Alt-Right candidate who could possibly emulate him or eclipse him. This could well herald the departure of the Alt-Right from any serious presidential candidacy, and a return to slates of more conventional Republican candidates, although McCarty (see chapter 4 in Vol 1) also considers the possibility of 'Trumpism' being a longer term prospect.

Apart from Trump and the US context, arguably the biggest threat to the Alt-Right generally is itself. The Alt-Right is only fully appealing to a minority of voters. Although some aspects of its ideology have a broader appeal, such as immigration control, anti-globalisation of trade, and not exporting jobs, most other aspects only appeal to extremists. Expecting a populace to vote for an Alt-Right party or candidate whose manifesto includes ideas and policies they find objectionable is unrealistic, and so such candidates may resort to linguistic camouflage. Their attempts at moderating their campaigning language are likely to be undone by sufficient numbers of committed supporters who are only too ready to noisily communicate the unvarnished nastiness of the Alt-Right ideology. However, whether rhetorical assertions and propaganda of the Alt-Right are presented in a raw form, or disguised by euphemism or dissimulation, they are likely to fail to match the reality of most people. To most people, the Alt-Right ideology is regarded as a distasteful irrelevance, promoted by cranks and fixated zealots. In short, the Alt-Right is its own worst enemy.

In many countries, the Alt-Right has long demonstrated not only its fragmented character, with typically dozens of unconnected small groups, but also its fractious nature, with such groups competing for ideological recognition and supremacy as unequivocally the true representatives of the Alt-Right. See, for example, Lyons (2017), Michael (2008; 2014) and Neiwert (2017) on the Alt-Right ferment in the US. In the UK, defections between BNP, UKIP, Britain First, and EDL and the, at times, internecine wars between some of them have been legendary. In-fighting within the Front National senior levels in France in 2017 led to Philippot and his supporters quitting FN and forming a new party Les Patriotes. All such antics threaten not only their functionality and public credibility but also their membership numbers and finances.

Alt-Right Evolution

As already noted, the power relationships in society as desired by the Alt-Right rely on maintaining, and hopefully widening, inequalities between 'the deserving' (i.e. WASPs, the rich, the business/property owning classes, and those having an Alt-Right mind-set) and 'the undeserving' (i.e. immigrants, ethnic minorities, Muslims and other non-Christian religious minorities, the unemployed, the poor and low paid, the disabled, and those having a non-Alt-Right mind-set). As also noted earlier, the Alt-Right ideology is inherently conflicted by professing to offer 'freedom', but only to the 'deserving', while doing so via authoritarian and repressive means against the 'undeserving'.

Given such a predisposition and the relatively short history of the Alt-Right since 2008 (notwithstanding the history of its precursors), how is it likely to evolve? The final chapter Fascism and Our Future in Neiwert (2017) offered an insight. Although focussed on the US, there is much to draw on when considering other countries.

Neiwert considered first the history of fascism and its characteristics, before addressing how these have shown up in modern America and especially in the Trump era. He cited Paxton's (2005) consideration of fascist development, which noted that while fascism is defined by its ideology it can only be understood by also addressing what it does. Paxton also identified nine key characteristics that empirically have driven all fascist movements. Many of these have been identified throughout this book in relation to the Alt-Right, for example:

- Paranoid anxieties about invented or exaggerated threats leading to a sense of overwhelming crisis that demands radical, or even extreme, solutions.
- Dread of national decline as a combined result of perceived negative influences, such as liberalism, multi-culturalism, multilateralism, class conflict, immigration, and alien religions.
- A belief that one's national group is a victim of other groups (e.g. ethnic, religious, immigrants, elites) and that any action, without restriction, against such groups is warranted.
- The destiny and right of the 'deserving strong' to dominate, control and, if necessary, eliminate the 'undeserving weak' in a Darwinian supremacist struggle.

Neiwert (2017) identified six fascist traits in Trump:

Eliminationist rhetoric and actions: stopping categories of 'undesirables' alleged to threaten the safety and economy of the United States from entering the country; visa blocking of Muslims; building a wall along the Mexican border; dehumanizing Hispanic immigrants by labelling them "criminals", "killers", and "rapists"; plan to deport all 12 million undocumented migrants [note similar rhetoric and actions by Alt-Right leaders in Hungary and Italy].

Palingenetic ultra-nationalism: race-baiting, ethnic fearmongering, and assumptions of US exceptionalism; "we're going to take the country back"; labelling particular nationalities as "criminals", "killers", and "rapists"; labelling particular nationalities as "terrorists"; "Make America Great Again"; "America First" [note similar Alt-Right themes in UK, Hungary, Italy, Germany].

Deep contempt for both liberalism and mainstream conservatism: "cleaning the swamp"; blaming America's problems on the alleged corruption of traditional two-party politics, former Presidents, and political opponents (Democrat and Republican); dismantling legislation of the Obama administration based on hatred of Obama rather than on substantive evidence of its lack of efficacy.

Projecting America as a victim: assertions that America has become a victim of trade abuses by China and other countries; assertions that America had become a "laughingstock" in the eyes of the world; assertions that illegal immigrants are treating America as a 'soft touch' and abusing the country's hospitality through tax evasion, sex crimes, and other criminality [note Orban's similar claim that Hungary is a victim of the liberal multicultural values of George Soros and his alleged subversion of Hungarian national and religious identities].

Projecting himself as a lone man of destiny, America's saviour: an ego-maniacal conviction that he alone will save America using his supreme intellect and instincts and invented 'facts', while ignoring or denigrating scientific evidence and real facts that counter his prejudice; global warming denial; insistence that the American Health Care Bill is vastly superior to Obamacare, contrary to professional consensus; making impetuous foreign policy decisions and ill-advised threats against unfriendly countries, implying a countdown to war.

Contempt for perceived weakness in others: denigrating Senator John McCain as "not a hero" because he had been captured in the

Vietnam War; appearing to ignore 28 million citizens currently uninsured for health care and possibly a further 20 million citizens who may become uninsured under his proposed American Health Care Act; publicly mocking the disability of a disabled *New York Times* reporter; enthusiastically endorsing the pro-gun lobby and the National Rifle Association in ensuring ready uncontrolled availability of firearms to ordinary citizens, implying that gun controls only benefit weaklings; publicly denigrating Attorney General Jeff Sessions on *Twitter* for "weakness".

All of the above traits are also observable in Alt-Right leaders across Europe.

Andrew Sullivan's review of Sunstein's book on contemporary authoritarianism in America (Sullivan 2018; Sunstein 2018) charged Trump with being a "cult leader of a movement that has taken over a political party" [i.e. the Republican Party] and who "specifically campaigned on a platform of one-man rule". The implication is that, in parallel with actively pursuing a "creeping authoritarianism", Trump is also encouraging his elevation from being (in Neiwert's terms) simply a lone man of destiny as America's saviour to an almost god-like all-powerful status beyond question, challenge, or criticism.

However, while all of the above (Paxton's analysis, Neiwert's list, and Sullivan's characterisation) apply to Trump and his administration to varying degrees, Neiwert cautions about assuming that Trump is a full-blown fascist. He argued (as does the author in chapter 5 of Vol 1) that he is not a committed far-right ideologue but rather an opportunist who is comfortable with Alt-Right ideas and is happy to implement them in the furtherance of his self-aggrandisement and ambitions for the Trump brand. As Neiwert put it, "Trump's only real ideology is worship of himself, 'the Donald'". More graphically, Singer (2017) wrote that Trump carries around "the longest selfie-stick in the world". Real ideological fascists act out a rigid adherence to a consistent, totalitarian world-view that would involve paramilitary enforcement of the leader's will and diktats, whereas Trump, while enthusiastically echoing much of the far-right's nastier rhetoric, acts out only some aspects of their wishes and soft-peddles on fully endorsing their views. Occasionally, he has even condemned the far-right. This is the mark of a right-wing populist demagogue, an opportunist but not a fascist dictator.

Nevertheless, Trump's very seductiveness to voters feeling aggrieved and ignored by the mainstream political establishment is dangerous, in that it may encourage and embolden more hard-line elements to become more publicly assertive in their demands for a permanent Alt-Right stamp on the governance of the United States. The authors in Sunstein (2018) warned of the creeping authoritarianism of the Trump era. This possibility is already in evidence from protagonists such as Trump's Cabinet members, Steve Bannon, Richard Spencer, and failed senatorial candidate Roy Moore, as well as a slate of right-wing current or former congress members such as Michele Bachmann, Louie Gohmert, Steve King, Ted Cruz, and Ben Carson (e.g. Mudde 2017). Right-wing extremists such as Richard Spencer and former KKK leader David Duke have been fulsome in their public praise of Trump and his policies, and for the first time in years the KKK has reactivated its aggressive street protests. Trump's weak apologia and unwillingness to condemn the far-right thuggery evident in the fatal Charlottesville street attacks in August 2017 received much endorsement from right-wing extremists across the US.

Neiwert warned against what is evident so far, namely a proto-fascist right-wing populism à la Trump, being allowed to evolve into true fascism as a result of public brainwashing by a relentless exposure to Alt-Right ideology and propaganda. See also Cooper (2015). What today may seem extreme and repugnant to the majority of citizens, may eventually seem to them more reasonable, acceptable and normal, as happened in Nazi Germany and appears to be happening in contemporary Europe e.g. Hungary, Italy, Austria, Germany, Sweden, and Spain. Existing proto-fascist elements are becoming empowered. As Neiwert noted about Trump, intentionally or not ".....his alt-right-Tea Party brand of right-wing populism is helping these groups grow their ranks and their potential to recruit new members by leaps and bounds. Not only that, he is making thuggery seem normal and inevitable. And that <u>is</u> a serious problem".

Projected Scenarios for Alt-Right Evolution

The situations and conditions in each country are different, and it would therefore be nonsensical to project a common evolution for the Alt-Right for all countries. With this limitation in mind, the author has sought to identify a level of abstraction at which national differences are sufficiently unimportant to potential scenarios that may be posited.

The author puts forward five potential scenarios:

1. Despite winning some elections, the inability of the Alt-Right to retain seats and expand elected representation leads to it remaining a noisy, fragmented, minority protest movement, albeit harbouring hate criminals and violent elements. (i.e. current democratic order maintained).
   Possible examples: some US states; UK; France; Netherlands; Nordic states.
2. A slow rightward societal drift occurs and entrenchment into an illiberal democracy, relying on determined Alt-Right candidates, weak mainstream candidates, and populist Alt-Right votes. (i.e. elected autocracy).
   Possible examples: some US states; UK; France; Netherlands; Italy; Austria; Germany; Sweden.
3. Takeover of current democratic parties, institutions, and government by Alt-Right activists and supporters, using stealth infiltration and 'entry-ist' techniques, relying on inertia, complacency, or intimidation of mainstream parties. (i.e. coup by stealth, followed by pseudo-democracy or dictatorship)
   Possible examples: some US states; US federal government; Austria; Germany; Poland; Hungary; Russia.
4. Crisis leading to rapid collapse of current democratic order and opportunistic takeover of particular local/regional governments and possibly national government by Alt-Right elements, possibly using armed force. (i.e. opportunistic coup by separatists or other dissidents, followed by pseudo-democracy or dictatorship).
   Possible examples: some US states; US federal government.
5. Rapid takeover of particular local/regional governments and possibly national government by Alt-Right elements, using armed force. (i.e. armed coup planned by separatists and Alt-Right politicians and probably involving armed forces dissidents, followed by dictatorship).
   Possible examples: some US states; US federal government; Russia.

A confident prediction is not possible. However, on the balance of probabilities and based on the evidence presented in the preceding chapters, the most likely scenarios of those above are 1, 2 and 3. In the United States, for example, there has been evidence of all three scenarios in the making. Steve Bannon orchestrated a spectacular Alt-Right coup by stealth in getting Donald Trump elected as President. While there is no evidence of the US yet being turned into a pseudo-democracy or elected dictatorship, in Trump's first year in office there was much evidence of his determination to ensure a permanent rightward societal drift and entrenchment, into what (unless unchecked) might well eventually become a proto-fascist pseudo-democracy with harsh authoritarian policies relying on determined Alt-Right candidates, weak mainstream candidates, and populist Alt-Right votes. Frum, (2018) argued that Trump had been greatly enabled in this by tacit Alt-Right "appeasers" among Republican Party leaders and donors. Nevertheless, Verney (see chapter 8 in Vol 1) concludes that the current Alt-Right upsurge and electoral success in the US may only be temporary, as part of a historically long-wave waxing and waning cycle of far-right nationalism and nativism.

The senatorial candidature of Roy Moore for Alabama exemplified scenario 2 and doubtless, had he won, from his own public rhetoric and statements it is clear that he would have been very dictatorial against the human rights of Alabama citizens.

In other states, such as California and the New England states, scenario 1 prevails. However, as Paxton noted in chapter 3, the possibility cannot be ignored that some 'red states' may become so imbued with Alt-Right ideology that they withdraw from as much federal control as they are able i.e. pseudo-secession (scenarios 2 and 3). Alternatively, 'blue states' may adopt their own version of pseudo-secession (Blest 2017) by using state budgets and funds to ensure that only more liberal policies are enacted, while ignoring or side-lining any harsh Alt-Right federal policies. Any attempt at actual secession or any armed insurrection (scenarios 4 and 5) is unlikely and would almost certainly result in swift federal intervention to restore law and order and democracy. However, the net effect of scenarios 2 and 3 might be to divide the country into two different universes in conflict. Demographic changes would likely follow, as a result of people migrating to be with those having a similar world-view (Aaronovitch 2017) or because they are unable to tolerate the political, social or economic climate of the state where they live. Liberals would migrate from 'red states' to 'blue', whereas Alt-Right supporters would migrate from 'blue states' to 'red'. Two different confederacies may emerge: the Confederation of Liberal Progressive States, and the Confederation of Nationalist Conservative States. What such a polarised country would mean for America and the world in general is open to debate and beyond the scope of this book.

Scenarios 1, 2 and 3 are clearly evident in contemporary Austria, Germany, Italy, Hungary, and Poland. Italy also exhibits vestiges of pseudo-secession. For example, the far-right Lega strongly supports regional autonomy and federalism for Italy. Until relatively recently, Lega Nord discriminated against southern Italians for their alleged fecklessness and advocated secession of Italy's north (Padania) from Italy (Paravicini 2016). However, perhaps sensing a need for attractiveness to a national electorate, they changed their name to simply Lega (League) ahead of the 2018 general elections. Having achieved a huge electoral success (and now ruling in coalition with the populist far-right 5 Star Movement (M5S)), it is unlikely that Lega will pursue its erstwhile secessionist agenda and instead scenarios 2 or 3 will ensue. Nevertheless, despite exhibiting a Trump-like 'winners' worldview heavily favouring big business and not the working class or the vulnerable, the Lega and 5 Star coalition planned and embarked on a massive public spending programme which, on top of Italy's existing €2.3 trillion debt, heralded economic meltdown (Kington 2018c). This, and an evident anti-EU 'Italexit' agenda of the Lega Nord/M5S coalition, led to the EU threatening legal action and financial punishment for gross breaches of EU budgetary and fiscal regulation (*Reuters* 2018).

Conclusion

The Alt-Right ideology is all about ensuring inequalities between 'the deserving' (i.e. WASPs, the rich, the business/property owning classes, and those having an Alt-Right mind-set) and 'the undeserving' (i.e. immigrants, ethnic minorities, Muslims and other non-Christian religious minorities, the unemployed, the poor and low paid, the disabled, and those having a non-Alt-Right mind-set). Those inequalities can only be maintained and deepened via authoritarian and repressive means against the 'undeserving'. Thus, in professing to offer 'freedom', the Alt-Right ideology is inherently conflicted, as such freedom is offered only to the 'deserving'.

Conflicted ideology, making unsubstantiated and often contradictory assertions, and issuing inflammatory false propaganda are just some of the weaknesses of the Alt-Right that add to its central characteristic of racial, ethnic and religious intolerance manifested increasingly in intimidation of minorities, hate crimes, and violence. The majority population find the overall Alt-Right proposition objectionable and therefore refuse to vote for such candidates. However, although in most countries those having an Alt-Right commitment are a relatively small proportion of the electorate, there are some Alt-Right issues, such as fears relating to immigration, that are of concern to the broader population and which the Alt-Right readily exploits. This has seen an upsurge of support for populist Alt-Right parties or candidates, although significant electoral success has occurred only in some countries e.g. US, Germany, Austria, Hungary, and Italy. In other countries, despite robust campaigning, noisy rallies, and inflammatory rhetoric, the Alt-Right has been unable to secure any significant electoral success e.g. UK, Nordic countries, Holland, and France.

Nevertheless, in some countries (e.g. Hungary), ruling populist Alt-Right parties have secured an assured majority in the legislature by forming coalitions or cooperating with smaller hard-right parties. In others (e.g. Austria, Netherlands, Italy), manoeuvring by Alt-Right groups and parties to normalise their policies through mainstream parties, either through the latter copying them to attract votes or through coalition, is already on the increase. Such manipulation of the democratic process and electoral system is becoming an Alt-Right 'weapon of choice' to gain either formal power or strong influence. Such developments raise the prospect of a drift towards either elected dictatorship or coup by stealth, and ultimately a potential fascist state. In the United States, continued electoral success by the populist Alt-Right may result in a similar drift, and ultimately a 'permanent' separation of states into those that are liberal progressive and those that are nationalist conservative (i.e. Alt-Right controlled). The effects and implications of such potential developments are incalculable. However, overall, the author concludes that extreme scenarios involving coups and separatist splits are unlikely.

References

Aaronovitch, D. 2017. "Obama's Right: Hashtags Can't Change the World". *The Times.* December 28, 2017. Page 31.

Atkins, R. 2017. "Far-Right Leader Warns Against 'Islamification' of Austria". *Financial Times.* October 13, 2017. https://www.ft.com/.

Blest, P. 2017. "Blue-State Secession is Dumb and Cruel: All States Matter". *The Nation*, March 13, 2017.

Burleigh, M. 2018a. "There's Nothing Ordinary About the Populists". *The Times.* May 28, 2018. Page 24.

C4 News. 2018. "Exclusive: Court Documents Claim New Arron Banks Links with Russia". *Channel 4 News.* July 20, 2018. https://www.chanel4.com/news/.

Cooper, R. 2015. "Is Donald Trump Leading a Proto-Fascist Movement?". *The Week.* August 28, 2015. theweek.com/.

Cork, T. 2017. "UKIP Donor Likened to National Front After Calling for Muslim Immigration Ban and 'Levelling' of Mosques". *Bristol Post.* July 16, 2017. www.bristolpost.co.uk.

Day, M. 2015. Hungary's far-right Jobbik party wins first by-election. *The Telegraph.* April 13, 2015. https://www.thetelegraph.co.uk.

Frum, D. 2018. Trumpocracy: The Corruption of the American Republic. New York: Harper Collins.

Gatehouse, G. 2017. "Marine Le Pen: Who's Funding France's Far Right?" *BBC Panorama.* April 3, 2017. www.bbc.co.uk.

Green, J. 2017. *Devil's Bargain: Steve Bannon, Donald Trump, and the Storming of the Presidency.* New York: Penguin Random House Publishing.

Hackett, R. 2016. "Here are All the Billionaires Backing Donald Trump". *Fortune.* August 3, 2016. fortune.com.

Hermansson, P. 2017. *HNH Explains.... How the Alt-Right is Funded.* November 6, 2017. London: Hope Not Hate.

HT. 2017. "British Right-Wing Politician Nigel Farage Discusses Hungary, Orban, The EU , and Brexit". *Hungary Today.* June 15, 2017. hungarytoday.hu/.

Humphrey, A.S. 2005. "SWOT Analysis for Management Consulting". *SRI Alumni Newsletter*, 7–8. Stanford University. SRI Alumni Association.

Kington, T. 2018a. "Orban Poised to Win Poll After Anti-EU Campaign". *The Times.* April 7, 2018. Page 40.

Kington, T. 2018b. "Viktor Orban, Buoyed by his Election Triumph, is Making Life Ever Harder for Advocates of Free Speech in Hungary". *The Times.* April 16, 2018. Page 31.

Kington, T. 2018c. "Italy Faces Fresh Elections as Populists Are Sidelined". *The Times.* May 29, 2018. Page 26.

Learned, E.P., Christensen, C.R., Andrews, K.E., and Guth, W.D. 1965. *Business Policy: Text and Cases.* Homewood IL: Irwin.

Lyons, M.N. 2017. *Ctrl-Alt-Delete: The Origins and Ideology of the Alternative Right.* Somerville, MA: Political Research Associates.

Mason, R. and Syal, R. 2014. "Nigel Farage Deal with Polish Far-Right Party 'Raises Serious Questions'". *The Guardian.* October 21, 2014. https://www.theguardian.com/.

Michael, G. 2006. *The Enemy of My Enemy: The Alarming Convergence of Militant Islam and the Extreme Right.* Lawrence KA: University Press of Kansas.

Mudde, C. 2017. "Is the GOP a Far-Right Party?" The Blog. *Huffington Post.* February 28, 2016 updated 28 February 2017.

Neiwert, D. 2017. *Alt-America—The Rise of the Radical Right in the Age of Trump.* London: Verso.

Page, L. and Goldstein, D.G. 2016. "The Role of Subjective Beliefs in Preferences for Redistribution". *Social Choice and Welfare,* 47(1), 25–61.

Paravicini, G. 2016. "Italy's Far Right Jolts Back from Dead". *Politico.* February 3, 2016. https://www.politico.eu/.

Pasha-Robinson, L. 2018. "Steve Bannon Tells French National Front: 'Let Them Call your Racist..... Wear it as a Badge of Honour'". *The Independent.* March 12, 2018. https://www.independent.co.uk.

Pavia, W. 2018. "Trump's Latest Remarks on London Show How Fraudulent his Legend Is". *The Times.* January 13, 2018. Pages 40–41.

Paxton, R.O. 2005. *The Anatomy of Fascism.* London: Penguin Books.

Reuters. 2018. "Factbox: Timeline and Sanctions if EU Starts Disciplinary Budget Steps Against Italy". https://www.reuters.com/article/. (accessed November 18, 2018).

Rice, S.A. 1928. "The Distribution of Individual Political Attitudes". In *Quantitative Methods in Politics,* edited by S.A. Rice, 71–91. New York: Appleton-Century-Crofts.

Roston, A. and Anderson, J. 2017. "He Spent Almost 20 Years Funding the Racist Right. It Finally Paid Off". *Buzzfeed.* July 23, 2017. https://www.buzzfeed.com/.

Rushe, D. 2017. "Steve Bannon is Back at Breitbart. But Can His Page of Rage Survive an Ad Boycott?" *The Guardian.* August 25, 2017. https://www.theguardian.com/.

Schaeffer, C. 2017. "How Hungary Became a Haven for the Alt-Right". *The Atlantic.* May 28, 2017. https://www.theatlantic.com.

Sherman, G. 2017. "'I Have Power': is Steve Bannon Running for President?" *Vanity Fair.* December 21, 2017. https://www.vanityfair.com/.

Sherwood, H. 2017. "Evangelical Christians 'Uncritical' in Support of Trump, UK Bishop Says". *The Guardian.* December 28, 2017. https://theguardian.com/.

Singer, T. 2017. "President Trump and the American Selfie: Archetypal Defences of the Group Spirit". In *A Clear and Present Danger: Narcissism in the Era of President Trump*, edited by L. Cruz and S. Buser, 17–48. Asheville, NC: Chiron Publications.

Sullivan, A. 2018. "Can Trump be Impeached?" Books review. *New York Times.* March 12, 2018. https://www.nytimes.com/.

Sunstein, C.R. (ed). 2018. *Can It Happen Here? Authoritarianism in America.* New York: Dey Street Books/HarperCollins.

UKSC. 2017. *R (on the application of Miller and Dos Santos) versus Secretary of State for Exiting the European Union and associated references.* January 24, 2017. London: Supreme Court of the United Kingdom. https://www.supremecourt.uk/.

Vogel, K.P. 2016. "Behind the Retreat of the Koch Brothers' Operation". *Politico.* October 27, 2016. https://www.politico.com/.

Walker, P. 2018. "Arron Banks Inquiry: Why Is £8m Leave.EU Funding Under Review?" *The Guardian.* November 2, 2018. https://www.theguardian.com/politics/2018/nov/02/. (accessed November 18, 2018).

Waterfield, B. 2018. "Next EU Election Will Finish Liberal Elite, Says Orban". *The Times.* July 30, 2018. Page 25.

Watt, H. 2017. "Electoral Commission to Investigate Arron Banks' Brexit Donations". *The Guardian.* November 1, 2017. https://www.theguardian.com/.

Weirich, H. 1982. "The TOWS Matrix: a Tool for Situational Analysis". *Long Range Planning*, 15(2), 54–66.

Chapter 14:
Potential Strategies to Limit the Alt-Right Threat

By Alan Waring and Roger Paxton

Abstract

Overall, Alt-Right leaders, advocates, and opinion formers seek to subvert, persuade, and as necessary bully, mainstream and populist conservatives to permanently shift their allegiance firmly towards the far-right. Six overall objectives in combating potential Alt-Right domination and excesses are posited. To meet these objectives, five broad categories of preventive strategy are discussed in detail: 1. Legislative, law enforcement, and judicial; 2. Internet, social media, and related approaches; 3. Educational; 4. Political and economic; 5. Grassroots and mass action. A determined, multi-facetted response of 'muscular moderation' is advocated.

Key words: Alt-Right, authoritarianism, threat, prevention, moderation, strategies,

Addressing an Existential Threat

In this final chapter, the authors consider what strategies, and in what combination, may be required to limit the Alt-Right threat to western society and democracy. In doing this, the authors necessarily take a position that the Alt-Right ideology, policies, and activities represent not just a theoretical but also an existential threat—see e.g. Abramovitz (2018), Hackenbroich and Shapiro (2018), Neiwert (2017), and Roth (2018).

As previous chapters have shown, Alt-Right leaders, advocates, and opinion formers seek the normalisation of their ideology, so that its implementation in various forms is less likely to be challenged robustly in society. Alt-Right leaders and opinion formers are typically keen to portray their ideology and policies as a reasonable, fair, just, and necessary response to dangerous liberal ideas and weak mainstream governance. The Alt-Right seek to portray themselves as society's saviours, as the only protection against being overwhelmed and destroyed by foreigners and immigrants, and their alien ideas, creeds, and cultures e.g. the rhetoric of Marine Le Pen, Salvini, Orban, Strache, Gudenus, Gauland, Trump and other leaders. By subverting and persuading mainstream and populist conservatism to shift its centre of political gravity firmly towards the far-right, they seek to ensure a permanent Alt-Right stamp on national governance. In the Alt-Right coda, any and all means are permissible in pursuit of their ends, including lies, fake news, and invented 'alternative facts' as a means to subvert the gullible and the disaffected and encourage the already persuaded. To some of them and their supporters, violence and even murder are not off limits.

A major criticism of liberal western governments, mainstream politicians and political parties, institutions, public authorities, and corporate leaders, is that they generally fail to stand up to the Alt-Right or, worse, appear to be apologists for them, or worse still, endorse or collaborate with them. Indeed, Neiwert (2017) accused the liberal elites in the US of false moral superiority, condescension, and even contempt towards the parochial heartlands of the Alt-Right, while doing precious little to combat its rise. While this criticism is not unique to any one country, the US has provided a number of high profile examples of largely unchallenged Alt-Right excesses, and especially those involving President Donald Trump. Abramovitz (2018) also cited "violations of basic ethical standards by the new administration", Trump's admiration "for some of the world's most loathsome strongmen and dictators", and his threats to press freedom. He asserted that there had been "a faster erosion of democratic norms in the US than at any other time in memory". By behaving in this way, Trump went beyond being just a far-right appeaser and passive fellow traveller and demonstrated a more enthusiastic active participation.

The rise of the Nazis in Europe in the 1930s should be a sufficient warning from history that the more that liberal governments and mainstream society and its moderate leaders engage in appeasement, turning of blind eyes, and passive acceptance of and collaboration with far-right ideology, policies, and actions, the more that the Alt-Right will be encouraged and emboldened. As Rees (2005) noted, "....only with the collaboration, weakness, miscalculation, and tolerance of others could the Nazis come to power". Abramovitz (2018, 3) commented on the resurgent trend of "emboldened autocrats, beleaguered democracies, and the United States' withdrawal from its leadership role in the global struggle for human freedom". Roth (2018) and Hackenbroich and Shapiro (2018) also referred to the rise of autocrats and the populist challenge to democracy. As Neiwert concluded:

> "So it is vital for liberals, progressives, moderates, and genuine conservatives to link arms in the coming years to fight back against the fascist tide. It will require organizing, and it will require real outreach. And if this coalition wants to succeed, its members will need to break the vicious circular social dynamic that right-wing extremists always create, particularly in rural communities where their bullying style of discourse can stifle honest discourse. To do that, some self-reflection will go a long way". (Neiwert 2017, 375)

Neiwert's conclusion, of course, addresses the American context, in which both neglected rural and decaying industrial communities may be especially amenable to Alt-Right attentions. In other western countries, the urban-rural disjuncture may be less pronounced. However, the same concern about their pathological assertions, egregious conduct, and bullying style of discourse applies wherever the Alt-Right operates.

Overall, whatever strategies and methods are employed to thwart the Alt-Right, they will need to consider carefully the warnings of Kaltwasser (2017) and Capoccia (2005; 2013) about the paradox of potential self-destruction for democracy in its fight against nationalist authoritarian threats. Liberal democracy is meant to be pluralist and inclusive but, if in its defence it adopts a militant or repressive strategy against the Alt-Right threat internally, then it could appear to be illiberal and anti-democratic. A 'fighting fire with fire' approach may perversely aid the populist forces' discourse by enabling the latter to cast themselves and their supporters as victims. An accommodative rather than an oppressive approach (Kaltwasser 2017; Capoccia 2005) may therefore be preferable wherever justifiable, although clearly not to the extent that pathological outcomes result. If and when contain-and-convert approaches fail or are inappropriate, then contain-and-punish approaches must also be available.

Kaltwasser (2017) also warned against regarding both populist and more extreme elements as necessarily representing the same amorphous threat. For example, although sharing the same underlying loathing for what they regard as the dishonest and corrupt elite of the ruling-class political and economic 'Establishment', and the need to change or disempower it, many of the populist Alt-Right eschew the nastier rhetoric and violent tactics of their far- and extreme-right associates. As discussed in chapter 3, for example, during the Brexit referendum campaign the populist UKIP articulated widespread public concern in Britain about a perceived over-bearing and unaccountable EU, and posed legitimate questions. As UKIP was a properly registered and functioning political party within the British system of governance and representation of the people, their participation or 'incorporation' matched the short-term accommodative approach suggested by Kaltwasser (2017) and Capoccia (2005). However, in chapter 9, van der Valk graphically describes how such a political strategy ('poldering') in the Netherlands produced a counter-intuitive result.

With the above caveats in mind, an overall strategy to combat the full spectrum of potential Alt-Right domination and excesses would require such objectives as:

- Accommodating the populist Alt-Right as far as possible within the normal democratic process, while seeking via robust debate and education to limit their appeal, challenge their manifesto, and isolate their far-right and extreme-right associates.
- Resisting the normalisation of far- and extreme-right ideology and policies in society.
- Treating far- and extreme-right ideology as a social and political deviancy—a dangerously pathological belief system to be challenged robustly. As Vaughan (1985; 1986) has shown in another sphere, normalisation of deviance is likely to have an insidious and corrosive impact on the domain affected.
- Challenging the false assertions and absurdities of Alt-Right lies, invented facts, and fake news.
- Condemning the inhumanity of far- and extreme-right ideology and its intimidating aura, including its violent tendencies.
- Prosecuting all crimes having far- and extreme-right motivations to the fullest extent of the law and ensuring tough sentencing.

To address these objectives, this chapter considers the most likely scenarios for Alt-Right evolution i.e. the first three of the five potential scenarios identified in chapter 13:

1. Despite winning some elections, the inability of the Alt-Right to retain seats and expand elected representation leads to it remaining a noisy, fragmented, minority protest movement, albeit harbouring hate criminals and violent elements. (i.e. current democratic order maintained, but only with vigilance and sustained preventative strategies).
2. A slow rightward societal drift occurs and entrenchment into an illiberal democracy, relying on determined Alt-Right candidates, weak mainstream candidates, and populist Alt-Right voters. (i.e. elected autocracy, as in e.g. Hungary). Robust preventative strategies required.
3. Takeover of current democratic parties, institutions, and government by Alt-Right activists and supporters, using stealth infiltration and 'entry-ist' techniques, relying on inertia, complacency, or intimidation of mainstream parties. (i.e. coup by stealth, followed by pseudo-democracy or dictatorship). Robust preventative and response strategies required.

The other two scenarios identified in chapter 13 (i.e. involving either, crisis and opportunistic coup leading to pseudo-democracy or dictatorship, or planned armed coup followed by dictatorship) also require appropriate preventive and protective strategies. However, the latter fall primarily within the area of national security, and therefore hopefully state intelligence and security services are best able to monitor dissidents and terrorists and thwart coup attempts. Attempts by a book such as this to offer substantive advice on national security would be unrealistic. Nevertheless, whatever may be done to combat scenarios 1–3 might also assist in dampening down the precursors to, and limiting the receptive environment for, more extreme scenarios.

With the above scope in mind, the authors suggest preventative strategies in the following categories, which are not in any order and which need to be combined:

- Legislative, law enforcement, and judicial strategies
- Internet, social media, and related strategies
- Educational strategies
- Political and economic strategies
- Grassroots and mass actions

These categories match in part the four domestic responder categories identified by Kaltwasser (2017) for dealing with populist threats, to which he also added four external actor categories (foreign governments, supra-national institutions, transnational civil society actors, and international federations of political parties). It should be noted that the authors' five categories cover generic precursors to risk reduction and control, and not necessarily solutions for every specific risk identified in chapter 12 and earlier chapters. These latter risks will require more particular responses.

Legislative, Law Enforcement, and Judicial Strategies to Combat the Alt-Right Threat

Historical evidence shows that legislation, policing, and the criminal justice system, even in combination, are never likely to be able to deter, control, or modify egregious human behaviour to the extent desired. Nevertheless, such formal systems are essential in order to prevent anarchy, maintain law and order, and ensure public safety among other things (ECHR 1953). Moreover, such systems are also necessary to define and prescribe the envelope of societal acceptability, proscribe behaviours that are unacceptable, and determine punishments for offenders.

Nevertheless, it is arguable that one of the cynical weapons used by the Alt-Right, both against their opponents and as propaganda for public consumption, is to twist the precepts of democracy into arguments for societal and lawful acceptability of Alt-Right ideology, rhetoric, and actions. For example, the human right of freedom of speech, as enshrined in the constitutions of many countries, is manipulated by the Alt-Right to justify its exponents making speeches, issuing public rants, affixing public posters, and sending flyers, letters, e-mails, text and social media messages, that are suffused with blatantly racist and/or religious hatred, sometimes including threats of or incitement to violence—see examples in chapters 6 and 7. There seems to be little recognition among the Alt-Right that freedom of speech, as with other freedoms, has never been absolute and is conditional upon legal constraints aimed at protection of the public good. The European Convention on Human Rights (ECHR 1953), Article 10, identified the limitations to freedom of expression as encompassing instances that threaten the following:

- National security
- Protection of territorial integrity
- Public safety
- Prevention of disorder or crime
- Protection of health and morals
- Reputation or rights of others
- Laws against harassment, or incitement to crime, or libel and slander
- Disclosure of confidential information
- Maintaining the authority and impartiality of the judiciary

One of the earliest pieces of legislation seeking to limit freedom of expression that would otherwise threaten sections of society was Section 24 of the 1881 French press freedom law (FPL 1881), which proscribed incitement to racial discrimination, hatred, or violence on the basis of one's origin or membership/non-membership of an ethnic, national, racial, or religious group. This section is now absorbed into Article 13-1 of the 1990 law of the same name. After the European Convention (ECHR 1953), the UN International Convention (UN 1965) sought to outlaw hate speech and criminalize the membership of racist organizations. Further national laws followed e.g. the UK Public Order Act 1986 made it a criminal offence to "stir up racial hatred" using threatening, abusive, or insulting words or behaviour or written material, and the Malicious Communications Act 1988 (S1) and the Communications Act 2003 (S127) added more specific offences (CSC 2017). The UK Human Rights Act 1998 enshrined the European Convention in British law, and has since been amended to include hate crimes based on religion. The UK Criminal Justice Act 2003 also made sentencing 'uplift' provisions for some hate crimes. Although many states had already done so, the EU Framework Decision of 2008 (EU 2008) sought to require all EU Member States to criminalize hate speech and hate crime motivated by racism and xenophobia.

Similar developments have occurred in the US, the first being the 1968 Federal Hate Crimes Statute (USDoJ 2018). This was followed by the Patriot Act 2001 (S. 802), the Hate Crimes Prevention Act 2009 (the so-called Shepard and Byrne Act), as well as other statutes that also contain anti-discrimination and hate crime provisions.

Nevertheless, despite such a welter of legislation, there have been concerns by some (e.g. Walters 2017; Walters et al 2017) that either it does not go far enough, thereby leaving vulnerable groups unprotected, or the legislation does not work effectively enough. There are also counter-arguments that, no matter how repulsive, inflammatory, and dangerous some speech may be, it has a right to be made as a fundamental human right of free expression. This debate, and the limitations of an unfettered purist interpretation of 'freedom of speech', was examined at length in EHRC (2015). Overall, a purist interpretation of free expression has been widely rejected. Moreover, as bit by bit hate crimes are becoming more precisely defined and proscribed in legislation, the exclusion of hate crimes from free expression has become clearer and unequivocal.

Copsey et al (2013) examined hate crime specifically perpetrated by the far-right against Muslims in the UK, and included CPS (Crown Prosecution Service) data and data from the moderately successful Tell MAMA self-reporting scheme for victims of such crimes (see https://tellmamauk.org). The Copsey report noted a reluctance of victims to report alleged instances to the police, which indicated a problem of under-reporting. Overall, such instances were of low-level verbal abuse and harassment, with less than 10% involving extreme violence. Notably, 74% of incidents reported to Tell MAMA related to on-line abuse (Internet, social media, text messages), and often included threats of more direct action against the victim.

The Copsey report suggested that whereas most of the premeditated hate crimes and anti-Muslim campaigns were organized by far-right groups such as BNP, Britain First, and EDL, the numbers of committed members of such groups were too small to account for the number of low-level hate crimes. The latter were committed mainly by sympathisers-at-large, characterized by their "ordinariness", on an opportunistic or spontaneous basis. EDL were responsible for more complaints of on-line hate crime than all other far-right groups combined. However, as EHRC (2015) discussed in detail, there are perennial problems associated with definitions of offences, policing procedures, obtaining evidence, quality of evidence, witness intimidation, and so on, which combine to make successful prosecutions in this subject area difficult to secure, especially with low-level hate crime.

Greater success has been achieved in the UK in cases where prominent members of far-right groups, typically at political rallies, protest marches, or contrived confrontations, have made flagrantly racist and/or anti-Muslim public statements that were likely to inflame tensions and provoke violence. Examples include a string of criminal convictions of the leader of Britain First, Paul Golding, for offences relating to hate speeches, harassment, using threatening or abusive language, breach of a court order banning him from entering mosques, and wearing a political uniform (Ferguson 2017; Gibbons 2018b; Hopkins, 2016). Punishments have included fines, jail terms, and restraining orders. His deputy, Jayda Fransen, also has a list of convictions for similar offences (D'Arcy 2017; Gibbons 2018b; Paterson 2017; York 2016) and several further prosecutions were in process in 2018, one of which resulted in a 10-month jail sentence. Tommy Robinson (real name Stephen Yaxley-Lennon), ex-BNP and a founder of the English Defence League, has served jail terms for assault and also has convictions for contempt of court, drug offences, using someone else's passport, and mortgage fraud (Lusher 2017). His latest conviction (for contempt of court) on May 29, 2018 resulted in a 13-month jail term (Hamilton 2018a), later granted an appeal on procedural grounds not on substance (*Times* 2018). At the time of writing, a retrial was pending.

Success has also been achieved in arresting and prosecuting UK far-right terrorists. These include members and alleged members of the proscribed far-right terrorist group National Action. In 2017 and 2018, there were several waves of arrests of alleged National Action members, some of whom were also serving members of the British armed forces. Between early September 2017 and mid-January 2018, twenty-eight suspects were arrested and charged with membership of National Action, which carries a jail sentence of up to ten years. Of the 28, a number were also variously charged additionally with the commission, preparation, and instigation of acts of terrorism, and one (Jack Renshaw) was also charged with plotting to murder (initially the then Home Secretary Amber Rudd), a Labour MP, and a police officer, to which he pleaded guilty (Hamilton 2018b; Hamilton and Gardham 2018). The various trials arising (including Renshaw's) had not all concluded at the time of writing. Of those trials concluded, convictions were secured against all defendants and jail sentences of up to 8 years each were imposed.

Further, there have been calls in Parliament (Hansard 2016) for the UK government to consider making membership of or support for Britain First proscribed under the Terrorism Act 2000, to bring them into line with the already proscribed National Action and its offshoots NS131 and Scottish Dawn. While this has yet to happen, it is inevitable that Britain First, EDL and other such groups have been, and will continue to be, closely monitored by the various police, national security, and counter-terrorism branches. In Kaltwasser's (2017) terms, proscription as a repressive response may to some extent aid the self-image of extremists and their supporters. Nevertheless, government's over-riding duty to protect the safety of the public against extremist threats is likely to take precedence.

The relative success of intelligence-led action by the British police and security services in preventing acts of terror by far-right groups has not been matched by the ability to prevent lone-actor terrorists carrying out atrocities. Two prominent cases are the murder of Jo Cox MP by Thomas Mair in June 2016 (see details in chapter 5), who was sentenced to life imprisonment, the murder of Makram Ali and the attempted murders of nine others outside Finsbury Park Mosque on June 19, 2017, caused by Darren Osborne deliberately driving a van at speed at worshippers leaving the mosque. He was convicted as charged in February 2018 by jury (taking only one hour to decide) and sentenced to two concurrent life sentences with a minimum of 43 years to be served (Rawlinson 2018). The judge described him as having a "belligerent and violent character", his evidence in defence as a "pathetic last-ditch attempt" to blame the crime on two invented men, and his attack as "terrorism", even though he was not accused under terrorism legislation. Police described Osborne's actions as "devious, vile and hate-filled". Evidence was presented in court that Osborne had been heavily influenced by far-right websites (as Thomas Mair had been), and that only days before the attack he had received unsolicited general messages of encouragement for his beliefs from Tommy Robinson, the former EDL leader, and Jayda Fransen, the deputy leader of Britain First (Dearden 2018; Hamilton and Johnston 2018). Other similarities between Mair and Osborne were their lacklustre careers, misfit personalities, and apparent proneness to depression and being socially isolated, even though Osborne did have a family. However, unlike Mair, he also had numerous prior convictions (over 100), including theft and assault. They both blamed Britain's problems on immigrants and had developed a pathological hatred of Muslims.

However, the UK police were able to apprehend and convict the neo-Nazi white supremacist Ethan Stables, a young 'drop-out' who was on his way to attempt a planned machete slaughter of as many attendees as possible at an LBGT event in June 2017. In May 2018, in view of his severe mental illness and threat to society, Stables was sentenced to be detained indefinitely in a secure hospital under the Mental Health Act. Like Mair and Osborne, Stables had spent many months researching far-right websites on how to obtain or make firearms and explosives, and had amassed a stash of weapons, including knives, a machete and an axe, and bomb-making paraphernalia (Swerling 2018a and b).

The influence of far-right propaganda on Mair, Osborne, and Stables was also prevalent in the case of Anders Breivik, the notorious Norwegian far-right extremist who, on July 22, 2011, carried out the lone-actor terrorist bombing in Oslo which killed 8 people, and then went on to massacre 69 children and young people at a youth camp on Utøya island (see chapter 10). Of course, not all mass killings are far-right motivated or indeed politically motivated, but a high proportion have been far-right inspired (ADL 2018; Freilich et al 2014).

From the small number of lone-actor terrorism cases, it is not possible to readily identify an obvious way to prevent such outrages. As Jackson notes in chapter 5, prevention of this category of far-right terrorism points towards using a variety of existing professionals to better notice early signs of depression, mental disturbance, social isolation, blaming others, and anti-social or extremist rhetoric and behaviour in the individual patients and clients they deal with. This may result in better and earlier identification of potential 'risk' individuals, but on its own it may not ensure that appropriate public safety actions then follow. Therefore, beyond Jackson's suggested approach, is there also a case for a statutory notification of such suspicions to an appropriate authority for clear action? But what might that action to prevent terrorist acts comprise? For example, compulsory psychiatric evaluation and treatment, at best might only deal with a third of the cases, since roughly two thirds do not appear to suffer from mental health issues. Moreover, such a controversial move would require legislation, not to mention rigorous ethical procedures and doubtless considerable debate on the moral, ethical, medical, political, and legal issues arising. More work is required on developing appropriate practical strategies for preventing this kind of terrorism.

In addition, as noted above, evidence suggests that lone actor terrorists are typically influenced, if not provoked, by extremist images and propaganda they receive from far-right organizations, especially on-line via the Internet and social media. Such influence flows not only from generalised, anonymous narratives and imagery but crucially also involves the demagoguery of named far-right ideologues—the far-right leaders whose poisonous invective provides individual personalities vulnerable to radicalisation both a cause to rally to and a justification for violence in the name of that cause. Such remote 'heroes' may cleverly avoid any outright exhortation to violence and instead rely on ambiguous messages, innuendo, and suggestive hints, presumably in the hope that recipients will understand the subtext and act on it. The next section addresses the specific issue of such provocative agencies and intermediaries, from legal, practical, and politico-cultural perspectives.

Internet, Social Media, and Related Strategies

Nagle (2017, 120), concentrating on the spread and effects of social media, ended her book on a gloomy note, seeing no "easy way out of the mess that has been created". Others have been less pessimistic. The first kind of suggestion for action concerns regulation of the new media that have clearly contributed greatly to the rise of the Alt-Right. *The Economist* (2017) suggested firstly that social media companies could be held accountable, as newspaper publishers are, for the material they disseminate. Libel and ownership laws could be extended and deployed. Secondly, such companies could be required to make clear whether a post comes from a friend or trusted source; and thirdly, reminders could be displayed warning of the harm caused by misinformation. Howard and Kolanyi (2017) made similar, quite specific, recommendations: although *Facebook* and *Twitter* do not generate fake news, they should be held responsible for serving misinformation to voters, and helped to do better. This could be achieved without interfering with free speech in the United States, for instance by using the Uniform Commercial Code to make both advertisers and social media companies adhere to basic anti-spam and truth-in-advertising rules. Paid political content should come with clear disclosures, and information on this should be filed with election authorities. Social media are now so pervasive, powerful, and full of misinformation (often stoking confirmation biases) that the success of democracy requires urgent legislative action by governments to strengthen regulation of them. It will be essential that the sanctions contained within this legislation take account of the enormous wealth of the social media companies.

Therefore, is there a case for making those who in any way create, broadcast, disseminate, or publish far-right hate material (or indeed any hate material), liable for prosecution for this specific criminal offence? So far, when challenged by governments on this issue, Internet providers, search engine operators, and social media providers have claimed that they have no direct involvement in, or responsibility for, the content created by information providers and users, as they are not publishers but merely electronic communications facilitators. This claim to be entirely innocent and uninvolved has striking similarities to the *mens rea* legal defence once used by business owners and directors to avoid liability for corporate manslaughter. For example, in the event of a person being killed while at work, prosecution of an organization deemed responsible indirectly, by virtue of policy or managerial decisions, would nearly always fail because the prosecuting authority could not prove that any individual director knew or foresaw such a consequence. In Britain, the *mens rea* defence was removed by the Corporate Manslaughter and Corporate Homicide Act 2007, whereby the organization itself and individual senior executives are guilty of the offence if the way in which it was managed or organized by senior management led to a death (MoJ 2008; CPS 2018). A number of companies and directors have been successfully prosecuted under this Act and sentences have included jail terms, fines thus far in the range £385,000-£600,000, and compulsory 'name and shame' publicity orders (see e.g. Chan 2011). Although there is no upper limit to fines under this Act, sentencing guidelines suggest £20m for larger firms in view of their turnover and assets (SC 2016).

Many countries have been increasingly concerned at the reluctance of Internet providers, search engine operators, and social media providers to ban extremist content (e.g. Gibbs 2017). Thus far, although there have been some attempts to self-regulate, the evidence suggests that these have been superficial, slow, and ineffective. If this failure to self-regulate continues, despite pressure from governments, perhaps the only way to force such companies to behave responsibly is to legislate robustly against them (e.g. Griffin 2017). For example, a

Prevention of Hate Crime and Terrorism (Internet Provider and Social Media) Act could compel companies to ban extreme content or else be deemed guilty of aiding and abetting hate crime and/or terrorism. Using the corporate manslaughter legislation as an analogue guide, a *mens rea* defence would have to be removed, and individual senior executives deemed to be responsible would be made liable as well as the body corporate. As with corporate manslaughter, punishments for those convicted would need to be commensurate with both the gravity of the crime and their financial strength and assets. In view of the annual turnover of such companies being typically tens of billions of US$ (e.g. for 2016, *Google's* revenue totalled US$89.5bn, and *Facebook's* was US$27.64bn—https://www.statista.com), fines would need to be proportionately large. Jail sentences for convicted individuals would also need to reflect the gravity and extent of the offence, as well as the person's attitude e.g. repeat offender, lack of remorse. The use of international arrest warrants may become necessary, if offenders seek to evade jurisdiction. There may even be a case for a compulsory public register of offenders, similar to that employed in the UK for serious sex offenders, whereby registration may be for a fixed number of years or for life.

The continuing failure of such companies to effectively curb extreme content led to the British Prime Minister, Theresa May, telling world leaders at the 2018 World Economic Forum (January 2018) that these companies must do much more, and that "No one wants to be known as the terrorists' platform or the first-choice app for paedophiles" (Coates and Blakely 2018). She added that, if necessary, their major investors should force them: "Investors can play a vital role by considering the social impact of the companies they are investing in. They can use their influence to ensure these issues are taken seriously". There was an implication that if self-regulation continued to fail, then legislation would be inevitable and damaged investors would have only themselves to blame for failing to act. In February 2018, the chief marketing officer of the Unilever group, which spends over US$9 billion annually on marketing, of which one third is on digital advertising, threatened to withdraw its advertising from digital media companies unless they ceased distributing extremist, offensive, and illegal content (Gibbons 2018a).

The interim report on Disinformation and 'Fake News' (HoC 2018) by the British House of Commons Digital, Culture, Media and

Sport Committee expressed strong concerns about 'fake news'; using the word 'crisis', and seeing it as presenting risks to our democracy and values. The Committee was particularly troubled by "the relentless targeting of hyper-partisan views, which play to the fears and prejudices of people, in order to influence their voting plans and behaviour". This was an interim report, and therefore had no power to result in changes immediately, but it correctly described the existing legal framework as no longer fit for purpose. Legislative changes are therefore likely to be proposed and accepted following publication of the final report. In addition to the misuse of electronic communications to disseminate hate, the use of a vast set of *Facebook* data without participants' consent and seeking to manipulate voting intentions, revealed in early 2018 and described in chapter 11 of Vol 1, is a further and glaring illustration of the need for tighter regulation.

Thus, closing the "justice gap" probably needs to go much further globally than the scoping issues for hate crime identified by Walters (2017) and Walters et al (2017) in relation to the UK, and address the powerful commercial interests that control the vectors of hate dissemination known to potentiate radicalisation and extremist violence (of any kind: far-right, far-left, ISIS or whatever).

Educational Strategies to Combat the Alt-Right Threat

Common sense suggests that education ought to be a prominent component within any overall strategy to combat any form of pathological or extreme ideology, whether left-wing, right-wing, religion-based, or whatever character. See, for example, DARE (2017a), OSCE (2011), and several speakers in PCPRCI (2012). Kaltwasser (2017) also suggested education as a long-term accommodative response to populist forces. One of the common findings of PCPRCI (2012, 9) relating to Europe was that "The reason why the youth is in most cases more receptive to the ideas of the radical right is the lack of systemic education of democratic norms and values in schools, as well as the lack of fostering a debating culture in primary schools, high schools and universities alike (especially in Eastern Europe)". Education would be anticipated to provide models of attitudes and behaviour that are not only socially acceptable and law-abiding but also safer and more respectful of others. As Neiwert (2017) noted, loss of respectful engagement is a characteristic of the Alt-Right era.

As one important initiative, the EU DARE (Dialogue About Radicalisation and Equality) project (DARE 2017b) aims to significantly enhance understanding of why and how some young people become radicalised with the potential for engagement in violent extremist ideologies and behaviours. One objective is to develop new evaluation and intervention tookits to counter radicalisation effectively.

However, 'education' to counter extremism would need to target not only school children up to age 18 but also many other identifiable categories likely to be vulnerable to adoption of pathological or extremist ideas, e.g. non-school students, long-term unemployed, the low paid, the socially isolated, those having personality or mental disorders, those with grievances, and especially those who fall into several of these categories. With such a range of different targets, it is likely that preventive educational needs, objectives, and methods would also vary.

At school level, Davies (2008) argued that formal education alone does little to prevent people from joining extremist groups, nor does it equip young people with skills needed to identify and analyse extremism. Like PCPRCI (2012), she argued that much more than descriptive literacy about such threats is needed, and that young people need to be taught how to think critically and constructively about human rights and societal, social, and political issues and how to apply such skills outside of school. In a way, it was a call in part for a modernised and expanded version of the Civics classes that were widespread in British schools in the 1960s. In Britain, the government's Prevent strategy for schools introduced under the Counter-Terrorism and Security Act 2015 placed a duty on schools and childcare providers to, among other things, build children's resilience to radicalisation: "....schools can build pupils' resilience to radicalisation by providing a safe environment for debating controversial issues and helping them to understand how they can influence and participate in decision-making. Schools are already expected to promote the spiritual, moral, social and cultural development of pupils and, within this, fundamental British values" (Prevent 2015, 8–9). The Department of Education also supplies schools and childcare centres with standard guidance and practical resource packs on the Prevent duties.

Nevertheless, as Davies (2008) noted, any such educational efforts in relation to schools need constantly to keep abreast of the fast-moving extra-curricular global communications technologies (e.g. Internet, social media), a theme identified earlier by UNESCO (2003, clause 17), in its nine priorities for the development of new educational approaches and teaching materials to combat intolerance and extremism.

In addition, policies of tolerance and inclusion in schools whereby all faiths are welcomed may be in danger of being inverted by determined parents and their supporters whose views and beliefs are intolerant and exclusive (Bennett 2018). Cases have been cited by the chief inspector of Ofsted (Office for Standards in Education) (Spielman 2018), who accused some parents and community leaders of seeing schools as vehicles "to indoctrinate impressionable minds with extremist ideology". She called on head teachers to face down and "tackle those who actively undermine British values". Further, she urged "Rather than adopting a passive liberalism, that says 'anything goes' for fear of causing offence, school leaders should be promoting a muscular liberalism".

The development among school children of constructively critical analytical skills advocated by Davies raises a parallel concern about university students. However, in recent years, the problem has been much less to do with such students becoming far-right enthusiasts (although a minority appear to have been), and much more to do with a growing tendency to protest and demand that university lecturers must not include any content in their lectures that these so-called 'snowflake' students consider objectionable, and that university authorities should ban lecturers or speakers whose intellectual views they do not like. Numerous press articles, on both sides of the Atlantic, attest to the level of concern, e.g. Burden (2018); Collins (2017), Fox (2016), Heller (2016), Sullivan (2018), and Turner (2017). In the polarised yah-boo 'snowflake' setting in universities, what emerges is not uplifting (Barber 2017; Turner 2017).

Turner (2017) reported that the Universities Minister in Britain now required universities to uphold free speech on campus or face being blacklisted, fined, suspended, or ultimately deregistered by OFS. Thus, combatting pathological or extreme ideologies at university level has become complicated by a battle of contradictory certitudes that seeks not to inform, enlighten, engage, and persuade by strength of facts and argument, but to bully, banish, and expunge with the weight of self-absorbed ignorance. For the time being, it would seem that success for an educational strategy at this level against far-right extremism will remain muted.

In the UK, the Prevent (2011) strategy drawn up by government addressed all forms of radicalisation and extremism, not just far-right. As mentioned above, it included a clear educational focus (Prevent 2015), but the latter addressed only one of Prevent's three over-riding objectives, namely supporting sectors and institutions where there are risks of radicalisation. Prevent as a whole has been criticised by prominent politicians such as Diane Abbott MP (e.g. Khomami 2016) for allegedly failing to effectively rein in the rise of the far-right. Essentially, Prevent is a multi-pronged multi-agency political strategy devolved to local authorities which, in addition to educational initiatives, involves schools, the police, community workers, and a wide range of local voluntary projects (*BBC* 2017). Latest government figures (Home Office 2018) for the period 2015 to 2016 show that more than one third of referrals to Prevent related to far-right concerns.

While UK educational strategies to prevent extremism, such as Prevent (2015) and Davies (2008), may be working at school and community levels and, according to Lambert (2017), at non-university further education level, it would be optimistic to expect large numbers of committed Alt-Right and far- and extreme-right adults in the population at large to convert into moderates as result of educational efforts. As Johnson (2017) observed on US strategies against the far-right, "We sometimes assume that education works such that if people know better, they will do better. We ask, 'How can we train people out of this?' We are missing so much because our strategies have been limited". Some adults may respond to education, and some may even undergo a dramatic conversion and then work tirelessly to counter far-right extremism (e.g. Small Steps 2018). While necessary and to be encouraged, such educational efforts are unlikely to persuade the majority of hard-core far-right activists to recant, de-radicalize, and convert to moderate attitudes and behaviour. For these, perhaps realistically only a combination of containment and punishment is possible.

Political and Economic Strategies to Combat the Alt-Right Threat

The strategies considered in this section are those that could be adopted by mainstream and moderate politicians. Grassroots political strategies, mass political opposition and similar actions are discussed in a later section. In pursuit of the objectives set out at the start of this chapter, this section is concerned with three time scales:

- What can be done immediately.
- From a US perspective, what is needed in the short to medium term to (among other things) prevent Trump's re-election in 2020 (and the consequent further institutional solidification of the Alt-Right).
- What can be done to arrest the longer term rightward shift globally, of which the US Alt-Right and Trump are currently prominent indicators.

Tackling the Alt-Right Overall

By analogy with economics, factors contributing to the rise of the extreme right (and which also can be targeted to counter it) may be categorised as supply-side or demand-side (Mudde and Kaltwasser 2017). The supply-side comprises what is provided or offered to the electorate: that is, the populist leader or leaders, and the messages and promises made. The demand-side constitutes the characteristics and circumstances of the electorate that lead them to find these messages relatively appealing. Mudde and Kaltwasser identified four sectors within the institutions of mainstream politics that are able to challenge the supply side of extreme-right politics: (1) mainstream politicians, (2) institutions dedicated to protecting fundamental rights, (3) news media, and (4) supranational institutions. Politicians and influential people and organizations in other countries should be added as a fifth category. This section concentrates on political institutions, but inevitably touches on all the above institutions, which are addressed in other sections. It is logical to begin with the demand side, to review the concerns and characteristics of the people that politicians need to address with the messages and policies they supply.

There is a broad consensus that economic inequality is a main contributor to the rise of the far-right. Vast amounts of evidence, presented by Piketty (2014), Stiglitz (2013), and others, demonstrate this strong association and make the case for policies of investment, stimulation and growth, and more progressive tax structures, in place of long-term austerity. These findings are supported and extended by Wilkinson and Pickett's (2010) similarly huge international data set showing a strong relationship between economic inequality on the one hand, and various measures of mental and physical health, personal and social wellbeing, and (most relevant here) trust, social cohesion and political stability, on the other. A second factor, closely related and also widely commented on, is the sense of alienation from mainstream politics and politicians, and being left behind, culturally as well as economically. As Kaltwasser (2017, 500) said, "Many citizens are angry at the establishment and feel betrayed by mainstream political forces". The effect has been described as "a crisis of political legitimacy" (Hawkins et al. 2017), and its importance in fuelling the rise of populism around the world has been widely noted. The point was demonstrated vividly in chapter 3 of Vol 1 by Hochschild's (2016) research in rust-belt America where people reported feeling like 'strangers in their own land'. A third, and also related factor, is the vast political gulf in American society, from the government down. When politicians can barely agree on anything, including a budget, it is not surprising that many people completely reject those on the other side of the political fence, believing that they have nothing in common and nothing to say. Linked to this is a fourth point that is a main part of the reasons for this rejection; the huge gap in values and moral concerns that divides Americans. Fifth, there is no doubt, as previous chapters have shown, that public life has been morally degraded by the culture of fake news and post-truth. There is also the deeper problem, touched on in chapter 11 in Vol 1, labelled by political philosopher Michael Sandel (2013, 13) as "the moral vacancy of contemporary politics", and related to what he called 'market triumphalism'—the belief that all of our interactions can be governed by market mechanisms. These are the themes, emerging from earlier chapters, to which politicians need to respond.

Moving to the supply side, it is clear at the outset that in the US the Republican Party during the Trump administration has had much greater power than the Democrats to deal with all of these five demand themes and thus limit the Alt-Right threat. Not only have the Republicans had a monopoly of power in government, but also membership of the Alt-Right overlaps with that of the Republican Party. It is clear also that Trump, the Alt-Right figurehead, was able to retain power both in the short and longer term, not just because he retained grassroots support, but also because he has had the continuing support of most of the Republican Party establishment. Around the world, despite occasional instances of mainstream political parties forming alliances with the far-right in order to moderate their actions, by far the most common strategy has been to refuse alliances and directly attack them (Mudde and Kaltwasser 2017). Examples are the response of all British parties, including the Conservatives, to such far-right parties as British National Party, and the Belgian cordon sanitaire around the far-right VB (Vlaams Belang), with refusal of any collaboration.

Similarly, as discussed in chapter 9, the Dutch mainstream parties rejected any collaboration or collusion with the populist PVV and far-right parties. However, applying the 'poldering' concept (Bruning 2016), the mainstream parties instead chose to absorb the Alt-Right ideas of such parties and present them as their own, arguably as a cynical attempt to appease and attract populist voters. Thus, noble attempts at engagement with and inclusion of Alt-Right opponents in mainstream political processes may unintentionally result in a rightward shift of mainstream parties' centre of political gravity—not what these parties really want but exactly what the Alt-Right parties want as a stepping stone to a more permanent far-right governance. Clearly, great care and caution are required in any attempts to attenuate radical-right parties by engagement and inclusion.

Tackling the US Alt-Right

In America, however, mainstream Republicans (both politicians and supporters) have chosen overwhelmingly to collude with the Alt-Right, as represented by the Trump administration. Republican politicians—including Senators Bob Corker, Ted Cruz, Lyndsey Graham, Rand Paul and Marco Rubio—who earlier opposed Trump's presidential nomination and criticized him, but then joined his administration, or just stopped criticizing, may have been seeking to moderate his views and actions. Alternatively, of course, they may have been less principled, simply seizing the opportunity to gain or retain power. This second interpretation is more plausible. With few dissenters, the Republican Party stood by as Trump repeatedly displayed bigotry, ignorance and contempt for science, facts, and the compromises required for democracy to function.

Support for Trump is robust. Coppins and Godfrey (2017) investigated Republican Party support for him, focusing on his statements after the violence and killing at the Charlottesville rally in August 2017 and, in particular, his failure for four days to voice any condemnation of the violent white supremacists, and then to do so only in the most reluctant and insincere manner. They asked 146 Republican state party Chairs and National Committee members two questions: whether they were satisfied with the President's response, and whether they approved of his comment that there were "some very fine people" who marched alongside the Ku Klux Klan and neo-Nazis. Only seven of the 146 expressed any criticism or disagreement. Chapter 3 of Vol 1 showed how the party has moved over several decades to a position of extreme nationalism, but even so, other chapters have also shown that the recent rise of the Alt-Right and the Trump presidency represented a step change. As Republican politicians turned a blind eye to Trump's repeated assaults on truth, tradition and morality, they placed the short-term success of their party and their own political careers before the values espoused in the American Constitution, and before military and climate security. As Freedland (2017) said, Trump is the face and voice of a deeper Republican malaise that has been evident for several decades, as described in Vol 1 chapter 3.

It seems unlikely, therefore, that Republican politicians and mainstream Republican supporters will rediscover the party's deepest values and oppose Trump and the Alt-Right. However, there is still the remote possibility that, if things in the Trump White House worsened further, mainstream Republican politicians might decide that enough is enough. A number of potential breaking points emerge. First, Trump might adopt a more reckless and aggressive stance, perhaps towards North Korea or Iran, leading to military action, or the imminent threat of it. Second, Trump might go beyond his previous history of derogatory remarks about judges who hand down decisions that are inconvenient for him, and interfere actively in the judicial process. This would be a direct assault on American democracy and the rule of law. Third, if extreme weather events and the resultant damage continue or worsen, and as more and more scientific evidence of human-induced climate change accumulates, it might become impossible to avoid facing the devastating and complex consequences of climate change denial. Fourth, if the President showed further and more explicit support for white supremacists and other anti-democratic movements, the resulting widening divisions and the risk of civil unrest would become inescapable. Fifth, although Robert Mueller's investigation into alleged collusion between the Trump team and high level Russian actors aiming to influence the outcome of the 2016 presidential election had not concluded at the time of writing, its findings might expose Trump and close associates to charges of unconstitutional or illegal conduct. The response of Trump and his supporters to such an outcome is unpredictable, but clearly any attempts to evade due legal process would likely meet powerful opposition. According to Cohen (2018), the institutions of government on which the President depends are demoralized by his behaviour rather than being swayed to support him. These institutions are unlikely to crumble or give way easily under pressure from the President. However, none of these potential breakpoints can be relied upon. Other political strategies must be considered.

For now, by far the most likely source of opposition to Trump and the Alt-Right is the Democratic Party. Supply-side strategies by them would need to address the demand factors summarised, aiming first to challenge the messages blaming the establishment, previous governments, immigrants and black people for economic decline and cultural changes. Second, they would need to tackle the enormous influence of Donald Trump, whose charisma, plain speaking and ability to empathize with ordinary people, have clearly magnified the impact of these messages. Making such challenges effective is enormously difficult, and a different approach is needed from the one led by Hillary Clinton in the 2016 Presidential contest. A different message and a different messenger, both of which are able to engage with Republican supporters, would be essential components of a successful challenge. The Democratic party has been concerned rightly with possible illegal interference with the 2016 Presidential election, but perhaps insufficiently concerned to examine what the party itself might have got wrong (Lears 2018), and what it needs to do differently to strengthen resistance to Trump and the Alt-Right, both in the immediate term and in order to win the 2020 election. Four areas for action emerge that will last beyond the contemporary Trump era.

First, learning not only from Trump's success but also from the growing world-wide worries about the negative consequences of economic globalization and neo-liberalism, there is an urgent need for the party to review its economic policies. A longer-term economic strategy is needed that is optimistic but realistic and which, unlike Trump's, would lift people in the economic middle and bottom, as well as achieving growth, and with fairer tax structures. The Democrats may need to proclaim policies centred on longer term investment, especially in rust-belt areas suffering from industrial decline which makes them responsive to Trump's promises to make America great again. Such policies would provide economic security and would be fairer and thus contribute to repairing social divisions and distress. It will be essential to explain how this approach will yield lasting and widespread gains, in contrast to Trump's support for such twilight industries as coal mining, the economic benefits of which inevitably will be short-term and will also exacerbate climate change.

Second, the Democratic Party's campaigning style and the style of its candidates would need to counter the perceived remoteness of mainstream politicians. Both the messenger and the message are central to Trump's continuing popularity. There are lessons here also from the Brexit campaign in Britain. The Remain campaign concentrated on predicted economic damage from Brexit, but the crucial factors favouring the Leave side seem to have been less tangible, more basic and emotional: freedom for Britain to make its own decisions and close its borders rather than obeying European Union bureaucrats, even if Britons are worse off as a result. Defeating the radical right in Europe and America requires energetic use of the range of media, and more attention to emotions and values as well as economic facts and promises.

Next, emotional and moral divisions need to be overcome, especially in America. Opposition politicians should take more account of the values of people likely to be attracted to the Alt-Right. Haidt's (2012) research, discussed in chapter 2 and Vol 1 chapter 3, revealed that the value sets of Americans on the political left and right are so different that they hardly overlap, and the result is little mutual understanding or respect, let alone room for agreement. Mainstream politicians on both the left and the right need to acknowledge and respect the importance of individual freedom, nationalism, loyalty and authority to very many people. These are the values that are distorted and used to draw people into the Alt-Right. In a similar vein, considering possible actions by other politically concerned people, as well as politicians, Neiwert (2017) and other writers reviewed in the Grassroots section below saw a great need for closer connection with the concerns of blue collar Trump supporters. These approaches aimed at bridging the political and social divide are all much needed for several purposes—to challenge the rise of the Alt-Right in the immediate term, as part of a strategy for the next election, and, in the longer term, beyond electoral politics to rebuild social harmony.

Lastly, there are the problems of the erosion of moral standards in public life. There is a clear need not just to show understanding of such right wing values as loyalty and authority, but also to promote and display other shared values that are threatened but perhaps hidden rather than destroyed by the post-truth culture. Politicians and other opinion leaders could, and arguably should, do more to counteract the slide of public morals that has been visible alongside and within this culture. Doing so requires the perhaps optimistic assumption that most people, of almost all political shades, share the belief that truth is better than lies, and share a desire to do what is right, rather than what just benefits them. These values are easily drowned out by the loud public voices of selfishness and political convenience, but they could begin to be revived if mainstream politicians took pains to demonstrate honesty, consistency, transparency and concern for others in both actions and words.

Turning from political institutions, Mudde and Kaltwasser's (2017) second sector is institutions whose function is the protection of fundamental rights. The most powerful of these in America is the Supreme Court. Its independence was demonstrated when it struck down Trump's travel ban on people from six Muslim-majority countries (although in December 2017 it allowed a revised version of the ban to be imposed until multiple legal challenges are resolved). Its independence is not assured, however (see Vol 1 chapter 10). New nominations have to be approved by the Senate, and this approval process was handled differently in 2016, following the sudden death of a Supreme Court judge. For the first time, the Republican-dominated Senate refused even to grant Obama's nomination a hearing. As discussed in Vol 1 chapter 11, for liberal democracy to function requires the acceptance of norms and conventions as well as compliance with legal necessities. Levitsky and Zitblatt (2018) saw this erosion of state institutional norms, such as the treatment of Obama's Supreme Court nominee, as the greatest threat to American democracy and mainstream politics.

The third sector is the news media, whose importance in the rise of Trump and the Alt-Right has been widely discussed. Van Donselaar (2003), reviewing European responses to the radical right, suggested influencing public opinion through education as an effective method, but with the news media in America and widely elsewhere firmly controlled by the political right, this is difficult. Political strategies to limit the Alt-Right threat therefore must pay close attention to the media. The survival of democracy requires governments to legislate to ensure politically diverse news media in the face of the continual advance of *Fox News* and other right-wing sources. Such interventions are discussed in detail in earlier sections of this chapter.

The fourth sector, supranational organisations, such as the European Union (EU), the Organization of American States, and the United Nations, can bring moral pressure, retaining and displaying the values of internationalism and mutual aid which Trump and the Alt-Right reject with their America-first approach. It might be argued that moral pressure is unlikely to have any effect, precisely because it is this moral stance that is being rejected. At the very least, however, these supranational organizations should ensure that they do not follow the new American path or show active support for it. Maintaining their existing principles will also provide a message of hope and encouragement to the American opposition to the Alt-Right. The same considerations apply to politicians and other leaders outside America.

This section concludes with only guarded optimism. The greatest potential to counter US Alt-Right risks rests with the Republican Party, but so far this Party has overwhelmingly colluded with them, and ordinary Republican voters are largely untroubled by Trump and his support for the Alt-Right. The possibility of change in the Republican Party remains nevertheless. For the Democratic Party opposition, much evidence is available on the reasons for the rise of Trump and the Alt-Right, and for their Party's failure in the 2016 election. There is much they could do to improve their standing in opposition and in preparation for the next Presidential election and beyond.

Grassroots and Mass Action Strategies

Although the nature and causes of populism are the subject of much recent research, as Kaltwasser (2017) remarked, there is little research on how to respond to them. History may be instructive though. In the case of grassroots actions in relation to extremist right wing political movements, twentieth century history contains powerful and glaring object lessons. The importance of mass support in the rise of radical right political leaders is illustrated by the familiar but still striking newsreels of the adulation of Hitler and Mussolini, and it is unlikely that the adulation was all based on fear. There is a pressing need to learn, firstly because of the similarities, noted by Neiwert (2017) and others, between Trump's style and rise and those of familiar right-wing demagogues. Like twentieth century (and contemporary) demagogues, Trump retains strong core support in the face of repeated inconsistencies and demonstrated falsehoods. A survey (Blakely 2018) found that nine out of ten Republican voters believed Trump's first year a success, and four out of ten called it "a major success". In addition, the current rise of the far-right internationally, along with the changing geopolitical power balance, signals a troubled and uncertain historical period. We need to learn everything possible to deal with these threats.

Grassroots and mass actions refer here to what ordinary people rather than politicians and decision makers can do. Timothy Snyder (2017, 9) summarised how history can help: "History does not repeat, but it does instruct". Snyder drew twenty lessons from the politics of the twentieth century to guide actions against what he saw as a serious current threat of tyranny. The central idea, emphasised concisely by Stephan and Snyder (2017), is that tyrants' tactics, and the road to tyranny, require the consent of large numbers of people e.g. contemporary Russia. Conversely, and most importantly here, it should be possible for tyranny to be thwarted by grassroots movements and mass withholding of consent. The first lesson therefore is: don't obey in advance. This means taking stock of existing values and the existing sense of patriotism rather than unthinkingly accepting new standards and new interpretations of patriotism. Hitler's rise was made easier, for instance, by 'anticipatory obedience' on the part of ordinary Austrians even before the Anschluss (annexation) of Austria. A second main theme in Snyder's often overlapping twenty lessons is personal courage. It often requires bravery to stand up and express a contrary opinion, to display a political poster when your neighbours all disagree, to object to racist or otherwise offensive statements, or to remove offensive material on public display. Courage may be aided by the realisation that if nothing is done, and the Alt-Right threat continues to grow, public life will become much more constrained and so, if opposition is delayed, it will require much more courage later, or will become simply impossible.

Another broad recommendation is civil resistance, and specifically non-violent resistance. There is strong evidence for the effectiveness of non-violent refusal to comply with anti-democratic government actions and new unacceptable norms. In an international study of 323 violent and non-violent resistance campaigns from 1900 to 2006, Stephan and Chenoweth (2008) found that 53% of the non-violent campaigns succeeded, compared with 26% of those who offered violent resistance. They argued first that non-violence enhances domestic and international legitimacy, and encourages wider participation and therefore greater pressure on the government. Second, when a non-violent rather than violent campaign is met with state violence and repression, the state action tends to backfire, reducing government support both domestically and abroad. A third theme from Snyder is defending institutions. When politicians or news media chip away at the independence of the judiciary, for instance (which Trump repeatedly comes close to, as noted earlier), this must be vigorously opposed. Every encroachment of this kind makes the next one less noticeable and therefore easier to get away with. Fourth, large numbers engaging in civil resistance and attracting the participation of diverse groups can separate authoritarian rulers from such pillars of support as economic elites, government workers and even the armed forces. The involvement of large numbers allows the growth of a virtuous circle, not only in terms of further increasing numbers but also by empowering other groups and influential people who are likely to be invigorated and their voices amplified. Snyder (2017) and Stephan and Snyder (2017) stressed the need for a longer-term and strategic approach. This means persevering in the face of short-term setbacks, and learning from similar events and experiences elsewhere, noting the huge information resources that are now immediately accessible.

Other points are about uniting in opposition. This involves concerned people channelling their fears, anger, and frustration into constructive action by joining appropriate civil or political groups. Such collective action brings collateral social and psychological gains, as well as being more effective politically. Sennett (2013), for example, reviewed extensive historical and sociological evidence on the benefits of cooperation as opposed to isolation or competition. The most basic kind of constructive, collaborative, grassroots political action is voting, and of course if all the people who are now horrified by Trump as President had voted in the 2016 election, he would have got nowhere near the Presidency. Voting, rightly seen as a civic duty, is a small action with great importance in safeguarding the health of all democracies, beyond the current dangers posed by Trump and the Alt-Right. Uniting also involves collaboration between opposition groups and movements. It is obvious that disunity very often hinders opposition and liberation movements.

The idea of unity links also to the vast and potentially dangerous social and political divide in America. An important suggestion concerning a possible additional cause of this divide was made by Parker (2018), seeking to understand why, in spite of decades-long general shifts in values towards tolerance and social liberalism, anti-democratic beliefs persist in what he called 'the mass public'. Parker suggested, on the basis of current research, that reactionary conservatism is passed from one generation to the next. The lesson he drew is that this effect will diminish with the continuing relative shrinking of the white, Anglo-Saxon, Christian, heterosexual, native-born demographic segment in America. This could take many years, however, and much damage could be done by the Alt-Right in the interim. Another possible lesson is that this tentative finding reinforces the need for engagement with this group. Neiwert (2017) also advised empathy rather than rejection of, or disconnection from, the concerns of blue collar Trump supporters. He argued that it need not be inconsistent or insincere for liberals to pay explicit respect to some central traditional rural values, such as community, common decency and respect for traditions. A related recommendation was made by Mudde and Kaltwasser (2017)—engaging with populists such as the Alt-Right by taking into account issues raised by them, rather than seeking to ostracize or fully oppose them. One aim of all such approaches would be to undermine the populist depiction of remote comfortable elites. Neiwert (2017, 371) expressed it thus: "If Americans of goodwill—including mainstream conservatives who recognise how their movement has been hijacked by radicals—can learn to start talking to each other again, and maybe even pull a few Alt-Americans out of their abyss along the way, then perhaps we can start to genuinely heal our divisions instead of relegating each other into social oblivion and, maybe eventually, civil war". Neiwert (2017, 372) went on to advocate "powerful non-defensive communication" as a style of talking to Alt-Right supporters. This involves gathering information, genuinely trying to understand the views expressed, and seeking to make the interaction a dialogue. Lilla (2017), castigating Democrats for their fragmentation into the identity politics of interest groups, urged them to "come down from the pulpit" to mix with Republican supporters. These proposals may all seem unrealistic, and such interactions may be unsuccessful or even counter-productive if handled badly, as van der Valk warned (see chapter 9), but Neiwert's worry is evidently that the current situation is so serious and dangerous that all reasonable remedies should be tried.

To conclude this section, history suggests that grassroots and mass actions have great potential, which is often unrealised. Compliance and inaction, and therefore the failure of opposition to the rise of the Alt-Right, are common, and for good reasons, some of which are clear. Resistance requires engagement and empathy with political opponents, and also commitment, courage and organization—often in greater quantities than people are able or prepared to give. However, every person who makes a contribution in these ways makes it easier for others, and more likely that others will follow. Each grassroots effort can therefore be seen as potentially doubled, and so is doubly worthwhile.

Conclusion

The evidence clearly suggests that the Alt-Right in western liberal democracies is not a movement whose often passionate beliefs are all benign and who always offer a reasonable, fair, just, and necessary antidote to liberal ideas and mainstream governance. Although the Alt-Right portrays itself as society's saviour, it deviates from and resides outside traditional conservatism which it seeks to subvert. Overall,

Alt-Right ideology requires widening of social inequalities, so that Alt-Right protagonists and their 'heroes' (winners/predators) are able to dominate society, government, and the economy and grab the benefits, all at the expense of their enemies (losers/victims) i.e. the vulnerable, the poor, immigrants, minorities, and anyone not sharing an Alt-Right world-view. The Trump presidency has provided one clear example of this, others being the current ruling regimes in Austria and Hungary, the AfD party in Germany, and the Lega Nord/M5S coalition in Italy. The more extreme elements of the Alt-Right seek to impose a minority world-view on the majority of the population (just as do the hard-left and IS). Overall, Alt-Right leaders, advocates, and opinion formers seek to subvert, persuade, and as necessary bully, mainstream and populist conservatives to permanently shift their allegiance firmly towards the far-right. The Alt-Right consider any and all means to be permissible in pursuit of their ends, which includes both flagrant and subtle defamation in the form of fake global conspiracy propaganda against Jews and Muslims, a warning eloquently put by Finkelstein (2018). For the far- and extreme-right elements, intimidation, hate crimes and violence are also acceptable tactics. Subversion and manipulation of representative democracy to gain power and influence is a hallmark of the Alt-Right (as it is also of the hard-left).

To combat such a multi-facetted determined threat on the scale posed by the Alt-Right in recent years requires an equally determined and multi-facetted response. There are no panaceas or easy solutions. All of the categories and kinds of defence strategy suggested in this final chapter will be needed and applied in the best combinations identifiable. In this battle of moderation against authoritarianism and extremism, there is no guarantee that success will always result. Inevitably, some initiatives will fail but, overall, the weight of determination and momentum will seek to ensure all the rest succeed. The Ofsted chair called for "muscular liberalism" to combat intolerance (Spielman 2018). Certainly, in combatting a strident and emboldened Alt-Right, muscular moderation needs to replace the quiet laissez-faire tolerance of the moderate majority, lest it be mistaken for acquiescence, weakness and lack of resolve. However, muscular moderation must not be allowed to descend into a blanket oppressive or repressive intolerance no better than that of the Alt-Right. Nor, in the thirst for votes, should mainstream parties allow engagement and inclusion of the populist Alt-Right to displace moderate policies in favour of harsh or pathological ones.

References

Abramovitz, M.J. 2018. "Democracy in Crisis". *Freedom in the World 2018.* Washington DC: Freedom House. www.freedomhouse.org.

ADL. 2018. *Murder and Extremism in the United States in 2017.* ADL Center on Extremism Report. New York: Anti-Defamation League.

Barber, M. 2017. "Universities Must be Places of Intellectual Discomfort". *Time Higher Education.* November 23, 2017. https://timeshighereducation.com/.

BBC. 2017. "Reality Check: What is the Prevent Strategy?" *BBC News.* June 4, 2017. http://www.bbc.co.uk/.

Bennett, R. 2018. "Extremists Use Schools to 'Pervert' Education. British Values Undermined, Warns Ofsted Chief". *The Times.* February 1, 2018. Page 1.

Blakely, R. 2018. "Trump's First Year has been a Political Circus Like no Other". *The Times,* January 20, 2018.

Bruning, H. 2016. "Polder and Politics". *Open Democracy.* February 25, 2016. https://www.opendemocracy.net/.

Burden, E. 2018. "Rees-Mobbed as Event Turns Nasty". *The Times.* February 3, 2018. Page 5.

Capoccia, G. 2005. *Defending Democracy: Reactions to Extremism in Inter-War Europe.* Baltimore: John Hopkins University Press.

Capoccia, G. 2013. "Militant Democracy: the Institutional Bases of Democratic Self-Preservation". *Annual Review of Law and Social Science,* Vol 9, 207–226.

Chan, S.P. 2011. "History of Corporate Manslaughter: Five Key Cases". *The Telegraph.* February 18, 2011.

Coates, S. and Blakely, R. 2018. "May: Investors Must Force Tech Giants to Ban Extreme Content". *The Times.* January 25, 2018. Page 1.

Cohen, E. 2018. "Trump's Lucky Year: Why the Chaos Can't Last". *Foreign Affairs,* January 20, 2018.

Collins, P. 2017. "Snowflake Students Must Learn How to Argue". *The Times.* October 20, 2017. www.thetimes.co.uk.

Coppins, M. and Godfrey, E. 2017. "The Republican Establishment Stands behind Trump". *The Atlantic,* August 24, 2017.

Copsey, N., Dack, J., Littler, M. et al. 2013. *Anti-Muslim Hate Crime and the Far Right.* Report 3, June 2013. Centre for Fascist, Anti-Fascist, and Post-Fascist Studies. Teesside University.

CPS. 2018. *Corporate Manslaughter.* Crown Prosecution Service. https://www.cps.gov.uk/. Accessed January 25, 2018.

CSC. 2017. *Hate and Abuse on Social Media.* Commons Select Committee on Home Affairs. UK Parliament. April 27, 2017. https://publications.parliament.uk/pa/cm201617/cmselect/cmhaff/609/60904.htm. Accessed January 25, 2018.

D'Arcy, S. 2017. "Jayda Fransen: Deputy Leader of Far-Right Group Britain First Arrested Over Speech in Belfast". *The Independent.* November 19, 2017. http://www.theindependent.co.uk/.

DARE. 2017a. *Modernising Education in European Democracies.* DARE communication to the European Parliament on modernisation of education. November 24, 2017. Democracy and Human Rights Education in Europe. Berlin: DARE.

DARE. 2017b. *Dialogue About Radicalisation and Equality.* European Commission Horizon 2020 Research and Innovation Program. Grant Number 725349. Manchester UK: University of Manchester.

Davies, L. 2008. *Educating Against Extremism.* Stoke-on-Trent UK: Trentham Books. www.ucl-ioe-press.com.

Dearden, L. 2018. "Finsbury Park Attack Trial Live: Witnesses Describe Darren Osborne's Alleged Van Ramming to Court". *The Independent.* January 24, 2018. http://www.theindependent.co.uk/.

Dror, I.E. and Fraser-Mackenzie, P.A.F. 2008. "Cognitive Biases in Human Perception, Judgment, and Decision Making: Bridging Theory and the Real World". In *Criminal Investigative Failures,* edited by Kim Rossmo, 53–67. Abingdon Oxon UK: Taylor & Francis.

ECHR. 1953. *European Convention on Human Rights.* Strasbourg: Council of Europe.

EHRC. 2015. *Freedom of Expression.* Equality and Human Rights Commission. February 2015. Manchester UK: EHRC. https://www.equalityhumanrights.com/.

EU. 2008. *EU Framework Decision on Combating Forms and Expressions of Racism and Xenophobia by Means of Criminal Law.* Council of EU. 2008/913/JHA. November 28, 2008. Brussels: EU.

Ferguson, A. 2017. "Britain First leader and Deputy Charged by Police in Belfast". *The Guardian.* December 14, 2017. www.theguardian.com/.

Finkelstein, D. 2018. "George Soros and the Roots of Antisemitism". *The Times.* February 14, 2018. Page 27. https://www.thetimes.co.uk/.

Fox, C. 2016. "Generation Snowflake: How we Train our Kids to be Censorious Cry-Babies". *The Spectator.* June 4, 2016. www.spectator.co.uk.

FPL. 1881. *Loi sur la Liberté de la Presse.* 29 July 1881. Subsumed within 1990 law. Paris: Legifrance. https://www.legifrance.gouv.fr/. Accessed January 23, 2018.

Freedland, J. 2017. "Donald Trump isn't the Only Villain—the Republican Party Shares the Blame". *The Guardian*, March 3, 2017.

Freilich, J. D., Chermak, S.M. Gruenewald, J. et al. 2014. *Far-Right Violence in the United States: 1990–2013.* National Consortium for the Study of Terrorism and Responses to Terrorism (START). June 2014. College Park, MD: START.

Gibbons, K. 2018a. "Drain the Swamp or Lose Advertising, Tech Giants Warned". *The Times.* February 13, 2018. Page 10. https://www.thetimes.co.uk/.

Gibbons, K. 2018b. "Britain First Pair Jailed for Harassment". *The Times.* March 8, 2018. Page 17. https://www.thetimes.co.uk/.

Gibbs, S. 2017. "EU Warns Tech Firms: Remove Extremist Content Faster or be Regulated". *The Guardian.* December 7, 2017. www.theguardian.com/.

Griffin, A. 2017. "Theresa May to Create New Internet that would be Controlled and Regulated by Government". *The Independent.* May 19, 2017. www.theindependent.co.uk.

Hackenbroich, J. and Shapiro, J. 2018. *Opportunities Amid Disorder: Europe and the World in 2018.* European Council on Foreign Relations. London: ECFR.

Haidt, J. 2012. *The Righteous Mind: Why Good People are Divided by Politics and Religion.* London: Allen Lane.

Hamilton, F. 2018a. "EDL Founder Jailed for Court Rant". *The Times.* May 30, 2018. Page 7.

Hamilton, F. 2018b. "'Neo-Nazi' On Trial Over Plot to Murder MP". *The Times.* June 13, 2018. Page 5.

Hamilton, F. and Gardham, D. 2018. "Far-Right Plotter Wanted Police to Kill Him". *The Times.* June 14, 2018. Page 19.

Hamilton, F. and Johnston, N. 2018. "Killer's Hatred Fuelled by Web Searches for Far-Right Leader". *The Times.* February 2, 2018. Page 7.

Hansard. 2016. "Prevention and Suppression of Terrorism". House of Commons. *Hansard.* December 14, 2016. www.parliament.uk.

Hare, J.P. 2017. *Strategies Against the Far Right. Reporting Back and Moving Forward.* Conference June 15–18, 2017. Conference proceedings. S. Ehmsen and A. Scharenberg (eds). New York: Rosa Luxemburg Stiftung.

Hawkins, K., Read, M., and Pauwels, T. 2017. "Populism and its Causes". In *The Oxford Handbook of Populism*, edited by C.R. Kaltwasser, P. Taggart, P.O. Espejo and P. Ostiguy. Oxford: Oxford University Press.

Heller, N. 2016. "The Big Uneasy—What's Roiling the Liberal-Arts Campus?" *The New Yorker.* May 30, 2016. www.newyorker.com.

HoC. 2018. *Disinformation and 'Fake News': Interim Report.* Digital, Culture, Media and Sports Committee. Report HC 363. July 29, 2018. London: House of Commons.

Hochschild, A.R. 2016. *Strangers in Their Own Land: Anger and Mourning on the American Right*. New York: The New Press.

Home Office. 2018. "New Figures Show Improved Referrals to Prevent and Rise in Far-Right Concerns". Press Release. March 27, 2018. *Home Office*. London. https://www.gov.uk.

Hopkins, S. 2016. "Britain First leader Paul Golding and Deputy Leader Jayda Fransen Arrested Following Luton 'Christian Patrol'". *The Huffington Post*. February 15, 2016.

Howard, P. and Kollanyi, B. 2017. "Who was Fed Most Junk News in the US election? It was Swing-State Voters". *The Observer*, October 1, 2017.

Johnson, T. 2017. "Fighting the Right Through Education". In *Strategies Against the Far Right. Reporting Back and Moving Forward*. Conference June 15–18, 2017. Conference proceedings, edited by S. Ehmsen and A. Scharenberg, 14–15. New York: Rosa Luxemburg Stiftung.

Kaltwasser, C.R. 2017. "Populism and the Question of How to Respond to It". In *The Oxford Handbook of Populism*, edited by C.R. Kaltwasser, P. Taggart, P.O. Espejo and P. Ostiguy. Oxford: Oxford University Press.

Khomami, N. 2016. "Prevent Strategy Failing to Rein in Rise of UK's Far Right, says Diane Abbott". *The Guardian*. November 21, 2016. https://www.theguardian.com/.

Lambert, S. 2017. "In Defence of Prevent: Why Britain's Anti-Radicalisation Strategy Must be Reformed Rather than Scrapped". *FE News*. December 20, 2017.

Lears, J. 2018. "What We Don't Talk About When We Talk About Russian Hacking". *London Review of Books*, 40(1), January 4, 2018, 15–18.

Levitsky, S. and Zitblatt, D. 2018. *How Democracies Die: What History Reveals About Our Future*. New York: Crown.

Lilla, M. 2017. *The Once and Future Liberal: After Identity Politics*. New York: HarperCollins.

Lusher, A. 2017. "EDL Founder Tommy Robinson to Address One of America's Most Prestigious Universities". *The Independent*. October 9, 2017. www.theindependent.co.uk.

MoJ. 2008. *Corporate Manslaughter and Corporate Homicide Act 2007*. Circular. February 19, 2008. London: Ministry of Justice.

Mudde, C. and Kaltwasser, C. R. 2017. *Populism: A Very Short Introduction*. Oxford: Oxford University Press.

Nagle, A. 2017. *Kill All Normies: Online Culture Wars from 4chan and tumblr to Trump and the Alt-Right*. Winchester, UK: Zero Books.

Neiwert, D. 2017. *Alt-America—The Rise of the Radical Right in the Age of Trump*. London: Verso.

OSCE. 2011. *Guidelines for Educators on Countering Intolerance and Discrimination Against Muslims: Addressing Islamophobia Through Education. Jointly with Council of Europe and UNESCO.* Office for Democratic Institutions and Human Rights (ODIHR). October 28, 2011. Warsaw: ODIHR.

Parker, C. 2018. "The Role of the Radical Right in the United States of America". In *The Oxford Handbook of the Radical Right,* edited by J. Rydgren. Oxford: Oxford University Press.

Paterson, S. 2017. "Britain First Deputy Leader Jayda Fransen Arrested for Appearing on Neo-Nazi Radio Show while Facing Trial for Causing Religiously Aggravated Harassment". *Daily Mail.* October 15, 2017.

PCPRCI. 2012. *How to Tackle the Far Right—Delusions and New Proposals.* Research and Conference Summary, October 11, 2012. Friedrich Ebert Stiftung and Political Capital Policy Research and Consulting Institute. Budapest: PCPRCI. www.politicalcapital.hu.

Piketty, T. 2014. *Capital in the Twenty-First Century.* Cambridge, MA: Belknap Press.

Prevent. 2015. *The Prevent Duty. Departmental advice for schools and childcare providers.* June 2015. London: Department of Education.

Rawlinson, K. 2018. "Darren Osborne Jailed for Life for Finsbury Park Attack". *The Guardian.* February 2, 2018. https://www.theguardian.com/.

Rees, L. 2005. *The Nazis: A Warning from History.* London: BBC Books.

Roth, K. 2018. "The Pushback Against the Populist Challenge". Pages 1–3. In *World Report 2018—Events of 2017.* Human Rights Watch. New York: HRW.

SC. 2016. *Health & Safety, Corporate Manslaughter, and Food Safety and Hygiene Offences. Sentencing Guideline.* London: Sentencing Council for England and Wales. https://www.sentencingcouncil.org.uk.

Small Steps. 2018. *The Small Steps Story.* London: Small Steps Consultants. https://smallstepsconsultants.com.

Sennett, R. 2013. *Together: The Rituals, Pleasures and Politics of Cooperation.* London: Penguin.

Snyder, T. 2017. *On Tyranny: Twenty Lessons from the Twentieth Century.* London: Bodley Head.

Spielman, A. 2018. *Speech on Diversity, Ethical Leadership and Faith Schools.* HM Chief Inspector, Ofsted. Church of England Foundation for Educational Leadership. February 1, 2018. London: Ofsted.

Stephan, M.J. and Chenoweth, E. 2008. "Why Civil Resistance Works: The Strategic Logic of Nonviolent Conflict". *International Security,* 33(1), 7–44.

Stephan, M.J. and Snyder, T. 2017. "Authoritarianism is Making a Comeback. Here's the Time-Tested Way to Defeat it". *The Guardian,* June 20, 2017.

Stiglitz, J.E. 2013. *The Price of Inequality.* London: Penguin.

Sullivan, A. 2018. "We All Live on Campus Now". *New York Magazine*. February 9, 2018. nymag.com.

Swerling, G. 2018a. "Nazi Spent Seven Months Plotting Gay Massacre". *The Times*. February 6, 2018.

Swerling, C. 2018b. "Nazi Sympathiser Who Plotted Gay Slaughter Detained in Hospital". *The Times*. May 31, 2018. Page 17.

The Economist. 2017. "Do Social Media Threaten Democracy?" *The Economist*. November 4, 2017.

Times. 2018. "Guidance on Proceedings for Contempt of Court". In re Yaxley-Lennon (aka Tommy Robinson). England and Wales Court of Appeal judgement [2018] EWCA Crim 1856 judgement August 1, 2018 published August 9, 2018. Law Report. *The Times*. August 9, 2018. Page 49.

Turner, C. 2017. "Students Should be Made to Feel 'Uncomfortable' So They Can Learn, Chair of Office for Students Says". *The Telegraph*. November 23, 2017. www.telegraph.co.uk.

UN. 1965. *UN International Convention on Elimination of All Forms of Racial Discrimination*. Office of Legal Affairs. New York: UN.

UNESCO. 2003. *Development of an Integrated Strategy to Combat Racism, Discrimination, Xenophobia and Related Intolerance*. General Conference, 32nd Session. Paris: UNESCO. http://www.unesco.org/.

USDoJ. 2018. *Hate Crime Laws*. US Department of Justice. Washington DC. https://www.justice.gov/. Accessed January 23, 2018.

van Donselaar, J. 2003. "Patterns of Response to the Extreme Right in Western Europe". In *Right-Wing Extremism in the Twenty-First Century*, edited by P.H. Merkl and L. Weinberg, 272–292. London: Frank Cass.

Vaughan, D. 1985. *Controlling Unlawful Organizational Behaviour: Social Structure and Corporate Misconduct*. Chicago, Ill: University of Chicago Press.

Vaughan, D. 1996. *The Challenger Launch Decision: Risk, Technology, Culture and Deviance at NASA*. Chicago, Ill: University of Chicago Press.

Walters, M. 2017. "A New Hate Crime Act is Needed to Address Vast 'Justice Gap' for Hate Crime in England and Wales". *International Network for Hate Studies*. www.internationalhatestudies.com. Accessed January 15, 2018.

Walters, M., Wiedlitzka, S., Owusu-Bempah, A. et al. 2017. *Hate Crime and the Legal Process: Options for Law Reform*. October 2017. Brighton UK: University of Sussex.

Wilkinson, R. and Pickett, K. 2010. *The Spirit Level: Why Equality is Better for Everyone*, edited by P. H. Merkl and L. Weinberg. London: Penguin.

York, C. 2016. "Jayda Fransen Guilty: Britain First Deputy Leader Convicted of Religiously Aggravated Harassment". *The Huffington Post*. November 3, 2016.

Glossary

A

ADL: Anti-Defamation League, a US-based organization formed in 1913 and dedicated originally to combatting anti-Semitism in the US. Subsequently, ADL broadened its scope to address all forms of hatred and injustice based on religion, ethnicity, nationality, or minority membership.

AfD: Alternative für Deutschland, the largest populist Alt-Right party in Germany.

Alt-Lite: A notional grouping within the Alt-Right (in the US) that allegedly displays less harsh and more populist characteristics than the far- and extreme-right, as described by the ADL (Anti-Defamation League).

Alternative-Right (Alt-Right): (1) as an ideology, the spectrum of right-wing world-views outside traditional conservatism, which begins with a dissatisfaction with the mainstream political process and character and frustration by perceived impotence of traditional conservatism, and runs through populist, hard-right, ultra-right, and extreme-right ideology; (2) as an identifiable group, those having such world-views.

Aryan Nations: An extremist far-right group in the US, proscribed as a terrorist organization.

Atlanticism: A belief in or support for the mutual benefits of political, economic, and military cooperation between western Europe and the United States i.e. the status quo since 1945.

autochthonous: indigenous; relating to an original native inhabitant.

authoritarianism: (1) A belief in or support for strict obedience to the authority of a particular orthodoxy, dogma, individual, or group, at the expense of personal freedom. (2) The overbearing and intimidating tactics frequently displayed by authoritarians.

autistic hostility: fantasised hostility, whereby an individual imagines that another party is hostile towards them, and so typically provokes a hostile reaction in the individual.

B

bounded rationality The inherent limitations on what an individual or group can know and understand about a particular topic. Decision-making is thus constrained by limited information (which also may be inaccurate or biased), limited capacity to process that information (which capacity may also be subject to biases), and limited time.

Breitbart News: A leading news and propaganda organ of the populist Alt-Right in America.

Brexit: The formal departure of Britain from the European Union, predicated on a referendum vote on June 23, 2016 and the implementation of the departure implementation programme started on March 29, 2017 with a formal Brexit date of March 29, 2019.

Brexiteer: A person strongly committed to Brexit.

C

Charlottesville: A town in Virginia, US, in which on August 12, 2017 far-right militants, some armed with guns and other weapons, attacked a peaceful counter-demonstration. One person was killed when a far-right supporter driving a car deliberately rammed the crowd at speed. Charlottesville became synonymous with civic resistance to far-right violence and intimidation.

climate change: A permanent change in the climates around the world, thought by scientists to result from outputs of uncontrolled industrial processes and other human activity.

confirmation bias: The result of an individual (often pre-consciously) seeking out and/or interpreting information that tends to confirm their preconceptions about a particular topic, while also avoiding, ignoring or rejecting information that tends to disconfirm those preconceptions.

conjunctural analysis: Identification and analysis of the intersections or conjunctures of various patterns of action in relation to e.g. production, exchange, communication, organization, and enquiry.

conservatism: Adherence to traditional, normative values and a reluctance to welcome change. See political conservatism.

control: Action taken by a system to maintain its activity or output at a pre-determined level, rate or quality.

corporate governance: The set of values, principles, systems, and processes by which companies and organizations are directed and controlled in order to protect the interests of owners, shareholders and other stakeholders. Corporate governance is a primary responsibility of the board of directors.

corruption: (1) UNCAC definition: an abuse of (public) power for private gain that hampers the public interest. (2) EU definition: requesting, offering, giving or accepting, directly or indirectly, a bribe or any other undue advantage (to any public official), or prospect thereof, which distorts the proper performance of any duty or behaviour required of the recipient of the bribe. Some jurisdictions treat all forms of such behaviour as corruption, even involving companies or individuals and no public official.

corruption of the spirit: Corruption exhibited by a culture in which members lack the will or encouragement to act professionally, ethically and efficiently or to challenge manifest wrongdoing.

crisis: For an organization, a period of intense and often dramatic conflict and uncertainty about a topic which is central to the organization's current existence and involving loss of control and, if unresolved, possible collapse and chaos. Frequently, a crisis involves acutely unstable conditions and often leads to enforced major change in the organization.

culture: A set of unwritten and usually unobtrusive attitudes, beliefs, values, rules of behaviour, ideologies, habitual responses, language, rituals, 'quirks' and other features which characterize a particular group of people; cultures may be identified at different levels e.g. nations, localities, societies, professions, organizations, departments, interest groups.

D

Da-esh: Acronym of al-Dawla al-Islamiya al-Iraq al-Sham, the Arabic term for Islamic State in Iraq and Syria (known in the west as ISIS).

due diligence: The exercise by a party to a relationship, contract, transaction or deal which seeks to demonstrate an appropriate and adequate degree of searching examination of an individual or entity to establish their probity, honesty and bona fides, and to uncover any hidden relevant facts, from which it may be reasonably deduced whether or not that party should proceed with the relationship, contract, transaction or deal.

E

economic nationalism: An ideology favouring protectionist policies that emphasize national domestic control of the economy, labour, capital resources, and foreign trade, at the expense of foreign interests.

entryism: Infiltration of a political party by members of another group, with the intention of subverting its policies or objectives, whether unobtrusively or by achieving manifest control.

environment: (1) In relation to global warming, the macro-level natural physical environment of the world, such as its oceans, forests, land masses, ice masses, and climate. The physical environment may be envisaged as comprising a systemic hierarchy of interacting component systems, each contributing to the next higher level. (2) A particular lower level within the global physical environment, at which pollution or other adverse effects are often observable or detectable by the human senses, although not always.

Establishment: The Establishment is a euphemism for an ill-defined group in society perceived as exercising undue power and influence over matters of policy, opinion, or taste, and seen as being resistant to change.

Europhile: A shorthand descriptor for anyone who favoured the UK's continuing EU membership.

Eurosceptic: A shorthand descriptor for anyone who had doubts about the UK's continuing EU membership. Gradually became the general term for anyone who definitely wanted the UK to quit the EU.

exceptionalism: The concept of a particular nation being inherently different to others in many key respects e.g. morally, politically, economically, militarily, culturally. The notion of US exceptionalism extends the idea to assert that the US is not just different but also superior to other nations, a status that will never change.

F

fake fact: A falsehood invented malevolently to challenge a real fact, with the purpose of casting doubt on the real fact or on the credibility of those using or disseminating the real fact, and thereby influencing public opinion.

fake news: The deliberate fabrication and dissemination of plausible but false news stories, or stories comprising a mixture of fact and damaging fiction, in order to assist in a black propaganda campaign against a political or other target, and thereby influence public opinion.

fascism: An authoritarian, nationalistic right-wing system of government characteristically formed around an iconic national leader whose ideology, policies, demagoguery, and actions both epitomize and justify their pathological nature.

Fidesz: Populist far-right political party in Hungary.

Five Star: The populist Alt-Right political party in Italy. Also known as M5S.

fraud: The abuse of position, or false representation, or prejudicing the rights of someone for personal gain. The essence of such fraud is a deliberate act of deception intended to permanently deprive another party of a valued asset (money, shares, property, elected post etc) which is rightly theirs. Most jurisdictions automatically treat all fraud as a criminal offence as well as a civil offence but a few jurisdictions are reluctant to treat fraud as warranting criminal investigation and proceedings.

Front National: The largest populist Alt-Right political party in France. In March 2018, the party proposed a name change to Rassemblement National (National Rally).

G

globalisation: The economic process of increasing global inter-dependency and integration of markets, products, location of production and product sources, and flows of money, ideas, human resources and technology, beyond the control of any one country.

global warming: A gradual rise in air and sea temperatures resulting from industrial and other human activity and having ultimately devastating effects on the planet and human existence; now thought to be irreversible but possibly still controllable through multilateral action by states, 190 of which signed the Paris Climate Accord to that end.

governance: The set of values, principles, systems, and processes by which an entity is directed and controlled in order to protect the interests of all stakeholders.

groupthink: A tendency for groups to form a consensus attitude and view on a particular topic. Typically, such a consensus forms around an authority figure, even when that figure's views may not always be supported by facts or be in the group's best interests.

H

hazard: A physical entity, substance, condition, activity or behaviour which is capable of causing harm.

hazard identification: The process of identifying a hazard and analyzing how it may cause harm, as a preliminary step in risk assessment.

hegemony: All-consuming application of power.

holism: The study of whole entities, and especially attributes conferred only by the whole and which are not attributable to particular components, as in 'the whole is greater than to sum of its parts'. Holism encompasses the concepts of emergence, synergy, and systemic properties.

heuristic: An assessment technique using experience or rules-of-thumb.

I

immiseration: Economic impoverishment.

interventionism: A foreign policy seeking to determine and control other regimes, events, conflicts, national and regional allegiances, and outcomes—all to suit one's own strategic interests.

isolationism: A foreign policy seeking to better protect a nation's own strategic interests by not intervening in other nation's problems.

J

jihad: Arabic word meaning 'struggle' or 'fight'. (1) an individual's inner struggle to comply with conscience and religious ideals; (2) the Sunni Muslim concept of holy war in defence of or propagation of Islamic values.

Jobbik: Far-right political party in Hungary, having a white supremacy, Christian identity, anti-Semitic, and anti-Muslim credo.

jus sanguinis: the legal principle of citizenship determined not by place of birth but by at least one parent being a citizen.

jus soli: 'right of the soil', the legal principle of citizenship determined by birthright.

K

KKK: Ku Klux Klan, a far-right neo-Nazi organization in the US, having a white supremacy, Christian identity, anti-Semitic, and anti-Muslim credo.

L

laïcité: French approach to secularism.

Les Patriotes: Breakaway party from Front National in France, formed in 2017 by Florian Philippot, formerly number 2 in Front National. Philippot represented a more professional realpolitik faction that for a time dominated FN, but who were beaten in an internal power struggle by a nativist authoritarian faction seeking a more radical activist stance for FN.

M

madman theory: A theory of war and diplomacy attributed to President Richard Nixon and his collaborator Henry Kissinger in the late 1960s, whereby a president seeks to shock, unnerve and inhibit an adversarial counterpart abroad by pretending to be so deranged and unpredictable that, at all costs, he should not be provoked.

major accident hazard: A hazard which in a single incident could result in the death or injury of large numbers of people and/or major damage to property and/or environment. Such hazards may be either natural in origin or human-created. Typically, human-created major hazards are named and defined by legislation e.g. EU Major Hazards Directive.

management system (1) A notional system relating to management of an organization or operation. (2) A structured systematic means for ensuring that an organization or a defined part of it is capable of achieving and maintaining high standards of specified performance.

Militant Tendency: A hard-left Marxist-Leninist-Trotskyist 'entryist' faction active within the British Labour Party during the 1970s and 1980s. Many Militant Tendency members of the Labour Party were eventually expelled from the Party and a number of leading Militant figures joined the Socialist Party of England and Wales.

misogynist: A person who dislikes, disparages, or is prejudiced against women.

Momentum: A hard-left faction increasingly active within the British Labour Party since Momentum's formalisation in 2015. Whereas many senior Momentum figures are self-affirmed Marxist-Leninsts and/or sympathetic to the old Militant Tendency ideas, Momentum has gained wider support from ordinary Labour Party members who favour Party leader Jeremy Corbyn and his views. Both Momentum and Jeremy Corbyn have also attracted much public criticism for their reluctance to eradicate anti-Semitism in the Party.

multiculturalism: The concept of recognition of and acceptance of the presence of several distinct cultural or ethnic groups within a society.

multilateralism: A belief favouring negotiations and agreements with at least three other parties as a means to better protect one's own interests. One foreign policy option.

N

narcissism: Deriving gratification by seeking affirmation from others that one's vain or egotistical admiration of one's own attributes is warranted.

National Action: An extremist far-right group in the UK, proscribed as a terrorist organization.

National Alliance: An extremist far-right group in the US, proscribed as a terrorist organization.

nationalism: The belief that national identity should be given political importance, that nations have rights to both autonomy and sovereignty, and that members of the nation should collaborate in defence of these rights.

nativism: A belief that the interests of native-born or long-established inhabitants of a country should be protected whereas those of immigrants should not.

neo-con: Abbreviation for neo-conservative. The Neo-Conservatives arose in the 1960s among hawkish US politicians disillusioned with Democratic foreign policy. The movement blossomed during the period 1970s-early 2000s and peaked in 2003 during the G.W. Bush administration. Neo-con ideas became absorbed into the Tea Party and then the Alt-Right.

neo-fascist: Contemporary follower of fascist ideology, applied to a modern context.

neo-Marxist: Contemporary follower of Marxist ideology, applied to a modern context.

Northern League: Populist and far-right political party in Italy, with nationalist, regional secessionist, and ant-immigrant policies. Also known in Italian as Lega Nord, Lega, and Carrocio.

O

opportunity risk: See speculative risk.

organizational learning: A cumulative, reflective, experiential process through which all members of an organization learn to understand and continuously interpret the organization, its strengths and weaknesses and its successes and failures, so as to modify systems and behaviour and improve outcomes.

P

palingenesis: Exact replication, recreation, or rebirth.

palingenetic ultranationalism: Generic fascism defined by its core myth, namely that a 'national rebirth' will be achieved by revolution.

Pamyat: Russian extreme far-right and neo-Nazi political group once significant in the late Soviet era, now largely dissipated.

PEGIDA: An acronym of the German far-right nationalist and anti-Islam movement Patriotische Europäer gegen die Islamisierung des Abendlandes, which translates as Patriotic Europeans Against the Islamisation of the West.

poldering: A term used in the Netherlands to describe attempts by a mainstream political party to engage and include all competing or even hostile parties in the democratic process, with the ultimate aim of not only mollifying and tempering their impact but also reaching common agreement. See Bruning (2016).

political conservatism: Adherence to traditional, normative values and a reluctance to welcome change, plus extolling the virtues of individual endeavour and self-reliance as well as favouring free enterprise, private ownership, low taxation and socially conservative ideas. Political conservatism emphasizes personal responsibility and eschews collectivism and any kind of socialist or left-wing agenda, such as an emphasis on public spending, high taxation of businesses and high earners, trades union power and a de-emphasis on defence spending.

populism: (1) The political primacy of the ideas, interests, fears, views, and opinions of the general public at the expense of those of the prevailing or ruling political class. (2) Direct democracy as opposed to representative democracy. (3) A polite euphemism for a belief in 'elective dictatorship'.

post-truth: Relating to or depicting circumstances in which objective facts are less influential in shaping public opinion than appeals to emotion and personal belief. Typically, arguments and positions based on fake facts and fake news.

producerism: A belief that those who produce tangible wealth are of higher value to society than those who either inherit wealth or who are otherwise non-productive. Neiwert (2017) attributed a 'producerist' view to US populist Alt-Right supporters who see themselves as hard-working patriots compared to the worthless, non-contributing 'others' below them who should be 'eliminated'.

proto-fascism: (1) Early ideas that preceded the birth of unequivocal fascism in the 1930s (i.e. pre-Hitler, Mussolini, Franco). (2) Contemporary right-wing authoritarian ideas and behaviour that could develop and migrate into fascism.

psychopath: A person who causes harm to others without self-recognition of his or her harmfulness, no empathy for those harmed, and no conscience, remorse or guilt about it. Ruthless 'end justifies the means' and 'what can I get away with?' behaviour is often the hallmark of a psychopath. Psychopaths are usually unable to form any kind of normal emotional or social bond with anyone, although they may create a false cloak of normality.

pure risk: An absolute risk or one which relates only to harm. With a pure risk, the best that can happen is that nothing bad happens.

Q

QRA: Quantified Risk Assessment. Risk assessment techniques based on scientific and mathematical relationships, typically applied in high risk contexts relating to nuclear, chemical, aviation and other major accident hazards, or to complex financial or economic forecasting risks.

R

Rassemblement National: New name proposed in March 2018 for Front National in France; meaning 'National Rally'.

realpolitik: A system of political decision-making based on pragmatism rather than ideological or moral principles.

risk: (1) The probability or likelihood that (for a pure risk) a specified hazard will result in a specified undesired event, or (for a speculative risk) a specified event or course of action will result in a specified gain or enhancement and/or specified loss or detriment. (2) For pure risks, the product of the potential severity of hazard consequences and the probability that the undesired event will occur. (3) In undisciplined parlance, an alternative term for 'threat' or 'hazard'.

risk acceptability: Use of criteria, usually formally agreed criteria, to determine whether a particular level of risk is acceptable. Often assumes that acceptability determined by risk specialists broadly matches public acceptability, but this assumption may not be born out.

risk acceptance: The fact of accepting a particular risk or level or risk. May not mean that all those accepting a risk actually regard the risk as acceptable if their options are constrained or compromised or they are under duress.

risk appetite: The amount of risk that an individual or an organization is willing to seek or accept in pursuit of its long-term objectives i.e. the propensity to take speculative risks.

risk assessment: The process of estimating and evaluating a risk in order to determine whether current risk strategies are appropriate and adequate.

risk cognition: see risk perception.

risk evaluation: The process of interpreting risk estimates and the overall results of a risk assessment.

risk management: The overall process of ensuring that risk exposures are managed in the most cost-effective and cost-efficient way.

risk perception: A comprehensive term applied to an individual's sensory perception, and cognitive processes, including thinking, reasoning, evaluating, comparing, judging, learning and deciding; alternative term for risk cognition.

risk reduction: A strategy seeking to reduce risk levels by prevention and control techniques.

risk strategy: An approach to risk seeking the best combination of avoidance, deferment, reduction, retention, transfer, sharing and limiting of risk exposures.

risk tolerability: Relating to a level of risk that is neither unacceptably high nor negligible but somewhere in between. A tolerable risk level is typically less than ideal but enables a trade-off of time, cost, and effort against risk reduction and control benefits up to a pre-set limit.

S

salvation model: A model which, if adopted, proponents imagine and expect will offer instant and long-term protection without too much effort.

Schengen Accord: The 1985 Schengen Agreement abolishing border checks of travellers between those EU Member States that are signatories to the Agreement. Not all Member States are Schengen signatories.

self-regulation: The purposeful and active interpretation and practical implementation by an organization of goal-directed legislation which applies to it, as opposed to waiting for external compliance enforcement by regulatory authorities.

snowflake: A pejorative term for someone in young adulthood who exhibits a precious, over-protected, self-indulgent, and non-resilient personality with a high sense of entitlement, and who believes strongly that they should not be exposed to any information, ideas or persons which they might find objectionable—otherwise they might 'melt'.

sociopath: A lesser form of psychopath with broadly similar characteristics but, unlike a psychopath, a sociopath can usually form some emotional and social bonds with family and friends and even colleagues but, although often functioning well socially among such people, he or she may show callous indifference to strangers and behave harmfully towards them without conscience.

sovereignism: A belief in a self-creating and self-sustaining system of liberty for all, formed by a pragmatic, eclectic, evolutionary combination of socialism, communism, and capitalism.

speculative risk: A risk which may have both beneficial and/or detrimental outcomes e.g. investment, human resources, product innovation, mergers and acquisitions, foreign policy. Also known as opportunity risk.

strategic risk: A risk which may damage or disrupt significantly an organization's overall business/corporate strategy or the organization itself.

subjective risk: A personal view of a risk. In a sense, all risk is subjective as risk is a perceptual and cognitive phenomenon i.e. it exists entirely in the minds of individuals.

subsidiarity: The organisational principle that decisions and actions should be devolved to the lowest level that is appropriate. For example, the principle provides for EU legislation issued in the form of Directives to be implemented by the Member States through their own legislation and enforced locally.

sub-system: An identifiable component of a system which itself has all the characteristics of a system.

system: The concept of a recognizable whole consisting of a number of parts which interact in an organized way; characterized by inputs, outputs, processes, a boundary, an environment, an owner, emergent properties, control and survival; addition or removal of a component affects both the component and the system.

T

Tea Party: A right-wing movement within the US Republican Party, many of whose supporters moved closer to the Alt-Right during and after the 2016 Presidential election campaign of Donald Trump.

threat: An alternative term for 'hazard' used in some areas of risk such as security and politics. Also sometimes used interchangeably with 'risk'.

Troika: Of Russian origin, the term applied to the tri-partite group comprising the EU, the European Central Bank, and the International Monetary Fund, which together are responsible for formulating any financial bailout programme deemed necessary for the protection of an EU Member State in grave financial difficulties and heading towards state bankruptcy.

Trumpism: A unique fusion of style and substance that, in the person of Donald Trump, has proven to hold out significant potential for electoral success in American politics. McCarty argues that while offering little new as a political ideology, Trumpism is most closely aligned with paleo-conservatism and thus may be understood as a kind of neo-paleo-conservatism.

U

unilateralism: A belief in making decisions and taking actions without agreement with, or possibly even consultation with, others. One foreign policy option.

unilateral interventionism: Taking a predominantly unilateral stance and intervening or not, case by case, as determined by what is perceived to be in one's own interests. One foreign policy option.

V

Volkskörper: Literally the 'people's body', or racial corpus, originating in Nazi terminology.

W

WASP: white, Anglo-Saxon, protestant; a reference to a class of Americans who are either self-ascribed or ascribed by others as having a superior status in the US compared to other classes; WASPs are traditionally perceived as ultra-conservative.

Weltanschauung: Of German origin, meaning 'world-view'.

world-view: A complex set of perceptions, attitudes, beliefs, values, opinions, and motivations which characterize how an individual or group of people interpret the world and their existence; a set of characteristic biases.

About the Editor and Authors of Vol 1 and Vol 2

Editor and Primary Author:

Dr Alan Waring: risk analyst and author, UK; international risk management consultant to government departments, institutions and large corporations 1986–2016; books include *Corporate Risk and Governance* (2013), Gower/Routledge, and *Managing Risk* (1998), Thomson/Cengage, co-authored with Ian Glendon; Visiting Professor at European University Cyprus (2014–2016), Adjunct Professor at Hong Kong Baptist University (2006–2008), and International Risk Consultant, Tsinghua University, Beijing (2006–2008); special interest in countering risks associated with the populist- and far-right.

Contributing Authors:

Dr Bernhard Forchtner: Lecturer, School of Media, Communication and Sociology, University of Leicester, UK; formerly a Marie Curie Fellow at the Institute of Social Sciences, Humboldt University of Berlin, 2007–2013, conducting project on far-right discourses on the environment; co-author with C. Kølvraa of "Extreme Right Images of Radical Authenticity: Multimodal Aesthetics in History, Nature and Gender in Social Media" in *European Journal of Cultural and Political Sociology* (2017).

Dr Gabriel Goodliffe: Assistant Professor, Department of International Relations, Instituto Tecnológico Autónomo de Mexico (ITAM), Mexico; specializing in comparative politics and political economy, populist and radical parties, and the French extreme right and Front National; author of *The Resurgence of the Radical Right in France: from Boulangisme to the Front National* (2012), CUP.

Dr Paul Jackson: Senior Lecturer, Department of History, University of Northampton, UK; specializing in fascism and the extreme right; curator of the Searchlight Archive on extreme-right groups; editor of Bloomsbury's *A Modern History of Politics and Violence* series; author of *Colin Jordan and Britain's Neo-Nazi Movement: Hitler's Echo* (2017), Bloomsbury.

Dr Antonis Klapsis: Adjunct Lecturer, Hellenic Open University, Greece; Academic Coordinator, Centre of International and European Political Economy and Governance, University of Peleponnese; former Visiting Fellow, Wilfried Martens Centre for European Studies, Brussels; author of five books, including *An Unholy Alliance: the European Far Right and Putin's Russia* (2015), Wilfried Martens Centre.

Dr Timothy McCarty: Assistant Professor, Political Science and International Relations, University of San Diego; research interests in democratic theory, politics of taxation, moral responsibility, and politics & literature; he has published work on the politics of complicity, political thought in the work of Vladimir Nabokov, right-wing radicalism, and is preparing a monograph on the relationship between taxation and citizenship in democratic thought and practice.

Özgur Özvatan: Research and Teaching Fellow, Department of Social Sciences, Humboldt University of Berlin, Germany, and a research fellow at the Berlin Institute for Integration and Migration Research; PhD candidate at the Berlin Graduate School of Social Sciences researching how far-right discourses in western Europe and Turkey shape EU-Turkey relations.

Dr Roger Paxton: Clinical psychologist, formerly Associate Director of R&D and Psychological Services in the UK National Health Service, and Honorary Senior Lecturer at Newcastle University, UK; chair of the British Psychological Society's ethics committee. Special interest in political psychology in relation to the populist right and far-right.

Dr Markus Rheindorf: Lecturer, Department of Applied Linguistics, University of Vienna, Austria; an applied linguist with extensive work on cultural studies and on discourse in politics, the media, and the sciences; has held a fellowship at the International Centre for Cultural Studies in Vienna and the Amsterdam School of Cultural Analysis.

Dr Emily Turner-Graham: Academic researcher and writer on the far- and extreme-right, Australia; former lecturer and researcher at Melbourne, Deakin and Latrobe universities; numerous publications on both the historical and contemporary extreme-right in Britain, Germany, and Australia; author of *'Never Forget that You Are a German': Die Brücke, 'Deutschtum' and National Socialism in Interwar Australia* (2011), Peter Lang Verlag.

Dr Ineke van der Valk: Senior Researcher, Faculty of Governance and Global Affairs, University of Leiden, Netherlands, specializing in racism, Muslim discrimination, Islamist and right-wing extremism, ethnic relations, the history of immigrants, and diversity in multicultural societies; has studied far-right political discourse in France and the Netherlands; participant in the EU DARE (Dialogue About Radicalization and Equality) project.

Prof Kevern Verney: Professor in American History and Associate Dean—Research, Faculty of Arts and Sciences, Edge Hill University, UK; author, co-author, or editor of numerous books and publications on the history of civil rights in the US, e.g. *Black Civil Rights in America* (2000), Routledge, *The Debate on Black Civil Rights in America* (2006), MUP, and *Barack Obama and the Myth of a Post-Racial America* (2013), Routledge, co-edited with Prof Inderjeet Parmar and Dr Mark Ledwidge; co-organizer 2010–2014 with Prof Parmar and Dr Ledwidge of the Barack Obama Research Network, partnered with the universities of Warwick and Middleburg; current research includes race and the politics of policing during the Obama presidency, and immigration and race issues under the Trump administration.

Prof Ruth Wodak: Emerita Distinguished Professor and Chair in Discourse Studies, Lancaster University, UK, and Professor in Linguistics, University of Vienna, Austria; visiting professor at several universities in the US and across Europe; recipient of numerous awards and distinctions, including the Wittgenstein Prize for Elite Researchers (1996), the Kerstin Hesselgren Chair of the Swedish Parliament at Örebrö University (2008), the Grand Decoration of Honour in Silver for services to the Republic of Austria (2011), and the Willy Brandt Chair at Malmö University (2017); prolific author of academic articles and books, including *The Politics of Fear. What Right-wing Populist Discourses Mean* (2015), Sage, *Rightwing Populism in Europe: Politics and Discourse* (2013, with M. KhosraviNik and B. Mral), and *Analyzing Fascist Discourse. Fascism in Talk and Text* (2013, with J. Richardson).

Index

ibidem Press

Waring, Alan

The New Authoritarianism

Vol 1: A Risk Analysis of the US Alt-Right Phenomenon

This volume considers from a risk perspective the current phenomenon of the new Alt-Right authoritarianism and whether it represents 'real' democracy or an unacceptable hegemony potentially resulting in elected dictatorships and abuses as well as dysfunctional government. Contributing authors represent an eclectic range of disciplines, including cognitive, organizational and political psychology, sociology, history, political science, international relations, linguistics and discourse analysis, and risk analysis. The Alt-Right threats and risk exposures, whether to democracy, human rights, law and order, social welfare, racial harmony, the economy, national security, the environment, and international relations, are identified and analyzed across a number of selected countries, including the US, UK, Austria, France, Germany, Netherlands, Norway, and Russia. Potential strategies to limit the Alt-Right threat are proposed.

11/2018, 468 pages

Paperback, € 45,90 / $50.00
ISBN 978-3-8382-1153-4

e-book, € 30,99 / $30.99
ISBN 978-3-8382-7153-8

ibidem Press | Leuschnerstr. 40 | 30457 Hannover | Germany
Phone: +49 (0) 511 2 62 22 00 | Fax: +49 (0) 511 2 62 22 00 | sales@ibidem.eu | www.ibidem.eu

"This two-volume edited work (volume I dealing with the US scene and volume II with the European context) by Dr. Alan Waring is like building a tapestry. Threads are put together in a skillful and professional way to create a whole. I regard this phenomenal work to be a major contribution to our understanding of the risks facing democracies from the rising new authoritarianism. I can safely predict that it will establish itself and remain a major reference book for generations to come. A must-read. Highly recommended."

Emeritus Professor Antony A. Vass, Criminologist, Penologist, Legal Consultant, Sociologist, Psychologist and Psychotherapist

"This looks to be a most timely examination of the nature and rise of the Alt-Right phenomenon. The fact that it deals with trends on both sides of the Atlantic, whilst offering political and psychological context, will doubtless help to ensure a wide readership. The chapters on the United States deal with highly topical and important issues, and as someone who teaches US Politics at undergraduate and post-graduate level, I can see how these topics would be very suitable for classroom use. I very much enjoyed reading the material and found it to be engaging and informative throughout."

Dr Clodagh Harrington, De Montfort University

"Waring provides a fascinating insight and a counterpoint to 'armchair expertise'."

Professor George Boustras, Professor in Risk Assessment, European University Cyprus, and Director of the Center for Risk and Decision Science

About the Editor:

Dr Alan Waring, main contributor and editor. Originally qualifying and practicing as an industrial chemist, in mid-career he switched to management and social sciences. PhD 1993 at Westminster University jointly with Aston Business School, for an ethnographic study of three cases of organizations undergoing substantive change.

International risk management consultant on range of corporate, strategic and operational risk issues to government departments, institutions and large corporations 1986–2016. Reports contributed to several public enquiries on major disasters. More than 80 assignments in 14 countries.

ibidem-Verlag / *ibidem* Press
Melchiorstr. 15
70439 Stuttgart
Germany

ibidem@ibidem.eu
ibidem.eu